The
MAKING *of the* GULF WAR

The
MAKING *of the*
GULF
WAR

*Origins
of Kuwait's
Long-Standing
Territorial
Dispute
with Iraq*

H. RAHMAN

ITHACA
PRESS

THE MAKING OF THE GULF WAR
Origins of Kuwait's Long-Standing Territorial Dispute with Iraq

Ithaca Press is an imprint of Garnet Publishing Limited

Published by
Garnet Publishing Limited
8 Southern Court
South Street
Reading
Berkshire RG1 4QS
UK

First edition

ISBN 0 86372 207 5

British Library Cataloguing-in-Publication Data
A catalogue record for this book is available from the British Library

Jacket design by David Rose
Typesetting by Tiger Typeset
Maps drawn by GEOprojects (UK) Limited

Printed in Lebanon

Contents

CONTENTS

Map 1

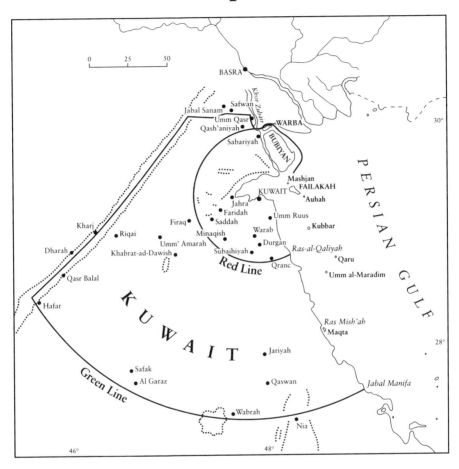

The inner and outer limits of Kuwait's territories as defined by the Red and Green Lines respectively in the unratified Anglo-Ottoman Convention, 29 July 1913

Source: Based on the map produced by the Foreign Office, Research Department, May 1954, PRO FO 371/114644

Map 2

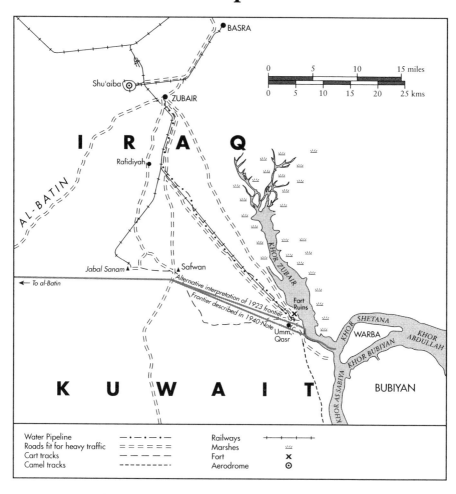

Iraq–Kuwait frontier as interpreted in 1923 and as described in the 1940 Note

Source: Based on the map produced by the Foreign Office, Reasearch Department, January 1948

Map 3

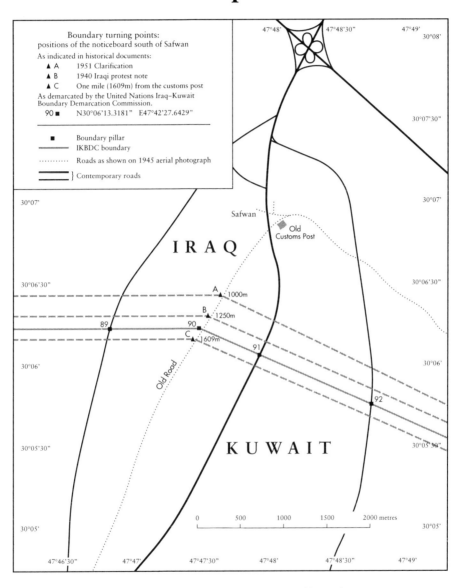

The new Iraq–Kuwait international land boundary

Source: **Based on United Nations Map No 3786, May 1993**

Map 4

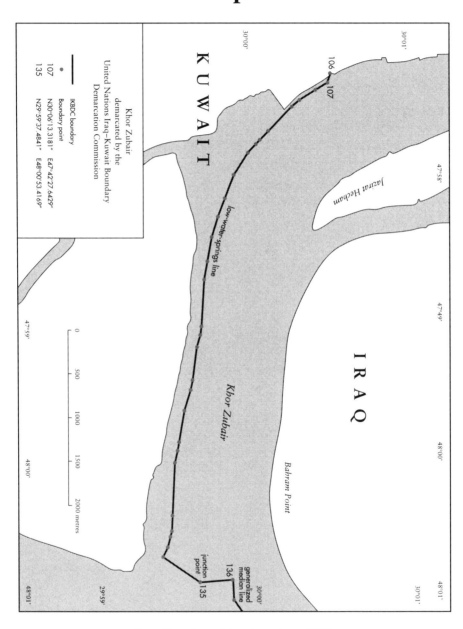

Map 5

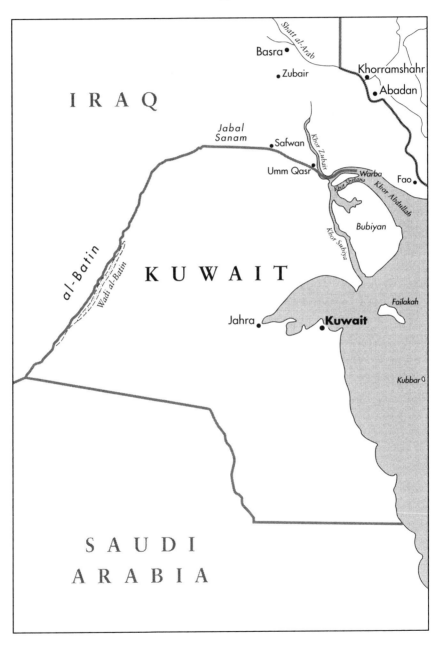

Iraq–Kuwait frontier as defined by the Iraq–Kuwait Boundary Demarcation
Commission (IKBDC), April 1992

Glossary

Baath Party	A pan-Arab socialist party founded in Syria in 1943. Different factions of the Baath (meaning Renaissance) Party hold power in Syria and Iraq.
Emir	Governor, military commander, ruler. Title used by the Kuwaiti as well as some other rulers in the Gulf since 1961.
Hashemite	A descendant of Hashem, the great-grandfather of the Prophet Muhammad.
Liwa	Province.
Majlis	Assembly or Parliament.
Mufti	Highest religious adviser.
Mutasarif	A government official immediately below governor.
naqib	Chief or leader.
Pasha	Ottoman official title given to ministers or provincial governors.
Qadah	Ottoman local government division.
Qadi	Judge.
Qaimaqam	Deputy Governor.
Rafidain	Civil Order.
Sanjak	Ottoman administrative division.
Sheikh	Title given to members of the ruling families of the Arabian Gulf, to the chief or head of an Arab tribe, family or village and to religious leaders.
Sultan	Ruler.
Vilayet	Ottoman province.
Wali	Governor.
Wazir	Minister.

Preface

To understand the Iraqi annexation of Kuwait in August 1990 it is first necessary to go back to the beginning of the twentieth century when the Ottoman authorities in Basra adopted a robust foreign policy, extending their influence further south as far as Safwan, Umm Qasr and Bubiyan Island, and in so doing raised the question of the status of Kuwait and its territorial limits. The Ottomans did so in response to the growing British power in Kuwait following the conclusion of the Exclusive Agreement of 1899, which governed Britain's relations with Kuwait until 1961. Before the conclusion of this agreement, Kuwait had attracted the attention of the great powers due to both its position as a meeting point of East-West trade and German aspirations for the location of a railway terminus there. The growing British and Ottoman interests in Kuwait in particular and the Gulf in general eventually led to the conclusion of the Anglo-Ottoman Convention of 1913, which, in addition to settling other Gulf issues, defined the territories of Kuwait.

Following the collapse of the Ottoman Empire after the First World War, Kuwait gained a new status with a well-defined boundary, and a new Iraq was created under a British mandate which was eventually terminated in 1932. Even before Iraq's emergence as an independent state, the Iraqis had been indulging in anti-Kuwaiti propaganda and had launched campaigns for the annexation of the Sheikhdom. Therefore, Saddam Hussein's invasion of Kuwait on 2 August 1990, in violation of international law and the UN Charter, was not an act undertaken on the spur of the moment; it was rather a well-planned move to accomplish the unfulfilled objectives of his predecessors. Although Kuwait existed as a separate entity long before Iraq, its annexation to Iraq had been in the minds of almost all previous Iraqi rulers on the grounds that Iraq was the natural heir to the Ottoman legacy in the region. Fuelled by this perception, they coveted Kuwait because of its strategic location at the head of the Arabian Gulf. Saddam Hussein felt strong enough to fulfil this long-cherished Iraqi desire because of the comparative stability of his regime and his success in building up a huge army during its protracted war with Iran.

Moreover, being more ambitious than previous Iraqi leaders, he nurtured the dream of becoming the undisputed leader of the Arab world, or at least of the Arab Mashreq. But Saddam Hussein's Kuwaiti adventure backfired because he miscalculated world opinion and US government resolve. In the event, the abortive invasion, while bringing about complete economic and political isolation to Iraq, paved the way for the UN demarcation of Kuwait's northern frontier in 1993 for which Kuwait had been struggling for more than half a century. It was the conflicting and imprecise definitions of the Iraqi–Kuwaiti frontier, dating back to the Ottoman period, as well as Britain's interpretations of these definitions and its failure to demarcate the frontier which were at the root of the Iraqi invasion of Kuwait in 1990. So it seemed.

A large number of books have been written about the Iraqi–Kuwaiti problems before, during and after the Gulf crisis, but there is no study that examines in detail the long-standing border dispute between the two countries which contributed crucially to Iraq's rationale of its invasion of Kuwait. This book attempts to fill this lacuna, provides a detailed chronological account of the protracted Iraqi–Kuwaiti territorial dispute and sets this account against the background of the origins of the Gulf War which led to Iraq's acceptance of the UN-demarcated boundary in 1994.

In writing this book, unpublished British official correspondence preserved in the India Office Library and Records and the Public Record Office in London as well as other contemporary sources have been extensively used. While India Office and Foreign Office records are invaluable aids for understanding the British perceptions of the undemarcated Iraq–Kuwait boundary, the Joint Planning Staff's papers and the Cabinet's conclusions are also essential for an understanding of the British commitment to the long-term defence of Kuwait against the background of repeated claims to the country by the Iraqi Prime Minister Abdul-Karim Qasim in 1961. Some secondary works are also important in assessing the development of the frontier dispute since 1961. While HRH General Khaled bin Sultan's book gives an Arab perspective of the war in the Gulf, General Schwarzkopf's memoirs, General de la Billière's work as well as contemporary local dailies and CNN war reports provide interesting accounts of the war and its consequences.

The idea of writing this book came to me during the Gulf crisis when I was myself present in one of the Gulf states and witnessed the overflight of Coalition air missions on their way to the war zone. Moreover, more than a decade of extensive study and research in the inter-Gulf territorial disputes has helped me to acquire knowledge about the complicated boundary issues of the region – a thorny legacy of the British Empire – and enabled me to describe Iraq's long-standing claims on Kuwait that ultimately tempted Saddam Hussein to make his disastrous move on the Emirate.

I take this opportunity to express my gratitude to Professor Malcolm Yapp, an eminent Middle East historian of international repute, for his encouragement and various suggestions in writing this book. I am grateful to HE K. P. Fabian, the Indian Ambassador to the State of Qatar, and Professor A. Karim, the former Vice-Chancellor of the University of Chittagong, Bangladesh, for their valuable comments. I would like to thank Professor J. A. Allan, Department of Geography, School of Oriental and African Studies, University of London, for his keen interest in this book. Majed Saleh al-Kholaifi of the Trade and Economics Department, Diwan Amiri, State of Qatar, and my colleague Ibrahim Salahi deserve special thanks for their encouragement throughout the writing of this book. My family is a constant source of inspiration, particularly my eldest daughter Nadia who assisted me in collecting large amounts of source material for this study during the Gulf crisis.

1

The Strategic Importance of Kuwait and Anglo-Ottoman Rivalry

From the eighteenth century onwards, Kuwait emerged as one of the most thriving ports in the Arabian Gulf due to its location at the head of the Gulf, becoming a meeting point for East–West trade and commerce. However, in addition to its strategic location the commercial potentialities of Kuwait made it the victim of the rivalry of foreign powers. Ottoman attempts to absorb the Sheikhdom and Russo-German designs on that part of the Gulf spurred Britain to establish its authority in Kuwait by concluding a secret treaty in 1899 whereby Kuwait could expect some degree of protection though not a formal one. However, despite the Sheikh of Kuwait's acceptance of Britain's pre-eminence in the Sheikhdom, the Ottomans persisted with their efforts to control Kuwait and to support German endeavours to extend the proposed Berlin–Baghdad railway to Kuwait. Disregarding British protests, the Ottomans increased their interference in the Sheikhdom following the involvement of Sheikh Mubarak of Kuwait in the affairs of Najd, the central and eastern plateau of Arabia. And ironically, just after reaching an understanding with Britain to preserve the status quo in Kuwait, the Ottomans proceeded to encroach Kuwaiti territory.

The foundation of the autonomous Sheikhdom of Kuwait dates from the year 1752 when the settlers elected Sheikh Sabah (I) bin Jaber as their first ruler. Sheikh Sabah was the eldest member of the Al Sabah family, a branch of the Utub tribe, who came to Kuwait at the beginning of the eighteenth century from central Najd. Gradually Sheikh Sabah extended his authority from Kuwait town to Khor al-Kaffi along the Arabian coast and various tribes such as Al Ali and Al Muntafiq amongst others acknowledged his suzerainty.[1] The Sheikh also developed Kuwait

---

1. See J. A. Saldanha, *Precise of Kuwait Affairs, 1896–1904* (Calcutta, Government of India, 1904), p. 1. For the system of government in Kuwait, see J. Crystal, *Kuwait: the Transformation of an Oil State* (Boulder, Colorado, Westview Press, 1992), pp. 7–14.

into one of the wealthiest and most important trading centres in north-eastern Arabia. This was possible due to the geographical location of the country with its excellent natural harbour. Indeed, the Sheikhdom reached its zenith as a flourishing port following the decline of Basra after its occupation by the Persians in 1776, leaving Kuwait as the sole transit port for Indian trade with Baghdad, Aleppo (in Syria) and Constantinople.[2]

While the fall of Basra increased the commercial importance of Kuwait, it also marked the beginning of British relations with the Kuwaitis. The British desert mail from the Gulf to Aleppo began to be dispatched from Kuwait instead of Zubair because of the Persian occupation. Although this route was discontinued in 1779, the British East India Company, owing to its differences with the Ottoman authorities in Basra, transferred its factory from Basra to Kuwait, where it remained until August 1795. This selection of Kuwait by the British as a place safe from Ottoman intrusion clearly shows that the Sheikhdom had ceased to be an Ottoman dependency by 1793.[3] More than a quarter of a century later, in December 1821, as a result of the difficulties with the Ottoman authorities in Baghdad, the British Residency at Basra was transferred to the Failakah Island, a Kuwaiti possession at the entrance of the harbour of the town of Kuwait. It remained there until the conclusion of a peace treaty with the Pasha of Baghdad in 1822.[4]

The British considered Kuwait a safe haven owing to its comparative peace and prosperity, and, recognizing the potential of Kuwait's

---

2. J. G. Lorimer, *Gazetteer of the Persian Gulf, Oman and Central Arabia* (Historical), Part 1B (Calcutta, Government Printing, 1908), p. 1001.
3. *Ibid.*, pp. 1002–4.
4. It is important to note that not only the British but also other powerful regional chiefs considered Kuwait as a safe haven in case of difficulty with other powers. For example, in 1837 Sheikh Thamir, chief of the Kaab tribe in Arabistan, took temporary refuge in Kuwait when the Ottoman occupied his town of Muhammarah. The Sheikh once again took asylum in Kuwait in 1841, following his expulsion from Arabistan by the Persian Governor of that province. In 1844, the Persian dissidents from Fars province and Kharg Island took shelter on the Kuwaiti island of Failakah. *Ibid.*, pp. 1008–12. See also Saldanha, *Precise of Kuwait Affairs*, p. 1 and Richard Schofield, *Kuwait and Iraq: Historical Claims and Territorial Disputes* (London, Royal Institute of International Affairs, 1991), p. 8.

strategic location, both Lieutenant Edmunds, the Assistant Resident at Bushire in Persia, and Lieutenant Felix Jones of the Indian Navy chose it as a probable site when the removal of the British naval and military stations from Kharg Island became necessary in 1839 in order to re-establish friendly relations with Persia. However, Lieutenant Arnold Kemball, the Officiating Political Resident, who toured the northern Gulf and produced a report in January 1845, did not share these views as he considered the Sheikhdom unsuitable for a military base due to the poor quality of its water, although because of its excellent harbour it might be used as a coaling station in the near future.[5] Although no British military base was established in the Sheikhdom, non-official con-tacts between the rulers and the British officials continued. In 1863 and 1865, during the rule of Sheikh Sabah bin (II) Jaber (1859–66), Lieutenant Colonel Lewis Pelly, the then Officiating Resident in the Gulf, visited Kuwait and produced two remarkable accounts about it. Describing its early history and its flourishing trade Pelly wrote:

> No doubt, much of the prosperity of Koweit may be due to posi-tion and to the comparatively healthy climate: it was in ancient days the point where the sea trade took to caravans or river carriage; it still maintains its natural advantages, and, although I would not recommend the artificial forcing of trade from its present course, I will still keep an eye on Koweit for future purposes. It is, in my opinion, by no means impossible that Koweit, under the effective development of the Gulf trade, would become the terminus for our sea-going steamers, a Coal Station, and a Telegraph Station. The more you analyse the question, the more will you be probably struck by the fact that the trade of the East and West has a marked tendency to resume its old lines under improved means of transit. Koweit appears to me a preferable port to Basrah for the same reasons that Karachi is preferable to Tatta. The climate of Basrah is fatal, that of Koweit comparatively good. The water of Koweit, it is true, is brackish, yet fever is unknown. Dysentery and ophthalmia are rare; and when men commence begetting new families at 80

---

5. See A. B. Kemball, 'Memoranda on the Resources, Localities and Relations of the Tribes Inhabiting the Arabian Shores of the Persian Gulf' in R. Thomas (ed.), *Arabian Gulf Intelligence: Selections from the Records of the Bombay Government*, new series, vol. XXIV (New York, The Oleander Press, 1985), p. 110.

and die at 120, the climate cannot be considered as prematurely exhausting.[6]

Pelly had, therefore, identified Kuwait as a possible commercial port that could be more advantageous than that of Basra in serving as a meeting place of East and West trade in addition to its suitability for the siting of lines of communication for the British Empire.

Pelly's second report, which he produced during his journey to Riyadh through Kuwait in 1865, dealt with the economic and commercial importance of Kuwait to British India as well as to the whole Gulf region. The Resident considered Kuwait as "one of the most thriving ports" in the Gulf owing to its growing economic activity. The last portion of the report, in which he considered the head of the Khor Abdullah inlet as an alternative location to Kuwait for a railway terminus from the Mediterranean, is both significant and remarkable. Pelly observed:

> It seemed to me that the Khore Abdullah leading up in to the Zubair creek might possibly hereafter be preferred by sea-going steamers to the present channels leading up to Busrah. The entrance of Khore Abdullah is wide and sufficiently deep. I anchored at the head of the Zubair creek, close alongside the bank, in four fathoms of water. From the head of the Zubair creek, a railway might reach the Mediterranean in a direct line of some 800 miles.[7]

Pelly's far-sighted observations about the strategic importance of the Khor Abdullah were sadly overlooked by his successors. Even the British officials who initiated formal Anglo-Kuwaiti relations in 1899 stopped at Kuwait without venturing beyond its horizon. It was not until some thirty years later that the Germans made a careful study of Pelly's prophecy about the Khor Abdullah.

In April 1866, formal Anglo-Kuwaiti commercial relations began when the steamers of the British India Steam Navigation Company started to call frequently at Kuwait. These dealings, however, became a cause of anxiety for the Ottoman authorities in Mesopotamia (later to

---

6. As quoted in Saldanha, *Precise of Kuwait Affairs*, p. 2.
7. *Ibid.*, p. 3.

become Iraq), who were concerned that such contacts might eventually bring further prosperity to Kuwait at the expense of the economy of Ottoman Basra and started gathering statistics to prove this. Therefore, Sheikh Sabah, fearing the Ottoman reaction, requested that the British authorities suspend the visits of the company's vessels to his port. Although the Ottomans had no right to object to the extension of British trade within the limits of Kuwait, the service was eventually suspended upon the recommendation of Kemball on 26 June 1866.[8]

Therefore, Kuwait's relations with Ottoman Mesopotamia should be examined against the background of Sheikh Sabah's fear of the Ottomans. Several reports had been produced by various British officials in the Gulf concerning Kuwait's relations with the Ottoman Empire. It is important to note within this context that the relocation of the British East India Company's factory from the Ottoman province of Basra to Kuwait indicates that Kuwait was far from being under Ottoman jurisdiction. John Gordon Lorimer, the eminent British civil servant and gazetteer, confirmed this. He argued: "From the selection of Kuwait as a place of retreat from the Turks, it is clear that, whatever may have been the case in 1775, it was not in any real sense a Turkish dependency in 1793."[9] However, Lieutenant Kemball gave his own account of the relations between Sabah and the Turks. He stated that the Sheikhdom maintained close contact with the Ottoman authorities in Baghdad and that Kuwaiti vessels flew the Ottoman flag. The Sheikh received an "annual allowance of 200 Karahs of dates" from the Ottomans in return for his undertaking to protect Basra from any foreign aggression.[10]

Although Kemball reported that Kuwaiti ships carried the Ottoman flag, he gave no reason for them doing so and nowhere implied that the Sheikhdom was subservient to the Ottomans. In 1852, when Kemball became the Resident in the Gulf, he stated more categorically that, unlike other littoral states in the Gulf, Kuwait enjoyed full independence even though its inhabitants used the Ottoman flag. In addition, the Sheikhdom was still responsible for the defence of Basra

---

8. *Ibid.*, p. 5.
9. Lorimer, *Gazetteer*, (Historical), p. 1004.
10. Kemball in Thomas, *Arabian Gulf Intelligence*, p. 110.

under the terms of an agreement entered into by the two parties.[11] This independent status of Kuwait, with no legal link with the Ottoman Empire, may easily be corroborated with a map drawn by William Gifford Palgrave who visited Central and Eastern Arabia between 1862 and 1863. Palgrave's map makes a distinction (by use of a different colour) between Kuwait and the countries subject to the Ottoman Empire.

In 1863, Lieutenant Colonel Lewis Pelly, the Officiating Resident in the Gulf, reconfirmed this position of Kuwait with regard to the Ottomans. Pelly also gave reasons for the use of the Ottoman flag by Kuwaiti vessels, which he confirmed had been previously flying their own distinctive Arab flag. The use of the Kuwaiti flag had brought economic disadvantage to Kuwaiti exports entering Bombay, where the authorities levied higher taxes on ships flying the Kuwaiti rather than the Ottoman flag. This economic inconvenience prompted Kuwaiti mercantile ships to change their colour.[12] In other words, the Kuwaiti vessels flew the Ottoman flag not for any political reason but simply for their own economic benefit. A recent study on Kuwait reconfirmed that there was no special arrangement or agreement between Kuwait and the Ottoman state for Kuwaiti vesssels to fly the Ottoman flag. They did so in order to protect their own interests by safeguarding the security of their vessels in Gulf waters where the British had ceased to recognize any native Arab flags other than the "white-pierced" flag prescribed in the 1820 General Treaty of Peace.[13] Furthermore, there is no evidence to suggest that the Kuwaitis used any such flag on land during that time. In fact, Kuwait enjoyed more independence in the 1860s than ever before, a status corroborated by the report of W. P. Johnstone, the British Agent

---

11. See A. B. Kemball, 'Statistical and Miscellaneous Information connected with the Possessions, Revenues, Families etc. of the Imam of Muscat, the Ruler of Bahrain and of the Chiefs of the Maritime Arab States of the Persian Gulf' in Thomas, *Arabian Gulf Intelligence*, p. 29.
12. Saldanha, *Precise of Kuwait Affairs*, p. 2.
13. Abdullah al-Ghunaim, Mufid Shehab, Gamal Zakariyya Qasem, Mohammad Murci Abdullah and Ahmed al-Mayyal, *Kuwait: Statehood and Boundaries* (Kuwait City, Kuwait Foundation for the Advancement of Sciences, 1992), p. 54. For the British-prescribed flag for the Trucial Sheikhdom (excluding Kuwait), see A. B. Kemball, 'Treaties with the Arab Tribes in the Persian Gulf' in Thomas, *Arabian Gulf Intelligence*, p. 76.

at Basra, which he produced on 4 April 1866, following his visit to the Sheikhdom. Johnstone was firmly convinced that "rather than submit to a Turkish government at Koweit, the [Kuwaiti] people to a man would abandon the place."[14] In submitting this statement to London on 18 April 1866, Kemball (the then ex-Resident), once again discussed the status of Kuwait, asserting that the Sheikhdom had never accepted Ottoman suzerainty:

> Unlike Bahrein, Koweit has never avowed the suzerainty of the Porte and has never been recognized to be a Turkish dependency; but in the very weakness of the Suzerain originated a policy in its part, which while affording the surest guarantee of virtual independence relieved the Feudatory from contracting engagements to other foreign powers. This policy has hitherto been justified by the character and conduct of the dominant family. Their Port being free, their commercial relations have involved no responsibilities and, strong enough to cause their rights to be respected by neighbouring cognate Principalities, they have uniformly avoided any cause of umbrage or offence to the Government which now for nearly half a century has exercised paramount authority in the Persian Gulf: I am unable to call to mind a single instance of maritime irregularity committed by the inhabitants of Koweit during that period and even in the matter of the slave trade wherein their obligations were equivocal, the remonstrances of English functionaries have always been received by them with deference and ostensibly at least have not remained without effect.[15]

Kemball's straightforward statement on the political status of Kuwait makes it clear that the Sheikhdom was not, at that time, under Ottoman jurisdiction. However, Kuwait's relations with the Ottomans began to take a new turn with the appointment of Midhat Pasha as the Governor of Baghdad in 1869, who formulated a grand strategy to bring the length of the Arabian shore of the Gulf under Ottoman suzerainity. The dynastic rivalry in Najd between Abdullah bin Faisal and his brother Saud provided Midhat with the opportunity to fulfil his objectives in the north. Dislodged by Saud in 1870, Abdullah sought Ottoman assistance through Sheikh Abdullah (II) bin Sabah, the

---

14. For more details, see Saldanha, *Precise of Kuwait Affairs*, pp. 3–4.
15. *Ibid.*, p. 5.

Kuwaiti ruler, to subdue Najd. Midhat Pasha immediately sent an expedition with the assistance of Abdullah bin Sabah who supplied 300 vessels and personally accompanied the expedition. The Sheikh's wholehearted support of Ottoman expansionism was spurred by his fear of Saud's ambitions in Kuwait. Midhat Pasha soon defeated Saud's forces, and the authority of the Ottoman Empire was established throughout al-Hasa province including Katif and Uqair. Although the Ottomans were unable to extend their direct rule in Najd, they later stabilized their hold over it by proxy through the Al Rashid family. It was reported that Sheikh Abdullah bin Sabah was rewarded with considerable tracts of land with palm groves in Fao for his military assistance to the Ottomans and for encouraging Sheikh Jasim bin Muhammad bin Thani of Qatar to fly the Ottoman flag on Qatari territory. As a result of this, Ottoman troops landed in Doha in 1871.[16] Towards the end of 1871, Midhat Pasha visited Kuwait to confer on Abdullah the title of the Qaimaqam (Deputy Governor) of Kuwait, stating that he should remain at the head of the Kuwaiti government, that the Qadis and the Muftis should retain their positions and that the administration of Kuwait should remain unchanged.[17] Thus the Ottomans made no attempt to bring the Sheikhdom under their direct control despite their predominant position in Eastern Arabia.

Following the extension of the Ottoman suzerainity over al-Hasa and Katif, Midhat Pasha introduced administrative reforms in the newly conquered territory. J. A. Saldanha, a civil servant of the Government of India, quoting the "precise" on the Ottoman expansion along the Arab littoral, gave a clear picture of the administrative arrangement:

> In 1875 this newly conquered territory [Hasa and Katif] called by the Turks Nejd, along with Basrah, Nasariyah, the centre of the Montefik country and Kurna and Amarah were constituted with an independent vilayat called the Basrah vilayat and Nasir Pasha – the Montefic Sheikh – was appointed the first Vali thereof.[18]

---

16. Lorimer, *Gazetteer*, (Historical), pp. 1014–15. See also Saldanha, *Precise of Kuwait Affairs*, p. 6.

17. See the Memorandum on the dependence of the village of Kuwait on the High (Turkish) Government, unnumbered, n.d., R/15/5/5.

18. Quoted in Saldanha, *Precise of Turkish Arabia Affairs, 1801–1905* (Simla, Government of India, 1906), p. 27.

No mention was made about the inclusion of Kuwait into this newly formed Vilayet of Basra. Midhat Pasha apparently could not do so as the Sheikhdom was neither conquered nor annexed. In 1884, the Basra Vilayet was reconstituted into four separate administrative units: Basra, Najd and al-Hasa, Nassriya and Amarah. In 1889, the boundaries of the Basra Vilayet were defined by the *Gazetteer of Baghdad* as:

> North – The boundary dividing Basrah Wilaiat [Vilayet] from that of Baghdad – lies between Kut and Amara, and crossing the Tigris below Kut, passes above the Hai country in Mesopotamia to Nasiria (Montefik), and thence crosses the Euphrates to the Shamia desert. Thus the lower boundary of Kut, the river Hai and a point below Samawa divides the two Walaiats [Vilayets].

> South – The Persian Gulf.

> East – A line from the Jabal-Himrin hills to the town of Mohammerah, and thence down the Shat-el-Arab to the Persian Gulf, divides the Wilaiat [Vilayet] from Persia. The left bank of the Shat-el-Arab is Persian territory.

> West – The boundary ends at a place to the south of Nejd called Birich.[19]

Thus the *Gazetteer of Baghdad* also excluded Kuwait from the boundaries of the Basra Vilayet and the limit of the southern boundary of this Vilayet was set at the waters of the Gulf.[20]

Although Kuwait was not included under the Basra administration, Sheikh Abdullah maintained cordial relations with the Ottomans.[21] In view of the Sheikh's pro-Ottoman leanings, the British authorities in the Gulf considered Kuwait as being "under the exclusive influence, if not the sovereignty of the Porte".[22] However, according to the Kuwaitis, this Kuwaiti–Ottoman entente during the reign of Sheikh Abdullah was

---

19. *Ibid.*, p. 28.
20. This contrasts with some other studies. For example, see Schofield, *Kuwait and Iraq*, pp. 12–13.
21. See the Memorandum on the dependence of the village of Kuwait on the High (Turkish) Government, unnumbered, n.d., R/15/5/5.
22. Lorimer, *Gazetteer*, p. 1016.

nothing more than a religious affiliation between the Sheikh and the Ottoman Sultans, who during the nineteenth century claimed authority over all Muslims owing to their succession to the Abbasid Caliphs. In fact, the Ottoman Caliphate was considered the highest religious authority in the Islamic world until its collapse after the First World War.[23] Furthermore, the Ottoman Sultans were the custodians of the holy places in Makkah and Medina prior to the establishment of the Saudi dynasty and Muslims all over the world tacitly acknowledged this fact. Nevertheless, Kuwait's religious affiliation with the Ottomans was confusing and unclear to the British authorities in the Gulf, who had been advocating since 1878 a policy of recognizing Ottoman suzerainity on the Arabian coast from Basra to Uqair. However, the British government in London declined to adopt this policy on political grounds. Sheikh Abdullah bin Sabah died in 1892 and was succeeded by his brother Sheikh Muhammad bin Sabah. Sheikh Muhammad continued the policy of his predecessor with regard to the Ottomans, while the British still failed to understand the true nature of the Ottoman religious influence over Kuwait.[24]

However, an act of piracy committed against a native Indian ship, the *Haripasa*, on 22 August 1895, off the Fao brought about a significant change in the British perception of Kuwait and raised the question of its status with regard to the Ottomans. As the land in the vicinity of Fao was owned by the Sheikh of Kuwait and the offending pirates were living there, Captain Whyte, the British Consul at Basra, recommended that the Ottoman government should be asked to instruct Sheikh Mubarak al-Sabah (who succeeded Muhammad in May 1896) to surrender the pirates and that if he did not comply, he was to pay compensation. Sir Philip Currie, the Ambassador in Constantinople, opposed this representation, arguing that there were ample grounds to believe that Sheikh Mubarak was "in reality an independent potentate and only nominally subject to the Sultan", and it would therefore be unwise to request the Porte to make the Sheikh produce the pirates.[25] In view of

23. Al-Ghunaim *et al.*, *Kuwait: Statehood and Boundaries*, p. 62. See also M. E. Yapp, *The Making of the Modern Near East 1792–1923* (London, Longman, 1987), p. 375.
24. See the Memorandum by Harcourt, 'Respecting Kuwait', no. 7696, 29 October 1901, L/P&S/18/B133.
25. Saldanha, *Precise of Kuwait Affairs*, p. 9.

these conflicting opinions, the British Foreign Office told Currie that it did not want to hold the Ottomans responsible for the piracy of the Kuwaiti subjects given that Britain had never admitted that the Sheikhdom was under the protection of the Ottoman government.[26] Eventually, following unofficial Anglo-Ottoman discussions in Constantinople over the *Haripasa* incident, it was decided to deal with Sheikh Mubarak directly rather than through the Ottomans. On 9 May 1897, Lord Salisbury, the Foreign Secretary, directed the Resident to warn the Sheikh that he would be responsible for any act of piracy against British shipping committed by his subjects.[27] Salisbury's directive was, therefore, a turning point in the evolution of British policy towards Kuwait, as it was "deemed to amount to a repudiation of the shadowy suzerainty of the Porte over Koweit, and would be driving the thin end of the wedge towards a British protectorate of Koweit".[28]

Prompted by the Foreign Secretary's instruction Colonel Malcolm Meade, the Resident in the Gulf, dispatched his deputy J. C. Gaskin to Kuwait on 5 September 1897 to convey Britain's warning to Sheikh Mubarak. The Kuwaiti ruler instantly denied the allegation, arguing that his subjects were not involved in piracy in the Shatt al-Arab. However, Sheikh Mubarak made a significant overture in telling Gaskin that the Ottomans wanted to absorb Kuwait and to avoid this he wished to place his Sheikhdom under British protection. If this was agreed to, he was prepared to cooperate with Britain in maintaining law and order in that part of the Arabian Gulf. The Sheikh added that although he had been flying the Ottoman flag and that his predecessors had accepted the Ottoman title of Qaimaqam, no treaty had ever been signed with the Ottomans. As Meade believed that the Ottoman influence over Mubarak's predecessors constituted no real obstacle to the extension of British influence, he was inclined to accept Mubarak's proposal.[29] To convince London of this, he advanced the following reasons:

> Koweit possesses an excellent harbour, and will, under our protec-
> tion, undoubtedly become one of the most important places in the

---

26. *Ibid.*, p. 10. See also B. C. Busch, *Britain and the Persian Gulf, 1894–1914* (Berkeley, University of California Press, 1967), p. 99.
27. Saldanha, *Precise of Kuwait Affairs*, p. 11.
28. *Ibid.*, p. 11.
29. *Ibid.*, p. 14.

Persian Gulf. Apart from the chances of its being the sea port for the projected railway from Port Said, which is under consideration and which the possession of Koweit would enable us to protect, the trade with the interior is already considerable, and will greatly increase. At present, in spite of the Sheikh's assertions, it is regarded as a centre of piratical expeditions, and therefore, endangers our trade with the Shat-al-Arab. Finally, it is said that it is a great slave emporium, and that our efforts to put a stop to the slave trade are more or less barren of results, as long as slaves can be marched across Arabia, and shipped at Koweit for Turkey and Persia.

Piracy and the slave trade would receive a blow if we brought the place under our protection, and it would also enable us to exercise a supervision over its trade which would undoubtedly advance our interests in the Persian Gulf.

As far as we are concerned, it seems advisable to fall in with Sheikh Mubarak's views, and to extend to Koweit and its ruler the protection enjoyed by Bahrain and other places on the Arab Coast.[30]

Meade was arguing for a protection treaty with Kuwait similar to that with Bahrain which had been concluded in May 1861, binding Bahrain to abstain from war, piracy and the importation of slaves by sea, on condition of protection against similar aggression. In addition, British subjects were to be permitted to trade with Bahrain on payment of an *ad valorem* duty of five per cent on their goods. It should be mentioned here that in March 1892, Bahrain signed a further treaty with Britain promising not to enter into any agreement with any other power than the British; to disallow the residence within its territory of the Agent of any other power; and neither to "cede, sell, mortgage" nor otherwise "give for occupation" any part of its "territory save to the British Government".[31] Similar treaties were signed with the seven Trucial States (Ras al-Khaima, Abu Dhabi, Dubai, Sharjah, Fujairah, Umm al-Qaiwain and Ajman).[32] Nevertheless, Meade's arguments for closer

---

30. *Ibid.*, pp. 14–15.
31. C. U. Aitchison, *A Collection of Treaties, Engagements and Sanads Relating to India and Neighbouring Countries* (Delhi, Manager of Publication, 1933), vol. XI, pp. 234–8.
32. *Ibid.*, p. 256–7.

Anglo-Kuwaiti relations failed to convince the British government, which was still not disposed to interfere more than necessary in order to maintain the peace of the region or to bring Kuwait under its protection.[33]

Meade, however, was undeterred by this response. In November 1897, he put forward further reasons in support of his campaign for the extension of British power to the Sheikhdom, arguing that a protection treaty with Kuwait would bring enormous benefits to the British Empire due to its strategic location. If the British government refused to do so, Meade argued, Mubarak would eventually turn towards the Porte for such an arrangement "or seek protection elsewhere, in either case changing the status quo" to Britain's disadvantage.[34] Meade's position was further boosted by reports of a concentration of Ottoman troops near Basra at the end of 1897, and of an alleged Russian plan to acquire a coaling station in Kuwait in early 1898.[35] However Meade's repeated arguments in favour of a British protectorate over Kuwait failed to convince the India Office to reverse the policy of non-intervention in Kuwait.[36]

However, by the middle of 1898 the British government was forced to reconsider its position as a result of an attempt by the Russian Count Vladimir Kapnist to obtain permission from the Ottoman government for the construction of a railway from Tripoli (in Syria) to Kuwait. This information was confirmed by the British Embassy in Constantinople in August. In November, Lord Curzon, following his appointment as the Viceroy of India, produced a memorandum stating that the "Russian design along with the possible increased German

---

33. See the Memorandum by Harcourt, 'Respecting Kuwait', no. 7696, 29 October 1901, L/P&S/18/B133.
34. *Ibid.*
35. Lorimer, *Gazetteer*, (Historical), p. 1022. See also Saldanha, *Precise of Kuwait Affairs*, p. 18.
36. The India Office was responsible at this time for overseeing the affairs of the Gulf through the Government of India (owing to its proximity to the Gulf). In fact, the Government of India had been managing the affairs of the Gulf since 1834 through its Bushire Political Residency. As Kuwait had not yet been brought under the jurisdiction of the Government of India, British relations with the Sheikhdom had still to be placed on a formal footing. As such the Sheikh remained paramount in the conduct of the foreign and internal affairs of Kuwait.

activity in the Gulf" would definitely "challenge" Britain's hitherto uncontested supremacy in the Gulf.[37] The newly appointed Viceroy therefore emphatically requested British protectorate status for Kuwait:

> I am of opinion that a tacit recognition (and a fortiori much more the effective realization) of Turkish, or, indeed, of any alien authority at Koweit, might be fraught with danger to British interests in the Gulf, and would cause us trouble in the future. For even though Turkey did not assert her authority, she could (and is very likely even now negotiating to) part with her assumed rights to other parties or Powers . . . I believe that we still have time to avert any such danger, and the step I recommend is the extension at a convenient and, if possible, an early opportunity of the British Protectorate to Koweit, whose Sheikhs have constantly asked for it for years and would welcome it, in the same way as it is applied to Bahrain.[38]

Lord Curzon's prophetic formula for Kuwait was accepted by the India Office, which held inter-departmental discussions on the issue. The Foreign Office immediately expressed its willingness to support the Government of India by diplomatic action should it think that a protectorate over Kuwait might be established without difficulty. Having received the Foreign Office's assurance, Lord George Hamilton, the Secretary of State for India, cabled the Government of India on 24 December 1898:

> Foreign Office would approve of protectorate on the understanding that responsibilities for its assertion and maintenance and for control devolved on the Government of India and if you think that it could be undertaken without difficulty or inconvenient extension of duty of Police devolving on your Government in the Gulf, I should like to know the opinion of the Government of India with special reference to present state of affairs at Koweit and to the measures you could take to make protectorate effective relying on Her Majesty's Government for support at Constantinople diplomatically.[39]

---

37. Busch, *Britain and the Persian Gulf*, p. 105.
38. As quoted in *ibid.*, pp. 106–7.
39. Saldanha, *Precise of Kuwait Affairs*, p. 18.

No sooner was it reported that Count Witte, the Russian Finance Minister, had given his backing to the Kapnist railway project, than Lord Salisbury (without waiting for the reply to Lord Hamilton's communication) moved swiftly and with the utmost secrecy. On 6 January 1899, Curzon was instructed to take immediate steps to conclude a treaty with Sheikh Mubarak. Accordingly, Meade at Curzon's instruction proceeded to Kuwait, and on 23 January the secret agreement was signed. The Kuwaiti ruler agreed not to accept any foreign representative or agent in his country nor to "cede, sell, lease, mortgage or give for occupation or for any other purpose any portion of his territory" to any foreign power or subjects of any power without the prior consent of the British government.[40] In return for these concessions, Meade, on behalf of the British government, assured "Mubarak, his heirs and his successors of the good offices" of the support of the British government. In addition, a payment of 15,000 rupees (£1,000) was made to the Sheikh.[41] The agreement was ratified by the Government of India on 16 February 1899.

However, this treaty, the Exclusive Agreement, still fell short of establishing a formal British protectorate over the Sheikhdom, as Britain reckoned to do so would provoke an unfavourable reaction from the Ottomans, with whom the British government was on friendly terms. Accordingly, the agreement did not spell out Britain's assumption of responsibility for the Sheikhdom's foreign affairs nor did it explicitly guarantee the security of Kuwait against foreign attack. Furthermore, it gave no guarantee for the protection of the Al Sabah family's property in the Ottoman territory near Fao, which was gradually being absorbed by the Ottomans. Yet despite these omissions, Britain over time began to treat the Sheikhdom as one of its protected territories with Anglo-Kuwaiti relations governed by the terms of this agreement until the Sheikhdom achieved full independence in 1961.

Although the Ottomans were unaware of the conclusion of the agreement, Meade's visit to the Sheikhdom in January 1899 greatly

---

40. The full text is in Appendix I.
41. Meade to Mubarak, unnumbered, 23 January 1899, R/15/1/472. See also Mubarak to Meade, unnumbered, 2 February 1899, R/15/1/472; and the 'Communication', Meade to the Brothers of Sheikh Mubarak, unnumbered, 22 January 1899, R/15/1/472.

alarmed them. While increasing their forces at Basra in March 1899, the Ottoman Quarantine Officer there complained that Meade's landing at Kuwait was a violation of Ottoman sanitary regulations. Meade rejected this allegation and argued that no effective or regular quarantine existed at Kuwait and that in any case the quarantine arrangements of the Ottoman Sanitary Board in Constantinople in no way implied any sort of Ottoman jurisdiction or rights over Kuwait. In view of the Ottoman build-up at Basra, Meade then requested the immediate presence of a strong naval force at Kuwait. Although an imminent attack on Kuwait was considered unlikely as the hot weather was approaching, the Secretary of State for India authorized the presence of a naval force in the Gulf.[42] At the same time Mubarak, emboldened by the conclusion of the secret treaty, took provocative measures against the Ottomans. In May 1899, the Sheikh established a customs department in Kuwait and imposed a five per cent *ad valorem* import duty on all goods arriving from Basra and other Ottoman ports, which had been previously exempted from duty. The Porte retaliated in September by announcing the appointment of an Ottoman harbour master for Kuwait port and the establishment of their own custom-house at Kuwait as well as their intention to connect Fao with Qatif by a telegraph line through Kuwait. It was also reported that the Ottoman military authorities at Basra were demanding military action against Kuwait.[43]

Britain's reaction was unequivocal in its support of Mubarak's actions. Under instruction from the Foreign Office, Sir Nicholas O'Conor, the British Ambassador in Constantinople, warned the Porte on 8 September 1899 that since Britain had friendly relations with Sheikh Mubarak any attempt on the part of the Ottoman government to establish customs control at Kuwait without the prior consent of the British government would have wider repercussions. As a result of this warning, the Ottomans relented and decided to try to win over the Kuwaiti ruler by guile. The new wali of Basra, Mohsin Pasha, who replaced the hard-liner Hamdi Pasha in early 1900, reversed the aggressive approach of his predecessor by pursuing a "clever policy of gaining a hold" on Sheikh Mubarak by conciliatory measures. On his recommendation, Sultan Abdul-Hamid II conferred on Mubarak the

---

42. Saldanha, *Precise of Kuwait Affairs*, pp. 22–4.
43. *Ibid.*, p. 25–6.

title of Pasha and fixed 150 karas (1 kara = approximately 1½ tons) of dates as his annual subsidy.[44] No evidence exists, however, as to whether Sheikh Mubarak accepted this favour.

Meanwhile, Baron Von Marschall, the German Ambassador in Constantinople, persuaded the Porte to issue a decree on 25 November 1899 granting the Anatolian Railway Company a preliminary concession to construct a railway line from Konya to Baghdad. The Anatolian Railway Company was established in 1888 by two German financiers, Herr Kaula of the Wurtembergische Bank and Dr George Siemens, the Director of the Deutsche Bank, to construct a railway line from Constantinople to Angora. Germany's main objective behind the construction of railway projects in the Ottoman Empire was to exploit the Ottoman markets for its own rapidly growing industry. On the other hand, Sultan Abdul-Hamid II favoured the Baghdad railway project as he believed the scheme, once in operation, would make a significant contribution to the economic development, unification and security of his Asian domains. Therefore, the Sultan permitted a commission of experts appointed by the Anatolian Railway Company to survey the route for the possible expansion of the projected Konya–Baghdad line to the Gulf. The commission, headed by Herr Stemrich, the German Consul-General in Constantinople, arrived in Kuwait in early January 1900, with the Sultan's approval, in search of a terminus for the planned Berlin–Baghdad Railway. The commission selected Kadhamah at the head of Kuwait bay as a suitable site for the terminus and attempted to open negotiations with the Sheikh for its purchase. When Sheikh Mubarak refused to negotiate, the commission recommended its acquisition directly from the Ottoman Sultan.[45]

Britain was concerned that if the Germans established their railway terminus in Kadhamah, which was the best harbour in the entire Gulf and the most suitable for a military base, it would be difficult to dispossess them of it later if this became necessary. Therefore, upon the Foreign office's recommendation, Lord Salisbury, now the British Prime Minister, immediately agreed to disclose the nature of the existing Exclusive Agreement to Germany. Accordingly, on 10 April 1900, O'Conor told Baron Von Marschall, the German Ambassador in

---

44. *Ibid.*, pp. 26–8.
45. *Ibid.*, pp. 28–9. See also Lorimer, *Gazetteer*, (Historical), pp. 1026–7.

Constantinople, that Britain had an agreement with Kuwait, which although not opposed to the status quo, prohibited the ruler from making concessions to any other power without the prior consent of the British government. Von Marschall, however, declined to accept this restriction. He argued that the agreement would not prevent the construction of a railway as the Sheikhdom was still "a part of the Ottoman Empire". This unrealistic assertion compelled O'Conor to tell him that although Britain was averse to distrupting the status quo, the Kuwaiti ruler was "not a free agent". Later that day, O'Conor saw Tawfiq Pasha, the Ottoman Foreign Minister, and told him that since Britain had "certain agreements" with Kuwait, it would not allow any other power to have rights or privileges over Sheikh Mubarak's territory. As the Pasha raised no questions, the Ambassador believed that the Ottomans were already aware of the nature of the Exclusive Agreement of 1899. Despite these warnings, the Anatolian Railway Company made preparations for the construction of a pier at Kadhamah, once again raising the question of the international status of Kuwait. In June 1900, Sir Frank Lascelles, the British Ambassador in Berlin, clarified Kuwait's position to Chancellor Von Bulow informing him that Sheikh Mubarak had been enjoying "a large measure of independence", having maintained no political or administrative links with the Ottoman state.[46] As a result of this diplomatic representation, the Anatolian Railway Company made no immediate attempt to continue with the project.

In May 1900, while Sheikh Mubarak was concluding another secret treaty with Britain prohibiting the importation and exportation of arms into and from Kuwait,[47] he involved himself in the dynastic rivalries between the houses of Saud and Rashid. Following an unsuccessful revolt in 1891 by the Wahhabi Imam Abdul-Rahman ibn Faisal Al Saud against the Rashid family, the Imam sought refuge in Kuwait together with his son Abdul-Aziz (who later became the first king of Saudi Arabia). In October 1900, Mubarak extended his wholehearted support to Abdul-Aziz ibn Saud in raiding Ibn Rashid's territory, angering Ibn Rashid to such an extent that he openly threatened an attack on Kuwait.

---

46. Lorimer, *Gazetter* (Historical), p. 1027. See also Busch, *Britain and the Persian Gulf*, pp. 193–4; and Memorandum by Harcourt, 'Respecting Kuwait', no. 7696, 29 October 1901, L/P&S/18/B133.
47. Aitchison, *A Collection of Treaties*, p. 262.

Mohsin Pasha, who had been waiting for a chance to boost Ottoman prestige in Kuwait, at once intervened and persuaded Ibn Rashid, through his emissaries, not to attack Kuwait. Thereupon, Mubarak was asked to meet the wali of Basra, which he did on 17 November 1900. As a result of this encounter, relations between the Sheikh and the Ottoman authorities were reinforced, so much so that Sheikh Mubarak even promised to abstain from having relations with "foreign powers".[48]

The arrangement was, however, short-lived. Ibn Rashid, who could not relinquish his grievance against Mubarak, attacked the Bedouins loyal to Kuwait in the deserts of Dahanah and Summan in December 1900. In response, Mubarak and his ally, Abdul-Aziz ibn Saud, undertook fresh preparations for an attack on Najd, which alarmed Lieutenant Colonel Charles Kemball, the Acting Resident. Kemball, concerned that a second crisis might provide the Ottoman Empire with an excuse for a greater degree of interference in the affairs of Kuwait, wrote to Mubarak on 10 December 1900 requesting that he did not pursue an aggressive policy towards Ibn Rashid. Kemball added: "It seems to me that you are pursuing a dangerous policy by continuing to provoke the Emir of Najd and I again counsel you to keep quiet."[49] Ignoring this advice, Mubarak, in February 1901, joined with Abdul-Rahman and Abdul-Aziz and together proceeded as far as Riyadh, the capital of Najd. By mid-February, the joint forces captured Riyadh and Abdul-Aziz ibn Saud was installed as its governor. Following this, Mubarak continued on towards Hail, where he met Ibn Rashid in a major battle, which ended in the Sheikh's total defeat. He returned to Kuwait on 31 December 1901.[50]

Mubarak's defeat prompted further Ottoman attempts at interference in Kuwait. In April 1901, A. C. Wratislaw, the British Consul in Basra, reported on the movement of troops from Baghdad to Basra under the command of the Ottoman Field Marshal, Muhammad Pasha, suggesting that the Porte was about to use force to depose Mubarak. In a pre-emptive move the British dispatched the gunboat HMS *Sphinx* to

---

48. Lorimer, *Gazetteer*, (Historical), p. 1028. See also Saldanha, *Precise of Kuwait Affairs*, pp. 31–2.
49. Saldanha, *Precise of Kuwait Affairs*, p. 34.
50. *Ibid.*, p. 35.

Kuwait with Kemball on board to demonstrate British support of Mubarak, while O'Conor was instructed to warn the Porte to refrain from any action against the Sheikh in view of Britain's "special arrangement" with him. To avert a possible Anglo-Ottoman armed clash, the astute Mohsin Pasha ordered the Field Marshal to halt the advance towards Kuwait, and proceeded to Kuwait in person on 19 May 1901. The wali pressed the ruler to accept the presence of a small Ottoman garrison in Kuwait for his own protection – an offer Sheikh Mubarak politely refused. Mohsin Pasha's unsuccessful military mission in Kuwait eventually led to his replacement by Nuri Pasha as wali and military commander at Basra in October 1901.[51]

Mohsin's request for an Ottoman garrison to be stationed in Kuwait spurred Sheikh Mubarak to seek a permanent British protectorate over Kuwait and 28 May 1901, the Sheikh formally applied to the Resident, through the commander of HMS *Sphinx*, for such protection.[52] Both Kemball and Curzon immediately gave their unqualified support to the proposal, arguing that a permanent British protectorate would protect Mubarak against attack from either the Ottoman Empire or from Ibn Rashid. However, Lord Lansdowne, the British Foreign Secretary, who believed that Britain could preserve its position in Kuwait without establishing a protectorate, opposed it on the grounds that the declaration of a British protectorate might arouse serious opposition not only from the Ottoman Empire but also from Germany. Lord Hamilton, the Secretary of State for India, agreed. On 23 July 1901, the Viceroy was informed of London's decision not to proclaim Kuwait a protectorate,[53] shelving the idea without discussion.

The British government's rejection of Mubarak's request for protectorate status intensified the debate over both the international status of Kuwait and of the siting of the Berlin–Baghdad railway project. On raising these issues with Sir Frank Lascelles, Dr Rosen of the German

---

51. *Ibid.*, pp. 35–6. See also Busch, *Britain and the Persian Gulf*, pp. 199–200; and Memorandum by Harcourt, 'Respecting Kuwait', no. 7696, 29 October 1901, L/P&S/18/B133, p. 12.
52. Commander, HMS *Sphinx*, to the Resident, unnumbered, 29 May 1901, R/15/1/474.
53. Busch, *Britain and the Persian Gulf*, pp. 201–2. See also Saldanha, *Precise of Kuwait Affairs*, p. 37.

Foreign office told the Ambassador that Germany still considered Kuwait the most suitable site for the terminus of the railway and that the German Emperor himself was interested in the scheme. He therefore wanted clarification about reports that Britain was planning to annex Kuwait. Explaining the reasons behind Britain's "special arrangements" with Mubarak, Lascelles attempted to relieve German apprehensions and reiterated his earlier assertion:

> His Majesty's Government had no intention of annexing, or even proclaiming a protectorate over, Koweit. Our position in the Persian Gulf has rendered it advisable for us to make special arrangements with the Sheikh of Koweit, who, although technically a subject of the Sultan, enjoyed a considerable amount of independence.[54]

The reference to Sheikh Mubarak as an Ottoman subject infuriated Hamilton, the Secretary of State for India, who brought the Ambassador's unauthorised statement to the attention of the Foreign Secretary. As a result, Lascelles was warned not to make such remarks in the future as the Germans might take advantage of them to argue that the Ottoman Sultan could occupy Kuwait.[55]

While the attention of the British government was focused on the proposed railway, the attitude of the Ottomans towards Kuwait became increasingly hostile. Concentrating a large military force on the Euphrates, the Ottoman sloop of war *Zuhaf* entered Kuwait harbour on 24 August 1901. Britain immediately took the necessary measures in order to defend Kuwait. Captain E. R. Pears, the commander of the British gunboat HMS *Perseus*, which was then in Kuwait bay, warned the captain of the *Zuhaf* that any attempt by Ottoman forces to land on Kuwaiti shores would be prevented by force if necessary. While the Ottoman captain attempted to justify his mission by arguing that the whole area from Fao to Qatar, including Kuwait, was Ottoman territory, Captain Pears informed him that the British government regarded Kuwait as being independent. Consequently, the captain of the *Zuhaf*

---

54. Lascelles to Lansdowne, no. 191, 30 July 1901, L/P&S/19.
55. Busch, *Britain and the Persian Gulf*, pp. 202–3. See also Memorandum by Harcourt, 'Respecting Kuwait', no. 7696, 29 October 1901, L/P&S/18/B133.

kept his forces aboard and went ashore himself the following day. He then had a meeting with Sheikh Mubarak, at which he attempted to obtain a pledge from the Sheikh accepting Ottoman suzerainty. Failing to obtain this, he left for Fao, threatening Mubarak with future punishment.[56]

Pears's military intervention precipitated an Anglo-Ottoman diplomatic crisis. On 29 August 1901, Tawfiq Pasha, the Ottoman Foreign Minister, summoned O'Conor, the British Ambassador in Constantinople, and strongly protested against Pears's behaviour. The Foreign Minister then demanded to know whether Britain intended to establish a protectorate over Kuwait. O'Conor assured him that Britain had no intention of doing so, provided that the Ottomans did not force Britain's hand by interfering with Sheikh Mubarak, with whom Britain had a "special arrangement". Heated exchanges continued between the two sides until 9 September 1901 when both governments agreed to maintain the status quo of Kuwait. This agreement was reached on the understanding that, in return for the Ottoman government not sending any troops to Kuwait, Britain agreed to abstain from occupying the Sheikhdom or establishing a protectorate over it.[57]

Within three months, however, the Ottomans violated the terms of this status quo arrangement. On 3 December 1901, the naqib of Basra, acting on the Sultan's order, travelled in person to Kuwait and bluntly told Sheikh Mubarak that he could either go to Constantinople and enjoy the status of a member of the Council of State on a high salary or leave the Sheikhdom empty-handed. Alternatively, he could stay in Kuwait on condition that he severed his links with the British government and accepted Ottoman protection with some Ottoman soldiers stationed there. The naqib's threat was apparently to serve the interest of Ibn Rashid, who had already taken up position in the area down from Hafar towards Safwan, on the frontier between Ottoman Iraq and

---

56. For more details on Pears's heated argument with the captain of the *Zuhaf,* see extract from a letter, Pears to the Senior Naval Officer in the Gulf, unnumbered, 25 August 1901, R/15/1/474. See also Lorimer, *Gazetteer,* (Historical), p. 1030.

57. For more details, see Saldanha, *Precise of Kuwait Affairs,* pp. 40–1; see also Memorandum by Harcourt, Respecting Kuwait, no. 7696, 29 October 1901, L/P & S/18/B133, pp. 14–5.

Kuwait. Sheikh Mubarak tactfully avoided giving any immediate reply to the naqib's ultimatum and sought Kemball's advice on the matter.[58]

Captain Simon, the Senior Naval Officer, who was already in Kuwait, instantly reassured the Sheikh on behalf of Kemball that he could rely on Britain's support to defend his country against the Turks. As the Sheikh, who expected a definite pledge of support from Britain, was not satisfied with this mere assurance, Captain Simon met with the naqib and informed him that it was he who forbade the Sheikh to answer his ultimatum as this constituted a violation of the Porte's understanding with London to preserve the status quo in Kuwait. On hearing this, the naqib left Kuwait empty-handed on 4 December.[59] Two days later, HMS *Sphinx* arrived at Kuwait with a letter for the Sheikh from Kemball embodying the substance of a telegram from Lord Hamilton, the Secretary of State for India. The telegram reassured Mubarak that the British government would not remain silent if the Sheikhdom was attacked by the Turks. The telegram read:

> There can be no reason for fresh assertion of Sultan's rights or for attempt to further define them, which, if not superfluous, must clearly involve alteration. The action of the Nakib appears to constitute distinct violation of Sultan's promise, and in these circumstances His Majesty's Government are prepared to support Sheikh, and will not tolerate an attack by Turkish troops or ships on Koweit. Sheikh should not leave Koweit and should continue to observe his engagements with us.[60]

Simultaneous representations against the naqib's activities in Kuwait were duly made to the Ottoman government. The Porte, however, immediately denied all knowledge of the naqib's initiative, and assured the British government that it had no intention of either sending troops to Kuwait or disturbing the status quo.[61]

---

58. Lorimer, *Gazetteer*, (Historical), p. 1031. See also Sheikh Mubarak to Kemball, unnumbered, 3 December 1901, L/P&S/19; and Saldanha, *Precise of Kuwait Affairs*, pp. 46–8.
59. Captain Simons to Rear Admiral Day H. Bosanquet, unnumbered, 14 December 1901, L/P&S/19.
60. As quoted in Saldanha, *Precise of Kuwait Affairs*, p. 48.
61. See *ibid*.

Despite this explicit pledge, the status quo arrangement was soon on the verge of collapse when the Ottomans made direct encroachments on Kuwaiti territories. This happened in late January 1902, when Turkish forces occupied Safwan and Umm Qasr (64 kilometres north-north-east of Kuwait City on the Khor Abdullah) and established military garrisons there. Perceiving this move as a direct threat to Kuwait, Sheikh Mubarak immediately sought Britain's help in ejecting the Ottomans under the terms of the 1899 agreement, arguing that these areas were within the boundary of Kuwait's territory and had belonged to Kuwait for a long time.[62] The Sheikh said that while Umm Qasr was originally occupied by a subject of Kuwait in 1862, Safwan had permanently been inhabited by 10 Kuwaiti families for the last 40 years and had always paid tribute to Kuwait. He added that these two areas had never been occupied by the Ottomans.[63] Careful not to press the Turks for immediate withdrawal from these places, O'Conor, at Lansdowne's instruction, simply told Tawfiq Pasha, the Ottoman Foreign Minister, on 8 February 1902, that the authority of the ruler of Kuwait had hitherto existed in Umm Qasr and Safwan and, therefore, the Ottoman occupation of these places was a contravention of the terms of the Anglo-Ottoman understanding of September 1901, which prohibited Ottoman military encroachments on Kuwait's territory. Tawfiq Pasha, who was not even aware of the geographical location of these places, assured O'Conor that the occupation of Umm Qasr and Safwan was not directed against the Sheikh, as the Ottoman government had relinquished all ideas of attacking Kuwait. The Foreign Minister stated that the occupation, particularly in the case of Umm Qasr, which was close to the shore, was instead prompted by the desire of the Anatolian Railway Company to keep a free passage to the sea. He informed the Ambassador that the company was no longer interested in Kuwait as a terminus for fear of it falling into the hands of a foreign power, which would deny the railway access to the sea. O'Conor replied that there was no reason for such speculation as the British government had never

---

62. Sheikh Mubarak to Lt Col Charles Arnold Kemball (Acting Resident), unnumbered, 22 July 1901, R/15/1/475. See also Government of India to Hamilton, unnumbered, 28 January 1902, L/P&S/19.
63. Government of India to Hamilton, unnumbered, 11 February 1902, L/P&S/19.

raised any objection to a terminus at Kuwait and, indeed, had no intention of doing so, provided the railway went there with Britain's approval and the consent of the Kuwaiti ruler.[64]

As the Ottoman motive behind the occupation of Safwan and Umm Qasr was not quite clear, the British gunboat *Sphinx*, under the command of T. W. Kemp, arrived at Umm Qasr on 15 February 1902 to assess the situation and also the commercial potentialities of Umm Qasr. On landing there, Commander Kemp found an Ottoman camp with 40 men and, opposing it, a camp of some 70 Bedouins belonging to Sheikh Mubarak. As the Sheikh's contingent was ready to attack the Ottomans, Kemp dissuaded them from doing so. He then extensively toured the area and noted that the shores of the harbour of Umm Qasr would provide a better location than the shores of Kuwait harbour for the terminus of the proposed Berlin–Baghdad railway. Pointing out the natural advantages of Umm Qasr, Kemp stated that it was "quite land-locked and a good anchorage", and that it could easily be turned into a suitable commercial harbour for ships of all sizes, so long as the Khor Abdullah was surveyed and buoyed.[65] Despite Kemp's favourable report and his assessment of the Qasr as a valuable commercial asset, Britain took no action to expel the Ottoman forces stationed there in order to avoid a direct military confrontation with them.

As the British registered no strong protest against the deployment of the troops at Safwan and Umm Qasr, the Ottomans, in early February 1902, made a further advance as far as Bubiyan Island. The island, which was uninhabited, is approximately 42 kilometres long and 19 kilometres wide and lies at the north-western corner of the Arabian Gulf and Khor Abdullah, separating it from the mouth of the Shatt al-Arab. Bubiyan Island is about 1.6 kilometres away from Kuwait and 5 kilometres from Ottoman Iraq. The Ottoman force, consisting of 20 men and an officer, established its garrison at Ras al-Qaid, the eastern-most point of the island. Sheikh Mubarak instantly claimed Bubiyan as Kuwait's on the grounds that his subjects occupied it annually for

---

64. O'Conor to Lansdowne, no. 56, 13 February 1902, L/P&S/19.
65. For the full text of Commodore Kemp's report, see the enclosure in Captain Pelham to Rear Admiral Bosanquet, unnumbered, 22 February 1902, L/P&S/19.

fishing and paid him rent. Kemball, who considered both the Khor Abdullah and Bubiyan as within the limits of Kuwait, supported the Sheikh. He argued that Britain should instruct the Ottomans to leave Bubiyan without delay, as failure to do so would encourage a further Ottoman advance possibly to Subiya.[66]

O'Conor's opinion, however, differed from that of Kemball, in that he did not consider the Sheikh's arguments to be sufficiently convincing to justify his claims to Umm Qasr and Bubiyan. Reporting to London, O'Conor argued that it would be difficult to interpret the action of the Turks in Bubiyan or Umm Qasr as constituting a disturbance of the status quo in Kuwait and that the British should be content with maintaining the Sheikh's authority over Kuwait. Endorsing O'Conor's recommendation, the Foreign Office made no demand for an Ottoman withdrawal from either Umm Qasr or Bubiyan.[67] The Ottomans, encouraged by this lack of opposition, decided to move on Haqaijah and Subiya, two important areas on the mainland opposite Bubiyan Island. Kemball, without waiting for London's authorization, asked Sheikh Mubarak to occupy these places at once to head off the Ottomans. The Sheikh complied in March 1902 by deploying his armed forces there,[68] and justified his actions by arguing that Haqaijah and Subiya belonged to him as some of his subjects had always lived there. Kemball, anxious to check the Ottoman advance before it became a direct threat to Kuwait, defended Mubarak's claims to Haqaijah and Subiya in his dispatch to the Government of India:

> The Sheikh's claim to this place [Haqaijah], and also Subiya, inde-
> pendently of his relations with Turkey, may, perhaps, be not much

---

66. Kemball to the Foreign Secretary, Calcutta, no. 316, 3 March 1902, quoted in Saldanha, *Precise of Kuwait Affairs*, p. 54. See also Kemball to the Foreign Secretary, Calcutta, no. 308, 25 February 1902, quoted in Saldanha, *Precise of Kuwait Affairs*. For the geographical features of Bubiyan Island, see J. G. Lorimer, *Gazetteer of the Persian Gulf, Oman and Central Arabia* (Geographical and Statistical), Part 2A (Calcutta, Government Printing, 1908), p. 324.

67. Lord George Hamilton (Secretary of State for India) to Curzon, unnumbered, 12 March 1902, in Saldanha, *Precise of Kuwait Affairs*, p. 54. See also Hamilton to Curzon, no. 340, 14 March 1902, quoted in Saldanha, *Precise of Kuwait Affairs*.

68. Curzon to Hamilton, no. 343, 17 March 1902, quoted in Saldanha, *Precise of Kuwait Affairs*, p. 54. See also Foreign Office to India Office, unnumbered, 15 March 1902, L/P&S/19.

stronger than his claims to Um Kasr and Bubiyan, but their occupation by the Turks would undoubtedly cause him great anxiety, and I am of opinion that his claims to them should be upheld.[69]

Kemball's firm support for Mubarak prompted London to re-examine the whole question of Kuwait. In a memorandum of 21 March 1902, Lansdowne attempted to clarify Britain's obligation to the Sheikh under the terms of the 1899 Exclusive Agreement, stating that when Britain made its pledge of "good offices" it had thought in terms of Kuwait proper. "No one knows where his possessions begin and end", the Foreign Secretary remarked; he therefore felt it necessary to tell the Porte as well as the Sheikh that British obligations to Kuwait did not "extend beyond the district adjoining or close to the bay of that name", and that the British government should "endeavour to obtain the adhesion of the Porte and of the Sheikh to an approximate definition of that district". However, on 24 March, the Foreign Secretary instructed O'Conor to remind the Porte that Britain was obliged to give Mubarak its support against attacks or attempts to encroach upon his territories or to diminish his privileges. Lansdowne then confirmed that Britain had no right to place any obstacles in the way of the extension of the railway from Baghdad to the Gulf or to Kuwait, or indeed any other location which might be selected as its terminus. However, British assistance would be conditional upon British business receiving a share at least equal to that of any other power as regards orders for materials and construction contracts as well as for management of the line. The Ambassador was further asked to make it clear to the Porte that British cooperation was essential in order to secure the goodwill of the Sheikh and his tribesmen.[70]

The following day, O'Conor met the Grand Vizier and informed him of Britain's anxiety over the Ottoman encroachments upon the Sheikh's territories, which had greatly diminished his prestige. The Ambassador also clarified the British stance on the proposed extension of the railway, stating that the Ottomans could count upon Britain's

---

69. Kemball to Government of India, unnumbered, 16 March 1902, L/P&S/19.
70. Memorandum by Lansdowne, unnumbered, 21 March 1902, L/P&S/19. See also Lansdowne to O'Conor, no. 54, 24 March 1902, L/P&S/19.

support on certain conditions. In response, the Grand Vizier explained that the underlying reason behind the advance to Safwan, Umm Qasr and Bubiyan was the Ottoman belief that Britain intended to deny the railway access to the Gulf. Since his conversation with O'Conor had seemed to convince the Grand Vizier that Britain had no such motive, the Ambassador was assured that the Ottoman government would abide by the terms of the status quo arrangement of 1901 and cease all efforts to disturb the existing order.[71] On 1 April, Tawfiq Pasha reiterated this to O'Conor. Denying the reported dispatch of troops to Subiya and Haqaijah, he reassured the Ambassador that the Porte was determined to respect the status quo arrangement and to end all further encroachments on the Sheikh's territory. However, he fell short of giving an assurance of an Ottoman withdrawal from the newly occupied territories. In light of this omission, Tawfiq Pasha was reminded that the occupation of Umm Qasr and Bubiyan "could not be regarded as in any way prejudicing the Sheikh's rights and authority over them". O'Conor did not hesitate to warn the Foreign Minister that Britain would take military action in the event of any further Ottoman encroachments.[72]

As a result of this warning, the Ottomans abandoned any idea of making further moves on Mubarak's territory and instead adopted a different tactic. The Ottoman authorities at Basra incited Sheikh Mubarak's three arch-enemies – Yusuf al-Ibrahim of Dora and the Sheikh's two dissident nephews, Adhbi bin Muhammad and Hamud bin Jarrah, who had withdrawn to Basra – to launch a series of attacks on the border at Safwan as well as on Subiya. Hostilities continued against the Sheikh until the British government brought pressure to bear on the Ottomans to expel the two nephews from Basra in December 1902.[73] While Adhbi and Hamud resolved their differences with Sheikh Mubarak, Yusuf joined forces with Ibn Rashid, who having failed to recapture Riyadh from Ibn Saud, threatened the Sheikh and, on 20 December 1902, made a surprise attack on his tribesmen who resided in the vicinity of Jahra. Mubarak immediately proceeded to Jahra with a large number of his followers, a development which was regarded by the

---

71. O'Conor to Lansdowne, no. 144, 25 March 1902, L/P&S/19.
72. See O'Conor to Lansdowne, no. 153, 1 April 1902, L/P&S/19.
73. Saldanha, *Precise of Kuwait Affairs*, pp. 64–5.

Ottoman authorities at Basra as a direct threat to Zubair. Therefore, on 18 January 1903, Kemball, at London's instruction, persuaded the Sheikh not to take any military action against Ibn Rashid as this might entail direct confrontation with the Ottomans. Accordingly, Mubarak refrained from attacking Ibn Rashid (whose power was declining as a result of his wars with Ibn Saud). With Sheikh Mubarak's son, Jaber, in firm control of Jahra, Ibn Saud accompanied by his brother Muhammad paid a visit to Kuwait to consult with Sheikh Mubarak in March 1903. This signalled "the end of the alarms caused by Ibn Rashid", according to Lorimer.[74] Over time, Sheikh Mubarak's internal position greatly improved and anxiety over the stability of the local situation gradually diminished.

Conclusion

While Sheikh Mubarak was able to improve his position at home, his position with the Ottoman Empire remained unchanged, as it showed no sign of withdrawing from Umm Qasr and Bubiyan. Kuwait, there-fore, was still at the mercy of foreign powers. Its strategic location on the one hand, and the German desire to establish a railway terminus at Kadhamah, on the other, did not engender stability. Although Kuwait maintained close contact with the Ottoman state during the nineteenth century, there was no valid reason to consider it as under Ottoman juris-diction or administration. Even Midhat Pasha in the 1870s made no attempt to establish Ottoman administration in the Sheikhdom or bring it under the Basra Vilayet, though he maintained cordial relations with Sheikh Abdullah (II) and his successor.

Subsequently, the assumption of power by Sheikh Mubarak was a turning-point in the history of modern Kuwait as he successfully resisted, with British help, Ottoman interference in his country. British strategic requirements in Kuwait, arising out of the growing Russo-German designs in the Gulf in addition to Britain's apprehension of losing Kuwait either to the Ottomans or another foreign power,

---

74. See Lorimer, *Gazetteer* (Historical), p. 1037. See also Saldanha, *Precise of Kuwait Affairs*, pp. 60–3; and Kuwait Agent to Kemball, unnumbered, 22 December 1902, L/P&S/19.

eventually forced a favourable response to Sheikh Mubarak's call for protection by the conclusion of the Exclusive Agreement in 1899, which defined the British position in Kuwait. While the agreement did not install a formal protectorate over Kuwait, it established a predominant position for Britain in the country. However, as Britain remained non-committal as regards the formal protection of Kuwait, the Ottomans persisted with their military threats against the Sheikhdom despite British protestations, while the Germans for their part, intensified their efforts for the construction of the proposed railway terminus there.

Anglo-Ottoman diplomatic wranglings over Kuwait continued until both parties agreed in September 1901, to maintain the status quo. To the surprise of the British and the Sheikh, however, the Ottomans soon violated the terms of this arrangement by occupying Safwan, Umm Qasr and Bubiyan, thereby posing a direct threat to Kuwait. The Ottomans did so because they were convinced that Britain intended to block all access to the Gulf for the proposed railway. Despite the Sheikh's claims to these locations, Britain did nothing to eject the Ottomans except to lodge diplomatic protests.

2

The Status of Kuwait
and its Northern Frontier

In response to Turkish encroachments on Kuwaiti territory to safeguard the interests of the Baghdad Railway Concessionaires in the Khor Abdullah inlet, Britain remodelled its policy in Kuwait by appointing a Political Agent in the Sheikhdom. The secret Bandar Shuwaikh Lease Agreement of 1907 facilitated a further strengthening of the British hold over Kuwait, thereby effectively debarring other powers from gaining any political and commercial advantages in the country. Though Sheikh Mubarak readily accommodated British interests, London was reluctant to recognize his claims to Warba, Bubiyan, Safwan and Umm Qasr. But the Sheikh's tireless struggle to assert his ownership of these islands and locations raised both the question of Kuwait's status and the issue of its territorial limits – particularly its northern frontier – more forcefully than ever. The Anglo-Ottoman debates over Kuwait as well as other Gulf issues continued until the signing of a convention in 1913, which defined the territories of the Sheikhdom and recognized the Sheikh's right of ownership to Warba and Bubiyan as well as to other islands and islets. Turkey's declaration of war against Britain and its allies in October 1914, brought about a significant change in the British perception of Kuwait. After the war, Turkey renounced its claims on Kuwait, and in 1923 a boundary line between Kuwait and the newly established Iraq was delineated. This boundary line was reconfirmed in 1932, by an exchange of letters between Iraq and Kuwait.

The emergence of Kuwait with a defined territory should, therefore, be discussed against the background of British policy towards the proposed Berlin–Baghdad railway scheme and the continuous Ottoman hold over Umm Qasr and Bubiyan. The first quarter of 1903 witnessed intensified efforts on the part of the Anatolian Railway Company to obtain permission to extend the Berlin–Baghdad line to Basra. In March 1903, the company was able to conclude a definitive concession ement with the Ottoman government for the construction and peration of an extension of the line from Konya in Turkey to Baghdad and Basra.[1] Although the project never wholly materialized, the awarding of the contract intensified European rivalries in the Middle East. The promoters of the scheme soon offered Britain a 25 per cent share in the project provided that Britain made the necessary customs arrangements, which included allowing an Ottoman custom-house at Kuwait. Although the Foreign Office initially gave serious consideration to the offer, it eventually backed out because of a hostile press campaign as well as unfavourable public opinion in Britain against the whole scheme which would allow German penetration into the Gulf.[2]

The Foreign Office's recommendation not to join in the Baghdad Railway project prompted Britain to remodel its policy towards Kuwait in a way that would increase its involvement beyond the status quo arrangement. This marked change on the part of the British government was due to its conviction that if the promoters of the railway project developed the Khor Abdullah inlet as the terminus of the railway without Britain's participation, it would jeopardize Britain's economic and political interests as it would provide Germany with legitimate grounds to challenge Britain's monopoly in that part of the Gulf. Following a six-month-long debate on the best way to strengthen the British position in Kuwait, with ideas ranging from placing it under the jurisdiction of the Consul at Basra to the stationing of an Agent in Kuwait, Lord Curzon, the Viceroy of India, arrived in Kuwait at the end of November 1903.[3] This was his first visit to the Sheikhdom and the first by such a high-ranking British dignitary. The visit consolidated Britain's influence in Kuwait and "placed in a clear light" Sheikh Mubarak's cordial relations with the British Empire. The Viceroy, however, looked beyond the horizon of Kuwait. On 30 November, the steamer RIMS *Lawrence*, with Lord Curzon on board, entered the Khor Abdullah and sailed on to the junction of the Khor Umm Qasr and Khor Zubair.[4] The Viceroy was convinced that "all the anchorages in Umm Kasr and round Warba Island were greatly preferable to Koweit and would afford an impregnable

1. J. C. Hurewitz, *Diplomacy in the Near and Middle East: A Documentary Record 1914–1956,* vol. 1 (New York, Octagon Books, 1972), pp. 252–63.
2. Busch, *Britain and the Persian Gulf,* pp. 222–3.
3. *Ibid.,* p. 224.
4. Lorimer, *Gazetteer* (Historical), p. 1038.

harbour". Curzon concluded that the Ottomans should be told to withdraw their garrison at Ras al-Qaid on Bubiyan Island. If they did not, Britain would assist the Sheikh in establishing a Kuwaiti post at the northern end of Bubiyan to counterbalance the Ottomans at Umm Qasr and Ras al-Qaid and would inform the Porte that Britain considered Bubiyan as belonging to Sheikh Mubarak.[5]

As the Viceroy continued his campaign for an Ottoman withdrawal from Bubiyan Island, where the garrison then consisted of some six men in total, the Foreign Office eventually instructed O'Conor to remind the Ottomans that their military post at Ras al-Qaid violated the terms of the status quo understanding of 1901. Accordingly, on 16 May 1904 the Ambassador told Tawfiq Pasha, the Ottoman Foreign Minister, that if the Ottomans failed to withdraw their forces from Bubiyan, Britain would have no alternative but to support the Sheikh in establishing his own garrison on the island. Although the Foreign Minister acknowledged the Sheikh's enjoyment of some "sort of semi-independence" over Kuwait, he declined to accept his claims to Bubiyan unless he produced proof showing that the island belonged to him. To this O'Conor replied that Britain fully accepted Sheikh Mubarak's claims to Bubiyan, a place where the Ottomans had never even pretended to exercise any kind of authority.

Despite this protest, the Ottomans showed no sign of retreat.[6] While maintaining their hold over Bubiyan, they involved themselves more heavily than ever in the renewed struggle between Ibn Rashid and Ibn Saud when the latter captured Buraida and Unayza in the interior of Arabia. In May 1904, the Ottomans dispatched a well-equipped brigade of 4,200 troops in support of the retreating Ibn Rashid. This Ottoman support in reviving the seriously weakened position of Ibn Rashid alarmed William St John Broderick, the Secretary of State for India. He believed that if Ibn Saud were defeated, a possible attack on Kuwait from the direction of Najd was very likely, which would destroy Sheikh Mubarak's influence and lead to the establishment of Ottoman supremacy in Najd. As a result, Broderick quickly appointed Captain

5. Saldanha, *Precise of Kuwait Affairs*, pp. 73–4.
6. Schofield, *Kuwait and Iraq*, pp. 30–1.

Stuart Knox as the temporary Political Agent in Kuwait in order to strengthen British authority there.[7] The India Office defined his main duties and responsibilities as follows:

> His first objects should be to cultivate and maintain close and friendly relations with Sheikh Mubarak and the principal personages in Koweit. The interests of British trade and traders at Koweit and in the adjacent tracts of Arabia should be safeguarded, and a vigilant watch kept over the proceedings of the Turks on the boundaries of Koweit territories. Matters tending to show an intention, on the part of the Turks or any other Power, to interfere with, or disturb, the existing status quo or anything which would lead to a belief that any other Powers have designs on, or in connection with, possible harbours within or without Koweit territory should at once be reported. Special regard in this respect should be paid to Khor Abdulla and the waters round Bubiyan Island and Um Kasr.[8]

In addition to these tasks, Captain Knox was also to try to ascertain the efficacy of Sheikh Mubarak's occupation of Haqaijah and Khor Subiya. Furthermore, he was to endeavour to secure early and accurate information on the struggle for supremacy in Najd between Ibn Saud and Ibn Rashid. At the same time O'Conor was instructed to tell the Ottoman government that it should refrain from taking any action which might further disturb the status quo in Arabia and restrain Ibn Rashid from embarking on a course of action which might endanger peace in the region.[9]

As soon as Captain Knox arrived in Kuwait on 6 August 1904, the Porte strongly protested that "the presence of a British Officer at Kuwait was in contradiction with the agreement arrived at to maintain the status quo in those regions." When on 3 November 1904, the Ottoman Grand Vizier Farid Pasha demanded the immediate withdrawal of Knox from Kuwait, Walter Townley, the Chargé d'Affaires in Constantinople, justified Knox's appointment as a necessary measure in view of the continued maintenance of the Ottoman military post on Bubiyan Island.

---

7. Secretary of State for India to the Viceroy, no. 1748-EA, 29 May 1904, quoted in Saldanha, *Precise of Kuwait Affairs*, p. 86.
8. The Under-Secretary (to the Government of India) to P. Z. Cox (the Resident in the Gulf), no. 2918-EA, 7 September 1904, R/15/5/59.
9. *Ibid.*

The Grand Vizier defended the Turkish position by arguing that "the military post had been established on the island for the protection of the fishermen on the coast, and that Sheikh Mubarak had never established any claim to the island, which was a barren, uninhabitable waste." Although Townley did not accept this explanation,[10] the Ottomans persisted with their protests against Knox's appointment with such vehemence that the British government decided to withdraw him in order to avert souring relations with the Ottoman government.[11] Knox left Kuwait in May 1905.

Though Britain withdrew its Agent from Kuwait (ostensibly) in deference to the status quo arrangement, the Ottomans still maintained their hold over Bubiyan. Therefore, in June 1905, Britain decided to give active support to Sheikh Mubarak in establishing a military post on the north-west of the island to balance the Ottoman garrisons there and at Umm Qasr. Sir Percy Cox, the Acting Political Resident in the Gulf, arrived in Kuwait in June 1905 to submit this proposal to Sheikh Mubarak, who accepted it on condition that the British government would give him full moral support and inform the Ottomans of its recognition of his claim to Bubiyan Island. In addition, the Sheikh set out the following conditions (as noted by Cox):

(a) That [the British] Government should maintain a Political Agent at Koweit (i.e. as a practical permanency) to give him support and advice.

(b) That [the British] Government should occasionally send a man-of-war to Koweit and up the Khor Abdullah.

(c) That [the British] Government should defray the cost of the guards' quarters – estimated at Rs 500/-, and of their maintenance @ Rs 100/- per mensem.[12]

In other words, the British government should bear the initial cost of the proposed establishment of the military post and protect Mubarak from any Ottoman reprisals.

---

10. Walter Townley to Marquess of Lansdowne, no. 851, 3 November 1904, R/15/5/59. See also Lansdowne to Townley, no. 377, 2 November 1904, R/15/5/59.

11. Foreign Office to India Office, no. 48, 25 November 1904, R/15/5/59.

12. Cox to S. M. Fraser (Secretary to the Government of India), no. T/10, 11 June 1905, R/15/5/68.

No sooner than Cox expressed his willingness to fulfil these conditions, Mubarak expanded his demands. The Sheikh wanted to establish not one, but three posts with British support. While the first should be located on the easternmost point of Ras al-Qaid (about two kilometres north-east of the existing Ottoman garrison), the second post might be established on the north-easternmost point of Bubiyan, south of the eastern extremity of Warba Island, which Mubarak also claimed as his territory. The third position, to which he attached great importance due to its strategic location, would be the Jaziret es-Soof or "Wool Island", one of the islands almost due east of Umm Qasr. Sheikh Mubarak laid claim to this island on the grounds that Kuwaiti wool merchants had been using it as a depot for the export of wool for very many years. The establishment of these three posts was due to Mubarak's natural desire to strengthen his legal and military positions both in and around the islands of Warba and Bubiyan. As Cox had no authority to support Mubarak in any other posts except the one on the north-east of Bubiyan, he refused to listen to Mubarak's arguments in favour of establishing three. However, he referred the Sheikh's proposal to London, which declined to take any immediate action until the Committee of Imperial Defence had examined the matter in connection with the question of the terminus of the Baghdad Railway.[13]

Meanwhile, a German team of engineers was proceeding to Kuwait to examine the site for the proposed railway scheme. This convinced the British government that the Germans were interested in extending the proposed line to Kuwait and it ordered Knox to return immediately to Kuwait in order to keep a vigilant watch on the Germans and also to make a thorough study on the proposed railway.[14] Knox, who arrived back in Kuwait in October 1905 after a five-month absence, concluded after making an extensive tour of the Sheikhdom that if the proposed railway was extended to Kuwait, the most suitable place for a terminus was either Kadhamah or Bandar Shuwaikh (just to the south-west of Kuwait). Knox's views were largely accepted by Vice-Admiral Edmund S. Poe, who himself surveyed the Gulf, including Kuwait, in April 1906.

---

13. See *ibid.* See also Foreign Office to India Office, no. 1, 9 August 1905, R/15/5/68.
14. Extract from a letter from India Office to Foreign Office, no. 40, 6 October 1905, R/15/5/68.

Rejecting both Warba, which completely flooded at high tide, and Umm Qasr, whose approach was too far from the sea, Poe recommended Bandar Shuwaikh as the site for the railway terminus, which he considered more suitable than Kadhamah not only because of its excellent location but also because of its strategic importance to the defence of Kuwait. Poe said: "The anchorage in question [at Bandar Shuwaikh] is the real harbour of Koweit, and the adjacent foreshore would be the proper site for a railway station, should a railway ever come to Koweit."[15]

Following Poe's recommendation, the India Office conducted a series of consultations with both the Foreign Office and the Government of India. In July 1907, the Cabinet, reversing earlier policy, eventually decided to participate in the Baghdad railway project and recommended the purchase of a plot of land on the foreshore of Bandar Shuwaikh with a view to securing it for a terminus of the proposed railway.[16] Accordingly, the Political Agent was instructed to start serious negotiations with Sheikh Mubarak for the lease of a rectangular plot at Bandar Shuwaikh, some 3,750 yards along the shore by 300 yards in width. He was further asked to secure from the Sheikh a right of future pre-emption over Warba Island and its north and south anchorages, with the adjacent foreshores, within a distance of three nautical miles of the island, so far as they lay within his territory. The main reason for such pre-emption was due to Britain's desire for commanding "all possible railway outlets on [the] western shore of the head of the Gulf".[17]

Negotiations between Knox and Mubarak took place towards the end of August 1907, and culminated in the conclusion of the secret Bandar Shuwaikh Lease Agreement on 15 October. Mubarak agreed to lease in perpetuity the strip of land at Bandar Shuwaikh to the British government for Rs. 60,000 per annum, granting it the right to relinquish the lease at any time should it wish to do so. He further agreed to

15. Vice-Admiral Edmund S. Poe to the Government of India, Enclosure 3 in no. 4, 19 May 1906, L/P&S/18/B.166a. See also Poe to Government of India, Enclosure 2 in no. 11, 26 April 1906, R/15/5/68.

16. John Morley to the Government of India, Enclosure 1 in no. 8, 26 June 1907, R/15/5/68; India Office to Foreign Office, no. 8, 17 July 1907, R/15/5/68; and Foreign Office to India Office, no. 9, 20 July 1907, R/15/5/68.

17. Government of India to Morley, Enclosure 2 in no. 11, 27 August 1907, R/15/5/68; India Office to Foreign Office, no. 11, 11 September 1907, R/15/5/68.

give the British government the right of pre-emption over the sale or lease of the following: the territory within a radius of 8,000 cubits from the boundary of the leased lands; the entire island of Shuwaikh and its surrounding foreshore (except the fishing nets); the entire island of Warba and its surrounding foreshore; and all the lands and the foreshore in the direction of Kadhamah to a distance of two sea miles. In return for these concessions the British government was to confirm that it recognized the town of Kuwait and its boundaries as belonging to the Sheikh and his heirs.[18]

Although the granting of the right of pre-emption over Warba Island in the Bandar Shuwaikh Lease Agreement implied British recognition of the Sheikh's jurisdiction over the island, Kuwait's ownership of Warba still remained uncertain. To resolve this vital question, an interdepartmental committee meeting was held in London in October 1907. The committee, emphasizing the importance of investigating the Sheikh's claim to Warba in view of his granting Britain the right of preemption over the island, made the following recommendations:

> We therefore recommend, if diplomatic considerations permit, that the Sheikh of Koweit should be invited to specify the nature of his claims to Warba Island, to which he is understood frequently to have referred; and that the continued occupation of Bubiyan Island by a Turkish post, in derogation of the Sheikh's territorial claims (which have been recognized and supported by His Majesty's Government), should be neutralized by the establishment forthwith of a Koweiti post, with the countenance of His Majesty's Government, on Warba Island, or, if that should prove undesirable, on the northern shore of Bubiyan Island, if practicable, we would even recommend the establishment of posts on both islands.
> We desire to emphasize the importance which we attach to the effective assertion of the Sheikh's territorial claims to Bubiyan.[19]

The committee, therefore, not only felt it necessary to solve the question of Warba but also emphasized the importance of recognizing the Sheikh's claim to Bubiyan. Its recommendations were largely accepted

---

18. See the text in the *Persian Gulf Historical Summaries: 1907–1953–4, (PGHS)*, vol. II (Gerrards Cross, Archive Editions, 1987), pp. 236–42.

19. See Memorandum by Foreign Office, 'Respecting British Interests in the Gulf', no. 9161, 12 February 1908, L/P&S/18/B166.

by the Admiralty which reiterated: "While it would be desirable to assert any rights which the Sheikh might possess in respect of Warba Island, his jurisdiction over Bubiyan should be resolutely supported [by the British government]."[20]

Due to the Admiralty's favourable observations on the question of Warba, it was decided in November 1907 to ascertain the validity of Sheikh Mubarak's claim to the island. Accordingly, in the following May Knox began investigating the ownership of Warba and asked Mubarak to provide evidence in support of his claim to the island. On 7 June, Mubarak submitted his official claim, maintaining that the island was "the property of Kuwait and it was the place of erection of fishing nets of the people of Kuwait for two hundred years". Knox, however, declined to accept these arguments and requested Mubarak to submit concrete proof to support his statement.[21] Sheikh Mubarak, in justifying his claim, argued that the "mainland swamp between Fao and the Khor Zubair was his property" and there was "incontrovertible proof of this fact in the deed of settlement" between himself and the sons of the former ruler of Kuwait. He further stated that the boundaries of the above-mentioned mainland swamp belonging to Kuwait were Khor Abdullah and the sea (the Gulf) to the south and the creek, to the west. This creek he contended to be the Khor Zubair, explored in 1907 by a British survey party.[22]

In addition to Warba, the Sheikh also reiterated his claim to Umm Qasr on the grounds that during the reign of his great grandfather, Sheikh Jaber al-Sabah (1814–59), a Kuwaiti subject called Ahmed bin Rizk, had built the fort there and dug the wells. Extra proof, to which Mubarak attached great importance, was the very existence of Wool Island, immediately opposite Umm Qasr, where Kuwaitis used to wash their wool. Sheikh Mubarak's arguments in support of his claims convinced Knox to submit this favourable recommendation:

> To sum up, I venture to record the opinion that Sheikh Mobarak's claim to the ownership of Warba island is a very strong one, and

---

20. *Ibid.*
21. Correspondence between Sheikh Mubarak and Major Knox, unnumbered, 7 June 1908, R/15/5/68; 'Examination of Witnesses in Enquiry on the Ownership of Warba Island', unnumbered, 7 June 1908, R/15/5/68.
22. Knox to Cox, no. 295, 9 June 1908, R/15/5/18.

that the general considerations recorded above are worthy of credit and could be established with little trouble. I regard the private ownership of Warba island as undoubtedly vested in Sheikh Mobarak as . . . proved so by deeds recorded in a Turkish court of law. The proofs to the ownership of Umm Qasar would have to be examined and the considerations, advanced by Sheikh Mobarak will undoubtedly have great weight, as will also his de facto occupation of the western bank of the Khor Sabiya, as evidenced by the old settlements of Araifijiya, Hogaija and Sabiya, the numerous wells dug by Koweit Araibdar and the actual status quo, as evidenced by the grazing rights of Koweit Araibdar and the Sheikh's authority throughout this tract. The analogy of Bubiyan, which I regard as undoubtedly Koweit property and at least as independent of Turkish control as Koweit itself will have great weight in deciding the ownership of Warba island.[23]

In other words, Knox was in favour of recognizing Mubarak's ownership of Warba on the principle of proprietary right and also on the supposition that Warba was an offshoot of Bubiyan. Therefore, the ownership of the island should follow that of Bubiyan.[24] John Gordon Lorimer, in the Geographical and Statistical part of his *Gazetteer of the Persian Gulf, Oman and Central Arabia*, which was published at this time, also stated that the ownership of the island of Warba "would naturally follow that of Bubiyan".[25] The Government of India, however, rejected these views on the grounds that the Sheikh had never occupied the island. They opted to refrain from deciding upon the matter until further enquiries had been made.[26] Thus on 17 March 1909 Knox asked Sheikh Mubarak to produce further evidence in support of his claim to Warba.[27] Although the Sheikh had none to offer, the Government of India maintained in a memorandum in December 1910 that since the island of Warba "is separated only by a narrow channel from Bubiyan, it might fairly be argued on geographical grounds that the ownership of Warba followed from that of Bubiyan".[28] Despite this view, no firm decision was taken on the

---

23. *Ibid.*
24. *Ibid.*
25. Lorimer, *Gazetteer* (Geographical and Statistical), Part 2B, p. 1061.
26. Minto-Kitchener to Viscount Morley (Secretary of State for India), no. 168, 10 September 1908, R/15/5/18.
27. Knox to the Resident, no. 153, 17 March 1909, R/15/5/18.
28. As quoted in Schofield, *Kuwait and Iraq*, p. 37.

ownership of the island as the British government intended to reopen negotiations with the Ottomans on both the proposed railway and the status of Kuwait.[29]

Evidence supporting the Kuwaiti claim to the ownership of Bubiyan Island was more conclusive than that of Warba. During the course of the investigation, some leading figures of the Awazim tribe categorically told Knox that the fishing nets on Bubiyan belonged to them and that they had documents to prove this. These fishing rights on the island were granted to them by Sheikh Abdullah al-Sabah, Mubarak's ancestor, and no Kuwaiti ruler had yet reversed this grant. This straightforward statement in support of Mubarak's claim to Bubiyan was accepted unreservedly by Knox:

> I may be permitted to record here the very favourable impression I formed of the Awazim witnesses. Their evidence was clear and to the point and obviously untutored. I think a mere perusal of their statements will convince a disinterested observer of this fact. No one with any regard to truth will be able to deny that an ancient grant of fishing rights was accorded to the Awazim fishermen by Sheikh Mobarak's great-grandfather and that his order has been universally respected to the present day. I hope shortly to obtain written evidence that these rights are capable of inheritance and transfer and that the forum which habitually deals with such cases is the old Shari'a Court of Koweit, in which the hereditary Kazi is of the Atsani family and which depends for the execution of its decrees on the executive action of the Sheikhs of Koweit. This will go far to establish the ancient ownership of the Sheikhs of Koweit in Bubiyan island and the unwarranted encroachment of the Turkish authorities in establishing, in spite of remonstrances, a post there, flanked on all sea sides, by the Awazim properties.[30]

In short, the Awazim tribe of Kuwait had enjoyed hereditary fishing rights in Bubiyan for generations and these rights had been granted to them by the Kuwaiti Sheikhs, whose authority in doing so had hitherto never been challenged by any power. All the same, the British government hesitated to raise the question of the ownership of Bubiyan with

---

29. Deputy Secretary to the Government of India (Simla) to the Resident, no. 884-EA, 29 April 1910, R/15/5/18. See also Busch, *Britain and the Persian Gulf*, p. 313.
30. Knox to Cox, no. 295, 9 June 1908, R/15/5/18.

the Ottomans and did not permit the Sheikh to establish his authority over the island.[31] Similarly, no attempt was made to ascertain Sheikh Mubarak's claim to Umm Qasr and Wool Island, even though Knox had testified to the fact that the "land from Umm Gasar down the coast... [was] regarded as the grazing ground of the Koweiti Arabs and that Sheikh Mubarak's will throughout the region is law".[32]

However, the British government remained indecisive over all of these Kuwaiti claims as it was still studying the territorial boundaries of the Sheikhdom. In February 1908, prior to Knox's examination of the nature of the Sheikh's various claims, the Foreign Office produced a lengthy memorandum on British interests in the Gulf, acknowledging that the limits of Kuwait had never been accurately, or indeed even approximately, defined. Although the memorandum clearly summarized the nature of the Sheikh's claims – on the south extending as far as Muslamiya Bay and on the north including Safwan, Umm Qasr and Subiya on the mainland as well as the islands of Warba and Bubiyan – it gave no judgement on the actual limits of the Sheikhdom.[33] Alternatively, Lorimer's masterpiece, the *Gazetteer of the Persian Gulf, Oman and Central Arabia* (which was published a few months after the circulation of this memorandum for the guidance of civil servants in India), gave a vivid picture of the boundaries of Kuwait. Lorimer largely based his meticulous work on his own journey to the hinterland of Kuwait during the early part of the century, and his findings were subsequently confirmed by surveys of the Government of India.[34]

Lorimer considered the northern and southern frontiers of the Sheikhdom as fixed. This eminent civil servant of the Indian Government defined the northern boundary of Kuwait as passing immediately south of Umm Qasr and Safwan:

> On the north the most advanced Turkish outposts upon the main-
> land are at Umm Qasr and Safwan and the influence of the Shaikh
> of Kuwait is unquestioned up to the very walls of those places; we

---

31. The Deputy Secretary to the Government of India to Arthur Presscott Trevor (the Resident in the Gulf), no. 884-EA, 29 April 1910, R/15/5/18.
32. Knox to Cox, no. 295, 9 June 1908, R/15/5/18.
33. See Foreign Office, 'Memorandum Respecting British Interests in the Persian Gulf', no. 9161, 12 February 1908, L/P&S/18/B.166; see also FO 881/9161.
34. Lorimer, *Gazetteer* (Geographical and Statistical), Part 2B, p. 1058–9.

may accordingly consider the frontier on this side to be a line running from Khor-as-Sabiyah so as to pass immediately south of Umm Qasr and Safwan to Jabal Sanam and thence to the Batin.[35]

In his account, Lorimer eliminated any possible doubt regarding the correct position of the Sheikhdom's northern frontier *vis-à-vis* Safwan and Umm Qasr. He considered as the southern boundary a line running "westwards from Jabal Manifah on the coast to the Nairiyah hill at the north-western corner of Radaif". Although Lorimer found difficulty in drawing the limits of the Sheikh's territories on the remaining sides, he considered the Sheikhdom to be "bounded between Jabal Sanam and Hafar by the Batin, and that south of Hafar the border is the line dividing Summan from Dahanah as far south as the point where that line is intersected by the route from Warbah to Riyadh". Lorimer then went on to list the number of islands and islets belonging to Kuwait and stated these to be Warba, Bubiyan, Failakah, Mashjan, Auhah, Kubbar, Qaru and Umm al-Maradim.[36] From this he estimated the size of the whole Sheikhdom. Lorimer concluded its "length from north-north-west to south-south-east is about 190, and its breadth from east-north-east to west-south-west about 160 miles". Lorimer can therefore be credited as the first to clearly define the maritime and land boundaries of the Sheikhdom of Kuwait.

Despite the publication of Lorimer's findings, the British government made no immediate move to recognize the territorial limits of the Sheikhdom. However, by 1911, it saw the necessity of drawing the boundary of Kuwait based largely upon Lorimer's thesis. This was due to Britain's earnest desire to participate in the Baghdad Railway project as an equal partner, thereby controlling the southernmost section of the line. As a result, on 18 January 1911, Sir Edward Grey, the British Foreign Secretary, outlined a new approach to deal with the Ottomans regarding the problem of Kuwait, in that it should be worked out within the broader context of the railway. To this end, he was ready to recognize Ottoman suzerainty over Kuwait provided the Ottomans permitted Sheikh Mubarak's control of local customs and guaranteed the tenure of his palm groves at Fao (which could not be registered in his name

---

35. *Ibid.*, p. 1060.
36. *Ibid.*, p. 1061.

because of his refusal to declare himself an Ottoman subject). Grey's idea of recognizing Ottoman suzerainty was also dependent upon Ottoman agreement to joint Anglo-Ottoman control of the proposed railway terminus.[37]

On 1 March 1911, the Porte submitted a memorandum to the British Ambassador in Constantinople suggesting that the Ottoman government was ready to use Kuwait as the railway terminus provided Britain recognized Kuwait as an integral part of the Ottoman Empire. The memorandum also suggested that the railway should be internationalized with a 40 per cent share for Turkey and a 20 per cent stake each for Britain, Germany and France.[38] While no immediate response was made to the Porte's proposal, Robert Crewe-Milnes, the Secretary of State for India, reiterating the views of the Resident and the Government of India, set some severe conditions to any concession to the Porte with regard to the status of Kuwait. These were:

1. The securing for Britain of predominant control in the Baghdad–Kuwait section of the railway.
2. A binding assurance that Kuwait would be the terminus.
3. The joint Anglo-Kuwaiti control of the harbour and port.
4. A satisfactory agreement between the Sheikh and the Porte as to the divisions of customs and transit duties.[39]

Should these primary conditions be met the British government would be prepared to admit Ottoman suzerainty over Kuwait on the further condition that the Ottoman government recognized (a) the Sheikhdom's

---

37. Contrary to the Foreign Secretary's approach, *The Times* published an article on 28 January 1911 tracing the long history of an independent Kuwait. The article was based on a biography of Midhat Pasha, written by his son, and argued that Midhat had himself acknowledged his failure in bringing the Sheikhdom under Ottoman influence and that Sheikh Mubarak had skilfully preserved the independence of Kuwait by maintaining a balance between the two great powers, the Ottoman and the British empires. See 'Turkey and Koweit: the claim of suzerainty', *The Times*, 28 January 1911. See also Schofield, *Kuwait and Iraq*, p. 38. For Sir Edward Grey's ideas of recognizing Ottoman suzerainty in Kuwait, see Busch, *Britain and the Persian Gulf*, p. 322.
38. Busch, *Britain and the Persian Gulf*, p. 324. See also Schofield, *Kuwait and Iraq*, pp. 38–9.
39. R. Ritchie to the Under-Secretary of State for Foreign Office, unnumbered, 3 March 1911, R/15/5/65.

autonomy in respect of its internal administration; (b) the validity of the Exclusive Agreement of 1899; and (c) the territory of Umm Qasr, Bubiyan and Warba as being part of Kuwait (entailing the withdrawal of the Ottoman military posts and other symbols of authority from these areas).[40]

While a number of inter-departmental meetings were held to consider both the territorial limits of Kuwait and a reply to the Porte's proposal of 1 March, an agreement was signed between the Ottoman government and the Railway Company to extend the railway only as far as Basra, thereby ending the possibility of using Kuwait as a terminus. However, on 29 July 1911, the Foreign Office sent a memorandum to Hakki Pasha, the Ottoman Ambassador in London, outlining not only the status of Kuwait but also the British position on the Baghdad Railway and the whole of the Arab littoral of the Gulf. Regarding the railway, the memorandum proposed that the Ottoman Empire, Britain, France, Germany and Russia should each receive a 20-per-cent share – the idea being to secure 60 per cent or a majority share for the three Entente Powers (Britain, France and Russia). The memorandum also stated that the Ottoman government should recognize Britain's absolute right to police the Arabian Gulf and renounce its claims to Qatar and Bahrain. In defining the status of Kuwait, the memorandum outlined the British position:

> His Majesty's Government could not consent to any interference with the succession or with the internal administration, or any infringement of the complete autonomy of the Shaikh. On the other hand, they are prepared to recognize Turkish suzerainty over Koweit, and to recognize the Shaikh as a Turkish Kaimakam, provided in other respects the status quo is guaranteed, and the validity of certain agreements which the Shaikh has concluded with the British Government is recognized; provided the islands of Warba and Bubiyan are admitted by Turkey to be within the confines of Koweit and Turkish military posts are withdrawn; and provided finally the Shaikh is admitted to the full and undisturbed enjoyment of any properties he may own or hereafter purchase on Turkish territory. Koweit would thus form a sort of enclave within, and forming a part of, the Ottoman Empire, but enjoying complete self-government under Turkish suzerainty.[41]

---

40. *Ibid.*
41. Memorandum communicated to the Ottoman Ambassador in London, no. 1,

In effect, the British were arguing for the return of the status quo as agreed with the Ottomans in 1901, with some additions. No mention was made of Sheikh Mubarak's claim to Umm Qasr, Safwan and Wool Island. Later in October 1911, copies of the Exclusive Agreement of 1899, the Agreement for the Suppression of the Arms Trade in Kuwait in 1900 and the Postal Agreement of 1904 (which prohibited Sheikh Mubarak from allowing any foreign power except Britain to establish a post office in Kuwait),[42] were dispatched to the Porte as indicated in the memorandum. However, no copy of the Bandar Shuwaikh Lease Agreement of 1907 was sent. Instead, only a vague reference was made that the British government held a lease of land from the Sheikh, as it was anticipated that any mention of British pre-emption rights over Warba might create problems in further negotiations with the Ottomans.

Many months later, on 15 April 1912, Hakki Pasha gave the Ottoman reply to the memorandum of July 1911 to the Foreign Office, in which many of the British proposals were either amended or rejected. The Porte was now willing to give an equal 25 per cent share in the railway between itself, Britain, France and Germany, reserving the chairmanship and casting vote for itself. No mention was made of Russia. The Ottoman government also wanted to institute dual policing of the Gulf, retain Qatar, gain effective sovereignty over Warba and Bubiyan and have the 1899 agreement replaced by a new convention. Further, the Porte was only prepared to guarantee Sheikh Mubarak's properties in Fao provided he accepted Ottoman citizenship. Denouncing the proposed limits of the Sheikh's territory, the Porte put forward its own definition:

> As regards Koweit limits, as represented and claimed by His Majesty's Government and forming a territory 160 miles broad and 190 miles long, these limits are all the less admissible seeing that the sphere of influence of the Sheikh does not extend beyond "Kiazimeh, Jahra and Sira". Above all the Shaikh's influence does not make itself felt beyond 20 kilometres, i. e. to the limits of the territory occupied by the great Ajman tribe.[43]

---

29 July 1911, R/15/5/65; Busch, *Britain and the Persian Gulf*, p. 28; and Schofield, *Kuwait and Iraq*, p. 39.

42. Aitchison, *A Collection of Treaties*, p. 263.

43. See the *aide-mémoire* communicated to the Foreign Office by Hakki Pasha, unnumbered, 15 April 1912, R/15/5/65. See also 'Precise of Negotiations'

The Ottoman reply was harsher than expected. It showed no sign of accepting Britain's point of view on Kuwait. Once again, therefore, Foreign Office and India Office officials had to come together and engage in lengthy discussions over the counter-proposals to be sent to the Ottomans. Both Alwyn Parker, the Assistant Head of the Foreign Office's Eastern Department, and Sir A. Hirtzel, the Secretary of the Political and Secret Department, were concerned that the effect of giving a quarter share to each of the four powers and the chairmanship and a casting vote to the Porte would be to strengthen the Ottoman–German positions in the railway. Moreover, Russia would insist on participating in the project in the event of French participation. As the Ottoman government was prepared to admit France but not Russia, the result would be a complete deadlock of which the only remedy was the omission of both powers. In that case, Britain and Germany would have to bear the entire cost of the railway project, including the construction of new ports. Therefore, the India Office, with the firm support of the Government of India, strongly opposed any British participation in the Baghdad Railway project on Ottoman terms as this was of no commercial advantage. More important politically, "the construction of the railway means the military and administrative consolidation of Turkey in Mesopotamia, with an increased tendency to seek influence in the Persian Gulf, and to extend control in Arabia, and an increased power of offensive against British interests, including Koweit."[44]

A memorandum was eventually produced expressing Britain's position on the outstanding issues and on 18 July 1912 Sir Edward Grey sent it to Tawfiq Pasha. The memorandum proposed that Britain was now fully prepared to withdraw its request for participation in the railway from Baghdad to Basra, if a satisfactory agreement was reached on other issues such as the status of Qatar, Britain's absolute right to police

---

between the Ottoman and the British government regarding Kuwait, unnumbered, 10 May–12 July 1912, R/15/5/65.
44. See 'Memorandum on the Baghdad Basra Railway' by India Office, unnumbered, 6 June 1912, L/P&S/18/B188. See also joint minute by Sir A. Hirtzel and Parker, no. 16000, 24 April 1912, R/15/5/65. For behind-the-scenes study and debates on the Ottoman proposal of 15 April 1912, see Busch, *Britain and the Persian Gulf*, pp. 331–5.

Gulf waters, to control surveying, lighting, buoying and pilotage and to conduct all quarantine arrangements. Reiterating Britain's willingness to recognize Ottoman suzerainty over Kuwait, the memorandum attached great importance to the Sheikh's ownership of Warba and Bubiyan:

> His Majesty's Government would be fully prepared to recognise Turkish suzerainty over Koweit and indeed to recognise the Shaikh as a Turkish Kaimakam, but they attach cardinal importance to the Islands of Warba and Bubiyan being admitted by Turkey to be within the confines of Koweit, to the withdrawal of the Turkish military post from Bubiyan, and to a recognition of the limits of Koweit in accordance with the indications contained in the accompanying memorandum.[45]

Annex 4 to this memorandum contained a description of Kuwait's territory and an accompanying map indicated its limits. As the study was mainly concerned with the northern frontiers of the Sheikhdom, it did not elaborate on the southern and western boundaries. In regard to the maritime possessions of Kuwait, which (according to the memorandum) consisted of the islands of Bubiyan, Warba, Failakah, Mashjan, Auhah and the islets of Kubbar, Qaru and Umm al-Maradim, the memorandum described the Kuwaiti–Ottoman land frontier as "a line running from Khor as-Sabiyah so as to pass immediately south of Umm Qasr and Safwan to Jebel Sanam and thence to the Batin".[46] This description was completely in line with Lorimer's definition of Kuwait's northern boundary as mentioned earlier.

However, it is evident from contemporary correspondence that Lorimer's definition of the Kuwaiti boundary was by no means acceptable to Sheikh Mubarak. The Sheikh still maintained that Safwan and Umm Qasr were his beyond a doubt.[47] Captain William Shakespear, the Political Agent in Kuwait, staunchly supported this claim, arguing that until their occupation of Umm Qasr and Safwan in 1902, the Ottomans had exercised no authority in either place. He stated that the Bedouins there had for many years been referring their disputes to Kuwait for

---

45. See the Memorandum, Grey to Tawfiq Pasha, no. 28322, 18 July 1912, R/15/5/65. See also FO 371/1485.
46. See Annex 4 to the Memorandum in *ibid.*
47. Sheikh Mubarak to P. Z. Cox, unnumbered, 22 April 1911, R/15/5/59.

settlement and not to Zubair in the north, and that all Arabs using the wells at Umm Qasr and Safwan had considered the Sheikh of Kuwait as the ruler responsible for the immediate "surrounding tract". From his exhaustive enquiries, Captain Shakespear was able on 9 August 1912 to define the northern boundary as follows:

> Starting from junction of Khor Sabiya and Khor Zubair boundary would pass along water way of latter so as to include Soof Island [Wool Island] opposite Umm Qasr in latter Khor. The line would then pass north of Umm Kasr wells and north of Safwan wells and Jabal Sanam to the Ratk ridge; then south-west along the Batin.[48]

Cox, the Political Resident, who found Shakespear's boundary line as more clearly defined than Lorimer's, endorsed it without hesitation. In his report to the Government of India, he reiterated that the Sheikh's influence undoubtedly extended "up to the walls of the fort at Safwan and this fact should receive recognition when the boundary is fixed".[49]

The authorities in London, however, were not prepared to make any substantial changes to the definition of Kuwait's boundary which had already been conveyed to the Porte. Serious negotiations commenced in February 1913 between Hakki Pasha on the one side and Alwyn Parker and Lowis Mallet, the Assistant Under-Secretary of State for Foreign Affairs, on the other. While these were going on, the Ottoman authorities at Basra asked Sheikh Mubarak in early March 1913 to give his version of the limits of his territory. The Sheikh responded that while Jubail al-Bahri was his southern limit on the coast, the northern boundary of his territory extended as far as Khor Abdullah and included Failakah, Warba, Bubiyan and their waters. He also included Umm Qasr as well as Safwan within this limit. From Safwan the boundary followed the Batin to include Hafar with the most southerly point just south of al-Garna. From this point the boundary

---

48. For more details, see 'Note on the Boundaries of the Kuwait Principality' by Captain Shakespear, no. C-62, 9 August 1912, R/15/5/65.

49. Cox to India Office, no. 843, 16 August 1912, R/15/5/67. See also Cox to the Secretary to the Government of India in the Foreign Department, no. 1727, 4 August 1912, R/15/5/67.

passed south of Antaa and met the coast at Jubail al-Bahri.[50] This definition was very similar to that arrived at by Captain Shakespear.

Despite Mubarak's clear-cut definition of Kuwait's territory, the British negotiators produced a draft agreement on 26 March 1913, which placed no importance on his testimony. This latest British draft again acknowedged the autonomous status of the Sheikhdom "under the suzerainty of Turkey", with the Sheikh as a Turkish Qaimaqam and proposed the appointment of an Ottoman agent in Kuwait. However, Kuwait's autonomy meant that the Ottoman agent could not interfere in the internal or external affairs of the Sheikhdom. As for the limits of the Sheikh's territory, these were referred to in the draft as follows:

> A line running north-west from the coast at the mouth of the Khor-es-Zubair up to and past but not including the walls of the fort at Safwan to Jebel Sanam and the Ar Ratq ridge.[51]

The islands of Warba, Bubiyan, Failakah, Mashjan, Auhah, Kubbar, Qaru and Umm al-Maradim were also included within these limits.[52] As the draft made no reference to Umm Qasr, it was amended on 31 March 1913, at the India Office's suggestion, by including "the forts at Umm Kasr and Safwan" instead of just "the fort at Safwan". However, it was made clear that the British government was unable to support the Sheikh's claims to Umm Qasr based on such a substitution. It also seems clear that Britain gave no consideration to Sheikh Mubarak's claim to Safwan.[53]

Following the receipt of this draft the Ottomans produced their own counter-draft in early May 1913. Immediately the negotiators got down to working out the differences. Kuwait was to be considered as an autonomous Qada of the Ottoman Empire and not to be referred to as a territory under Ottoman "suzerainty" or Ottoman "sovereignty". The Ottoman flag was to be flown by the Sheikh who was, however, to have

---

50. Cox to India Office, no. 388, 26 March 1913, R/15/5/65.
51. See the Kuwait Draft Agreement, no. 12978, 26 March 1913, R/15/5/67.
52. *Ibid.*
53. T. W. Holderness (India Office) to the Under-Secretary of State, Foreign Office, no. P1166, 31 March 1913, R/15/5/67.

the right to insert a distinctive emblem of his own design in the flag's corner. The Ottomans further conceded the Sheikh's ownership of Warba and Bubiyan. This draft was eventually initialled on 6 May 1913 by both parties.[54]

Subsequently Captain Shakespear was dispatched to obtain the consent of Sheikh Mubarak who had been completely excluded from the negotiations. The Political Agent met with the Sheikh in late May 1913 and explained the terms of the initialled document. Although Mubarak initially resented the continuance of the Ottoman military posts at Safwan and Umm Qasr, when he was informed that the British government was attempting to "secure the recognition of his boundary as touching these two places" and that the presence of a few Ottoman soldiers there did not make any practical difference anyway, the Sheikh "seemed inclined to agree". However, as soon as the Agent told him about the proposed appointment of an Ottoman agent in Kuwait, the Sheikh vehemently opposed the draft, arguing that this appointment was in contravention of the terms of both the 1899 and 1907 treaties, which he had faithfully observed. Sheikh Mubarak, who was extremely distressed by this unexpected proposal, "begged" Shakespear to immediately cable London to intimate his refusal to accept any Ottoman official, "under any guise" whatsoever, in his Sheikhdom.[55]

Captain Shakespear, who was extremely sympathetic to Sheikh Mubarak's position, wrote to Cox accusing London of surrendering Kuwait to the Porte:

> The Agreement, as it stands in the Draft, will in reality give nothing whatsoever to the Ruler of Kuwait or his people which they have not enjoyed for years, while to them it will appear – owing to the clause permitting a resident Turkish Agent – rather as a formal delivery of Kuwait in to the hands of Turkey by the Power which has hitherto safeguarded them from the menaces of that very Power. I confess even I find it difficult to avoid some such conclusion when the Agreement contains Clauses (a) acknowledging Turkish suzerainty, hitherto disputed, (b) permitting a Turkish official in Kuwait, hitherto strenuously opposed, (c) maintaining Turkish military posts, hitherto protested against as encroachments,

---

54. Busch, *Britain and the Persian Gulf,* p. 337.
55. Shakespear to Cox, no. 13-C, 28 May 1913, R/15/5/65.

(d) circumscribing boundaries hitherto unquestioned and actually maintained, and (e) recognizing the Ruler of Kuwait as a Turkish official, hitherto denied. In the effort to reconcile the Agreement, should it materialise as proposed, with the actually existing position, the Shaikh and his people will ask themselves the inevitable question 'what has induced the British Government to make this agreement concerning us, so seriously to our detriment, and that too when Turkey is of no account in the world?' The answer locally is obvious, viz., that Kuwait has been made use of by the British Government to obtain something else, a recognition of other claims elsewhere, a concession in regard to the Baghdad Railway, and the like. When it is remembered further that the Ruler of Kuwait has not been consulted during the negotiations, has not been informed as to their course, and is to be presented with a *fait accompli* of some such description, I submit it is not unreasonable to expect the deepest disappointment and resentment at our action. How that resentment will affect our future relations I am loathe to contemplate, but I feel sure that its effect will not be merely local – it will affect us along the whole Arabian littoral of the Persian Gulf by shaking the confidence which our support has hitherto inspired.

No amount of explanation will ever remove the impression that we have used Kuwait as a pawn to secure other advantages for ourselves, more especially if some such advantages later become manifest, as, for instance, a settlement in our favour of the Baghdad Railway question.[56]

Cox agreed with Shakespear and argued that the appointment of an Ottoman agent was clearly a modification of the status quo in Kuwait. He, therefore, urged the Government of India either to abandon this "agent clause" or at least find an alternative to it.[57]

However, the India Office, supported by the Government of India, was unmoved. Cox was instructed to go to Kuwait himself to accomplish the task as soon as possible and tell the Sheikh that he was not being "sacrificed in return for any quid pro quo" and that he must pay the price for the permanent establishment, on a treaty basis, of his position and the recognition of his enormous territorial claims.[58] Acting under these instructions, Cox held his delicate meeting with Sheikh

---

56. *Ibid.*
57. Cox to the Secretary to the Government of India, no. 948, 27 May 1913, R/15/5/65.
58. Secretary of State for India to the Resident, no. P, 6 June 1913, R/15/5/65.

Mubarak on 6 July 1913. Although the Sheikh "demurred somewhat" at the exclusion of Umm Qasr and Safwan, he soon resigned himself to their loss. Then the conversation was turned to the clause requiring him to receive an Ottoman agent. The Sheikh still showed no sign of compromise and resisted the clause, arguing that it was one of the specific and chief features of his previous agreements with Britain that he should not receive the agent of any foreign power, with the exception of Britain but including the Ottoman Empire. In response the adroit Resident argued that the "agent clause" was essential in order to achieve Turkey's recognition of his administrative autonomy. Eventually, Cox obtained Sheikh Mubarak's agreement to the clause, on the stipulation that Cox was to confirm to him in writing that the British government would give him "efficacious support in case of need against the activities and intrigues" on the part of the Ottoman agent. Cox did so at once without any hesitation and on the following day the Sheikh sent his letter of acceptance.[59]

With the formalities completed, an agreement on all outstanding issues in the Gulf was finally reached with the Ottoman government and the historic Anglo-Ottoman Convention was signed on 29 July 1913. The fifth part of this convention dealt with Kuwait, Qatar and Bahrain. There were 10 articles concerning Kuwait, Articles 5 to 7 defining the territories and status of the country.[60] The inner and outer limits of the Sheikh's territories were respectively defined by a red circle and a green line on the map annexed to the convention. All the islands, including Warba and Bubiyan, and islets as mentioned in the British draft of March 1913, were included in Article 5 of the agreement.[61] Article 7 defined the northern frontier of the Sheikhdom:

> The line of demarcation runs north-west from the coast at the mouth of the Khor Zoubeir and passes immediately south of Um-Kasr, Safwan and Jabel Sanam, leaving these places and their wells to the Vilayet of Basra; and reaching the Batin the line follows it towards the south-west to Hafar-el-Batin ...[62]

---

59. Cox to the Secretary to the Government of India, no. 2102, 10 July R/15/5/65. See also Cox to Mubarak, no. 300, 6 July 1913, R/15/5/65 and Mubarak to Cox, unnumbered, 7 July 1913, R/15/5/65.
60. For full text, see Appendix II.
61. See Article 5 in Appendix II.
62. Article 7 in Appendix II.

In this way the northern boundary of Kuwait was delimited, clearly dividing it from that of the Basra Vilayet. This definition was identical in substance to Lorimer's description in the *Gazetteer of the Persian Gulf, Oman and Central Arabia.* The starting point of the line was retained as the mouth of the Khor Zubair but the line itself was defined as passing immediately south of Umm Qasr and Safwan rather than as "up to and past . . . the walls of the forts at Umm Qasr and Safwan" as mentioned in the amended British draft of March 1913. Accordingly, the actual meaning or intention of the Green Line was unclear.

Still, the 1913 convention did regularize the status of Kuwait for the first time and recognized the Sheikh's ownership of the islands of Warba and Bubiyan for which he had been fighting since the beginning of the century. However, the convention was not ratified due to the outbreak of the First World War in August 1914 and the entry of Turkey into the war the following October against the Allies. As soon as Britain declared war, Sheikh Mubarak issued a declaration of loyalty to Great Britain on behalf of himself and his tribes. He placed his men and ships at Britain's disposal and expressed his earnest desire to expel the Ottomans from the islands at the mouth of the Shatt al-Arab which he claimed as lawfully his. In response to this unswerving loyalty and cooperation, Major Stuart Knox, the then Political Resident, issued a statement on 3 November on behalf of the British government, giving the following assurances to Sheikh Mubarak:[63]

> In return for the valuable co-operation which we expect from you, I am authorized by the Government, in the event of success and, insha Allah [God willing], we shall succeed, to assure you again that Basra will never again be subject to Turkish authority.
> I am further to give your Excellency personally the following special assurances:
> (1) The date gardens which you now possess between Fao and Gurnak shall remain in the full possession of you and your heirs and for ever be immune from taxation.
> (2) You are guaranteed by the Great British Government against all consequences of your attack against Safwan, Umm Kasr and Bubiyan.

---

63. See the Memorandum by John W. Field (Foreign Office), no. 11880, 29 March 1922, L/P&S/12/3737.

(3) Koweit shall be recognised as an independent principality under British protection.

This declaration, therefore, changed the status of Kuwait from a so-called Ottoman Qada to a de facto independent entity under British protection. These undertakings were extended to both Sheikh Jaber bin Mubarak upon the death of Sheikh Mubarak in November 1915 and to Sheikh Salem bin Mubarak upon Sheikh Jaber's death in February 1917. It is known that Sheikh Mubarak occupied Bubiyan immediately at the outbreak of war, but it is not clear whether he also occupied Safwan and Umm Qasr at the same time. In any case, the Sheikh actively cooperated with the landing of British Indian troops at Basra following the expulsion of the Ottomans from Safwan and Umm Qasr. Eventually, the British brought the whole of Mesopotamia under their effective control and established their own administration headed by the veteran Sir Percy Cox.[64]

Towards the end of the war, however, Britain reviewed its wartime assurances to the Arabian chiefs including the Kuwaiti Sheikh. A Foreign Office postwar memorandum, giving the interpretation of the 1914 declaration, reconfirmed the Kuwaiti ownership of Umm Qasr, Safwan and Bubiyan:

> Our assurance practically commits us to recognizing Sheikh Salim's sovereignty over Safwan and Umm Kasr, as well as Bubiyan. But since the Sheikh is in a trucial relationship with us, our position at Basra would in no way be injured by this, nor does the possession of these forts by the Sheikh appear to conflict with any other British interests.[65]

The collapse of the Ottoman Empire after the war once again raised the question of the status of Kuwait, as Britain had promised in November

---

64. In 1913, Ottoman troops were ejected from the whole eastern province of al-Hasa by Ibn Saud and in early 1915 the Ottomans abandoned Doha, anticipating a British attack. See also V. Lutsky, *Modern History of the Arab Countries* (Moscow, Progress Publishers, 1969), p. 394 and 'Status of Certain Groups of Islands in the Persian Gulf' by J. G. Laithwaite, no. B-399, 27 August 1928, FO 371/52259.

65. 'Memorandum: British Commitments (during the war) to the Gulf Chiefs' by Foreign Office, no. 11794, n.d., L/P&S/10/606.

1914 to recognize it as an independent 'principality' under its protection. The Civil Commissioner in Baghdad mooted the idea of declaring a British protectorate over Kuwait. This proposal, however, was opposed by the Government of India, which argued that such a move might be viewed by the neighbouring Arab states and other powers as a definite step towards formal annexation. Moreover, it would involve Britain in heavy military and financial obligations. These views were accepted by London and the issue of Kuwait's *de jure* status remained unresolved.

Having failed to bring the Government of India round to his line of thinking, the Civil Commissioner in Baghdad instead suggested that a jurisdictional Order in Council be issued to establish British jurisdiction over British subjects and foreigners within the principality of Kuwait. Although the proposal was attractive to the India Office, it preferred to wait until the machinery for the administration of Mesopotamia under the British Mandate had been set up. The Foreign Office agreed with this view, and the question of Kuwait's status was allowed to rest until October 1925 when the Order in Council was issued.[66]

The San Remo Conference of April 1920 settled the question of the administration of the former Ottoman territories in the Middle East. Britain obtained a mandate over Iraq which, prior to 1920, had never existed as a separate and independent political entity. On 10 August 1920, the Turkish government signed the Treaty of Sèvres, surrendering all its former non-Turkish provinces, including Kuwait. Article 132 of the treaty specifically mentioned this undertaking:

> Outside her frontiers as fixed by the present Treaty, Turkey hereby renounces in favour of the principal allied powers all rights and title which she could claim on any ground over or concerning any territories outside Europe which are not otherwise disposed of by the present treaty. Turkey undertakes to recognise and conform to the measures which may be taken now or in the future by the principal allied powers, in agreement where necessary with third powers in order to carry the above stipulation into effect . . . [67]

---

66. 'Memorandum, Koweit, 1908–1928' by India Office, no. P4224/28, 1 October 1928, L/P&S/18/B.395 pp. 5–6.
67. Hurewitz, *Diplomacy in the Near and Middle East*, vol. II, p. 87.

In view of Turkey's severance of all links with its former territories, the Colonial Office, which was made responsible for overseeing the affairs of the Arab littoral of the Gulf Sheikhdoms as well as Iraq in early 1921, brought up the question of the legal status of Kuwait with the Foreign Office in July 1921. In reply, the Foreign Office clarified the status of Kuwait:

> From the legal point of view and on the supposition that there was no intention of including Koweit within the boundaries of Mesopotamia [that is Iraq], the status of that territory would seem to be governed by article 132 of the Treaty of Sèvres [quoted above].[68]

This clearly meant that Britain had not so far conceived of Kuwait as being part of Iraq, but had left the door open for a possible turn-about. However, the Treaty of Lausanne of July 1923 removed this option by affirming that there was no intention of including Kuwait within the boundaries of Iraq.[69]

On 23 April 1921, Faisal, the second son of Sharif Hussein of Makkah, who had lost his throne in Syria in 1920 at the hands of the French armed forces in the Levant, was installed by Britain as the first Hashemite king of Iraq. Britain then regularized its position in Iraq by signing the Anglo-Iraqi Treaty on 10 October 1922 confirming Britain's right to appoint British advisers in the Iraqi administration, protect foreigners, assist the Iraqi army, advise on financial matters and influence external relations. However, because of pressure from Iraqi nationalists, this treaty was revised on 13 January 1926 and again on 14 December 1927, scaling down Britain's control over economic and military matters. In addition, Britain pledged its support for Iraq's application for membership of the League of Nations. In 1930, a Labour government in Britain opened negotiations with the Iraqi government to settle all outstanding questions, including that of Iraqi

---

68. 'Memorandum: Koweit, 1908–1928' by India Office, no. PZ4224/28, 1 October 1928, L/P&S/18/B395.
69. Alan de Lacy Rush (ed.), *Records of Kuwait: 1899–1961*, vol. VII (Oxford, Archive Editions, 1989), p. 399. For the full text of the Treaty of Lausanne, see Hurewitz, *Diplomacy in the Near and Middle East*, vol. II, p. 120.

independence. In June the High Commissioner, Sir Francis Humphrys, and the Iraqi Foreign Minister, Nuri al-Said signed a treaty which was to run for 25 years, granting Britain the right to maintain three air force bases in various parts of the country; Britain would also continue to provide instructors for the Iraqi army and supply them with the necessary arms and equipment from Britain. Further, both parties agreed to "full and frank consultation in all matters of foreign policy which might affect their common interests". In return for these privileges, Britain proclaimed Iraq's full independence after terminating the mandate and supporting its entry into the League of Nations in 1932.[70]

As for Kuwait's boundary issue, it is necessary to go back in time to trace the course it took during the decade leading up to Iraq's independence in 1932. The limits of Kuwait's northern frontier and the boundary between Kuwait and Najd came up for consideration at the Oqair Conference which took place during November and December 1922. This was attended by Sir Percy Cox (the High Commissioner in Baghdad), Major James More (the Political Agent in Kuwait), Subih Beg (the Iraqi Minister of Communication and Works), Ibn Saud and his aide Abdullah Damluji. In addition to settling the Iraq–Najd frontier, the conference eventually reached a settlement which defined the boundary between Kuwait and Najd as follows:

> The frontier between Najd and Kuwait begins in the West from junction of the Wadi al Aujah (W. al Audja) with the Batin (El Batin), leaving Raq'i (Rikai) to Najd, from this point it continues in a straight line until it joins latitude 29° and the red semi-circle referred to in Article 5 of the Anglo-Turkish Agreement of 29th July 1913. The line then follows the side of the red semi-circle until to reach a point terminating [sic] on the coast south of Ras al-Qali'ah (Ras el Kaliyah) and this is the indisputable southern frontier of Kuwait territory. The portion of territory bounded on the North by this line and which is bounded on the West by a low mountainous ridge called Shaq (Esh Shakk) and on the East by the sea and on the South by a line passing from West to East from Shaq (Esh Shakk) to 'Ain al 'Abd (Ain el Abd) and thence to the coast north of Ras al Mish'ab (Ras Mishaab), in this territory the Governments of Najd and Kuwait will share equal rights until

---

70. For full text, see Hurewitz, *Diplomacy in the Near and Middle East*, vol. II, p. 178–81. See also George Lenczowski, *The Middle East in World Affairs* (London, Cornell University Press, 1980), pp. 268–9.

through the good offices of the Government of Great Britain a further agreement is made between Najd and Kuwait concerning it.[71]

In this way the conference at the Arabian seaport redefined Kuwait's
southern frontier with Najd, in the process significantly changing the
frontier as defined in the unratified Anglo-Ottoman Convention of
1913. Sheikh Ahmed bin Jaber al-Sabah, who became the Kuwaiti ruler
in March 1921, upon the death of Sheikh Salem, signed the agreement
in January 1923.[72]

Having settled his boundary with Ibn Saud, Sheikh Ahmed now
sought to fix the exact frontier between Kuwait and Iraq. He wrote to
Major More in April, requesting a ruling on the matter. The Political
Agent at once wrote back asking him to indicate the line he himself
wished to claim.[73] The Sheikh immediately replied as follows:

> It is the same as that claimed by the late Shaikh Salim in the
> Appendix to his letter to you dated the 3rd Muharram 1330 (17th
> September 1920); namely: from the junction of the Wadi al-'Aujah
> with the Batin; eastwards to the south of the wells of Safwan, Jabal
> Sanam, and Umm Qasr, to the shore of the islands of Bubiyan and
> Warbah, and along the coast to the present Najd-Kuwait Frontier.
> Included in this are the following islands of the sea: Maskan,
> Failakah, 'Auhah, Kubbar, Karu and Umm al-Maradim. These are
> the boundaries of Kuwait which I claim. [74]

On the same date, More forwarded this claim to the High
Commissioner in Baghdad stating that Sheikh Ahmed was indeed
claiming the northern portion of the Green Line of the (unratified)
Anglo-Turkish agreement as the frontier of Kuwait with Iraq.[75] Bearing
this in mind, Cox personally redefined, in his reply to More, Kuwait's
frontier with Iraq based on Article 7 of the convention of 1913:

---

71. See the Enclosure in J. C. More to the Secretary to the High Commissioner for
    Iraq, no. 15-S, 26 January 1923, L/P&S/10/937.
72. H. R. P. Dickson, *Kuwait and Her Neighbours* (London, George Allen & Unwin,
    1968), p. 279.
73. Sheikh Ahmed to More, unnumbered, 1 April 1923, R/15/1/523. See also More
    to the Secretary to the High Commissioner for Iraq, no. 52-S, 4 April 1923,
    R/15/1/523.
74. Sheikh Ahmed to More, unnumbered, 4 April 1923, R/15/1/523.
75. More to the Secretary to the High Commissioner for Iraq, no. 52-S, 4 April
    1923, R/15/1/523.

From the intersection of the Wadi-El-Audja with the Batin and thence northwards along the Batin to a point just south of the latitude of Safwan; thence eastwards passing south of Safwan wells, Jabal Sanam and Um Qasr, leaving them [i.e. Jabal Sanam and Umm Qasr] to Iraq and so on to the junction of the Khor Zobeir with Khor Abdullah.[76]

Cox also included in his definition all the islands and islets claimed by Sheikh Ahmed. On 19 April 1923, Cox instructed More to tell the Sheikh that the British government recognized "his claim to the frontier and islands". It is important to note here that Sheikh Ahmed included Safwan and Umm Qasr explicitly in his claim, but Cox's definition did not. Even so, the instruction specifically mentioned that the Sheikh's definition was "identical with the frontier indicated by the Green Line of the Anglo-Turkish Agreement of July 29th 1913".[77] Following the exchange of these letters, in consultation with the Iraqi national authorities, More, on behalf of Sheikh Ahmed, erected a large notice-board on the frontier near Safwan marked "Iraq–Kuwait Boundary" in order to demonstrate where the actual boundary ran.[78]

Although the frontier of Kuwait was delimited, Britain's obligations for the defence of the Sheikhdom had not yet been precisely defined. Therefore, in October 1928, the Government of India suggested that Britain's veiled protectorate in Kuwait should now be turned into a real one. The Viceroy of India, Lord Irwin (later to become Lord Halifax), advanced his own reasons in favour of such a move:

We are already saddled with defence commitment, and sterilization of foreign powers out of Koweit would always remain a necessity to us. Instead, should Iraq become independent, a British controlled Koweit would become an even greater necessity, not only to us, but to Koweit itself with two powerful neighbours [Iraq and Saudi Arabia] on her vulnerable frontier. Incidentally, this seems to be strong argument against the present tendency to link up the fate of Koweit with Iraq, and in favour of a reversion to Koweit's orientation towards India.[79]

---

76. Cox to More, no. 5405, 19 April 1923, R/15/5/209.
77. *Ibid.*
78. Dickson to R. F. Jardine, no. 79, 6 June 1932, R/15/5/184.
79. Viceroy to the Secretary of State for India, no. 2084-S, 16 October 1928, L/P&S/10/1271.

The Viceroy was arguing for a permanent protectorate over the Sheikhdom in order to preserve British supremacy in Kuwait and ward off interference from other local powers, particularly Iraq, whose attainment of independence was imminent.

However, Lord Irwin's arguments in favour of the establishment of a protectorate in Kuwait were not strong enough to convince Frederick Smith, the Secretary of State for India. In a memorandum to the Cabinet Sub-Committee of the Committee of Imperial Defence on 18 October 1928, Smith argued that it was not an opportune time to establish a formal protectorate in the Sheikhdom as such a move would invite international criticism of imperialism. Moreover, a Kuwaiti protectorate would be an extra burden on Britain as it was bound to involve the Empire in extra defence expenditure. Smith also believed that the undefined assurances of Britain's "good offices" given in 1899 was still a better means by which Britain could govern Kuwait without burdening itself with legal obligations. He further maintained that the undertaking of 1914 that Kuwait should be recognized as "an independent principality under British protection" had always been a matter of some doubt as to whether British obligations extended to the whole territory of Kuwait or just to the town of Kuwait. Smith preferred to leave things as they were for as long as possible. He wrote:

> I am inclined to think that it is better on the whole that matters should remain as they are, and that while endeavouring to secure so far as possible that Koweit shall not be identified with Iraq, we should defer consideration of the establishment of a formal protectorate until circumstances appear to make this move clearly desirable.[80]

This recommendation of not turning Kuwait into a formal protectorate was approved by the committee on 18 March 1929, without reservation.[81] In fact, no formal protectorate was ever established in Kuwait although, in practice, Britain treated it like one. This way, Britain could

---

80. See the Memorandum by the Secretary of State for India, no. PG16, 18 October 1928, L/P&S/10/1271. See also J. G. Laithwaite, the Under Secretary of State for India Office, unnumbered, 17 October 1928, L/P&S/10/1271.
81. See the final conclusion of the Persian Gulf Sub-Committee, 9th Meeting, 18 March 1929, L/P&S/10/1271.

enjoy pre-eminence in Kuwait without admitting formal responsibility for its defence.

Having therefore decided not to change the status of Kuwait, the British government turned its attention to Kuwait's boundary with Iraq. This was prompted by Iraq's application for membership of the League of Nations. As it was essential that applicants submit well-defined border lines with contiguous states at the time of applying for membership, the British government suggested that the existing Iraqi–Kuwaiti frontier as defined in the exchange of notes in 1923, should be reaffirmed in an exchange of letters between the government of Iraq and the ruler of Kuwait. This was to be achieved before the September 1932 session of the League.[82] Thus, Harold Dickson, the then Political Agent in Kuwait, was instructed to explain to the Sheikh the necessity of this reaffirmation of the existing Iraqi–Kuwaiti frontier. Accordingly, Dickson met the Sheikh on 6 June 1932. Sheikh Ahmed, who was already perturbed by the removal of the frontier sign at Safwan by the Iraqi frontier police just the day before, reacted sharply when the matter was raised. He argued that the British government was requesting something which had been settled almost a decade before. Sheikh Ahmed was convinced that this approach would induce Iraq "with her pseudo-Persian mentality" to ask for an alteration of the existing frontier, and when the Iraqis gained their final independence and joined the League of Nations, they would "become Turkish in spirit if not in actual fact". However, despite these reservations, the Sheikh was eventually persuaded.[83]

With the Sheikh's consent secured, Lieutenant Colonel Hugh Biscoe, the Resident, prepared the procedures for the proposed exchange of notes. It was suggested that the Iraqi Prime Minister should address the British High Commissioner in Baghdad, who should then send the proposal for reconfirmation to the Resident. Thereupon, it would be sent to Sheikh Ahmed through the Political Agent in Kuwait. The Sheikh's approval would then be transmitted to the Iraqi Prime Minister

---

82. J. E. Flood (Colonial Office) to the Under-Secretary of State (India Office), no. PZ2828/32, 11 May 1932, R/15/5/184. See also Minute by A. F. Morley, unnumbered, 17 May 1932, L/P&S/12/3737.
83. Dickson to Lt Col Hugh Vincent Biscoe (the Resident), no. 80, 7 June 1932, R/15/5/184.

through the same channels.[84] So, on 21 July 1932, Nuri al-Said, the Iraqi Prime Minister, wrote to Sir Francis Humphrys, the High Commissioner in Iraq, requesting him to obtain the agreement of Sheikh Ahmed to the following description of the "existing frontier" between Iraq and Kuwait:

> From the intersection of the Wadi el Audja with the Batin and thence northwards along the Batin to a point just south of the latitude of Safwan; thence eastwards passing south of Safwan wells, Jebel Sanam and Um Qasr leaving them to Iraq and so on to the junction of the Khor Zobeir with the Khor Abdullah. The islands of Warbah, Bubiyan, Maskan (or Mashjan), Failakah, Auhah, Kubbar, Qaru and Umm el Maradim appertain to Kuwait.[85]

The High Commissioner then referred Nuri al-Said's confirmation to Lieutenant Colonel Trenchard Fowle, the Officiating Political Resident in the Gulf, who passed it on to Sheikh Ahmed through Dickson on 10 July 1932.[86] The Kuwaiti ruler wrote back to the Agent a month later giving his reconfirmation: "We beg to inform you that we agree to reaffirm the existing frontier between Iraq and Kuwait as described in the Iraqi Prime Minister's letter."[87] Thus this exchange of letters in 1932 legally bound Iraq and Kuwait to abide unequivocally by the 1923 definition of the frontier.

With these formalities completed, Britain sponsored Iraq's entry into the League of Nations, terminating the decade-old mandate. On 3 October 1932, Iraq emerged as an independent state and in the following month a new government was formed under the premiership of Naji Shawkat. In July 1933, the Colonial Office transferred its responsibility for Iraqi affairs to the Foreign Office, while the India Office took full charge for overseeing the affairs of Kuwait as well as the other Gulf countries.

---

84. Biscoe to the Government of India, repeated to the Secretary of State for India, no. 344, 11 June 1932, R/15/5/184.
85. Nuri Sa'id to Francis H. Humphrys, no. 2944, 21 July 1932, R/15/5/184.
86. Fowle to Dickson, no. 528-S, 30 July 1932, R/15/5/184. See also Dickson to Sheikh Ahmed al Jaber al-Sabah, no. 128, 9 August 1932, R/15/5/184.
87. Sheikh Ahmed to the Political Agent, Kuwait, no. R560, 10 August 1932, R/15/5/184.

Conclusion

While the post-First World War settlement brought no major change in the status of Kuwait other than the reconfirmation of the pledge of 1914 that had identified it as an "independent principality" under British protection, it redefined the country's frontier without making any political or legal link with the newly created state of Iraq. The Iraqi Prime Minister's reconfirmation of Cox's Iraqi–Kuwaiti boundary line, which was itself based on Article 7 of the unratified Anglo-Ottoman Convention of 1913, left no room for further legal manoeuvring. While this convention recognized Kuwait's claims to Bubiyan and Warba, for which Kuwait had been struggling since the turn of the century, it deliberately ignored the Sheikh's historical claims to Safwan and Umm Qasr, despite the endorsement that this claim received from the British representatives stationed in the Gulf. Britain made this compromise with the Ottomans to achieve its objectives in the (abortive) Baghdad Railway Project and in the Gulf waters as well as other objectives in the area. However, after the war, Britain did recognize Kuwait's sovereignty over Safwan and Umm Qasr, although the Kuwaiti ruler made no attempt to physically occupy these two locations.

3

The Problems of Smuggling and Iraqi Territorial Encroachments, 1930–1939

Despite the reaffirmation of Kuwait's frontier brought about through the Exchange of Letters of 1932, relations between Kuwait and Iraq deteriorated sharply. Iraqi demands for the suppression of smuggling and their continuous encroachments within Kuwaiti territory soured the relationship between the two countries throughout the period after 1932. Several futile attempts were made to solve these problems and establish peace in the border area. However, as even the various British officials who played a pivotal role in the negotiations over the smuggling and the frontier violations differed in their views of how to approach them, these problems continued unchecked.

The Iraqi–Kuwaiti frontier became an issue for the first time in the beginning of January 1931, when it was reported by Abdul Jabbar Effendi, the Commandant of Police, Southern Desert, that four armed cars belonging to Kuwait had crossed the Iraqi frontier at Udhaiba on 25 December 1930. As soon as this was brought to the attention of Sir Francis Humphrys, the British High Commissioner in Baghdad, he lodged a protest on behalf of the Iraqi government with Sheikh Ahmed bin Jaber, through the Political Agent, requesting him to take disciplinary action against the perpetrators and to prevent any recurrence of such incidents. The Sheikh expressed his regret and immediately apologized, stating that his men had crossed the frontier in pursuit of criminals who had killed some Kuwaitis, without knowing the exact position of the borderline. He assured Dickson, the Political Agent, that no such incident would take place again.[1] Although the Sheikh managed

---

1. Commandant of Police, Southern Desert, to the Ministry of Interior, no. 19, 6 January 1931, R/15/5/184; R.S.M. Sturges (Political Secretary to the High Commissioner for Iraq) to Hugh Vincent Biscoe (the Resident), no. 1138, 30 January 1931, R/15/5/184; Sheikh Ahmed to Dickson, unnumbered, 8 February 1931, R/15/5/184; Dickson to Biscoe, no. 17, 14 February 1931, R/15/5/184.

to keep his word, the Iraqis intentionally complicated matters in the summer of 1932 by removing the notice-board which indicated the location of the frontier. As a result, Dickson, who had himself found the board at the Safwan police post, made a strong protest to R. F. Jardine, the Administrative Inspector at Basra. The Agent urged Jardine to investigate the matter and to replace the board at its original location, as it had been erected at the Sheikh's expense and served a useful purpose. Jardine, after informing Dickson that the Iraqi police had removed it by mistake, arranged for its replacement.[2]

Despite the animosity reflected in these frontier incidents, Sheikh Ahmed, in a bid to restore cordial relations, paid an official visit to Baghdad at King Faisal's invitation in the first week of September 1932 and was charmed by the courteous and generous reception accorded him by the King and his subjects during the visit. At the time of the Sheikh's departure, the King even conferred on him the "Order of the Rafidain".[3] However, despite the success of this visit, Iraqi–Kuwaiti relations began to deteriorate further as soon as Iraq emerged as an independent state in October 1932. The Iraqi customs department, largely staffed by British officers, was the main agitator in this regard. At the beginning of January 1933, the director of Iraqi customs complained to Sir Francis Humphrys, who had become the first British Ambassador to Iraq, that more than £60,000 worth of goods such as sugar, tea, cigarettes and tobacco had been smuggled into Iraq from Kuwait during 1932. Following this complaint, the Iraqi government proposed that an Iraqi customs official should be permanently stationed in Kuwait in order to protect its interest and that Kuwait should also permit Iraq to maintain patrols and guards on the Kuwaiti side of the frontier to control the overland smuggling. As these unreasonable demands were not acceptable to Sheikh Ahmed, tensions between the two countries continued to mount.[4]

Eventually, in May 1933, Dickson produced a detailed study on the problem of smuggling in Iraq. Stating that most of the tribesmen

---

2. Dickson to Jardine, no. 79, 6 June 1932, R/15/5/184; Dickson to Sheikh Ahmed, no. 118, 13 July 1932, R/15/5/184.
3. Dickson to Trenchard Fowle, no. 156, 9 September 1932, R/15/1/505.
4. Humphrys to Rendel, no. 72/2/33, 11 January 1933, R/15/5/158. See also *The Persian Gulf Administration Report for the Year 1933 (PGAR)*, vol. IX (Gerrards Cross, Archive Editions, 1986), pp. 65–6.

involved in the smuggling were either Iraqi, Persian or Saudi, he pointed out that the larger quantities of contraband goods entered Iraq overland through Kuwait's western boundary along the Batin. The trade was also carried on by small dhows, along the water channels surrounding the islands of Warba and Bubiyan to the entrance of the Shatt al-Arab and the northern shores of the Khor Abdullah. Dickson attributed two reasons for the continuation of this contraband traffic: first, the Bedouin of north-eastern Arabia considered Kuwait as their seasonal home and as the market for all their needs; and second, the Sheikhdom's trade and commerce would suffer if this traditional desert trade was stopped and that it would in turn serve a severe blow to the prestige of the Sheikh. Dickson suggested that if the Iraqis seriously wanted to stop the flow of this trade across their frontiers they should either reduce their higher custom duties or enlist the support of the tribes living in the border area by rewarding them for stopping the entry of any contraband goods into Iraq.[5]

With his study in mind, the Political Agent arrived in Baghdad in late July 1933, to discuss the problem of smuggling with the British Embassy staff. At the suggestion of the Chargé d'Affaires, George Ogilvie-Forbes, Dickson met with Monk, the Acting Iraqi Director-General of Customs. To his great surprise he found that Monk, although British, held deep Iraqi sympathies:

> His attitude, I fear, was that of the Englishman who has become more Iraqi than the real article. Kuwait was the sinner and must be punished. Iraq was the poor, suffering innocent party, struggling to do the right thing. Kuwait must be brought to her senses, either by the method of depriving her of her drinking water from the Shatt al-Arab, or by a policy of super frightfulness on all and sundry caught smuggling. This is to say by shooting out of hand any person so caught.[6]

After refusing to lower Iraq's high customs tariffs, Monk told Dickson that Kuwait was responsible for the smuggling and as a result should

---

5. Schofield, *Kuwait and Iraq*, pp. 69–70.
6. See the Note on the discussions held in Baghdad between Chargé d'Affaires of the Embassy and the Political Agent, Kuwait, in Dickson to the Resident, no. 179, 8 August 1933, FO 371/16852.

raise its customs duties to the Iraqi level and that, if necessary, the British government should force the Sheikh to do so. Dickson reacted angrily to this illogical suggestion as he was convinced that the so-called "contraband" entering Iraq from Kuwait "was nothing like as serious as the Iraqi Government tried to make out". He then offered a counter-proposal, insisting that Iraq should guard its own border by placing at least four customs posts on the 160 kilometres of the Iraq–Kuwait land frontier and by patrolling its frontiers with armed cars. If this measure proved insufficient Iraq should prohibit its merchants from either importing cargoes marked "Basrah option Kuwait" (which gave the option of unloading goods bound for Iraq at Kuwait) or exporting "bonded" cigarettes and tobacco to Kuwait, which the exporters brought back into Iraq with the help of Iraqi tribesmen. Monk's unfavourable reaction to these suggestions convinced Dickson that the Iraqi protests about smuggling "might not be unconnected with the Iraqi Government's desire to get control of Kuwait".[7]

A further deterioration of Iraqi–Kuwaiti relations followed a series of attacks, in September 1933, on Kuwaiti fishing boats by Iraqi armed launches in Kuwaiti waters. Sheikh Ahmed took these violations of his territorial waters more seriously when in the following month a Fao customs launch attacked a Kuwaiti boat just off Bubiyan Island, killing one man and wounding two others. The Sheikh strongly protested about the incident to the Agent, who referred the matter to Lieutenant Colonel Trenchard Fowle, the Resident in the Gulf. Fowle, in turn, placed the issue before Sir Francis Humphrys, the British Ambassador in Baghdad, who reminded Nuri al-Said, the then Iraqi Minister for Foreign Affairs, of the exchange of letters of 1932, which had specifically defined the boundaries of Kuwait to include Bubiyan Island. Humphrys then requested him to take all measures necessary to prevent further infringements. Yet the Foreign Minister's only response was to totally deny the allegations.[8]

---

7. *Ibid.* See also PGAR, p. 66.
8. For more details on Iraqi violations of Kuwaiti territorial waters, see: Sheikh Ahmed to Dickson, no. R-3/1235, 3 October 1933, FO 371/16852; Dickson to Fowle, no. PZ7361/33, 11 October 1933, FO 371/16852; Sheikh Ahmed to Dickson no. R-3/1271, 15 October 1933, FO 371/16852; Dickson to Fowle, no. 255, 18 October 1933, FO 371/16852; Dickson to Fowle, no. 263, 1 November 1933, FO 371/16852; Humphrys to Nuri, no. 686, 8 December

Despite repeated Kuwaiti protests, the incursions continued. It was reported, for example, that in May 1934, four Iraqi armoured cars entered Kuwaiti territory and roamed free for some ten days. During these incursions tents belonging to Kuwaiti subjects to the south of Safwan and the Batin Valley were surrounded and searched by Iraqis on the pretext that they were looking for smugglers. When the British embassy in Baghdad lodged protests on behalf of the Sheikh, the Iraqi government, as usual, denied the allegations arguing that smuggling from Kuwait had reached such "extensive proportions as constituted a menace to the trade of Iraq", thereby forcing the Iraqi government to "stem the tide of this smuggling by making frontier control more stringent".[9] The British government, however, refused to accept this explanation and made it clear that the investigations into the case should be "thorough and complete and that adequate assurance for the future be given as regards both Kuwaiti territory and territorial waters".[10]

As tensions mounted with each new report of border violations, the British seized the initiative by convening an informal conference in Kuwait on 24 September 1934 between the representatives of Iraq and Kuwait, in an attempt to resolve the problem. Gordon Loch, the Acting Political Resident, spoke on behalf of Sheikh Ahmed, while Naji al-Asil, the Director-General of Foreign Affairs, and Yahsin Ali, the Mutasarrif of Basra, represented Iraq. Loch opened the proceedings by stating that he was convinced that the government of Iraq sincerely wished to settle the smuggling question. The Iraqi delegation then put forward its proposals, which were as follows:

(a) the possibility of applying Iraq tariff in Kuwait with the technical advice of the Iraq Customs authorities, or

(b) the retention of the Kuwait tariff in Kuwait and the management of the Kuwait Customs by Iraqi Customs Officials in the employ

---

1933, FO 371/16852; Humphrys to Nuri, no. 690, 11 December 1933, FO 371/16852.

9. Sheikh Ahmed to Dickson, no. R-4/1506, 14 May 1934, R/15/5/129; British Embassy (Baghdad) to the Iraqi Ministry of Foreign Affairs, no. 10 (316-1/34), 31 May 1934, R/15/5/129; Iraqi Ministry of Foreign Affairs to the British Embassy, no. 1172/C, 15 July 1934, R/15/5/129.

10. Ogilvie-Forbes (British Embassy, Baghdad) to Tawfiq Beg al-Suwaidi, no. 410, 24 July 1934, R/15/5/129.

of the Shaikh of Kuwait, and that there should be a limitation of imports.[11]

Compensation would be given to the Sheikh if he agreed to accept either of these proposals. In response, Loch made it clear that there was no chance of establishing the Iraqi tariff, as it would be impossible to expect "the Kuwaiti population to accept such a measure peacefully".[12] However, he duly relayed the proposals to the Sheikh, who rejected them outright as a means by which to control not only Kuwait's customs but its trade as well. As Sheikh Ahmed showed no sign of flexibility, Loch suspended the meeting after just one day.[13]

Following this abortive conference, Nuri al-Said appealed to the British government to intervene more directly to solve the problem of smuggling which he alleged had reached 523 cases by the middle of 1934, causing a loss of £30,000 annually to the Iraqi treasury. In conversation with Humphrys on 11 December 1934, Nuri disclosed that if the Sheikh continued to take no action to suppress the smuggling, the Iraqi government would be forced to adopt the following measures unilaterally: first, the total prohibition of imports from Kuwait; second, the strengthening of the armed forces patrolling Iraq's land frontier; third, the placing of severe restrictions upon the entry of Kuwaiti vessels into Iraqi territorial waters; and finally, the withdrawal of the valuable customs concessions which were at the time extended to Kuwaiti commerce. As the implementation of these measures would seriously damage Kuwait's economy, which was already suffering from the decline of the pearl trade, the Ambassador suggested another conference, this time to take place in Baghdad and consisting of the local British representatives. He further suggested that if any formula produced by the conference received the approval of both the British and the Iraqi governments, it should be submitted to the Sheikh asking him either to accept it or face the consequences of his continued "obduracy".[14]

---

11. Note of an informal conversation between Colonel Gordon Loch and the Iraqi Representatives, unnumbered, 24 September 1934, R/15/5/129.
12. *Ibid.*
13. *Ibid.* See also the conversation between Loch and the Iraqi delegation, unnumbered, 25 September 1934, in *ibid.*
14. See Humphrys to John Simon (the British Foreign Secretary), no. 711, 16 December 1934, R/15/5/130. See also Nuri to Humphrys, no. C/2469, 10 December 1934, R/15/5/130.

This idea of holding a conference on smuggling in Baghdad was accepted by the British Foreign Secretary, Sir John Simon. In April 1935, he directed Sir Archibald Clark Kerr, the new Ambassador to Iraq, to proceed with this plan and to inform Iraq not to take any unilateral action until the British government made this further attempt to resolve the issue. Accordingly, on 11 April 1935, Kerr met Nuri al-Said and told him that the British government was unable to endorse Iraq's proposed measures against Kuwait for the suppression of smuggling as these were "wholly incompatible with the sovereignty of Kuwait". Although there were indications that the Iraqis had been organizing and financing the smuggling, Nuri al-Said defended the proposed action and maintained that Kuwait had been importing ten times more of certain commodities than it actually required. It was this excess capacity which was smuggled into Iraq, and thus if these extra imports were stopped there would be nothing to smuggle. Therefore, the Iraqi government wanted to secure the Sheikh's agreement to restrict these imports. However, the Ambassador made it clear that the British government was not prepared "to go beyond pressing the Shaikh to agree to the appointment of a British or British Indian Custom Director". Nuri al-Said was willing to accept this on condition that such a director "must be a *sine qua non* of a settlement".[15] A detailed discussion on this proposal then took place. From this came an agreement that the proposed director would be given special powers to take restrictive measures against the importation of certain articles into Kuwait. It was also agreed that the Sheikh should form a preventive service to work in cooperation with a fully organized frontier force maintained by the Iraqi government. In addition, a system of "land manifests" should be introduced. The entire cost of these measures would be met by Iraq. If the Sheikh gave his approval to them, a formal Iraqi–Kuwaiti conference would take place at Basra under British chairmanship.[16]

Following his visit to Baghdad, Fowle placed the proposals before Sheikh Ahmed. Considering these measures as contrary to the legitimate interests of Kuwait and its people, the Sheikh rejected them outright. He argued that the responsibility for checking smuggling across the frontier laid with Iraq and as such it was unfair to expect him to do their

---

15. Archibold Clark Kerr to John Simon, no. 198, 11 April 1935, R/15/5/130.
16. *Ibid.*

job for them. The Sheikh gave the following reasons for rejecting the proposals:

> Firstly – Kuwait would definitely lose all her trade with the interior, since it would be the business of the new Director of Customs to arrange this.

> Secondly – The whole of Arabia would understand that Kuwait had surrendered her liberty to Iraq, and so had become a vassal of her.

> Thirdly – I, the Shaikh, would be regarded as a traitor by all the members of my family as well as by all the people of Kuwait, and I would be execrated and possibly have to meet great difficulties and troubles.

> Fourthly – Bin Saud would himself say that 'The Shaikh of Kuwait has surrendered his State to Iraq . . .'

> Fifthly – With Kuwait trade gone, and I, the Shaikh, a traitor to my people, there will follow an exodus 'Hajir' from the town, of my leading citizens, notables and merchants . . . [17]

As he was unable to accept the Iraqi proposals Sheikh Ahmed found no reason for holding the conference. Fowle attempted to persuade the Sheikh that if he did not change his mind, Iraq would institute a complete blockade of Kuwait and might even place restrictions on the Kuwaiti boats which fetched drinking-water from the Shatt al-Arab.[18] As this warning failed to sway the Sheikh, Fowle found no reason to pursue the matter further and therefore recommended that the Iraqi government should be free to establish its blockade provided these measures were legal.[19] Although the Government of India endorsed Fowle's harsh recommendation, London refused to do so. Sir Samuel Hoare, the Foreign Secretary, was convinced that the Sheikh would eventually agree to a system of manifests for goods transported by sea. Therefore, he urged that the Iraqi government be advised to adopt a similar system of

---

17. Sheikh Ahmed to Fowle, unnumbered, 28 May 1935, R/15/5/130.
18. *Ibid.*
19. Fowle to the Government of India (Simla), repeated to the Secretary of State for India, no. C/193, 2 June 1935, R/15/5/130.

manifests for goods exported from Kuwait to Iraq by land on the understanding that Kuwait should set up three or four posts on the frontier
through which trade would be channelled into Iraq. All goods leaving
Kuwait consigned to or through Iraq would carry manifests which
would be issued on the authority of the Sheikh. It would then be up to
the Iraqis to deal as severely as they wished with those persons found
crossing the border either without manifests or at points other than the
proposed frontier posts. The Foreign Secretary believed that this new
system would go a long way in easing tension and therefore found no
justification for Iraq to take "extreme measures" against the Sheikh.
Thus, the Ambassador was instructed to push hard for an Iraqi acceptance of this new proposal.[20]

In presenting the idea of a system of manifests to the Iraqis, the
Ambassador made it clear that the onus of stopping the smuggling lay
entirely with Iraq. The Iraqis took this to justify the establishment of a
frontier police force to guard the land frontier without, however, intro-
ducing any system of manifests for goods imported from Kuwait.
Although no serious attempt was made to cross into Kuwait by land
following the establishment of this force, the encroachments into
Kuwaiti territorial waters continued. For example, in September 1935
the Fao customs launch again ventured into Kuwaiti waters at Thaabib,
to the north-west of Bubiyan Island, and attacked and arrested Kuwaiti
woodcutters, and seized their boat. Events such as this flagrant violation
of Kuwaiti territorial waters angered Sheikh Ahmed, who, frustrated at
the half-hearted British response to all his previous complaints, wanted
to personally deal with the matter:

> If the Iraq Government does not wish to believe what is taking
> place or has no desire to prevent the said launch from these
> infringements, we shall be compelled to seize it next time it enters
> our waters. Before doing anything so strong as this, however, we
> feel we ought to issue this warning and ask the Iraq Government
> not to raise objection, if we are compelled to take the law into our
> hand.[21]

---

20. Secretary of State for Foreign Affairs to the Ambassador in Baghdad, no. 175, 18
    July 1935, R/15/5/131. See also Government of India to the Secretary of State
    for India, no. 1492, 16 June 1935, R/15/5/131.
21. See Sheikh Ahmed to Dickson, no. R-4/2326, 24 December 1935, FO

This was the first time that the Sheikh had advocated direct action, and was the result of the continual failure of the British government to protect the territorial integrity of his country despite its assurances of 1914. Nevertheless, instead of supporting the Sheikh, the British government prevented him from taking any aggressive action against the Iraqi authorities.[22]

Yet this failure of the British government to check Iraqi encroachments into the Sheikh's territory, according to Fowle, was not only humiliating for the Sheikh but also "extremely damaging" to British prestige in the Gulf. For these reasons, he felt it necessary to protect Kuwait from any further Iraqi incursions:

> The Shaikh of Kuwait is under our protection, and one of our primary duties in this respect is to prevent encroachments of his territory, and ill-treatment of his subjects, by Foreign Powers. This we have obviously failed to do in regard to the outrages of the Iraqi Customs and Police Officials, since we have been able neither to obtain reparation for these outrages, nor to prevent their recurrence.[23]

As a result of Iraq's failure to exercise any effective control over its custom officials and its refusal to offer any compensation for their misdeeds, Fowle argued that the British government should, without further delay, take all measures, including the use of force if necessary, to protect the Sheikh's territory and territorial waters from further Iraqi violations and his subjects from maltreatment.[24]

London, however, declined to take a firmer line except for making a demand for some compensation, "ex-gratia or otherwise", for the Kuwaiti victims of the last raid, in the event of it being established that the incident occurred in Kuwaiti waters.[25] Despite his reservations, Sir Archibald Clark Kerr, protested about the Thaabib incident to the Iraqi Foreign Ministry on 19 April 1936. Iraq, however, argued that this

---

371/19967. See also Dickson to Fowle, no. C/4, 2 January 1936, FO 371/19967.

22. Fowle to J. C. Walton, no. DO 333-S, 5 May 1936, FO 371/19968.
23. Fowle to Kerr, no. C/5, 18 January 1936, FO 371/19967.
24. *Ibid.*
25. Foreign Office to Kerr, no. E-637/38/91, 3 March 1936, FO 371/19967.

incident had in fact occurred within Iraqi territorial waters, and as such the action taken against the Kuwaitis was in full accordance with Iraqi law. The ease with which Iraq was able to refute allegations of territorial violation was largely due to the absence of definite frontier marks between the two countries. In order to deny such an advantage to Iraq in the future, the Ambassador placed great importance upon marking the border and territorial water limits, at least at the salient point at the junction of the Khor Subiya and the Khor Zubair. The Sheikh of Kuwait should be brought into the operation by being asked to put as many ground marks or beacons as were feasible in order to enable Iraqi custom officers to determine the actual position of suspected Kuwaiti intruders at any given time.[26]

In addition, the Ambassador continued his efforts to bring an end to the frontier violations by personally calling on Yasin al-Hashemi, the Iraqi Prime Minister, on 20 May 1936, to request an enquiry into the Thaabib incident of the previous September. However, sidestepping Kerr's request, the Iraqi Prime Minister raised a new issue of the alleged smuggling of arms and ammunition from Kuwait. He argued that this smuggling was generating bitter resentment in Iraq against Kuwait as the arms had found their way to the anti-Iraq insurgents on the Euphrates. Kerr, however, rejected this allegation point-blank. Expressing his concern over the deterioration of Iraqi–Kuwaiti relations, the Ambassador pointed out that the existing Kuwaiti fear of Iraq's intended absorption of their Sheikhdom was one of the root causes of the present problem. Kerr was sure that if this fear could be assuaged then the atmosphere would be sufficiently conducive for nurturing a better understanding between the two countries. The Iraqi Prime Minister reacted sharply to this, arguing that although Iraq frequently spoke of an Arab Union, the "annexation of Kuwait had never been and was not now part of the practical policy of the Iraqi Government". The Iraqis wanted to be friends with the Sheikh and his people and had no plans to undermine his independence.[27] It is worth noting here, however, that at a meeting just two months earlier, on 16 March 1936, al-Hashimi had himself told Kerr that as an Arab he wished "to see

---

26. Kerr to Foreign Office, no. 86, 19 April 1936, FO 371/19968.
27. Kerr to Rendel, no. 100/12/36, 20 May 1936, FO 371/19968.

Kuwait absorbed by Iraq" as such an annexation would give Iraqi trade a safe outlet to the sea.[28]

Yet despite this denial of any official designs on Kuwait, al-Hashemi blamed Sheikh Ahmed for the bad relations existing between their two countries. He argued that the Sheikh was "acting in an unneighbourly and almost unfriendly manner by allowing his people to carry on smuggling into Iraq on a very large scale". In response, the Ambassador defended the Sheikh's position as it was difficult for him to intervene as Kuwait "lived largely on its entrepot" trade. If heavy restrictions were imposed upon this trade, many of the Kuwaiti merchants would be ruined financially.[29] Although the Iraqi Prime Minister disputed this, Kerr's opinion was accepted by George Rendel, the Head of the Foreign Office's Eastern Department, who believed that the Iraqis were acting most unreasonably in blaming the Sheikh, as the main reason for the smuggling was the "outrageously high tariff in Iraq comparing to an extremely low one in Kuwait". Accordingly, the only chance of checking smuggling was the removal of this tariff barrier.[30]

By continuing to press the Kuwaiti case, Kerr eventually persuaded the Iraqi government in July 1936 to appoint an enquiry commission headed by Major Cones, the British Deputy Inspector-General of Police in Baghdad, to investigate the Thaabib incident of September 1935. However, the findings of the investigation reflected the viewpoint of the Iraqi government. Cones reiterated that the arrested Kuwaitis had been engaged in smuggling while disguised as wood-cutters and their capture had taken place in the Khor Zubair, within Iraqi territory, some 3.2 kilometres from Umm Qasr. As there was nothing new in Cones's findings and as he had accomplished his task hastily without examining the Kuwaiti witnesses, Charles Bateman, the Chargé d'Affaires in Baghdad, believed his opinion to be biased. He therefore assured the Foreign Office that in future the British Police Inspector at Basra would be asked to investigate the Sheikh's complaints as and when they occurred and that the Sheikh would be encouraged to send his witnesses to Basra without any delay. At the same time, however, Bateman argued

---

28. See the Enclosure in Kerr to George Rendel, no. 100/8/36, 24 March 1936, FO 371/19968.
29. Kerr to Rendel, no. 100/12/36, 20 May 1936, FO 371/19968.
30. See Minute by Rendel, no. E 3233, 19 June 1936, FO 371/19968.

that it was a mistake for the British embassy to make representations to the Iraqi Foreign Ministry based "exclusively on the Sheikh's complaints", as this practice irritated the Iraqi government. He recommended that the embassy should only approach the Iraqis if the Political Agent was satisfied, after personally examining the Sheikh's witnesses, that there was a "strong prima facie case" for such representations.[31] Although this procedure was acceptable to the Foreign Office, it was thought that as Cones's report on the Thaabib case was "most favourable" to the Iraqis, they would not give a sympathetic ear to the Sheikh's complaints in the future. As a result, the Foreign Office agreed with Kerr's earlier suggestion that the border and the territorial water limits should be identified with a series of ground marks and beacons in order to avoid further incidents in the frontier zone.[32]

While the British government had been actively engaged in investigating the frontier violations, further incursions took place despite a considerable decline in smuggling. On 29 July 1936, Iraqi armed police confiscated commodities such as rice, flour and sugar from a party of Kuwaiti tribesmen travelling within Kuwaiti territory near Raudhat Umm al-Arish, to the south of Safwan. During the next two months Iraqi police carried out similar raids near Umm Niqqah, al-Anaq and Hinnabiyah. Other incidents had also taken place at sea. For example, on 29 and 30 August, the Iraqi customs launch trespassed into Kuwaiti waters by the western shore of Bubiyan Island at Bandur al-Adnya, situated approximately four kilometres north of Mashjan Island.[33] Despite Sheikh Ahmed's complaints, which were corroborated by witnesses, the Iraqis denied the charges. Yet pressed by the British Ambassador, the Iraqi authorities eventually agreed, in November 1936, to investigate the incidents and gave assurances that strict orders would be given to restrict the entry of the Iraqi force into Kuwait.[34]

---

31. Bateman to Eden, no. 365, 16 July 1936, FO 371/19968. See also the Enclosure in *ibid.*; Iraqi Ministry of Foreign Affairs to the British Embassy, Baghdad, no. 8106, 10 August 1936, FO 371/19968.

32. See Minute by Williams, no. E 4783, 8 August 1936, FO 371/19968.

33. Loch (Shiraj) to Prodrome (Baghdad), no. T 108, 27 August 1936, FO 371/19968. See also Loch to the Secretary of State for India, no. T/162, 12 September 1936, FO 371/19968; the Ruler of Kuwait to the Agent in Kuwait, no. R/5/223, 31 August 1936, FO 371/19968.

34. Bateman to Loch, no. 31/43/36, 21 September 1936, FO 371/19968. See also

Meanwhile, Fowle, the Resident, put forward a new proposal on 20 July 1936, to prevent further border violations. He suggested the establishment of a mixed commission to meet at Safwan, on the Iraq–Kuwait frontier, in order to investigate all the frontier incidents which had occurred between the two countries since April 1934. It was proposed that the Mutasarrif of Basra would represent Iraq and that the Political Agent in Kuwait would act for the Sheikh. The commission was to decide firstly who was to blame for the incident and secondly, what compensation, if any, was to be paid by the offending party. The decision of the commission would be final. If the representatives differed in their judgement on any particular incident, then the matter would be referred to an arbitrator, appointed by the British government.[35]

However, Fowle's proposal met strong opposition from Bateman, who found it not only impractical but, more importantly, unwise as any attempt to reopen past incidents would immediately meet with an Iraqi demand that enquiries should be extended to cover the loss of revenue to Iraq caused by smuggling from Kuwait. Further, the Iraqi government would not agree to the establishment of such a commission as it would deal only with the Sheikh's complaints against Iraqi officials and would offer no redress to Iraqi grievances against the Sheikh. According to Bateman, it was meaningless to pursue Fowle's suggestion further until some sort of comprehensive frontier agreement between the two countries was reached. He therefore recommended that past incidents should be forgotten and all energies put into persuading Iraq to demarcate the frontier so that there could be no excuse for "hot-headed Iraqi Officials" infringing the land or water frontier of Kuwait.[36]

In view of these criticisms of the proposed joint commission, the Foreign Office summoned Fowle to further explain his proposal. Accordingly, an inter-departmental meeting consisting of representatives

---

the Enclosures in de Gaury to Fowle, no. C-278, 5 October 1936, FO 371/19968; Kerr to Fowle, no. 109/32/36, 19 October 1936, FO 371/19968; Fowle to the Secretary of State for India, no. T/209, 28 November 1936, FO 371/19968.

35. Fowle to the Secretary of State for India, no. C/82, 20 July 1936, FO 371/19968.

36. Bateman to Eden, no. 401, 4 August 1936, FO 371/19968. See also Minute by Adams, no. E-5338, 2 September 1936, FO 371/19968.

of the Foreign Office and the India Office was held on 6 October 1936 under the chairmanship of George Rendel. Fowle, who attended the meeting, gave a detailed explanation of his proposal and defended it convincingly, reiterating that the commission should investigate both "past and future incidents". John Ward of the Foreign Office opposed this, however, as he believed that the raising of past incidents would lead to more problems than it would solve, not only because of the difficulties of obtaining reliable evidence about incidents going back as far as 1933 but also because the Iraqis would simply not agree to the idea of investigating the past. Rendel agreed and stated that the past incidents should be disregarded. He then suggested that the demarcation of the frontier should precede the setting up of the commission. Rendel believed that this was absolutely necessary not only because uncertainty as to the frontier's actual position was, as supported by historical fact, at the root of many of the incidents, but also because proper frontier demarcation would undoubtedly lead to an improvement in Iraqi–Kuwaiti relations. He thought that the frontier, which was laid down in documents and maps, could be easily demarcated on land by the use of pillars or obelisks and on the water by beacons and buoys. As there was a general consensus on Rendel's proposal, Fowle gave way.[37]

On 19 November 1936, Kerr was instructed to tell the Iraqi government that in view of the continued allegations of frontier violations, the Iraq–Kuwait border should be clearly demarcated as soon as possible. A committee to delimit and mark this frontier should also be set up prior to the creation of a small mixed local commission to deal with any incidents which might occur in the future.[38] However, as the Ambassador believed that the Iraqis would not accept these proposals until the problem of smuggling had been addressed, he declined to present them to the new Iraqi government headed by Hikmat Sulaiman (which had replaced Yasin al-Hashemi's Cabinet in October 1936). Kerr, therefore, suggested that an Iraqi–Kuwaiti anti-smuggling agreement based upon the proposed Kuwaiti–Saudi agreement, should be concluded before acting on the Foreign Office's latest proposals.[39] Fowle

---

37. See the Record of a Meeting held at the Foreign Office, no. E-6378, 6 October 1936, FO 371/19968.
38. Rendel to Kerr, no. 263, 19 November 1936, FO 371/19968. See also Fowle to the Secretary of State for India, no. 5030, 6 November 1936, FO 371/19968.
39. Kerr to Foreign Office, no. 296, 23 November 1936, FO 371/19969.

vehemently objected to this approach, as this would only serve to complicate matters further and create an unnecessary delay in the settlement of the problem of frontier violations.[40] The Foreign Office agreed that it would be "most undesirable" for the establishment of a frontier committee and the commencement of demarcation (if agreed upon) to await the conclusion of a detailed agreement on smuggling. Accordingly, on 3 December, Kerr was ordered not to broach the issue of smuggling, but rather to go ahead with the original idea of a committee to properly demarcate the Iraq–Kuwait frontier.[41]

Kerr, however, still refused to follow London's instruction and staunchly advocated his counter-proposal. On 6 December 1936, therefore, he cabled back to London arguing that it would be futile to seek Iraqi approval for the setting up of a mixed committee and for the demarcation of the frontier without first preventing smuggling.[42] The Foreign Office again disagreed and sought the opinion of the Resident, who argued that there was no valid reason to make the establishment of the mixed committee conditional on the settlement of the smuggling question.[43] The India Office, which was dismayed by Kerr's stubbornness, firmly backed Fowle as it believed there was no harm in convening another committee in an attempt to deal with the present incidents. However, when the India Office formally requested the Foreign Office to again urge Kerr to act upon Fowle's suggestions, it immediately and very surprisingly endorsed Kerr's view, and declined to issue any instruction unless the Sheikh agreed to open negotiations with the Iraqis on the issue of smuggling.[44]

Given this intra-governmental tussle between the Foreign Office and the India Office, Fowle had no other option but to agree to put pressure on the Sheikh to reach an agreement with the Iraqis similar to

---

40. Fowle to the Secretary of State for India, no. T/210, 28 November 1936, FO 371/19969.
41. See Secretary of State for India to Fowle, no. PZ8517/36, 3 December 1936, FO 371/19969. See also Foreign Office to Kerr, no. 279, 3 December 1936, FO 371/19969.
42. Kerr to Foreign Office, no. 312, 6 December 1936, FO 371/19969.
43. See Minute by Rendel, no. E-7619, 6 December 1936, FO 371/19969; Fowle to the Secretary of State for India, no. 5731, 14 December 1936, FO 371/19969.
44. Clauson (India Office) to M. S. Williams (Foreign Office), no. PZ8833/36, 24 December 1936, FO 371/19969.

the proposed Kuwaiti–Saudi Arabian trade canalization agreement.[45] The main features of this proposed agreement were: firstly, the issue of manifests in triplicate, one to be given to the head of the caravan, the second to the trade agent and the third to be kept in the local government office in Kuwait; secondly, the establishment of customs posts on the Saudi frontiers; thirdly, the establishment of a system to control the traders who would cross the Kuwait–Najd frontiers; and lastly, a Kuwaiti promise to give all possible assistance in the interest of both countries.[46] When the Political Agent told the Sheikh in late March 1937 that the British government wanted him to conclude an anti-smuggling agreement with Iraq along these lines in order to obtain Iraqi cooperation in the settlement of frontier disputes, the Sheikh reluctantly agreed to do so; but only after the conclusion of the proposed agreement with Saudi Arabia so as to be able to guage its success.[47] In other words, the Sheikh's consent to a Iraqi–Kuwaiti agreement on smuggling was entirely dependent on the successful implementation of a settlement with the Saudis. However, this would entail the lifting of the trade embargo imposed by Ibn Saud in 1922, which prohibited his subjects from trading with Kuwait because of his difficulties in collecting import duties on goods crossing the desert frontier between Kuwait and Najd, and the Sheikh's refusal to allow him to establish a Najdi custom-house in Kuwait town.[48] Although the embargo had had a serious impact upon the prosperity of the Sheikhdom, it became clear, by early April 1937, that the prospects of an early conclusion of the proposed Kuwaiti–Saudi agreement were remote due to the lack of progress in the negotiations. Accordingly, as Kerr was still of the opinion that the Iraqis viewed any solution to

---

45. See Minutes by Williams and Beneth, no. E-7996, 29 December 1936, FO 371/19969.
46. Sheikh Ahmed al-Jaber al-Sabah to Captain Gerald Simpson de Gaury (Political Agent, Kuwait), no. B-4/2384, 21 February 1936, R/15/5/112. See also de Gaury to Sheikh Ahmed, no. C1, 3 October 1936, R/15/5/113.
47. See Minute by E. R. Warner, no. E-1773, 2 April 1937, FO 371/20774. See also de Gaury to Fowle, no. 355, 28 March 1937, FO 371/20774.
48. Despite Ibn Saud's willingness to pay four per cent transit duty to the Sheikh, the Sheikh of Kuwait could not agree to the establishment of a Najdi custom-house in Kuwait Town due to his fear of the extension of Ibn Saud's influence in Kuwait (although the arrangement would not have been economically unsatisfactory). For more details on the customs dispute between Ibn Saud and the Sheikh of Kuwait, see *PGHS*, vol. I, p. 81.

the frontier problem as wholly conditional upon the prevention of smuggling, the Foreign Office agreed to defer taking any action on the outstanding Iraqi–Kuwaiti issues until Kuwait had concluded an agreement with Saudi Arabia. [49]

As the Ambassador, with the backing of the Foreign Office, made no attempt to deter the Iraqis from crossing the Kuwaiti frontier, the violations continued. In April 1937, the Resident once again drew the Ambassador's attention to further incursions into Kuwaiti territory – particularly a raid in the previous month by the Iraqi police carried out under the pretext of suppressing smuggling. Kerr once again declined to talk to the Iraqis about it, using the same excuse that they would not do anything about it so long as the smuggling continued.[50] Despite the Ambassador's stance, Fowle still continued his efforts to restore order in the border regions and maintained that all the past incidents should be enquired into by an Iraqi–Kuwaiti frontier committee in order to establish the truth. He again appealed to Kerr to press the Iraqis for a joint enquiry to include Gerald Simpson de Gaury, the Political Agent in Kuwait, if only to investigate any future incidents.[51] Kerr, however, objected to the idea of associating de Gaury in any enquiry and maintained that if only the Kuwaitis would cooperate to suppress smuggling there would be no difficulty in persuading the Iraqis to agree to joint action in other matters.[52] The Ambassador was undoubtedly trying to put all the blame for the smuggling on the Kuwaitis while Fowle, in defending the Kuwaiti position, accused the Iraqi government of not taking sufficient action in their own territory to stop the smuggling from Kuwait and reminded Kerr that in any case Kuwait was not legally bound to assist Iraq in the suppression of smuggling. The Resident advanced the instances of smuggling from Iraq into Persia to support his argument:[53]

---

49. Kerr to Foreign Office, no. 59, 16 April 1937, FO 371/20774. *Ibid.* See also Foreign Office to Kerr, no. 72, 12 April 1937, FO 371/20774. Minute by Rendel, no. E-2094, 1 May 1937, FO 371/20774.
50. Kerr to Fowle, no. 280/4/37, 29 April 1937, FO 371/20774. See also de Gaury to Fowle, no. C/104, 11 March 1937, FO 371/20774.
51. Fowle to Kerr, no. DO 364-S, 21 May 1937, FO 371/20774.
52. Kerr to Fowle, no. 260/9/37, 15 June 1937, FO 371/20774.
53. See Minute by T. Brenan, no. 3738, 9 July 1937, FO 371/20774.

The violations of Kuwait territory by Iraqi officials are definitely illegal acts. On the other hand there is no legal obligation on Kuwait to assist the Iraq Government to stop smuggling, and I should imagine there are very few instances of any country taking action on these lines for the benefit of its neighbour. I believe, for instance, that a certain amount of smuggling takes place from Iraq into Persia. I do not know whether the Iraq Government feel it incumbent on them to take action to stop this contraband trade.[54]

To this the Ambassador retorted:

The Iraqi government do accept responsibility for stopping smuggling into Persia and Persia have accepted the same responsibility towards Iraq, and a similar reciprocal arrangement exists between Persia and Turkey. In both instances these obligations form part of comprehensive frontier agreements.[55]

In short, Kerr admitted that Iraq, Persia and Turkey had been cooperating to stop smuggling as a result of frontier agreements. Yet despite the apparent success of these agreements in promoting inter-state cooperation, Kerr consistently ruled out any such agreement between Kuwait and Iraq as an essential prerequisite to a solution to the problem of smuggling between the two countries.

In the meantime, the Iraqi Prime Minister Hikmat Sulaiman, in early June 1937, bitterly attacked Kuwait over the alleged smuggling of 300 rifles into Iraq. This was based on an unsubstantiated press report of 3 June 1937.[56] In the following August, Abbas Mahdi, the Iraqi Acting Foreign Minister drew the attention of Oswald Scott, the British Chargé d'Affaires in Baghdad, to an arms smuggling incident which had allegedly occurred a month earlier on the Iraqi–Kuwaiti border and asked him to fully investigate the matter.[57] It is to be noted here that well before Mahdi's accusation against Kuwait, the issue of alleged gun-running had been investigated by de Gaury who concluded in November 1936 that there was no smuggling of arms from Kuwait into

---

54. Fowle to Kerr, no. DO 517-S, 6 July 1937, FO 371/20774.
55. Kerr to Fowle, no. 280/12/37, 21 July 1937, FO 371/20774.
56. Kerr to Rendel, no. 54/45/37, 7 June 1937, FO 371/20774. See also the extract from *al-Bilad*, 3 June 1937 in *ibid*.
57. Abbas Mahdi to Oswald Scott, no. C-2/94, 31 August 1937, FO 371/20774.

Iraq. The Political Agent even produced a list of the Iraqi subjects and organizations who were in fact responsible for the contraband trade, but the Iraqi government, despite repeated written complaints by its own high officials, took no action against them.[58] Even the former Iraqi Foreign Minister, Naji al-Asil, admitted in a clear statement after a visit to Kuwait on 10 November 1936 that no arms trafficking had ever taken place between Kuwait and Iraq. Following the publication of the press report of June 1937, both de Gaury and Fowle reconfirmed that there had been no change in the situation since the investigation of the previous November and questioned the validity of the Iraqi accusations of gunrunning.[59]

However, neither the Foreign Office nor the British Embassy in Baghdad paid much attention to the authorities in the Gulf and did not even ask the Iraqis to prove their allegations. Rendel even pleaded for an Iraqi blockade of Kuwait despite his suspicions that the smuggling was largely run by the Iraqis, in order to teach Sheikh Ahmed "a useful lesson".[60] Oswald Scott, the Chargé d'Affaires in Baghdad, even argued that al-Asil's statement of November 1936 did not reflect "the view of the matter usually taken in Iraq".[61] The India Office reacted sharply to Scott's interpretation of al-Asil's statement and reminded the Foreign Office that the former Iraqi Foreign Minister expressed "his conviction that recent reports of arms smuggling from Kuwait were entirely erroneous". As the Iraqis had failed to produce any evidence to the contrary, the India Office sought to uphold al-Asil's statement:

> We ourselves regard the statement, made as it was by the Iraqi Foreign Minister of the time, as of considerable importance as a protection against the many vague and unsupported accusations raised by the Iraqi Government about arms smuggling from

---

58. For the gist of the conversation between de Gaury and various Iraqi officials see Fowle to Kerr, no. DO 316-S, 27 March 1937, FO 371/20774.
59. See the Enclosure in Kerr to Fowle, no. 314/2/37, 19 March 1937, FO 371/20774. See also Fowle to Kerr, no. C/51, 7 April 1937, FO 371/20774 and Fowle to Kerr, no. 442-S, 8 June 1937, FO 371/20774.
60. See Rendel's Minutes, no. 3430/29/91, 21 June and 14 October 1937, FO 371/20774.
61. Scott to Olf Kirkpatrick Carore, Acting Political Resident, no. 135/5/37, 3 September 1937, FO 371/20774.

Koweit, and we should be reluctant to accept Scott's view that Dr. Naji's remarks should be interpreted merely as 'an admission that reports of open and active encouragement given by the Sheikh to arms smuggling were unfounded'.[62]

Yet despite the India Office's obvious opposition to Scott's view, the Foreign Office supported his misinterpretation of al-Asil's statement by its Chargé d'Affaires.[63]

While the Foreign Office and the India Office were engaged in this heated debate over arms smuggling, the Iraqi police carried out a serious raid on Udairi al-Khillah, a village about 40 kilometres inside Kuwaiti territory, on 15 October 1937. The raiders wounded several innocent Kuwaitis and killed 60 camels. The Iraqi police apparently did so while pursuing Iraqi smugglers carrying goods obtained in Kuwait. Sheikh Ahmed immediately protested against the incident and demanded urgent action. In response, the Political Agent visited the scene and questioned witnesses, and examined the bloodstains, cartridges and equipment left by the raiders. Following the submission of de Gaury's report, Fowle, who was convinced that there was systematic plan of armed Iraqi infiltration into Kuwait in order to catch smugglers before they reached the border, again demanded the establishment of a joint commission to investigate the incident.[64] Lord Zetland, the Secretary of State for India, endorsed Fowle's recommendation and urged the Foreign Office to make an immediate protest to the Iraqi government, demanding effective action to prevent any recurrence of such raids into Kuwaiti territory.[65]

Before issuing any instruction to Baghdad, the Foreign Office held an inter-departmental meeting on 1 November 1937, attended by both Kerr and Fowle, to discuss in detail the incident at Udairi al-Khillah in particular and the whole Iraqi–Kuwaiti situation in general. Rendel,

---

62. Gibson (India Office) to M. S. Williams (Foreign Office), no. PZ6924/37, 28 October 1937, FO 371/20774.
63. Rendel to Scott, no. E-6406/29/91, 4 November 1937, FO 371/20774.
64. Fowle to the Secretary of State for India, no. 995, 18 October 1937, FO 371/20774. See also Fowle to the Secretary of State for India, no. 994, 18 October 1937, FO 371/20774; Acting Political Resident to the Secretary of State for India, no. 998, 20 October 1937, FO 371/20774.
65. Gibson to the Under-Secretary of State for Foreign Office, no. PZ6892/37, 25 October 1937, FO 371/20774.

who chaired the meeting, first gave a brief description of the Iraqi penetration into Kuwaiti territory, then stated that a protest should be made to Iraq over the incident. Both Fowle and the India Office's representatives, Gibson and Symon, immediately raised the question of pressing Iraq for an enquiry. However, Kerr and the Foreign Office's representatives, Baggallay and Brenan, argued that it would be pointless to do more than to make a formal protest as the Iraqis would simply not agree to such an enquiry. As Rendel agreed with the latter position, the decision was taken to only make a strong protest about the incident Udairi al-Khillah.[66]

The meeting then turned to the problem of smuggling. Although Sheikh Ahmed was under no obligation to take any steps to stop the smuggling, Rendel argued that his attitude towards smuggling had left Britain unable to obtain from the Iraqis the settlement of any of the other outstanding issues such as the Sheikh's date garden which had been expropriated by the Iraqis in 1932. Fowle, backed by the India Office's representatives, strongly objected to this blatant anti-Kuwaiti assertion by arguing that the smuggling was carried out mainly by the Iraqis. Rendel replied that even if this was true, the Sheikh must bear the responsibility for the illegal trade, as the goods were imported through Kuwait from which he derived an enormous profit. Fowle did not accept these allegations and as he continued to press his support for the Sheikh, Rendel disclosed that unless Sheikh Ahmed reached an agreement with Iraq over smuggling, the Iraqis would impose a total blockade of Kuwait to cut off all trade. This would ruin the economy of Kuwait and it would be extremely difficult for Britain to secure the lifting of such a blockade once it had been imposed.[67]

The Resident then told the committee that the situation might be eased if only the Iraqis could be persuaded to agree to the demarcation of the border with Kuwait. Britain should therefore urge Iraq to accept a proposal for a frontier commission. Both Kerr and Rendel, however, instantly defended the Iraqi stance and pointed out that there was no reason why the Iraqis should agree to "anything at all in regard to Kuwait without a very substantial quid pro quo", which the Sheikh had

---

66. For the full text, see Minute of a Meeting in Gibson to Brenan, PZ7407/37, 16 November 1937, FO 371/20774.
67. *Ibid.*

consistently refused to offer them. Consequently, discussions continued until it was agreed: firstly, that no advantage would be gained by asking the Iraqis to agree either to the demarcation of the Iraqi–Kuwaiti frontier or to the establishment of a standing frontier commission at this stage; secondly, that Kerr should on his return to Baghdad ascertain the precise intentions of the Iraqi government regarding the proposed blockade; and finally, that the Sheikh should be warned to either face the ruinous consequences of a blockade or meet Iraq's wishes over the suppression of smuggling, thereby making it easier for the British government to bring about an earlier settlement of the question of his date garden.[68] Therefore, the meeting, which had been dominated by Rendel, greatly sided with Iraq in that, despite Fowle's efforts, it gave scant consideration to the problem of frontier violations or to border demarcation, but instead dealt almost exclusively with the question of smuggling. Following the conclusion of this inter-departmental meeting, the Chargé d'Affaires in Baghdad, at the Foreign Office's instruction, lodged a formal and strongly worded protest against the incursions into Kuwaiti territory by Iraqi armed police and demanded not only an early investigation and the punishment of offenders but also assurances against the recurrence of such raids.[69]

Avoiding any immediate response to this British protest, the Iraqi government instead made preparations for the imposition of a blockade on Kuwait, to be enforced by twelve or more armed cars and two aeroplanes. The aeroplanes would patrol the whole frontier at dawn each day and report any movement across the frontier to the armed cars which would then round up anyone spotted by the aircraft. Sir John Ward, the Director-General of the Iraq State Railway, was to conduct the operation. The blockade, however, did not take place.

Before communicating the conclusions reached at the meeting of 1 November 1937 to Sheikh Ahmed, Fowle requested that the Iraqis be informed of the Sheikh's willingness to negotiate an anti-smuggling agreement once the proposed Saudi agreement was up and running.[70] Sharing this view, the India Office managed to convince the Foreign

68. *Ibid.*
69. Foreign Office to Scott, no. 208, 4 November 1937, FO 371/20774.
70. Minute by R. G. A. Etherington Smith, no. 7336/29/91, 14 December 1937, FO 371/20774; Fowle to the Secretary of State for India, no. 1156, 14 December 1937, FO 371/20774.

Office to reverse its position. [71] On 1 January 1938, therefore, Kerr was instructed to present the Sheikh's position to the Iraqi government. Yet the Ambassador once again declined to do so as he believed the Iraqis would not view the Sheikh's pledge to negotiate only after the Saudi agreement was put into operation as a serious contribution to a solution of the problem of smuggling. [72] Resolute, Fowle cabled back to the Secretary of State for India on 11 January, requesting the proposed communication to the Iraqis be carried out "in fairness to Sheikh". [73] Lord Zetland, who did not understand Kerr's objection to such a "simple communication", recommended that the Foreign Office inform the Iraqi government of the Sheikh's stated position, as "the Iraqis should be given a chance to see that the Sheikh's attitude is not entirely unaccommodating". [74]

As a result, the Foreign Office, on 26 January, once again instructed its Ambassador to communicate with the Iraqi government. [75] It was only at this stage that Kerr felt he had no other option but to comply and accordingly, on 29 January 1938, he carried out the instruction. As he had anticipated, the Iraqi Foreign Minister received the proposal coolly and then went on to discuss the blockade. [76] Acting under the Ambassador's instructions, in September 1938, de Gaury informed the Sheikh of Iraq's plans to mount a trade blockade of Kuwait in the event of his failure to stop smuggling. Sheikh Ahmed, however, showed no signs of anxiety and reiterated that once agreement was reached to lift the Saudi blockade, he would then discuss the problem of smuggling with the Iraqis. [77]

In the meantime, on 28 March 1938, the Iraqi Foreign Ministry eventually replied to the British protest over the Iraqi raid on Udairi al-Khillah. The Iraqis denied all the charges and argued that the incident

---

71. J. P. Gibson to H. L. Baggallay, no. PZ8120/37, 22 December 1937, FO 371/20774.
72. Foreign Office to Kerr, no. 1, 3 January 1938, FO 371/20774. See also Kerr to Foreign Office, no. 4, 4 January 1938, FO 371/21813.
73. Fowle to Zetland, no. 34, 11 January 1938, FO 371/21813.
74. Gibson to Baggallay, no. PZ260/38, 17 January 1938, FO 371/21813.
75. Foreign Office to Baghdad, no. 10, 26 January 1938, FO 371/21813. See also Baggallay to Gibson, no. E-250/75/91, 26 January 1938, FO 371/21813.
76. Baghdad to Foreign Office, no. 11, 29 January 1938, FO 371/21813.
77. De Gaury to Fowle, no. 308, 30 September 1938, FO 371/21813.

had occurred within Iraqi territory. The reply categorically stated that the equipment, the bloodstains, the cartridges and all the other evidence found at Udairi al-Khillah were not traces of the fight itself, but rather of a halt made by the smugglers after they had retreated across the frontier into Kuwait. Despite this unsatisfactory Iraqi response, the new Ambassador to Iraq, Maurice Peterson, recommended that the matter should not be taken further as there had not been any other such incident.[78] Lord Halifax agreed that no useful purpose would be served by bringing further pressure to bear on the Iraqi government over the matter and sought the opinion of Lord Zetland. Despite sharing Fowle's opinion that the affray did take place inside Kuwaiti territory, Zetland reluctantly agreed with Halifax, and this decision was eventually communicated to Peterson on 14 July 1938.[79]

As no pressure was brought to bear on Iraq, its forces continued to violate Kuwaiti territory. For example, in June 1938, an Iraqi police patrol made frequent encroachments into the area around Qashaniya and Hanibiyah.[80] When on 13 August 1938, the British embassy complained to the Iraqi Foreign Ministry about these incursions, it simply denied the charges, as it had done repeatedly in the past, without making any investigations.[81] Instead Abbas Mahdi, the Acting Iraqi Foreign Minister, simply drew the attention of William Houstoun-Boswall, the Chargé d'Affaires, to the problem of smuggling from Kuwait, which he claimed was depriving Iraq of some £250,000 a year in customs duties. Mahdi felt that the British government should instruct the Sheikh to take appropriate action on his side of the border to put an end to the contraband traffic. Houstoun-Boswall assured the

---

78. Iraqi Ministry of Foreign Affairs to the British Embassy in Baghdad, no. 4550/2475/10, 23 March 1938, FO 371/21813. See also Maurice Peterson to Lord Halifax, no. 113, 28 March 1938, FO 371/21813.

79. Baxter to the Under-Secretary of State (India Office), no. E-2023/75/91, 25 April 1938, FO 371/21813. See also Fowle to Zetland, no. C/304, 4 May 1938, FO 371/21813; Gibson to the Under-Secretary of State (Foreign Office), no. PZ4473/38, 8 July 1938, FO 371/21813; Baxter to Peterson, no. 438, 14 July 1938, FO 371/21813.

80. De Gaury to Fowle, no. C-245, 12 July 1938, FO 371/21813. See also Fowle to the Ambassador, Baghdad, no. 477-S, 28 July 1938, FO 371/21813.

81. Iraqi Ministry of Foreign Affairs to the British Embassy in Baghdad, no. 19910, 13 December 1938, FO 371/21813. See also Peterson to Fowle, no. 307/17/38, 19 December 1938, FO 371/21813.

Minister that he would bring his complaint to the attention of the British government. In fact he strongly urged the Foreign Office to do something about the smuggling before it became more "troublesome, if not dangerous, later" by pressing the Government of India to persuade the Sheikh to take stronger action against the alleged smuggling. The Government of India, however, refused to do as it believed so the Sheikh was well within his rights in refusing to act to stop the smuggling.[82]

As no fresh Kuwaiti action was taken to prevent the smuggling, Tawfiq Suwaidi, the Iraqi Foreign Minister, raised the matter with Charles Baxter, the Head of the Foreign Office's Eastern Department, during a visit to London in October 1938. Suwaidi in fact resurrected the familiar, although unsubstantiated, Iraqi accusation that the smuggling from Kuwait into Iraq was not merely confined to merchandise but also included arms. Baxter, who was convinced that "no arms were entering Kuwait, at all events by sea", asked Suwaidi whether he could produce any evidence to support his assertion. With regard to the other forms of smuggling, Baxter told Suwaidi that the Iraqi government should check the smuggling itself by taking drastic measures against those organizations or individuals in Iraq who were assisting the smugglers. Having failed to convince Baxter of Kuwait's responsibility for the suppression of smuggling, Suwaidi instead pressed for a customs union between Iraq and Kuwait. However Baxter found this proposal totally unacceptable since such an "arrangement between a large State like Iraq and a small State like Kuwait, might be expected to undermine the independence of the smaller State". The Iraqi Foreign Minister then went a step further by suggesting that the northern borderline of Kuwait should be fixed further south so as to give the Iraqi frontier police more space in which to operate. This suggestion was equally as unacceptable to Baxter as it apparently would have involved the cession of about one-third of Kuwait to Iraq.[83]

Nevertheless, following Suwaidi's visit, Fowle was instructed to make a further investigation into the alleged arms smuggling and give

---

82. Houstoun-Boswall to Halifax, no. 447, 10 September 1938, FO 371/21813. See also Houstoun-Boswall to H. L. Baggallay, no. 14/12/38, 10 September 1938, FO 371/21813; Minute by Symon, no. E-5348/75/91, 20 September 1938, FO 371/21813.

83. See the Record of conversation with the Iraqi Minister for Foreign Affairs, no. E-5841/1982/93, 5 October 1938, R/15/5/208.

his opinion on the question of whether some stricter form of control over the sale of arms in Kuwait was necessary.[84] Following his visit to the Sheikhdom in February 1939, the Resident was convinced that the source of the arms smuggled to Iraqi tribes lay not in Kuwait but in Saudi Arabia or even in the soldiers of the Iraqi army themselves. He categorically stated that no arms were smuggled from Kuwait to Iraq either by land or by sea and concluded that the control of the sale of arms in Kuwait Town was entirely adequate. As a result of his findings, Fowle suggested that the Iraqi government should be asked to produce any evidence which might be in their possession regarding the alleged gunrunning.[85] Both the India Office and the Foreign Office endorsed the Resident's report as an adequate response to the Iraqi allegations and if they were to pursue this particular complaint in the future, they must produce detailed evidence in support of their accusations.[86]

While Iraq made no further attempt to raise the question of arms smuggling, its police made a series of incursions into Kuwaiti territory on 9, 15 and 20 March 1939 during which they opened fire on camps and a village. These outrageous violations took place about 5 kilometres north-west of Jahra, which itself is only 32 kilometres from Kuwait Town. The Agent personally visited the scene and on speaking with many independent witnesses who each confirmed the incidents, presented a full report to the Resident.[87] On receiving this, Fowle instantly referred the matter to both the Ambassador in Baghdad and the Secretary of State for India. He urged both of them to lodge strong and

---

84. Peel to the Secretary to the Government of India, no. PZ7168/38, 9 November 1938, FO 371/21813. See also William Rupert Hay (the Deputy Secretary to the Government of India) to Fowle, no. F114-N/38, 20 December 1938, FO 371/23180.

85. Fowle to the Secretary to the Government of India, no. C/98, 23 February 1939, FO 371/23180. See also Fowle to the Secretary to the Government of India, no. 102-S, 21 January 1939, FO 371/23180; Fowle to Peel, no. 47-S, 12 January 1939, FO 371/23180; Fowle to Peel, no. 648-S, 29 November 1938, FO 371/23180.

86. See Minute by Crosthwaite, no. 2254/66/91, 16 May 1939, FO 371/23181. See also Peel to Baggallay, no. PZ1808/39, 24 March 1939, FO 371/23181.

87. The Ruler of Kuwait to the Political Agent, no. R-6/1152, 17 March 1939, FO 371/23181. See also Political Agent, Kuwait to the Resident, no. C/114, 17 March 1939, FO 371/23181; Political Agent, Kuwait to the Resident, no. C/123, 22 March 1939, FO 371/23181; Fowle to Peterson, no. 228-S, 21 March 1939, FO 371/23181.

immediate protests with the Iraqi government, and suggested that the opportunity should be taken to press the Iraqis to cooperate in the demarcation of the frontier (which by this stage had assumed an added urgency due to the operations of oil companies on either side of the border).[88] Lord Zetland, who was convinced that a demarcated frontier would assist in checking the frontier violations by the Iraqi police, endorsed Fowle's recommendation and urged the Foreign Office to instruct the Ambassador in Baghdad to protest to the Iraqis as soon as possible.[89] Accordingly, on 25 March 1939, Houstoun-Boswall sent a note to Nuri al-Said, who at this time was the Acting Minister for Foreign Affairs, requesting an immediate investigation and the punishment of the offenders as well as stringent measures to prevent any recurrence of such incidents. The note also demanded an apology for the incursions by the Iraqi police into Kuwaiti territory.[90]

The Iraqi failure to make an immediate response to the British protests angered Sheikh Ahmed, who now wanted to protect his own frontier by establishing a control post near Safwan. Fowle immediately endorsed the Sheikh's plan as he believed that the repeated Iraqi violations of the Kuwaiti frontier and Britain's failure to prevent them had damaged British prestige not only in Kuwait but also in other Arab states, particularly in Saudi Arabia where Ibn Saud was keen to support Kuwait against Iraqi aggression. Fowle, therefore, believed that the establishment of a Kuwaiti frontier post at Rodha, about 19 kilometres south of the frontier at Safwan, for patrolling up to Jahra would prevent further Iraqi incursions. He urged the British government, as Kuwait's protecting power, to not only approve the establishment of the proposed post without delay but also to pledge full diplomatic and military support in the event of the use of force against the Sheikh.[91]

---

88. Fowle to the Ambassador in Baghdad and the Secretary of State for India, no. 148, 21 March 1939, FO 371/23180; Fowle to the Ambassador and the Secretary of State for India, no. 149, 21 March 1939, FO 371/23180; Fowle to the Secretary of State for India, no. 150, 22 March 1939, FO 371/23180.
89. Peel to the Under-Secretary of State, Foreign Office, no. PZ1818/39, 24 March 1939, FO 371/23180.
90. Houstoun-Boswall to Nuri, no. 125, 25 March 1939, FO 371/23181.
91. Fowle to the Secretary of State for India, no. 310-S, 6 April 1939, FO 371/23181. See also Fowle to the Secretary of State for India, no. 164, 26 March 1939, FO 371/23181.

Reserving comment, the India Office referred the proposal to the Foreign Office, where Symon viewed it as the only reasonable measure to stop the Iraqi police raids into Kuwaiti territory. However, he was opposed to the idea of providing military support to the Kuwaitis, which would have to come from the RAF bases in Iraq. Herbert Lacy Baggallay of the Foreign Office Eastern Department agreed with Symon and argued that although Britain was responsible for the preservation of the independence and integrity of Kuwait, it should not provide the Sheikh with military support against an encroachment by a police patrol from Iraq.[92] Houstoun-Boswall, the Chargé d'Affaires in Baghdad, was of the same opinion and suggested that orders should be given to the Kuwaiti police not to attack the Iraqi intruders if they were found within Kuwaiti territory but rather they should be told to return to the frontier.[93] Eventually, on 27 April 1939, an inter-departmental meeting under the chairmanship of Roland Peel, the External Secretary of the India office, approved the proposed scheme as a valuable deterrent against Iraqi incursions. A week later, Fowle was instructed to inform the Sheikh of this decision while making it clear that Britain was unable to use any of its armed forces against Iraqi intruders in view of the wider political and strategic implications of such support. Fowle was to explain that the British government would prefer the use of peaceful means to secure the withdrawal of Iraqi intruders from Kuwaiti territory and if this approach failed "diplomatic action might be taken".[94] Ironically, there was no mention of taking further measures if diplomacy failed to resolve any Iraqi–Kuwaiti border crisis. Indeed, the British government still remained non-committal to the protection of the Sheikh's territory from unauthorized Iraqi incursions. Nevertheless, while Houstoun-Boswall told the Iraqi Prime Minister about the intended post, Fowle wrote to the Sheikh on 21 May 1939 informing him of British approval for the establishment of a post at Rodha. Sheikh Ahmed, however, declined to implement the decision as he was worried the Iraqis might claim at some point in the future that Rodha marked the frontier

---

92. See Minutes by Symon and Baggallay, no. E-2854/66/91, 21 April 1939, FO 371/23181.
93. Houstoun-Boswall to Foreign Office, no. 160, 24 April 1939, FO 371/23181.
94. The Secretary of State to the Resident, no. PZ2643/39, 3 May 1939, FO 371/23181.

between their country and Kuwait. Instead, Sheikh Ahmed proposed that the post should be established on the northern Iraq–Kuwait frontier opposite Safwan. As this was unacceptable to Britain, no police post was established.[95]

In the meantime, Iraq sent its reply to the British protest over the frontier incidents of March 1939, which had initially brought about the idea of establishing a Kuwaiti frontier post. Unsurprisingly, the Iraqi government rejected the charges as an investigation by local officials had found that no violations of Kuwaiti territory had taken place. This time Houstoun-Boswall categorically refused to accept this Iraqi explanation as he was convinced the incursions had taken place. Therefore, on 18 April 1939, the Chargé d'Affaires officially wrote to Nuri al-Said, now Prime Minister urging him to establish an independent and authoritative enquiry without delay and that a full report of its findings should be communicated to him.[96] As no immediate response was forthcoming, Houstoun-Boswall met with Nuri al-Said two days later to press his case for an impartial enquiry. The Iraqi Prime Minister assured him that he would persuade his Minister of the Interior, Naji Shaukat – who was determined to create problems for Kuwait due to his dislike of Sheikh Ahmed – to nominate a special official for the task in association with the British Inspecting Officer of Police at Basra. After making this assurance, Nuri al-Said raised the question of smuggling from Kuwait. The Chargé d'Affaires attempted to reassure the Prime Minister that when the Saudi trade blockade of the Sheikh's territory was lifted, smuggling into Iraq would be considerably reduced. This, however, failed to convince Nuri al-Said who argued that the lifting of the Saudi blockade would "aggravate and not ameliorate" the problem of smuggling as the smugglers could then take their goods from Kuwait into Saudi Arabia and from there into Iraq. If this were to occur, the Iraqi government, he continued, would have to guard the whole frontier from the Khor Abdullah to the Jabal Anaiza, instead of just watching the Kuwaiti border. In response to these concerns, Houstoun-Boswall urged the Prime Minister to seriously consider the possibility of making early arrangements for the demarcation of the Iraqi–Kuwaiti frontier as one way

---

95. Sheikh Ahmed to Fowle, no. R/6-1176, 24 May 1939, R/15/5/184. See also Houstoun-Boswall to Foreign Office, no. 57, 11 May 1939, FO 371/23181.
96. Houstoun-Boswall to Nuri, no. 187, 18 April 1939, FO 371/23181.

of reducing smuggling. Nuri al-Said, however, showed no enthusiasm for this suggestion and argued it would do nothing to stop the smuggling.[97]

Discussions aimed at finding a solution to the problem of smuggling therefore continued. On 22 April 1939, the Iraqi Foreign Ministry sent an official note to the British embassy suggesting that the British government should take responsibility for the administration of customs operated in the Sheikhdom by placing its own officials to regulate imports there. This could be achieved either by raising the Kuwaiti tariff to correspond with Iraq's or by limiting Kuwaiti imports to quantities required for local consumption only. However, these proposals were simply the revival of those advanced by Suwaidi during his visit to London in October 1938. But this time the authorities in London made no immediate response to the suggestions. Instead, Houstoun-Boswall recommended that the British government should carefully re-examine the issue as he believed that the Iraqis had a "legitimate grievance".[98] The Foreign Office, however, found the Iraqi proposals unacceptable. In his minute of 16 May 1939, Ponsonby Crosthwaite of the Eastern Department put forward three valid reasons for not raising the Kuwaiti tariff: first, it would conflict with the terms of the Bandar Shuwaikh Lease Agreement of 1907 which limited the Kuwaiti duty on goods imported by British subjects to four per cent; second, it would create discontent in the Sheikhdom through the resultant price increases; and third, it would seriously affect the Sheikhdom's trade with the interior. Crosthwaite, however, was ready to approach the Sheikh, if the Iraqis so wished, for the introduction of a system of manifests for both land and sea traffic. Baggallay, a firm supporter of a system of manifests, suggested that if the Iraqis rejected this proposal out of hand they would have no option but to await the conclusion of the Kuwaiti–Saudi trade agreement, which would greatly reduce the level of smuggling from Kuwait into Iraq as those who were presently engaged in smuggling would be able to occupy themselves with the legitimate traffic which would then "spring up" with Saudi Arabia. As there was general agreement between

---

97. See Houstoun-Boswall to Halifax, no. 178, 20 April 1939, FO 371/23181. See also Houstoun-Boswall to Halifax, no. 179, 20 April 1939, FO 371/23181.
98. Houstoun-Boswall to Halifax, no. 210, 1 May 1939, FO 371/23181.

Baggallay and Crosthwaite, an instruction based on these lines was sent to Baghdad.[99]

Meanwhile as a result of continuous pressure from Houstoun-Boswall, the Iraqi government set up a special commission on 1 May 1939 to investigate the incursions of their police force into Kuwait in the previous March. The commission was headed by Jamil al-Azaawi, a senior official of the Ministry of the Interior, and its members were Darwish Lutfi, the Commandant of the Police Headquarters, and Major Arthur Sargon, the British Inspecting Officer of Police at Basra.[100] On 28 May 1939, the findings of the commission were sent to the British Embassy. These upheld the contents of the previous Iraqi note of 8 April by reiterating that no evidence was found to support the Kuwaiti allegations. This, however, failed to convince Sir Basil Newton, the new Ambassador to Iraq, as the enquiry had made no specific mention of the incursions of March 1939. Yet despite this, he too preferred to let the matter rest, as he considered it pointless to press for a further enquiry.[101]

However, unlike Newton, James Mackenzie of the Foreign Office's Eastern Department believed that there were practical advantages to be gained from continuing to apply pressure on the Iraqi government. If and when an incursion occurred again Britain could take the opportunity "to come down much more heavily" and insist that a commission, including the Political Agent in Kuwait, investigate the incident.[102] Symon went even further and rejected outright the findings of the Iraqi commission:

> I feel that we cannot accept the result of this committee of enquiry without further protest. For four years we have been complaining of these police incursions and have never received any satisfaction. If we swallow this report, it will be tantamount to an admission that our complaints were unfounded.[103]

---

99. See Minute by Crosthwaite, no. E-3334/66/91, 16 May 1939, FO 371/23181. See also Minute by Baggallay, no. E-3334/66/91, 23 May 1939, FO 371/23181.
100. Houstoun-Boswall to Foreign Office, no. 56, 5 May 1939, FO 371/23181.
101. See Newton to Halifax, no. 259/168/32/39, 31 May 1939, FO 371/23181. See also Iraqi Ministry of Foreign Affairs to the British Embassy in Baghdad, no. 7819/30/7, 28 May 1939, FO 371/23181.
102. See Minute by Mackenzie, no. E-4087/66/91, 13 June 1939, FO 371/23181. See also Fowle to the Ambassador, Baghdad, no. T/90, 18 May 1939, FO 371/23181.
103. Minute by Symon, no. E-4087/66/91, 13 June 1939, FO 371/23181.

Symon suggested that Newton should be instructed to inform the Iraqi government that in view of the evidence in Britain's possession, the British government was unable to accept the findings of the committee.[104] Baggallay, however, believed that as the commission included a British Commandant of Police, the Iraqis would be able to defend its findings against charges of bias or fabrication. Charles Baxter agreed, and on 20 June 1939 he recommended that the matter be left to rest.[105] Both the Resident and the India Office had little alternative but to reluctantly accept his decision.[106]

Conclusion

While the smuggling of goods from Kuwait was the main grievance of the Iraqi government during this period, it could have checked the smuggling by taking unilateral action within its own territory. Instead, despite the involvement of their own nationals in the contraband trade, the Iraqis continually blamed the Sheikh and demanded that he bring this activity to an end, at the cost of either Kuwait's economy or independence.

Although Britain, the so-called protector of Kuwait, made several (unsuccessful) attempts to solve the problem of smuggling, it did nothing about Iraqi violations of the Sheikh's territory. Instead of taking action against Iraq's constant denial of all charges, the British government followed a policy of appeasement despite holding evidence to the contrary. This inaction was largely due to sharp differences of opinion within the British government itself on almost all matters relating to the uneasy state of Iraqi–Kuwaiti relations. While embassy staff in Baghdad, supported by Foreign Office officials, posed as the protectors of Iraqi interests, the authorities in the Gulf, more specifically the Resident and the Political Agent, occasionally backed by the India Office, fought Kuwait's corner. This lack of coordination and cooperation among high-ranking British officials was one of the major

---

104. *Ibid.*
105. Minute by Baggallay, FO 371/23181. See also Minute by Baxter, no. E-4087/66/91, 20 June 1939, FO 371/23181.
106. Peel to Baggallay, no. PZ3873/39, 28 June 1939, FO 371/23181. See also Fowle to Newton, no. 578-S, 19 June 1939, FO 371/23181.

factors for the failure to develop genuine solutions to the problems of smuggling and territorial violations. As a result, antagonistic and inimical feelings stemming from both issues, compounded by the absence of a demarcated frontier, dominated Iraqi–Kuwaiti relations during the 1930s.

4

The War of Propaganda and Campaigns for Annexation, 1930–1939

Iraqi aspirations for the annexation of Kuwait became public following the emergence of Iraq as a sovereign and independent state. All the major Iraqi newspapers, backed by the government and the King, launched a series of campaigns for the annexation of Kuwait on the pretext of its alleged link with the defunct Ottoman Empire. This anti-Kuwait campaign was soon followed by a propaganda war broadcast under the personal direction of the King from his private broadcasting station. The years from 1930 to 1939 witnessed growing Iraqi pressures on Kuwait as reflected by their persistent efforts to build an Iraqi port on Kuwaiti soil as well as by their apparent planning for the invasion of the country.

In 1930, before Iraq had even emerged as an independent state, the Iraqis, particularly a group of Iraqi merchants in Basra headed by Hamid Bey al-naqib (who looked after the Kuwaiti ruler's business interests in Basra), were vocal in their support for the amalgamation of Kuwait with Iraq. Although confining their efforts at this stage to prominent Kuwaiti businessmen and the palm grove owners, these Iraqi propagandists urged Kuwait to accept the overlordship of Iraq, which would treat it well and allow it to retain its "quasi-independence". With British power in the Gulf waning, they argued, only Iraq could protect Kuwait from any future Najdi aggression.[1] Nevertheless, the Kuwaitis showed of enthusiasm for this Iraqi call for amalgamation.

The campaign for the annexation of Kuwait with Iraq inevitably attracted the attention of the British authorities in Baghdad. However, rather than discouraging such an idea, the Acting British High

---

1. Dickson to H. V. Biscoe (Political Resident), no. 223, 25 April 1930, R/15/5/126.

Commissioner, Major Hubert Young, fully supported it. In a dispatch to the Colonial Office in July 1930, he argued:

> His Majesty's Government, while making no overt act to encourage the absorption of Koweit by Iraq, should in fact assist any tendency there may be in that direction by assimilating their treaty relations with Koweit to the relations with Iraq under the new Treaty [the Anglo–Iraqi Treaty of Alliance of 30 June 1930] as soon as it has been ratified.[2]

However, Young's plea for the absorption of Kuwait by Iraq was unacceptable to Lord Passfield, the Colonial Secretary, who believed that the adoption of such an unrealistic suggestion would entail a complete reversal of British policy towards Kuwait. The Colonial Secretary was convinced that any closer union between Kuwait and Iraq would seriously jeopardize Britain's political and economic interests in the Sheikhdom as it would then naturally look to Baghdad rather than to London for guidance. Therefore, Passfield, after consulting with both Arthur Henderson, the Foreign Secretary, and William Wedgwood Benn (later to become Lord Stansgate), the Secretary of State for India, warned Young in October 1930, that the British government was determined to continue its policy towards Kuwait, namely that the Sheikhdom "should be maintained as a protected State entirely independent" of Iraq.[3] As a result of this reaffirmation of the British position, the British officials in Baghdad made no further attempt to align themselves with the Iraqi movement for the annexation of Kuwait.

The campaign for the annexation of Kuwait nevertheless intensified following Iraq's emergence as an independent kingdom. This campaign was spearheaded by the Iraqi press, with the full backing of the government, with the government daily, *al-Ikha' al-Watani*, played a leading role. On 16 May 1933, it ran its first leading article questioning the independent status of Kuwait and pleading for the unification of Kuwait with Iraq, arguing that until recently "Kuwait was a part and a non-separable part of the Basrah Liwa Province" and prior to the

---

2. O. G. R. Williams (Colonial Office) to the Under-Secretary of State (Foreign Office), no. 79171/30, 5 September 1930, R/15/5/109.
3. *Ibid.* See also Passfield to the Acting High Commissioner, unnumbered, 13 October 1930, R/15/5/126.

outbreak of the First World War the "colour on the map of the town of Kuwait was similar to that of Basrah".[4] It further argued, rather unconvincingly:

> The sound of telegrams is echoed in Kuwait in half an hour's time, and letters reach there within four hours by post. Experience and the existing state of affairs have both proved that Kuwait grieves at our sorrow, laughs at our happiness and lives again on hearing of Iraq's revival.[5]

Harold Dickson, the then Political Agent in Kuwait, believed that the article was inspired by government officials in order to arouse public consciousness about Kuwait.[6] As Rashid Ali al-Gaylani's government remained conspicuously silent following the publication, *al-Ikha' al-Watani* stepped up its campaign against Kuwait. In a second article on 20 August 1933, it urged Kuwait to unite with Iraq in view of their close connection "by blood, religion, proximity and business". Pointing to the bright and promising future augured by the strong possibility of an oil strike in Kuwait, it appealed to the youth of Iraq to seize the advantages offered by such an economic opportunity. It further added:

> Kuwait indeed is in dire need of persons who can promote the standard of education in it, for youth to add their efforts to those of their colleagues in Kuwait, and lastly for youth to emigrate and become a lasting link between the youth of Iraq and the youth of Kuwait. The benefits which would result from such an auspicious movement are too great to be defined.[7]

The article, a deliberate attempt to increase the Iraqi population in Kuwait, is an interesting example of the methods employed by Iraq in its attacks on Kuwait.

Throughout 1934, the Iraqi press became increasingly active and aggressive. For instance, on 31 January two similarly worded articles

---

4. See the translation of an article which appeared in *al-Ikha' al-Watani* (Baghdad, 16 May 1933) in Dickson to Fowle, no. 105, 20 May 1933, R/15/5/126.
5. *Ibid.*
6. *Ibid.*
7. See *al-Ikha' al-Watani* (Baghdad, 25 August 1933) in Dickson to Fowle, no. 201, 25 August 1933, R/15/5/126.

appeared simultaneously in *al-Thaghr* and *al-Ikha' al-Watani* under the name of one Omar al-Taibi. Although Kuwait had never been under the jurisdiction of the Vilayet Basra, al-Taibi stated that Kuwait was "one of the subordinate provinces of Basra" during the Ottoman rule over Iraq and that the Sheikhs of Kuwait had paid taxes to the Ottomans for their palm groves in Basra. Further, he openly advocated the annexation of Kuwait by Iraq for their mutual benefit:

> Under the circumstances . . . it should have been possible for the British government of the time to have helped in the annexation of Kuwait by Iraq on the understanding that the rulership should remain in the hands of the Al Sabah Amirs. Had this been effected, Kuwait, in view of its excellent geographical position, would have become a first rate sea port and harbour for Iraq; and Kuwait and Iraq together would have derived equal advantage at one and the same time.[8]

It would therefore appear that the central objective of the proposed annexation of Kuwait was to gain for Iraq the advantage of a first-class port as well as direct access to the Gulf.

These constant attacks upon Kuwait greatly perturbed Sheikh Ahmed. Fearing the eventual loss of his sovereignty to the Iraqis, he argued:

> There is little doubt that Iraq's policy today is to show her teeth and bite me one day, and the next day to fawn, and offer the advantages of peace, all with the one eventual idea of coercing my State and forcing me to come within her fold.[9]

As the Iraqi press continued its campaigns for the annexation of Kuwait, Sheikh Ahmed asked Dickson to lodge a formal protest with the Iraqi government.[10]

Following Britain's complaints, there was a pause in Iraq's anti-Kuwait propaganda. However, following the establishment of the Iraqi Ministry of Propaganda in 1935, the press resumed their crusade with

---

8. See the Enclosure in Dickson to Fowle, no. 378, 13 February 1934, R/15/5/129.
9. Ibid.
10. Sheikh Ahmed al-Jaber al-Sabah to Dickson, no. R-3/1433, 9 February 1934, R/15/5/129.

renewed vigour. On 12 August 1935, *al-Karkh*, a weekly newspaper in Baghdad, urged the Iraqi government to annex Kuwait alleging that most of the leaders of Kuwait "descend from Iraqi families; and above all it is directly connected with this country [Iraq]". In maintaining that Kuwait was an integral part of Iraq, the article continued:

> Affinity, uniformity of customs and manners and the bonds of blood, religion and language – all these firm connections leave no room for doubt in the fact that Kuwait is an integral part of Iraq and that it will remain so. Any contradictory idea should be rejected and should receive no attention at all.[11]

Inspired by the Ministry of Propaganda, similar articles appeared in the daily *al-Tariq* in various editions throughout August, September and October of 1935. As these contentious articles threatened to undermine the Sheikh's authority with his people, the Political Agent suggested that the Resident bring this "unfriendly and unfair propaganda" to the attention of the Iraqi government. However, when Fowle approached Yasin al-Hashemi, the Prime Minister, he simply dismissed the articles as "absurd rumours".[12]

Thus the Iraqi government refused to place any restriction on its press. Despite repeated British protests, their campaign against Kuwait continued unabated throughout 1936 and 1937. For example, on 18 May 1936, *al-Karkh*, in a front-page article directly blaming Kuwait for the high level of smuggling into Iraq, appealed to the Iraqi government to strike the name of Kuwait off the list of Arab principalities and to annex it to Iraq. Similar sentiments were expressed by *al-Iraq* in its edition of 16 June 1936 and in various editions of *an-Nas*, which launched an eight-month-long campaign against Kuwait in January 1937.[13] These continuous Iraqi press attacks on the Sheikhdom eventually convinced Captain de Gaury, the Political Agent in Kuwait, that the

---

11. See the translation of an article which appeared in *al-Karkh* (Baghdad, 12 August 1935), in Dickson to Fowle, no. 318, 12 August 1935, R/15/5/126.
12. See the translation of an article which appeared in *al-Tariq* (Baghdad, 27 August 1935) in Dickson to Fowle, no. 732, R/15/5/126. See also 'Newspaper Campaign in Iraq against Kuwait' in Dickson to Fowle, no. C-269, 5 September 1935, R/15/5/126.
13. See an-Nas, 19 January to 10 September 1937.

newspaper articles were part of a concerted campaign by the Iraqi government "to unsettle Kuwaities and increase their own [Iraqi] influence" in the Sheikhdom.[14]

However, in 1938 the Iraqi press got a direct foothold in the affairs of Kuwait. No sooner had some members of the Kuwaiti business community, headed by Yusuf al-Marzuq, launched an anti-government movement in the February, demanding the reform of education, public health, administration and finance, than the Iraqi press acted as their mouthpiece. Expressing its solidarity with the agitators and criticizing the living standards in the Sheikhdom, *al-Zaman*, a pro-government newspaper, on 3 April 1938, urged the Kuwaiti government to implement the proposed reforms. *Al-Istiqlal*, another pro-government daily, went a step further in appealing to the agitators to work for a union with Iraq which would "turn Kuwait into a prosperous progressive civilized country". After assessing the geographical and commercial position of Kuwait, the paper then called on the Iraqi government to annex it in order to make it "a junction of international communications and an excellent port". Sheikh Ahmed, understandably disturbed by the unprecedented ferocity of this Iraqi press campaign, directed his Private Secretary in May 1938 to write an open letter to *az-Zaman* in requesting the Iraqi press not to interfere in Kuwait's internal affairs and to end their anti-Kuwaiti propaganda. The publication of this letter, however, had little effect.

As the press continued their efforts to turn the Kuwaiti people against their government, Fowle also came to believe, as de Gaury did, that the press campaign "represented a part of an overall strategy aimed at annexing Kuwait to Iraq".[15] As the Resident had anticipated, the Iraqis soon developed a plan to increase their influence in the Sheikhdom. This was initially manifested in their attempt to construct a port in Kuwait. It was Suwaidi, who presented this ambitious proposal to James Morgan, the Chargé d'Affaires in Baghdad, in a conversation in March 1938. He argued that the lack of progress in the Iraqi–Persian

---

14. De Gaury to Fowle, no. DOC 246, 13 July 1936, FO 371/19968. See also 'Iraq–Kuwait Incidents' in de Gaury to Fowle, no. C-212, 12 June 1936, R/15/5/131.
15. Kamal Osman Salih, 'The 1938 Kuwait Legislative Council', *Middle Eastern Studies*, no.I (January 1992), pp. 71–2.

frontier negotiations and the potential for Persian interference with the Iraqi trade on the disputed Shatt al-Arab waterway, made an Iraqi port imperative with Kuwait as the obvious location. Accordingly, Suwaidi asked Morgan whether the British government would allow Iraq to extend its railway system through Kuwaiti territory to the coast in Kuwait Bay and to build a port there under Iraqi control, for which the Sheikh would be compensated. On 30 March 1938, Sir Maurice Peterson, on taking charge of the British embassy in Baghdad, sought Lord Halifax's authorization to discourage Suwaidi from such a course of action by persuading him to instead direct his attention to Sir John Ward's plans to extend the railway to Fao, which would enable Iraq to maintain a regular service between Fao and Karachi.[16] As Halifax favoured Peterson's suggestion he referred the matter to the relevant ministries and departments.[17]

All the authorities concerned in both London and the Gulf as well as the Government of India reacted unfavourably to the Iraqi proposal. The War Office for instance maintained that although an extension of the Iraqi railway line to Kuwait might eventually establish a vital link to Turkey, free from Persian interference, this would not be an adequate return for both the loss of trade in the Shatt al-Arab and the extension of Iraqi influence in Kuwait.[18] Similarly, the Admiralty raised strong objections to the project as it would inevitably push Kuwait increasingly under Iraqi control and render the Sheikhdom economically dependent upon Iraq. In addition, the Admiralty was not convinced that Persia would dare to interfere with Iraqi shipping on the Shatt al-Arab, due to the continuation of the Anglo-Iraqi Treaty of 1930, which guaranteed Iraq's security against any external threat. Therefore, the Admiralty also concluded that Iraq should be persuaded to abandon the proposed Kuwaiti project and instead concentrate on the option of a port at Fao.[19]

16. Peterson to Halifax, no. 116, 30 March 1938, FO 371/21860.
17. Baxter to the Secretary of the Admiralty, no. E-2094/2094/93, 2 May 1938, FO 371/21860. Similar letters were also sent to the Air Ministry, War Office and India Office, FO 371/21860.
18. The War Office's comments are in A. E. Widdows (War Office) to the Under-Secretary of State (Foreign Office), no. 0178/1087(M.O.1), 14 May 1938, FO 371/21860.
19. S. H. Phillips (Admiralty) to the Under-Secretary of State (Foreign Office), no. M-02976/38, 10 June 1938, FO 371/21860.

The Air Ministry, in agreeing generally with the War Office, added that Suwaidi's proposal was not entirely unconnected with certain Iraqi tendencies to dispute the independent status of Kuwait. As the project was designed "for some means of claiming sovereignty over Koweit", the Ministry wanted the British government to discourage Iraq from pursuing it further. However, as the Air Ministry acknowledged the military benefit of an Anglo-Kuwaiti-controlled port in Kuwait, in terms of its importance to British lines of communication through the head of the Arabian Gulf, it believed that it would be unwise to close the door on possible future negotiations.[20]

The Resident in the Gulf, however, was of a different opinion. Although Fowle considered an exclusively Iraqi-controlled port in Kuwait as totally out of the question, he was in favour of a port controlled by both Iraq and Kuwait under British guidance. In addition to resolving Iraqi shipping problems, Fowle reasoned that such an arrangement would not only financially benefit Kuwait resulting from a percentage share of the custom duties, but would also afford strategic advantages to Britain in the form of a modern rail-linked port. In short, Fowle was arguing for the tripatriate control of the port and urged that the proposal not be rejected before its careful consideration.[21] The Government of India, however, declined to endorse Fowle's suggestion as this might lead to increased Iraqi influence in Kuwait. Due to Kuwait's important position at the head of the Gulf, the Government of India considered it essential to preserve its independence. As a result, it strongly recommended that the Iraqi government, rather than being granted any concessions, should instead be clearly told that Britain would be unable to agree to any such scheme.[22] Lord Zetland, the Secretary of State for India, agreed and expressed his grave concern over "the danger of the extension of Iraqi influence to the detriment of the position of His Majesty's Government in Kuwait" which, he feared, would follow from such a railway and harbour development.[23] As there was general

20. Charles Evans (Air Ministry) to the Under-Secretary of State (Foreign Office), no. S-45102S.6, 12 July 1938, FO 371/21860.
21. Fowle to Sir Aubrey Metcalf, no. DO 278-S, 24 May 1938, FO 371/21860.
22. W. R. Hay (Deputy Secretary to the Government of India) to Lord Zetland, no. F297-N/38, 23 June 1938, FO 371/21860.
23. J. P. Gibson to the Under-Secretary of State (Foreign Office), no. PZ4484/38, 8 July 1938, FO 371/21860.

agreement between the various British authorities that the Iraqi proposal was unacceptable as it stood, Halifax instructed Houstoun-Boswall on the 15 August 1938 to inform the Iraqis that the British government was not "favourably disposed to a scheme on the lines suggested", since it did "not see how it could function without infringing the rights of the Sheikh". Halifax believed that Suwaidi would not insist upon his proposal as he had only done so in the past because of anti-government demonstrations in Baghdad in March 1938, following the ratification of the Iraqi–Persian Shatt al-Arab Border Agreement of 1937, and that tensions had now "died down".[24]

Contrary to this assumption, the Iraqis were determined to press ahead with their plan for a port in Kuwait. While the British government was assessing the proposal, the Iraqi Foreign Ministry on 11 August 1938, addressed a "secret and most urgent letter" to the various ministries concerned asking for their opinions on various aspects of the proposal, including the extension of the railway from Basra to Kuwait Bay. The Foreign Ministry's letter outlined the reasons for such requirements in Kuwait:

> In this connection, it is considered very necessary by this Ministry in view of economic, strategic and political reasons, that Iraq should obtain an undertaking from the British Government to grant her the freedom of export, import and other facilities at Kuwait to ensure for her such vital supplies and communications as may be needed in the event of the normal communications through Shatt-el-Arab being endangered. Such an undertaking is regarded as all the more necessary in view of the fact that the future administration of the Shatt is still the subject of discussion. In regard to the details of such undertaking, this Ministry desires to be furnished with the necessary information and advice thereon, due regard being taken of Iraq's economic, strategic and political interests.[25]

As soon as a copy of this letter was received by Sir John Ward, both the Director of Basra port administration and the Director-General of the Iraq State Railway (who was then in London), he secretly passed it to

---

24. Lacy Baggallay to Houstoun-Boswall, no. 462, 15 August 1938, FO 371/21860.
25. For the full text of the letter, see the Iraqi Ministry of Foreign Affairs to the Ministries of Finance, Defence, Economics and Communication, no. 13592/13592/10, 9 August 1938, FO 371/21860.

Herbert Lacy Baggallay of the Eastern Department in August 1938 informing him that the Iraqis were very keen to secure this alternative outlet in Kuwait and that Suwaidi intended to discuss it with Halifax during his forthcoming visit to London in October. Ward, who disapproved of the proposal to build an Iraqi port on Kuwait Bay, told Baggallay that if the British government so wished he was ready to divert the attention of the Iraqi government from Kuwait to the Khor Abdullah, which was equally capable of providing a good anchorage in this inlet, especially in the area lying to the north of Warba Island. In addition, if this option was chosen the expenses would be far less than those required to develop Kuwait Bay, since unlike the Bay, there was deep water right up to the shore. As Warba Island belonged to Kuwait, Ward proposed that Iraq might gain the island by making territorial concessions to Kuwait elsewhere.[26]

As the Foreign Office was now convinced that Suwaidi would raise the question of an Iraqi port in Kuwait, it referred the matter to the India Office and the service departments on 26 April 1938, suggesting that the whole subject should be re-examined at a meeting of the Middle East Sub-Committee before the Iraqi Foreign Minister's arrival in London.[27] Before proceeding further, however, the India Office sought the opinion of the Political Resident. In Fowle's absence, Hugh Weightman, the Officiating Resident, argued that if the Iraqis were determined to construct an alternative port outside the Shatt al-Arab, then they should be encouraged to do so in Kuwait rather than in the Khor Abdullah due to the strategic, economic and political advantages this offered. Weightman also believed that the negotiations for this port might provide Britain with an opportunity to secure a total renunciation of any claims on the part of Iraq to suzerainty over Kuwait.[28] Although this suggestion was attractive to the Government of India, it was rejected by the India Office since Britain "could not admit that any such claims

26. Minute by Baggallay, no. E-5577/2094/93, 23 September 1938 FO 371/21860. See also Baggallay to Peel, no. E-4994/2094/93, 26 August 1938, FO 371/21860.
27. Baggallay to Peel, no. E-4994/2094/93, 26 August 1938, FO 371/21860. See also the Secretary of State for India to the Government of India, repeated to the Resident, no. PZ6034/38, 2 September 1938, FO 371/21860.
28. Weightman to the Secretary of State for India, no. C-636, 10 September 1938, FO 371/21860.

had the slightest foundation in reality". In addition, Weightman's plea for British backing of Iraq's plan to build a port in Kuwait Bay met with strong opposition from the Foreign Office, which favoured the Khor Abdullah option.[29]

On 28 September 1938, the Middle East Sub-Committee met to take a final decision on the Iraqi proposal. The committee believed that in terms of practicability and cost, the Khor Abdullah was a more suitable site for a modern port than anywhere in Kuwait, in addition to its being nearer to the existing Iraqi railway system. Therefore, the committee decided unanimously that the Iraqi government should be told to construct a port on the Khor Abdullah, but also agreed to consider sympathetically any Iraqi request for port facilities in Kuwait if the Khor Abdullah option proved unsuitable. However, if this were to occur such a port would be controlled by the Anglo-Kuwaiti authorities in order to preserve the Sheikhdom's rights and interests. The minutes of the meeting read:

> It was, however, agreed that Taufiq Suwaidi could be told that if the Khor Abdullah does not on examination prove suitable for development, His Majesty's Government so far as they are concerned would be ready to give sympathetic consideration to a request from the Iraqi Government for harbour facilities in Koweit territory, with a railway connection to Iraq. It would, however, be necessary to point out that any such scheme would have to be framed in such a way and made subject to such conditions as would safeguard the political rights and interests of the Sheikhdom of Koweit, and that the Iraqi Government could not therefore expect to have the same control over a port there as they would have on their own territory.[30]

While these inter-departmental debates over Iraq's plan to establish an outlet to the sea were in progress, Abbas Mahdi, the Acting Iraqi Foreign

29. See Gibson to Baggallay, no. PZ6526/38, 26 September 1938, FO 371/21860. For the Government of India's comment on Weightman's suggestion, see Government of India to the Secretary of State for India, no. 1486, 20 September 1938 FO 371/21860. For the Foreign Office's unfavourable response, see Minute by P. M. Crosthwaite, no. E-5702/2094/93, 27 September 1938, FO 371/21860.
30. See the Minutes of the Meeting, no. ME(O) 62, 28 September 1938, FO 371/21860.

Minister, again raised the issue with Houstoun-Boswall. Mahdi elaborated on the previous arguments about the threats posed to Iraqi interests by possible Persian interference in the Shatt al-Arab and argued that it was Britain's duty "to do everything possible to obviate any such risk." The Chargé d'Affaires, however, informed Mahdi that the scheme was unacceptable to the British government as "it was felt that the rights of the Sheikh might be infringed thereby", but assured him that Britain was determined to maintain free communications in the Shatt al-Arab as both Britain and Iraq possessed a common interest there.[31]

After being informed of the British position, Suwaidi, who was at a meeting of the League of Nations in Geneva, then laid a formal claim to the whole Sheikhdom. In an *aide-mémoire* to R. A. Butler, the Under-Secretary of State for Foreign Affairs, dated 28 September 1938, Suwaidi argued that Kuwait presented a twofold problem for Iraq: first, it was an alleged "entrepôt" for arms traffic and smuggling; and second, it constituted a barrier to Iraq's access to the open sea. In response to the first problem Suwaidi's *aide-mémoire* suggested the establishment of an Iraqi–Kuwaiti customs union and the readjustment of Kuwait's northern frontier from its present latitude of about 30° N to a new position at a latitude of about 29° 35' N, in order to facilitate the prevention of smuggling.[32] However, this one measure entailed the cession of the whole northern part of Kuwait Bay, an area comprising about one-third of the total land area of Kuwait.

In his *aide-mémoire*, Suwaidi also advanced three practical reasons to support Iraq's claim to Kuwait: firstly, as a defence against the possibility of Persian disruption to Iraqi lines of communication in the Shatt al-Arab; secondly, due to the congestion in the Shatt al-Arab resulting from the expansion of the activities of the Anglo-Persian Oil Company's (APOC) activities at Abadan; and finally, because of Iraq's desire to extend the Tell-Koclink Baghdad section of the railway up to the shore of the Gulf to enable a fast passenger service to India.[33] In addition, Suwaidi justified Iraq's claim to Kuwait on so-called historical grounds. The Iraqi Foreign Minister argued:

---

31. Houston-Boswall to Halifax, no. 438, 7 September 1938, FO 371/21860.
32. See the Enclosure in Suwaidi to Butler, unnumbered, 28 September 1938, FO 371/21858.
33. *Ibid.*

> Just before the War of 1914–1918, Kuwait was an autonomous qadha of the Wilayat [Vilayet] of Basra. The Iraqi Government, as the successor of the Ottoman government in the Wilayats of Mosul, Baghdad and Basra, considers that Kuwait should properly be incorporated in Iraq. If incorporation should take place, Iraq would agree to maintain the local autonomy of Kuwait with a guarantee in the form of a special status, but of course without prejudice to Iraqi sovereignty.[34]

This was the first time that Iraq officially laid claim to Kuwait in the name of the defunct Ottoman Empire, despite the fact that such a claim was contrary to the terms of the treaties of Sèvres and Lausanne as well as the exchange of letters of 1932. It is to be remembered that Kuwait was never under the suzerainty of the Ottoman Empire and had long enjoyed the status of a virtually independent state. Moreover, the Sheikh of Kuwait had entered into an agreement with the British government in 1899 undertaking not to have relations with any other power except His Majesty's Government. All of Britain's agreements with Kuwait had been endorsed by the Anglo–Ottoman Convention of 1913 which had also granted Kuwait complete autonomy. The boundaries of the Sheikhdom were also fixed, clearly dividing Kuwaiti territory from the Basra Vilayet of the Ottoman Empire. After the First World War, the Allied powers had not attempted to include Kuwait "in any shape or form within the boundaries of Iraq" nor was there any decision that Iraq should include the Basra Vilayet as such.[35] In fact, the Allied powers maintained the status quo concerning the frontier of Kuwait as fixed in 1913 by the Anglo-Ottoman Convention. Therefore, Iraq had no justification for making any claim on Kuwait in view of this decision. This was reconfirmed by the Foreign Office in May 1938:

> Iraq in order to establish any claim to Koweit, whether in respect of suzerainty or otherwise, has to show some decision of the Allied Powers and the Powers concerned giving her these rights over Koweit, for all her claims must rest upon what these Powers allotted to her. There is nothing to indicate that these Powers even allotted Iraq any rights over Koweit, or even issued any decision allotting

---

34. *Ibid.*
35. See Foreign Office, 'Note on Iraq–Kuwait Frontier: Events Preceding to the Exchange of Notes of 1932', no. 2499/1391, 30 May 1938, R/15/5/207.

her the Basra Vilayet as such. From the moment when Iraq began to have an independent existence, which cannot be placed earlier than 1922, there was a frontier drawn with Koweit in the same sort of way as there was a frontier drawn with Trans-Jordan. The responsibilities of Iraq and His Majesty's Government under the Treaty of Alliance towards the Council of the League must, when they referred to Iraq, have referred to Iraq with these two frontiers then in operation. In 1932, when Iraq became a member of the League, the frontier with Trans-Jordan and the frontier with Koweit were confirmed by an exchange of notes in exactly the same way.[36]

In short, the postwar settlement negated the validity of any Iraqi claim to Kuwait and even questioned its right to Basra. Further, as the Iraq–Kuwait border was formally fixed by the exchange of notes in 1932, this afforded "Iraq no rights beyond it".[37] A Foreign Office minute of 1 October 1938 on the international status of Kuwait concluded that the arguments advanced by Suwaidi "had, in reality, little force" as the frontiers of Iraq had always been considered to be the de facto boundaries which had been in force since Iraq had become a sovereign state.[38] The India Office even went a step further in arguing that Suwaidi's claims to Kuwait were illogical in view of Britain's recognition of "the independence of Kuwait in return for its assistance against Turkey" in 1914.[39]

Given the lack of the historical and legal legitimacy of Iraq's claim to Kuwait, Lord Halifax, the Foreign Secretary, made it clear that the British government would find it extremely difficult to acknowledge any such Iraqi claim to sovereignty over Kuwait and even declined to discuss the issue when he met with Suwaidi in London on 4 October 1938. Consequently, the Iraqi Foreign Minister confined his discussion with Foreign Office officials to other more specific issues, such as smuggling (see Chapter Three) and the proposed construction of an Iraqi port in Kuwait Bay.[40] With regard to the latter subject, Suwaidi reiterated that

---

36. *Ibid.*
37. *Ibid.*
38. See Foreign Office, 'Note on the International Status of Kuwait', no. E-5806/1982/93, 1 October 1938, FO 371/21858.
39. See Gibson to Crosthwaite, no. PZ6804/38, 4 October 1938, FO 371/21813.
40. See the record of conversation with the Iraqi Minister for Foreign Affairs, no. E-5841/1982/93, 5 October 1938, R/15/5/208.

Iraq needed an additional commercial outlet to the sea in view of the threat posed by the possibility of Persian interference with navigation on the Shatt al-Arab. Unconvinced by this argument, Charles Baxter maintained that the Persians would not dare to interfere with shipping either in peace or wartime so long as the Anglo-Iraqi Treaty of Alliance remained in force. He further stated that Kuwait Bay was itself unsuitable for the site of a modern port due to the shallowness of its waters. Armed with a Foreign Office memorandum, he argued that such a project would be prohibitively expensive, as it would involve dredging on an enormous scale. Baxter then urged the Iraqi government to examine the possibility of constructing a port in the Khor Abdullah which in addition to being less expensive, would be nearer to the existing Iraqi rail system, and would also provide a far more suitable location for a modern port due to its deep-water approach and anchorage right up to the shore. Swayed by Baxter's logical arguments, Suwaidi agreed to examine the Khor Abdullah alternative on the condition that Sheikh Ahmed was prepared to cede part of his territory, namely Warba Island and the navigable channel between it and the open sea, to Iraq. Although Suwaidi was not laying a claim to Warba, he was still asking for an undue gesture of goodwill on the part of the Sheikh in order to enable the project. Due to the obvious implications of such a request, Baxter remained non-committal and stipulated that if Sheikh Ahmed agreed to such a sensitive proposal Iraq must compensate him and that such compensation "should quite evidently exceed in value the territory which they were asking the Sheikh to cede". When Suwaidi sought British permission to approach the Sheikh directly, Baxter refused to give it as it remained the case, as laid down in the terms of Exclusive Agreement of 1899, that the Sheikh had no authority to enter into direct negotiations with any other body except through the British government.[41] The conversation ended without making any further progress and Suwaidi returned to Baghdad empty-handed.

In the wake of Suwaidi's failed mission to London, the Iraqi press, actively supported by the King, redoubled its efforts in its propaganda campaign against Kuwait. Ghazi bin Faisal, who became the King of

---

41. *Ibid.* See also Foreign Office, 'Note on Desire of the Iraqi Government for an Additional Commercial Outlet to the Sea', no. E-5806/1982/93, 1 October 1938, FO 371/21858.

Iraq on 8 September 1933, personally directed the campaign. For instance, his own broadcasting station Qasr al-Zuhoor referred to Sheikh Ahmed as "an out-of-date feudal despot" whose backward rule contrasted with the enlightened regime existing in Iraq. It appealed to the youth of Kuwait to take "subversive action against authority", to fight for their freedom and to join with Iraq.[42] Simultaneously, the Iraqi press carried a number of anti-Kuwait articles. On 17 February 1939, an-Nas, in a leading article entitled 'Kuwait is a part of Iraq', demanded that the Iraqi army should march on Kuwait immediately to take advantage of the political disturbances there. Arguing that Kuwait was "a natural port and the only port of Iraq", the article added:

> It is Iraq's duty to protect that country and bring them back to their mother's arms, who is very anxious to welcome them with a warm kiss. Iraq should act quickly, in order that the chance should not be given to the foreigners to obtain their object in Kuwait.[43]

At this time, other more damaging steps were taken to destabilize Kuwait. For example, in the first week of February 1939, two radical members of Kuwait's Legislative Council[44] – Abdullah al-Sager and Khalid Abdul-Latif – as well as two extreme pro-Iraqi nationalists – Muhammad al-Barrak and Abdul-Aziz Abdul-Wahid – were invited to Baghdad as special guests of the Iraqi government and were warmly received on their arrival. In discussions with various ministers and Iraqi nationalist politicans, the conversation centred around plans to bring Kuwait and then Bahrain under direct Iraqi control, and from this to work hard for a unified Arab empire under an Iraqi umbrella. They also paid a visit to the royal palace where they received encouragement for their planned movement for unification from Rashid Ali al-Gaylani, the Court Chamberlain.[45]

---

42. Sir M. Peterson, *Both Sides of the Curtain* (London, Allen and Unwin, 1950), p. 38. See also de Gaury to Fowle, no. C-48, 13 February 1939, R/15/5/126 and de Gaury to Fowle, no. C-49, 14 February 1939, R/15/5/126.

43. 'Kuwait is a part of Iraq', *an-Nas*, 17 February 1939, quoted in *ibid*. See also the translation of a leading article by Rafael Bitti in *al-Bilad*, Baghdad, 9 February 1939, quoted in *ibid*.

44. For more details on Kuwait's Legislative Council of 1938, see Salih, 'The 1938 Kuwait Legislative Council', pp. 76–9. See also Jill Crystal, *Oil and Politics in the Gulf: Rulers and Merchants in Kuwait and Qatar* (Cambridge, Cambridge University Press, 1990), pp. 47–50.

45. It was later reported that Iraqi government officials had promised the disgruntled

As the anti-Kuwait campaign showed no sign of subsiding, the authorities in the Gulf attempted to bring some pressure to bear on the Iraqi government to halt the unrelenting and increasingly aggressive attacks. Maurice Peterson, the British Ambassador in Baghdad, called on Naji Shaukat, the Acting Prime Minister in the absence of Nuri al-Said (who was in London) on 21 February 1939, with a list of complaints concerning hostile Iraqi propaganda against Kuwait. Peterson pointed out that continued demands for the annexation of Kuwait by the Iraqi press could only lead to tension in Iraq's relations not only with its neighbours but also with Britain. In response, Shaukat explained his inability to take any action against the press, but that in any case attacks on the Sheikh of Kuwait were justified as he denied his people any effective participation in the government of the country while also failing to provide education, health or public services of any kind. The Ambassador totally refuted this allegation and stated that Iraq was mis-informed about Kuwait where "there might not be any modern schools, but there were good religious schools, the mosques were well-attended and public morality stood high". Nevertheless, Shaukat recommended that the British government should persuade the Sheikh to "develop a more enlightened government and administration for his country".[46]

Despite Peterson's protest, King Ghazi's Qasr al-Zuhoor continued its broadcasts attacking Sheikh Ahmed.[47] Seriously concerned by the ever-increasing regularity and severity of these attacks, the Political Agent developed a new strategy intended to deal with the Iraqi propaganda. The main features of de Gaury's proposed measures were that the British government should make a strong diplomatic representation to Iraq to protest against the propaganda; reaffirm its commitment to protect Kuwait; take steps to reintroduce trade between Kuwait and Saudi Arabia; ask Sheikh Ahmed to visit Saudi Arabia or alternatively invite Ibn Saud to Kuwait in order to publicly demonstrate the close

Abdullah al-Sager, the Mutasarif of Kuwait, or the future Kuwaiti seat in the Iraqi parliament after its annexation. See Air Liaison Officer (Baghdad) to Air Staff Intelligence (Habbaniya), no. 1/BD/28, 10 February 1939, R/15/5/126. See also de Gaury to Fowle, no. C-68, 24 February 1939, R/15/5/126.

46. Peterson to the Foreign Office, no. 21, 21 February 1939, FO 371/23180.
47. De Gaury to Fowle, no. C-68, 24 February 1939, R/15/5/126. See also de Gaury to Fowle, no. C-59, 23 February 1939, R/15/5/127.

relations between Kuwait and Saudi Arabia; make arrangements with the BBC's Arabic Service as well as Palestine Radio to transmit more favourable news on Kuwait in order to counter the Iraqi propaganda; and finally, station an armoured car contingent at Jahra for an indefinite period. The Political Agent urged the British government to immediately implement these measures in order to protect Kuwait from the impact of any further propaganda.[48] Fowle fully endorsed them as he was firmly convinced that a reconfirmation of Britain's undertaking to protect the Sheikhdom would have an "excellent effect both in Iraq and in Koweit".[49]

In line with these suggestions, and in reply to a question from Colonel John Allen, a Conservative MP, on the Iraqi radio and press attacks against the Sheikh of Kuwait, R. A. Butler, the Under-Secretary of State for Foreign Affairs, stated in the House of Commons on 8 March 1939, that the British government recognized the Sheikhdom as an independent country under British protection and assured the House that London had made urgent representations to Baghdad to "secure the cession of propaganda against the Sheikh".[50] On the same date, Maurice Peterson, acting on Foreign Office instructions, met with King Ghazi to express the British government's displeasure at the use of his private transmitting facilities for the dissemination of propaganda against Kuwait and insisted that the King disclose his real motives for "sponsoring these attacks". In defence of his position, King Ghazi presented the issue as one of national security. He argued that both he and his government were seriously concerned about the "influx of Persians into Kuwait" which they considered as a direct threat to Iraq's communications in the event of war. Peterson, however, declined to accept this as a valid justification for the King's interference in the internal affairs of Kuwait and reminded him that "matters of this kind were better handled through diplomatic channel than in the unfortunate manner which he has selected". Although Peterson received an undertaking from the King that he would amend his policy, Qasr al-Zuhoor continued its

---

48. De Gaury to Fowle, no. 6/69, 24 February 1939, R/15/5/126.
49. Fowle to the Secretary of State for India, no. T-51, 26 February 1939, FO 371/23180.
50. For the full text, see Sheikhdom of Kuwait, no. E-1777/66/91, 8 March 1939, FO 371/23180. See also Hansard Parliamentary Debates: House of Commons, 5th series, vol. CCCXLIV (London, HMSO, 1938–9), p. 2155.

anti-Kuwait programme of attacking the Sheikh and urging the annexation of Kuwait.[51]

Two days after the British Ambassador's audience with King Ghazi, Prime Minister Nuri al-Said, on the King's behalf, presented a plan to Peterson allegedly designed to improve relations between Iraq and Kuwait. This plan basically consisted of three distinct stages: first, a messenger would be dispatched to Kuwait with a friendly letter for the Sheikh; second, the Sheikh should reply by letter to the King; and third, the Sheikh would then be invited to Baghdad to receive an Iraqi civilian decoration from King Ghazi. Avoiding any direct reply, the Ambassador referred the proposal to the Foreign Office indicating his readiness to accept the first two stages of the proposal but rejecting the last. Although the Foreign Office was prepared to endorse Peterson's recommendation, it chose not to issue any instructions to Baghdad.[52]

The King, impatient with this delay, summoned Houstoun-Boswall, the Chargé d'Affaires, to the palace on 23 March 1939. During this audience at which Nuri al-Said was also present, Houstoun-Boswall was pressed to expedite the acceptance of Iraq's friendly overtures to Kuwait. He replied, however, that Sheikh Ahmed could not appreciate such overtures unless the Iraqis halted their "harmful propaganda" against the Sheikhdom. In response, the Prime Minister upgraded his previous proposal by replacing the sending of an ordinary messenger with an envoy dispatched directly by the King to advise the Sheikh on how to run the government and to convince him that King Ghazi's "sole idea was to render assistance in bringing that backward territory up to date". As this also failed to elicit a positive response from the Chargé d'Affaires, the King alleged that the Kuwaiti ruler employed Persian police and encouraged Persian immigration in order to enable him to repress his own subjects.[53] While Houstoun-Boswall rejected these allegations at the time, de Gaury, after a full investigation, later found

---

51. For more on Qasr al-Zuhoor's anti-Kuwait broadcasts, see the Enclosure in Fowle to the India Office, no. 244-S, 24 March 1939, FO 371/23181. See also Sir Reader Bullard (Jeddah) to Foreign Office, no. 39, 21 March 1939, FO 371/23180.

52. Peterson to the Secretary of State for Foreign Affairs, no. 66, 10 March 1939, FO 371/23180. See also Minute by Symon, no. E-1826/66/91, 13 March 1939, FO 371/23180.

53. Houstoun-Boswall to the Foreign Office, no. 91, 25 March 1939, FO 371/23181.

them to be groundless.[54] In a final bid, Nuri al-Said offered the services of the Iraqi police force to restore law and order in Kuwait, although Houstoun-Boswall told him that it was impossible to accept this in view of the Sheikh's bitter experiences of Iraqi police in the frontier incidents (see Chapter 3). These discussions only served to convince Houstoun-Boswall that the Iraqis were "aiming effectively to take over the protection of Koweit while nominally leaving the Sheikh and His Majesty's Government in their present position". He, therefore, felt that it was important to discourage the Sheikh from accepting the Iraqi offer of the so-called "messenger of friendship" to advise him on administrative matters until Iraq showed "proof of good faith by a genuine cessation of propaganda".[55]

Fowle, in agreeing with Houstoun-Boswall, reiterated that the arrival of either an Iraqi envoy or adviser in Kuwait would encourage pro-Iraqi demonstrations within the Sheikhdom and establish an "undesirable precedent". The Resident, therefore, recommended that the Iraqi government be told categorically that under the terms of the Exclusive Treaty of 1899, the Sheikh was precluded from receiving the representative of any foreign power except that of Britain. The Foreign Office endorsed Fowle's recommendation and made it clear that if the Iraqi government intended to make "any communication other than a message of mere courtesy" to the Sheikh they should do so through the British embassy in Baghdad. The Foreign Office further added that the British government would under no circumstances allow Iraq to interfere in the affairs of Kuwait and Iraq should therefore cooperate in an early demarcation of the frontier in order to reduce the tension between the two countries.[56]

Despite Iraq's public gesture of friendship, it was soon discovered that the Iraqi government had in fact made definite plans for the invasion of Kuwait following their failure to engineer a revolution there. The British Air Liaison Office at Basra first discovered the plot towards the end of March 1939, which was later independently confirmed by

---

54. Fowle to Peel, no. 436-S, 3 May 1939, FO 371/23181.
55. Houstoun-Boswall to Foreign Office, no. 91, 25 March 1939, FO 371/23181.
56. Fowle to Marquess of Zetland, no. 169, 27 March 1929, FO 371/23181. See also Foreign Office to Houstoun-Boswall, no. 98, 30 March 1939, FO 371/23181; and de Gaury to Fowle, no. C-143, 29 March 1939, R/15/5/127.

Royal Navy, Royal Air Force and Special Intelligence reports.[57] These invasion plans had been formulated by Iraqi government officials in collaboration with Kuwaiti opponents of the Sheikh. As a prelude to the occupation of Kuwait, a number of Iraqi armed cars were to make a sudden assault on Jahra – seen as the strategic key to Kuwait – and occupy the town. Simultaneously, five army battalions were to be deployed on the Kuwaiti border while the pro-Iraqi elements in Kuwait were to occupy other parts of the Sheikhdom.[58]

However, the plan was not put into operation due to the sudden death of King Ghazi in a car accident on 4 April 1939 and the resultant political instability in Iraq.[59] The British authorities in the Gulf took the matter very seriously and decided to formulate a strategy to defend Kuwait from what they now perceived as the very real possibility of an Iraqi attack. They differed however on the steps to be taken. While Fowle recommended that the British government reaffirm its undertaking to protect the Sheikhdom, Houstoun-Boswall argued that it would be seen as a sign of weakness for the government to emphasize its

57. Squadron Leader (Air Liaison Officer, Basra) to de Gaury, no. 1/65/292/9, 29 March 1939. See also de Gaury to Fowle, no. C-205, 5 May 1939, and Fowle to the Secretary of State for India, no. 246, 19 April 1939, FO 371/23181; the Enclosure in Fowle to Peel, no. PZ353/39, 23 May 1939, and Fowle to the Secretary of State for India, no. 158, 25 March 1939.

58. There were in fact only a few Kuwaitis, with estimates varying between 10 to 80, who wanted to join Iraq. Their leader was Abdullah al-Sager, a man who owned estates in Iraq, which he was frightened of losing. See R. Peel to H. M Eyres, no. PZ1978/39, 5 April 1939, R/15/5/127. See also Squadron Leader (Air Liaison Officer, Basra) to de Gaury, no. 1/65/292/9, 29 March 1939, R/15/5/127.

59. King Ghazi died on 4 April 1939 in a car accident leaving successive cabinets notoriously unstable. Nevertheless, the King's death relieved Iraqi–Kuwaiti tension a great deal. The Qasr al-Zuhoor radio broadcasting station was handed over to the government, and royal patronage of rebellious elements in Kuwait ceased. Palace pressure for the visit to Kuwait of a special messenger or envoy also disappeared. As Ghazi's successor, Faisal II, was a minor at that time, a regency was established under his uncle, Prince Abdul-Illah, who reigned until Faisal attained his majority in 1953 (although Prince Abdul-Illah remained a dominant figure in Iraqi politics until his assassination in 1958). There were many coups and counter-coups during this period. See H. B. Sharabi, *Government and Politics of the Middle East in the Twentieth Century* (New York, D. Van Nostrand, 1962), p. 153. See also Fowle to de Gaury, no. 213, 5 April 1939, R/15/5/127; de Gaury to Fowle, no. C-205, 5 May 1939, R/15/5/127; Houstoun-Boswall to Halifax, no. 178, 20 April 1939, FO 371/23181.

determination "to protect a protectorate, which is better left as a forgone conclusion".[60] As a result of these differing views, de Gaury devised another plan for the defence of Kuwait, which entailed the formation, with British assistance, of an efficient Kuwaiti tribal levy force to deter an Iraqi invasion. One British officer from the Indian Frontier Force and a British NCO should be employed under Kuwait's command to give the necessary training to the proposed force.[61]

Fowle forwarded de Gaury's defence scheme to the India Office, but felt the stationing of a small but permanent British force comprising of an armoured car detachment, would provide far more effective defence of Kuwait than the formation of a tribal levy. The Air Ministry was therefore asked to review the options and give its opinion on the possibility of deploying an armoured car detachment permanently in Kuwait. The Ministry concluded that since the armed car section at Shuaiba (just to the west of Basra) could reach Kuwait in around four hours in the event of a serious threat from Iraq, there was no justification for the stationing of British forces in Kuwait in peacetime. Moreover, such a permanent deployment of troops might be viewed by Iraq as a rather provocative step. The Ministry instead felt that cooperation between RAF armoured cars and aircraft and the local Kuwaiti forces was adequate to safeguard Kuwait.[62] In short, given that the outbreak of war with Germany was imminent, the British government did not want to take any action which might damage its friendly relations with Iraq.

Although no major Iraqi military movement took place, the Iraqi police once again crossed the frontier in April 1939 and the Basra port authorities provocatively erected posts for survey work within Kuwaiti territory (along the shore of the Bahaith Bay and the Khor Subiya) without obtaining permission from Kuwaiti authorities. De Gaury was convinced that these territorial violations were due to Prime Minister Nuri al-Said's ardent desire to annex Kuwait, and had been designed to demonstrate to Sheikh Ahmed that while on the one hand Iraq was able

---

60. Houstoun-Boswall to Foreign Office, no. 40, 20 April 1939, FO 371/23181.
61. See de Gaury to Fowle, no. C-205, 5 May 1939, R/15/5/127. See also Fowle to the Secretary of State for India, no. 246, 19 April 1939, R/15/5/127.
62. M. H. Ely (Air Ministry) to R. Peel (India Office), no. PZ4002/39, 26 June 1939, R/15/5/184. See also Peel to Ely, no. PZ3678/39, 19 June 1939, R/15/5/184.

to attack Kuwait, on the other the British were unable to protect the Sheikhdom from such an attack. As the continuation of anti-Kuwait activities was largely due to Britain's passive policy towards Iraq, the Agent, in May 1939, strongly recommended that Britain should move quickly and forcefully by demarcating the frontier, thereby rectifying its consistent failure to do so.[63] How Britain proceeded with this delicate problem of demarcation is the subject of the next chapter.

Conclusion

Iraq's hostile attitude towards Kuwait in the 1930s revealed its ulterior expansionist motives towards the Sheikhdom. In pursuing these aims the Iraqis resorted to the tactics of propaganda, together with acts of intimidation and interference, while consistently ignoring British demands to halt their anti-Kuwait campaign. Iraqi designs on Kuwait became clearer with its attempts to construct a port in Kuwait on the pretext of possible Persian interference with its trade on the Shatt al-Arab waterway. However, the campaign for annexation reached its zenith when the Iraqi government for the first time laid claim to the whole of Kuwait on unfounded historical and legal assertions. Iraq's last attempt to bring the Sheikhdom under its suzerainty during this period was a planned invasion of Kuwait. Although the Iraqis opted not to go ahead with the invasion following the death of King Ghazi, the chief architect of the plan, Britain took no countermeasures to defend Kuwait against possible attack, despite its earlier discovery of the plot, for fear of losing Iraqi cooperation in the likely event of the outbreak of war.

---

63. See Kuwait Intelligence Summary for the period 1 to 15 April 1939 in *Political Diaries of the Persian Gulf: 1938–1939*, vol. XIII (Oxford, Archive Editions, 1990), p. 320. See also de Gaury to Fowle, no. C-171, 14 April 1939, R/15/5/184; Fowle to de Gaury, no. 350-S, 15 April 1939, R/15/5/184; de Gaury to Fowle, no. C-207, 5 May 1939, R/15/5/127.

5

The Elusive Frontier Line and the Problem at Umm Qasr, 1935–1945

Although the British government, following lengthy internal discussions, took limited steps to demarcate the Iraqi–Kuwaiti frontier during the Second World War, they failed to make any tangible progress towards this end. The settlement of the frontier issue was further complicated by the Iraqi desire to construct a port at Umm Qasr to supplement their sole port at Basra. However, the problem of demarcation became even more acute when the British themselves decided to build a port in this disputed territory to serve their own wartime requirements. This chapter attempts to analyse the British efforts for the settlement of the frontier dispute against this background. It also endeavours to prove that the frontier dispute was further aggravated as a result of the divergent views that existed among the various British officials concerned in the affairs of Kuwait.

In order to discuss the problem of the demarcation of the Iraq–Kuwait border in detail it is first necessary to go back to 1935, when the Government of India raised the question in connection with its publication of a map prepared by the Survey of India, its cartographic department. In May 1935, the Director of Map Publication proposed that the frontier between Kuwait and Iraq should be shown as an undemarcated boundary on the Survey of India map. In view of this proposal, Dickson, the Political Agent in Kuwait, was instructed to establish the actual position of the Iraqi–Kuwaiti border as given by the 1923 definition, which had itself been reaffirmed by both Iraq and Kuwait in the exchange of notes in 1932. Yet in attempting to do so, the Agent found the wording of the 1923 definition to be "somewhat loose" and ambiguous. To illustrate this, Dickson reproduced the exact wording of the 1923 definition concerning the Sheikhdom's western and northern frontiers with Iraq:

From the intersection of the Wadi-el-Audja with the Batin and thence northwards along the Batin to a point just south of the latitude of Safwan; thence eastwards passing south of Safwan Wells, Jabal Sanam and Um Qasr, leaving them to Iraq and so on to the junction of the Khor Zubair with the Khor Abdulla.[1]

Dickson however pointed out that as the Batin Valley varied in width from 1.6 to 8 kilometres throughout its length, it would be difficult for British surveyors to fix a correct line "thence northwards along the Batin" on the proposed map. He therefore suggested, on 27 July 1935, that the borderline should run up the centre of the valley in order to give both sides "an equal share of this fertile grazing valley". Based on his local knowledge and existing practice in Kuwait, he then gave his own interpretation of the remaining portion of the text of 1923:

We here have always understood the northern boundary of the frontier to run in a 'due East and West straight line' from the Batin (centre line) to a point one mile South of Safwan Wells (where a large Notice Board exists on the side of the road which today marks the actual boundary). From there, the boundary continues, also in a straight line, but in a south-easterly direction to the junction of the Khor Zubair with the Khor Abdulla. The whole line thus drawn leaves each of the points known as Jabal Sanam, Safwan, and Um Qasr to Iraq, with a space of about a mile to spare.[2]

Dickson recommended that the Survey of India map should follow his "local interpretation" in fixing the line on the map so as to avoid any future "bone of contention between Iraq and Kuwait".[3]

Although Colonel Gordon Loch, the Officiating Political Resident, endorsed Dickson's interpretation without reservation and recommended that the delimitation of the Iraqi–Kuwaiti frontier be based

---

1. For the full text, see Percy Cox to More, no. 5405, 19 April 1923, R/15/5/209. See also Dickson to Fowle, no. C/262, 27 August 1935, R/15/5/184; 'Boundaries of Kuwait' in the Director (Map Publication Office, Survey of India, Calcutta) to the Foreign Secretary (Foreign and Political Department), no. 1612, 23 May 1935, R/15/5/184; the Foreign Secretary to the Government of India to the Under-Secretary of State for India (London), no. F169-N/35, 12 June 1935, R/15/5/184.
2. Dickson to Fowle, no. C/262, 27 August 1935, R/15/5/184.
3. *Ibid.*

upon it, Sir Archibald Clark Kerr, the British Ambassador to Iraq, opposed it on the grounds that Iraq might, "with good reason raise serious objection if the frontier line was adjusted solely based on the local views of Kuwait".[4] The Ambassador was worried that if Dickson's proposals were accepted and the borderline on the proposed map was drawn along the centre of the Batin, the water-hole at Hulaiba would probably be shown in Kuwait. He was convinced that Dickson's line would invite future trouble as the question of the frontier was likely to assume far greater importance on account of both the impending exploitation of oil in Kuwait and the preventive measures which the Iraqi government were planning to undertake in order to suppress smuggling across the border. He therefore recommended, on 30 October 1935, the rejection of Dickson's "unilateral interpretation" in favour of the maintenance of the Green Line of the Anglo-Ottoman Convention of July 1913 – on which the 1923 definition was based – in all official maps on which the frontier between Iraq and Kuwait was to be shown.[5]

Unable to reach an agreement, the authorities in London, faced with these conflicting opinions, requested Dickson to provide a further clarification of his proposed realignment. Accordingly, the Agent, in December 1935, forcefully defended his position by stating that the Ambassador's objection regarding the placement of Hulaiba was already answered by his formula, as it still placed the water-hole inside Iraqi territory by a hundred yards or so. As regards fixing the centre-line of the Batin as the frontier, he candidly argued that he was not attempting to "gain something for Kuwait at the expense of Iraq". He was convinced that the Ambassador would agree to his proposed line if he visited the valley as throughout its entire length there was "a deep and clearly defined motor car trace made by the RAF in 1929–30, which as near as possible forms an artificial demarcation line". He then once again appealed for the formal acceptance of the proposed line, which he still believed to be not only the fairest solution but also the one least likely to cause future argument.[6]

---

4. Loch to the Foreign Secretary to the Government of India, no. 699-S, 6 September 1935, R/15/5/184.
5. Kerr to Samuel Hoare, no. 378, 30 October 1935, R/15/5/184.
6. Dickson to Fowle, no. C/351, 13 December 1935, R/15/5/184.

The Foreign Office was eventually persuaded by Dickson's arguments and in January 1936, following an inter-departmental meeting, arrived at a decision on the issue. Defending the proposed frontier line, the Foreign Office reiterated:

> From Safwan to the Persian Gulf, His Majesty's Government see no reason to dissent from the frontier line which the Pol. Agent at Koweit has indicated as being locally accepted, namely, a straight line from a point one mile south of Safwan to the junction of the Khor Zubair and the Khor Abdullah, although there is room for doubt as to the exact way in which this line should appear on a map . . . In their view this line should be drawn straight from a point a mile south of Safwan to the tri-junction of the Khor Zubair, the Khor Shetana and the Khor as-Sabiya, since this point represents as nearly as possible the junction of the Khor Zubair and the Khor Abdullah.[7]

This observation seemed to concur with Dickson's local interpretation while dismissing the Ambassador's objection. Regarding Hulaiba, the Foreign Office made it clear that although the water-hole was not mentioned in any text defining the frontier or shown on the map attached to the Anglo-Ottoman Convention of 1913, it intended it to remain in Iraq. The Ambassador was then instructed to obtain the Iraqi government's acceptance of this proposed borderline.[8] Kerr, however, did not consider it politic to do so, and instead continued to press his objections to Dickson's proposals.[9]

In March 1936, the India Office asked the Government of India to go ahead with their proposed map showing the frontier line and clearly marking Hulaiba on the Iraqi side of the boundary. However, it stipulated that the frontier between Kuwait and Iraq should be shown "as an undemarcated boundary" on the Survey of India map and that a note should be made on the map explaining that the frontier was defined in 1923 and specifically reaffirmed by agreement between Kuwait and Iraq in 1932.[10] The map was eventually published in November 1938, but

---

7. G. W. Rendel to Kerr, no. 43, 22 January1936, R/15/5/184.
8. See *ibid.*
9. Kerr to Eden, no. 72, 8 February 1936, FO 371/19967.
10. J. C. Walton to Aubrey Metcalfe (Foreign and Political Department, Government of India), no. PZ1849/36, 27 March 1936, FO 371/19967. See

although it left Hulaiba in Iraq it mistakenly placed a Kuwaiti water-point, Qaqaiya, also inside Iraq. Gerald de Gaury, the Acting Political Agent, who noticed the error, suggested to Fowle that the Iraqi police be instructed to avoid entering Qaqaiya pending the final demarcation of the frontier.[11]

Meanwhile, on 4 April 1937, C. J. Edmonds, the principal British adviser to the Iraqi Ministry of the Interior, offered some suggestions for the demarcation of the frontier in an attempt to curb both the smuggling as well as the border incidents taking place in the frontier zone (see Chapter 3). He considered this an opportune time to do so in view of the departure of the hard-line Prime Minister Yasin al-Hashemi and the formation of a new Cabinet in October 1936 under the premiership of Hikmat Sulaiman, who had expressed his desire to settle all outstanding Iraqi–Kuwaiti issues. However, before taking the issue any further, Edmonds urged that the agreement of the Sheikh of Kuwait be sought to the interpretation of the following disputed points:

(a) In the Batin the frontier line follows the thalweg, i.e. the line of deepest depression.

(b) The 'point just south of the latitude of Safwan' shall be a point due west of a point situated one mile south of the palms of Safwan.

(c) From the Batin to the neighbourhood of Safwan the frontier is a straight line running due east to the above-mentioned point one mile due south of the palms of Safwan.

(d) The junction of the Khor Zubair and the Khor Abdullah means the junction of the thalwegs of these two waterways.

(e) The frontier from the above-mentioned point south of Safwan to the above-mentioned junction of the thalwegs is a straight line joining these two points.

---

also Deputy Secretary to the Government of India to the Director (Map Publication Office, Survey of India, Calcutta), no. F/169-N/35, May 1936, R/15/5/184.

11. De Gaury to Fowle, no. C/724, 19 December 1938, L/P & S/12/3737.

(f) From the above-mentioned junction of thalwegs to the open
sea the boundary follows the thalweg of the Khor Abdullah.[12]

These proposals were largely based on Dickson's formula and in fact
confirmed the existing practical interpretation. There was on the
Zubair–Kuwait road, about 1.6 kilometres south of Safwan, a board
marking the point where the road crossed the frontier. If the Sheikh
agreed to this interpretation the demarcation should be carried out
following the completion, where defective, of the triangulation along the
frontier zone and the formation of a joint commission to erect pillars,
which were to be visible from both sides along the whole length of the
land frontier.[13] Kerr found these interpretations to be "generally sound"
and referred them on to the Foreign Office.[14] However, London made
no attempt to either obtain the Sheikh's agreement to Edmond's
interpretation or to even approach the Iraqis with the interpretation.
This was apparently due to Iraqi unwillingness to open the issue
together with the appearance of a new government in Baghdad in
August 1937, headed by Jamil al-Midfa'i, an advocate of the anti-
Kuwaiti propaganda campaign (as discussed in the previous chapter).[15]

London's reticence over the demarcation question became a cause
of anxiety for Fowle, who had been pleading for the settlement of this
issue ever since he assumed charge of the Residency. In February 1939,
given the lack of any tangible progress, the Resident urged that the issue
of demarcating the frontier be raised with the Iraqis without further
delay in view of the drilling operations of the Basra Oil Development
Company in Iraq and of the Kuwait Oil Company (KOC) in Kuwait.
The discovery of oil by either company in territory claimed by the other
would obviously have serious consequences. Therefore, the only logical
step to avoid such an eventuality was an early demarcation of the
Iraqi–Kuwaiti frontier.[16] Yet even these arguments failed to convince the
authorities in London. The hesitation of the Secretary of State for India

---

12.   See the Note in Edmonds to Kerr, no. 480, 5 April 1937, FO 371/20774.
13.   *Ibid.*
14.   Kerr to Rendel, no. 387/3/37, 3 May 1937, FO 371/20774.
15.   For more details see *PGHS* (1937), vol. II, p. 91 and PGAR (1937), vol. IX,
      p. 37.
16.   Fowle to the Secretary of State for India, no. C/94, 22 February 1939, FO
      371/23180.

to take the matter more seriously again forced Fowle to cable him the following month, informing him that the present time was extremely suitable to press the Iraqis over demarcation as they were now "penitent at any rate outwardly, on the subject of anti-Koweit propaganda".[17]

As both Fowle and de Gaury pleaded for an early demarcation of the frontier,[18] the Foreign Office, at the recommendation of the India Office, directed Sir Basil Newton, the new Ambassador in Iraq, to prepare the ground for formal talks on the problem. Accordingly, on 1 July 1939, Newton prepared a draft proposal for the joint demarcation of the Iraqi–Kuwaiti frontier. This new formula, largely based on Edmonds's interpretation of the definition of 1932, advocated the formation of a joint Iraqi–Kuwaiti commission consisting of two representatives from each country with the necessary technical and other assistants to be nominated by the respective governments. In line with Edmonds's interpretation, the main task of the commission was firstly to complete where necessary the network of triangulation along the frontier zone from the intersection of the Wadi al-Auja with the Batin to the western extremity of the land frontier. Secondly, the commission was to organize the siting of frontier pillars, which were to be visible from both sides of the land frontier along its entire length and to mark with buoys (or other means which might be agreed upon) that part of the boundary "following the thalweg of the Khor Zubair, the Khor Shetana and the Khor Abdullah down to the sea". The first representative of each country should preside alternately over the meetings of the commission and in cases of disagreement between the representatives, they should refer the matter to their respective governments with a view to a solution being reached through diplomatic channels.[19]

The Foreign Office, expressing its willingness to accept this draft, referred it to the departments concerned for their comments. However, Fowle, who studied it at the India Office's invitation, objected to Newton's interpretation of the "point just south of the latitude of Safwan" (as defined in the 1932 exchange of letters) as the point situated 1.6 kilometres "due south of the most southerly palm of Safwan". Fowle

---

17. Fowle to the Secretary of State for India, no. 1141, 16 March 1939, FO 371/23180.
18. De Gaury to Fowle, no. C/207, 5 May 1939, R/15/5/127.
19. Newton to Halifax, no. 335, 1 July 1939, FO 371/23181. See also Enclosures in FO 371/23181.

maintained that the frontier at this point should be to the south of a board which had long marked the frontier between Kuwait and Iraq, but this was less than 1.6 kilometres from the Safwan palms. He argued that the exact location of the frontier at this point was of considerable importance to both countries in view of the possibility of oil being discovered in the immediate area around either side of the frontier. Apart from this, Fowle agreed with all of Newton's other points, but he suggested that the Sheikh of Kuwait be consulted before submitting the proposed interpretation of the frontiers to the Iraqis. Both the Government of India and the India Office agreed with Fowle and questioned whether it was in fact necessary for the "frontier line to run as much as a mile south of Safwan" as Newton had suggested.[20] Although the War Office initially declined to give its opinion due to its preoccupation with the war in Europe, eventually on 13 October 1939, at the Foreign Office's insistence, it submitted its views on the draft pro-posal. While it expressed its general agreement with Newton's interpret-ations, the War Office suggested that it would be prudent if the description of the point south of Safwan was based on more permanent landmarks than palm trees which might die or be cut down at any time.[21] In February 1940, with all the comments on Newton's proposal now ascertained, the Foreign Office concentrated its energies in produc-ing the procedures for the opening of talks with Iraq on demarcation.[22]

However, the Foreign Office's painstaking preparations for an early approach to the Iraqis were interrupted by the re-emergence of Iraq's campaign for a new port on the Gulf. In the first week of November 1939, Ali Jaudat Bey, the Iraqi Foreign Minister, discussed the matter with Newton. The Foreign Minister stated that his government had decided to construct wharves with moorings for two ships near Umm Qasr in view of the favourable results of a survey. Iraq also wished to

---

20. See Fowle to Peel, no. C/284, 1 August 1939, FO 371/23181; W. R. Hay (External Affairs Department, New Delhi), no. PZ7585/39, 21 November 1939, FO 371/24545; and Peel to Under-Secretary of State (Foreign Office), no. PZ375/40, 30 January 1940, FO 371/24545.

21. See Major Hall-Dare (War Office) to Eyres (Foreign Office), no. 0178/1036 (M.1.4), 13 October 1939, FO 371/23181; Eyres to P. K. Boulnois (War Office), no. E-4936/66/91, 27 July 1939, FO 371/23181; and Boulnois to Eyres, no. 6666, 22 September 1936, FO 371/23181.

22. See the Minutes by J. Z. Mackenzie, Eyres and Baggallay, no. E-413/309/91, 5 February 1940, FO 371/24545.

extend the railway line from Shuaiba to the new port thus providing it with a rail link to Basra.[23] This proposal was the result of the meeting between Suwaidi, the then Iraqi Foreign Minister and Charles Baxter, the Head of the Foreign Office's Eastern Department, in London in October 1938. Following Baxter's advice to study the possibility of constructing a port on the Khor Abdullah rather than in Kuwaiti Bay (as discussed in the previous chapter), Suwaidi instructed the Basra port authorities to carry out a survey to assess the feasibility of such an idea. On 14 July 1939, Colonel Sir John Ward, the Director-General of the Port of Basra, secretly handed a copy of the findings of the survey, including a chart of the Khor Abdullah, to Lacy Baggallay, one of the officials of the Eastern Department before it was submitted to the Iraqi government, in order to give the British government time to formulate a policy in advance. The survey revealed that there were two good sites for a port on the right bank of the Khor Abdullah, one on the north and the other on the south side of the Umm Qasr creek. (Even the creek itself, with the use of the dredgers of Basra port, could be easily developed into an excellent basin.) As Ward considered the southern side more suitable than the northern, he recommended that a port could be constructed just below Umm Qasr for a comparatively small sum and a railway line could be linked to it.[24] Yet he did recognize that such a recommendation was in itself problematic as he believed that although both the northern side and the creek itself lay in Iraq, the southern side – the optimal location for the port – was in Kuwait. After Ward handed over the survey he personally attempted to gain the support of Foreign Office officials for his proposal by pointing out that the additional or alternative facilities of such a port would be of significant strategic importance to Britain in the event of war.

Ward's survey therefore placed the Foreign Office in a difficult situation. Crosthwaite was worried that if the southern side of the channel proved to be in Kuwaiti territory, Britain would be faced with the problem as to whether it could influence Kuwait to cede it to Iraq in return for suitable compensation. The British government would also be faced

---

23. Newton to Halifax, no. 668, 14 November 1939, FO 371/23200.
24. Minute by Crosthwaite, no. E-5116/58/93, 15 July 1936, FO 371/23200. See also Baggallay to C. G. Jarrett (Admiralty), no. E/5116/38/93, 5 August 1939, FO 371/23200.

with the decision of whether it would be preferable for Iraq to have absolute control of the port and of its approaches or whether Kuwait should be permitted to have some form of control. Like Crosthwaite, Baxter, who had introduced the Iraqi Foreign Minister to the idea of a port on the Khor Abdullah, was now equally unsure of how best to proceed if the Iraqis requested the better southern side of the Umm Qasr creek. In view of their failure to reach a decision on a possible reply to the Iraqis, they recommended that the issue be placed before a meeting of the Middle East Official Sub-Committee.[25]

The committee met on 14 August 1939 under the chairmanship of Sir John Shuckburgh to assess the implications of Ward's Umm Qasr project. The representatives of the three service departments and all the other departments concerned were present. Baggallay, the Foreign Office representative, presented Ward's scheme and stated that the Foreign Office had no objection to the Iraqi development of a port at Umm Qasr and that the British government should not put any obstacles in their way. Although Peel, who represented the India Office, agreed with Baggallay, he also demanded that the rights of Kuwait must be safeguarded. C. G. Jarrett, in expressing the Admiralty's concern over the possible adverse effects on the traffic of the Shatt al-Arab, told the Committee that the Admiralty was not opposed to the scheme in principle provided that it did not hamper British oil traffic from Abadan. John Ward, who was also present at the meeting, assured Jarrett that the new port would not affect the oil traffic on the Shatt al-Arab provided that the refinery remained at Abadan. Ward's position was further boosted by F. J. Coleman, head of the Petroleum Department, who stated that as the prospect of discovering oil in southern Iraq was now very likely, a new port on the Khor Abdullah would provide a suitable outlet for this oil if a successful strike occurred. Major A. W. S. Mallaby, on behalf of the War Office, also spoke in favour of the scheme, although he argued against the use of any special pressure to bring it to fruition. Finally, Group Captain W. A. Coryton also expressed the Air Ministry's support for the establishment of the port.[26]

---

25. Minutes by Crosthwaite and Baxter, no. E-5116/58/93, 28 and 29 July 1939, FO 371/23200.
26. See the Minutes of the Meeting of the Middle East Official Sub-Committee, no. M.E. (O), 69th Meeting, 14 August 1939, FO 371/23200.

In short, no department was opposed in principle to the Umm Qasr project. However, the members of the committee were concerned that difficulties might arise if frontier adjustments were required to enable the development of the port, particularly if the Sheikh of Kuwait had to be asked to make territorial concessions. Nevertheless, Ward reassured the committee that if the maritime boundary passed down the median line or the thalweg of the Khor Abdullah it would be possible for shipping to move down to the sea in Iraqi waters without impinging on Kuwaiti waters since the navigable channel was sufficiently broad throughout. In summing up, Sir John Shuckburgh suggested that since the committee was not in a position to pinpoint the exact position of the frontier, Ward, on his return to Iraq, should place the results of his survey "unreservedly" before the Iraqis and that discussions as to the location of the frontier between Kuwait and Iraq in the vicinity of the Umm Qasr creek should await further action by the Iraqi government. There was general agreement to this suggestion.[27]

Therefore, upon his return to Baghdad John Ward submitted his survey to the Iraqi Ministry of Commerce and Works on 25 September 1939.[28] With the Iraqi government greatly impressed by these results, Ali Jaudat, the Iraqi Foreign Minister, raised the issue in early November with the British Ambassador. He stated that Iraq was not prepared to proceed with the project at Umm Qasr unless it secured sovereignty over both banks of the channel connecting it with the open sea. He therefore asked for British assistance in acquiring Warba and Bubiyan from Kuwait, which he considered merely as barren islands of no value to Kuwait. Sir Basil Newton – who was aware of the survey report as Ward had handed a copy to the embassy on the same day as he had submitted it to the Iraqi government[29] – pointed out that although these islands were barren, they represented in terms of area a considerable portion of the territory of Kuwait and that it would be folly to simply expect the Sheikh to cede them to Iraq without adequate compensation. Yet the Foreign Minister argued that as the islands were intrinsically worthless it

27. *Ibid.*
28. J. C. Ward (Port Director and Director-General of Navigation), no. C/58/39, 25 September 1939, FO 371/23200.
29. See the Enclosure in Chancery to the Eastern Department, no. 30/13/39, 26 September 1939, FO 371/23200.

would be unnecessary to compensate the Sheikh for their loss. He even went on to say that Iraq was "in a position to claim sovereignty over these Islands and even over the whole of Kuwait".[30] Newton, however, reminded him that the reaffirmation of the frontier contained in the exchange of notes between their two governments in 1932 quite clearly specified that the islands of Warba and Bubiyan belonged to Kuwait. He then warned the Foreign Minister that Iraq should not attempt to dispute the validity of the definition of the frontier contained in those documents. Consequently, Newton suggested that the best policy for the Iraqi government would be to study the whole problem from the point of view of providing Kuwait with a common interest with Iraq in the construction and development of this new port. As Ali Jaudat found this argument reasonable, he requested British cooperation towards this end.[31] Nevertheless, his conversation with the Iraqi Foreign Minister convinced Newton that given the complicated nature of the frontier question, a solution would be difficult to achieve:

> The problem of finding a suitable quid pro quo which Iraq could offer to Koweit for the cession of the two islands is clearly difficult to solve. The frontier on the west of Koweit follows the line of the well-marked natural feature of the Batin and could not conveniently be altered to make a territorial concession to Koweit, while any movement northwards of the line from the Batin to the Khor Abdulla would not only take the boundary dangerously close to Basra but would also cut off Iraq from access to the site of the new port itself. It would seem, therefore, that the quid pro quo must be economic and not territorial, and I venture to suggest that the question should be approached from that angle.[32]

In other words, the Ambassador was suggesting that Kuwait should cede the islands of Warba and Bubiyan to Iraq in return for economic compensation instead of any territorial concession. He, however, recommended this without first ascertaining the opinions of either the authorities in the Gulf or those of the Sheikh on the issue.

The Ambassador's recommendation for the Iraqi acquisition of Warba and Bubiyan, however, was not acceptable to the Foreign Office,

---

30. Newton to Halifax, no. 668, 14 November 1939, FO 371/23200.
31. *Ibid.*
32. *Ibid.*

which believed that Iraq could build a port on its own territory without the need of any territorial concession from Kuwait. Nevertheless, the Foreign Office was inclined to allow Iraq to have full control of the channel leading to Umm Qasr due to its belief that if Iraq was given the complete control of at least one good access route to the sea, "it would make for steadier conditions in that part of the world in years to come". It further believed that Kuwait's sovereignty over half of the waterway in the channel was of no practical use to the Sheikh, which would remain the case even if oil was discovered in greater quantities since Kuwait had other outlets. However, the Foreign Office did realize that absolute Iraqi control of the Khor Abdullah for the construction of the proposed port meant the cession of at least a small portion of the Kuwaiti mainland near the point at which the common frontier met the Khor which was only a little to the south of the Umm Qasr creek. Ironically, it thought that this was possible as it assumed that the Sheikh could be induced to relinquish this territory in exchange for financial compensation from Iraq. However, the Foreign Office was not prepared to take a final decision on the matter until the views of the authorities in the Gulf were canvassed.[33]

Charles Prior, Fowle's successor as Resident, was opposed to any territorial concession to Iraq either on the Sheikh's half of the waterway or on Bubiyan Island, irrespective of whatever financial inducement was offered. In a long letter to the India Office dated 8 February 1940, Prior warned that any extension of Iraqi influence in the region would be potentially dangerous to Kuwait as he was convinced that the Iraqis would "abuse their position and by bluff from without and intrigue from within seek to undermine Kuwait" until they realized their dream, namely the annexation of the Sheikhdom. Instead, to reduce the risk, the Iraqis should be encouraged to build the port within their own territorial waters. In any case, Prior was sure that Sheikh Ahmed would never accept such dangerous proposals:

> Bubiyan the Shaikh would never yield, no matter what compensation was paid, for, apart from any question of pride, its value as

---

33. See Minute by Crosthwaite and Baggallay, no. E-7601/58/93, 30 November and 4 December 1939, FO 371/23200. See also Foreign Office to the Under-Secretary of State (India Office), no. E-7601/58/93, 16 December 1939, FO 371/23200.

an oil territory is unknown. He could not accept money compensation for territory without serious loss of 'face' . . .

I am extremely doubtful if he would agree to hypothecate his right to the waterway, for, apart from questions of prestige, it would mean that any port developed by the Kuwait Oil Company for the oil which has already been found would be at the mercy of the Iraqis. Nor does it seem to me that it is in our interests that Iraqis should have undivided sway. As long as Kuwait, or rather ourselves, have a half share in the Khor Abdullah, Iraq has incentive to remain on good terms with us. They cannot say that the Kuwait share in the Khor Abdullah can ever be a danger. Far from an undivided Iraqi control of access to the sea making for steadier conditions in this part of the world, the Iraqis would become more intransigent than ever.[34]

In short, Prior was determined to keep the Iraqis out of Kuwaiti territory at all costs. Moreover, any absolute Iraqi control of the Khor Abdullah would create tension rather than establish "steadier" conditions in the region. The Resident criticized John Ward for devising such an ambitious and potentially dangerous project and stated that he had done so merely to serve his own interests and to protect his position and power in Basra. Even the British government did not escape criticism, with Prior accusing it of adopting a dubious policy towards the Sheikh in keeping him in the dark of all of Iraq's unjustified proposals. He therefore strongly recommended that the Sheikh be kept informed of all events and "reassured that he is not going to be asked to make concession against his will".[35]

While the Foreign Office still showed no sign of flexibility in its idea of surrendering Kuwait's rights in the Khor Abullah waterway, it instructed Prior, through the India Office, to place the matter before the Sheikh for his views. The Resident, who had been eagerly awaiting an opportunity to do so, approached Sheikh Ahmed in the third week of March 1940. However, the Sheikh, already well aware of the Umm Qasr scheme and the Iraqi designs on his territory, categorically refused to make any territorial concession to Iraq.[36] As he had no objection to the project being carried out in Iraqi waters, even though such a new port would adversely affect Kuwait's economy, he asked if the Senior Naval

---

34. Prior to Peel, no. C/93, 8 February 1940, R/15/5/208.
35. *Ibid.*
36. It was Haji Abdullah Williamson, a renegade Christian sailor and retired

Officer in the Gulf could examine the channel in order to discover whether the project could be situated entirely within Iraqi waters. Prior accepted the Sheikh's views without reservation.

The Resident's opposition to any territorial concession to Iraq was also supported by a plea from James Jameson, the Director of the APOC and KOC, to safeguard Kuwait's rights in the Khor Abdullah channel in order to provide the oil companies with an alternative export route in the event of any serious difficulty with Kuwait Bay. Armed with this argument, Prior sent two urgent cables to London on the same day requesting that the Sheikh's interests be protected by refusing Iraq permission to establish a port "infringing Kuwaiti territory". He further recommended the immediate demarcation of the borderline to determine where the frontier ran at this crucial point.[37] The Senior Naval Officer also backed the Resident's recommendation and stated that the military authorities should be kept informed of any new developments as they themselves might require a port on the Khor Abdullah as a point of disembarkation for British troops.[38]

The India Office joined forces with the authorities in the Gulf in arguing: "It is important for our position in the Gulf that Koweit should be stable and free from Iraqi influence." It added that no pressure should be brought to bear upon Sheikh Ahmed to cede any of his rights to the Iraqis and suggested that, in view of the Sheikh's refusal to make territorial concessions, the Iraqis should be told categorically that the British government was unable to help them in the acquisition of Kuwaiti territory either on land or sea. However, it had no objection to the Iraqis locating the port within their own territory. As a result, the India Office felt it essential to proceed with the demarcation of the Iraqi–Kuwaiti frontier as soon as possible since, "should the Iraqi Government decide to confine the scheme for a new port to Iraqi territory, the precise position of the boundary line in the neighbourhood of Umm Qasr may be of considerable importance."[39]

employee of the Anglo-Persian Oil Company, who in fact told the Sheikh of the need for the cession of some of his land for the proposed project in Umm Qasr. See de Gaury to Fowle, no. C/219, 9 May 1939, R/15/5/208.

37. Prior to the Secretary of State for India, no. ST209 and 210, 22 March 1940, FO 371/24559.
38. C-in-C, East Indies, to the Admiralty, no. 320, 30 March 1940, FO 371/24559.
39. Peel to the Under-Secretary of State (Foreign Office), no. PZ1779/40, 19 April

The Foreign Office had no choice but to reverse its policy and express its solidarity with the India Office in that there could be "no question of any attempt being made to force the Sheikh into ceding any part of his territory even in return for compensation, if he does not wish to do so".[40] On 22 May 1940, the Foreign Office instructed Sir Basil Newton to tell the Iraqis that as the Sheikh was utterly opposed to any territorial concession, they "must" site their proposed port within their own territory and must not endeavour to impress upon the Sheikh for the cession of any of his territory or rights in the waterway. The Ambassador was further requested to press the Iraqis for an early demarcation of the frontier. Three days later, this message was conveyed to the Iraqi Foreign Minister.[41]

Once this decision had been taken on Umm Qasr, the Foreign Office turned to examine the issue of demarcation which had laid dormant since February 1940. Bearing in mind Fowle's (the former Resident) criticism of Newton's draft proposal and the Sheikh's refusal to surrender any territory to Iraq for a port at Umm Qasr, the Foreign Office produced a new formula largely based on Cox's definition of 1923. The Foreign Office, contrary to Newton's suggestion but in line with Fowle's interpretation, was of the view that since the determination of the frontier at the point south of Safwan "by a reference to the most southerly palm" had always been a "somewhat unsatisfactory expedient", it preferred to adopt a reference to the existing post and notice-board to avoid any dispute with either Iraq or Kuwait. Eventually, on 5 May 1940, a new draft was produced making the definition as clear as possible:

(1) 'Along the Batin' the frontier line shall follow the thalweg, i.e. the line of the deepest depression.

(2) The point 'just south of the latitude of Safwan' shall be the point on the thalweg for the Batin due west of the point a

---

1940, FO 371/24559. See also Government of India to the Secretary of State for India, no. 831, 18 March 1940, FO 371/24559.

40. Baggallay to the Under-Secretary of State (India Office), no. E-1883/630/93, 4 May 1940, FO 371/24559.

41. Foreign Office to Newton, no. 156, 22 May 1940, FO 371/24559. See also Newton to Foreign Office, no. 245, 28 May 1940, FO 371/24559.

little to the south of Safwan at which the post and notice-board at present marking the frontier have been erected.[42]

(3) From the Batin to the neighbourhood of Safwan the frontier shall be a line along the parallel of latitude on which stands the above-mentioned point at which the post and notice-board have been erected.

(4) The 'junction of the Khor Zubair with the Khor Abdullah' shall mean the junction of the thalweg of the Khor Zubair with the thalweg of the north-westerly arm of the Khor Abdullah known as the Khor Shetana.[43]

(5) From the neighbourhood of Safwan to the junction of the Khor Zubair with the Khor Abdullah the frontier shall be the shortest line between the point defined in sub-paragraph (2) and the point defined in sub-paragraph (4). But if this line shall be found, when followed on the ground to strike the

42. It is to be remembered that this notice-board was originally placed in position by the Sheikh of Kuwait and the Political Agent in 1923. It was removed by the Iraqis in 1932 who later replaced it following a strong protest by the British government. It was again removed by the Iraqis in March 1939. However, on 9 June 1940, the Political Agent with the help of the Sheikh erected a board on the old spot in the presence of an Iraqi frontier officer. On 25 June 1940, the Iraqi government protested that the new board had been erected at a point far from the site of the old one at a distance of 250 metres within the Iraqi frontier. The British Embassy, however, on 3 August 1940, refuted the allegation and stated that the Kuwaiti authorities were satisfied that the new board had been placed on its original site. However, the Iraqis removed it. Up to this point no attempt had been made by the British to replace it for fear of damaging Anglo-Iraqi relations. See Galloway to Prior, no. C/266, 2 June 1940, R/15/5/185; Galloway to Prior, no. C/293, 20 June 1940, FO 371/91291; Iraqi Ministry of Foreign Affairs to the British Embassy, no. 2635/2635/7/2364, 25 June 1940, R/15/5/185; the 'Note Verbale' from British Embassy to the Iraqi Foreign Ministry, no. 356, 3 August 1940, R/15/5/185; and Newton to Halifax, no. 411, 3 August 1940, R/15/5/185.
43. Sir Basil Newton, the British Ambassador in Iraq, suggested that since the place below Umm Qasr, the Khor Zubair, was described on certain Admiralty charts as the Khor Umm Qasr, it would be more accurate to replace the term "Khor Zubair" with "Khor Umm Qasr". The Foreign Office overruled this arguing that in the same charts the westerly part of the Khor Shetana was described as the Khor Sakan. It therefore replaced the term "Khor Sakan" with the "Khor Shetana". See Baggallay to the Under-Secretary of State (India Office), no. E-1758/309/91, 5 May 1940, FO 371/24545.

right bank of the Khor Zubair before it reaches the point defined in sub-paragraph (4), it shall be modified in such a manner as to follow the low water-line on the right bank of the Khor Zubair until such a point on the bank immediately opposite the point defined in sub-paragraph (4) is reached, thus leaving the whole of the Khor Zubair to Iraq.

(6) From the point defined in sub-paragraph (4) to the open sea the boundary shall follow the thalweg of the Khor Abdullah.[44]

This draft was a substantial improvement on Newton's proposal of July 1939. Based on this new formula a final interpretation clarifying the definition was produced. On 9 June 1940, this fresh definition of the Iraqi–Kuwaiti frontier was placed before Sheikh Ahmed for his approval, which he gave without objection on 12 June.[45] With this obtained, the Ambassador was instructed on 31 July 1940 to formally present the proposal to Nuri al-Said, the then Iraqi Foreign Minister, in order to reach a joint demarcation of the frontier. Newton carried out the instruction on 7 October 1940.[46] This was the first time that the British government had presented an official note to Iraq expressing its earnest desire to achieve the demarcation of the frontier, the most delicate issue in Iraqi–Kuwaiti relations.

Eventually, on 21 November 1940, the Iraqi government replied to the British proposal. It argued that since it had been inspired by the Iraqi–Saudi frontier negotiations and, given that these had already been suspended, the Iraqi government considered it premature to open negotiations.[47] Newton, however, believed that this linkage of the

---

44. See Enclosure in *ibid.*
45. Political Agent to the Ruler of Kuwait, no. 199/4/6, 9 June 1940, FO 371/24545. See also the Ruler of Kuwait to the Political Agent, unnumbered, 12 June 1940, FO 371/24545.
46. For the full text, see Appendix III.
47. Iraqi Ministry of Foreign Affairs to the British Embassy, Baghdad, no. 2635/26/35/7/19684, 21 November 1940, FO 371/24545. Although Iraq and Saudi Arabia agreed to settle the line of their common frontier, including its eastern and western termination points, through a joint commission under Egyptian chairmanship, following the visit of Nuri al-Said (the then Iraqi Foreign Minister) to Saudi Arabia in the first week of April 1940, discussions on demarcation were suspended following disagreement on the question of fixing the point of intersection of latitude 32° north and longitude 39° east.

Iraqi–Saudi frontier negotiations with the proposed Iraqi–Kuwaiti frontier demarcation was merely a delaying tactic to provide the time for its demands on the islands of Warba and Bubiyan to be realized.[48] As the Ambassador had anticipated, the Iraqis argued, in March 1941, that the proposed demarcation should be preceded by the Kuwaiti cession to Iraq of the two islands in order to ensure Iraqi control of the approaches to Umm Qasr.[49] As a result, Iraq still neither accepted nor rejected the British proposal.

Meanwhile, the strategic importance of Umm Qasr was enhanced by the progress of the war in the Middle East and the British intention to build an emergency port there. The British military authorities in Iraq were worried that the Allied war effort in that part of the Gulf would be jeopardized if the Basra port – which could only be reached along the 112 kilometres of the narrow Shatt al-Arab channel – was closed by enemy action. Therefore, Umm Qasr was an obvious alternative to the Basra base. Following extensive reconnaissance, the Commander-in-Chief, Middle East, in late May 1941, sought the War Office's permission to immediately develop Umm Qasr.[50] Although the War Office agreed with this request, it could not issue an immediate sanction unless the Foreign Office cleared the way.[51] However, the Foreign Office, which was uncertain of the exact site where the military authorities wished to construct a harbour, was again faced with the political problem of where exactly the Iraqi–Kuwaiti frontier ran. As a port at Umm Qasr was particularly problematic, given that the consent of both countries was needed as neither of them had full control of the channel, a meeting of the Middle East Official Sub-Committee debated the issue on 22 July 1941. Whilst the committee felt that it would not be difficult to pursue the matter with the Iraqis as they themselves were keen to construct a port in Umm Qasr, the Sheikh of Kuwait on the other hand, who had previously refused outright to cede any of his

---

48. Newton to Halifax, no. 537, 29 November 1940, FO 371/24545. For more details of the Iraqi–Saudi boundary dispute, see Richard Schofield (ed.), *Arabian Boundary Dispute* (Gerrards Cross, Archive Editions, 1992), pp. 718–31.
49. *PGHS*, vol. II, p. 70.
50. C-in-C, Middle East, to War Office, no. Q(P)/67933, 28 May 1941, FO 371/27106. See also C-in-C, India, to the War Office, no. 7670/G, 17 June 1941, FO 371/27106.
51. Foreign Office to Baghdad, no. 675, 24 July 1941, FO 371/27106.

territory to the Iraqis for this purpose, might realistically be expected to react unfavourably. Nevertheless, the committee believed that he could be induced to comply if he was assured that his interests would be safeguarded and that the proposed project would be a totally British concern free from any Iraqi involvement. It thus decided that the British General Officer Commanding in Iraq should immediately pinpoint the exact location of the port in Umm Qasr.[52]

Following the conclusion of this meeting, Sir Kinahan Cornwallis, Newton's successor as the British Ambassador in Baghdad, was instructed on 24 July 1941 to send a preliminary communication to Iraq, which although to be couched in non-committal terms, was to make it clear that the project was being treated as a matter of urgent military necessity. The port was to be constructed under the orders of the British military authorities and for the course of the war it would remain under their control. Crucially, this communication was to avoid specifying who would control the port after the war in order to obtain Iraqi consent easily for the project by giving the Iraqis the impression that following the war they would have a ready-made port.[53] And indeed on 31 July 1941, when Cornwallis spoke to the Iraqi Minister for Foreign Affairs about the port, the latter welcomed the decision in the hope that Iraq might secure the port free of charge after the war.[54]

At London's instruction, the Political Agent in Kuwait made a similar approach to Sheikh Ahmed on 1 August 1941.[55] Yet as the Sheikh believed that any move to hand over the port to Iraq after the war would constitute an immediate threat to Kuwait and would endanger its territorial water rights, he therefore demanded that the port should be destroyed on the conclusion of the war. Sheikh Ahmed was however assured that his rights would be fully safeguarded both now and in any future arrangements for the disposal of the port following the war and that in no circumstances would Kuwait's sovereignty be infringed.

52. See the Minutes of a Meeting of the Middle East Official Sub-Committee, no. M.E. (O) (41), 3rd Meeting, 22 July 1941, FO 371/27106. See also Minutes by Baxter, no. E-3762/2687/93, 23 July 1941, FO 371/27106.
53. Foreign Office to Baghdad, no. 675, 24 July 1941, FO 371/27106.
54. Cornwallis to Foreign Office, no. 858, 31 July 1941, FO 371/27106.
55. Secretary of State for India to the Resident, no. 8791, 27 July 1941, FO 371/27106.

These assurances persuaded Sheikh Ahmed to give his formal approval to the project.[56]

At the same time the military authorities eventually selected a site for the proposed port. It was to be located directly south of Umm Qasr creek with the northern end of the proposed berth on the southern tip of creek. However, Cornwallis was convinced that this site lay within disputed territory. To avoid future problems, the Ambassador suggested, on 13 August 1941, that before a final decision was taken the exact position of the frontier in this area should be established by a demarcation commission as a matter of urgency.[57]

Once again the contentious issue of demarcation confronted the Foreign Office. Holding a series of inter-departmental discussions over the matter, the Foreign Office, though agreeing that it was essential for a demarcation commission to determine the exact position of the frontier in the Umm Qasr area, overruled the proposal for demarcation since the Iraqis had never showed any genuine interest in resolving the problem. Moreover, since the process of demarcation was a time-consuming matter it was impossible to tell the military authorities to delay starting work on the port until agreement had been reached on the position of the frontier. Accordingly, on 25 August 1941, Cornwallis was instructed to explore the possibility of building the port on an undisputed site in order to avoid any controversy.[58]

Upon receipt of this instruction, Cornwallis rather surprisingly amended his previous assessment of the location of the port by stating that the site was undoubtedly on the Iraqi side of the boundary line. The Ambassador's revised position followed a close examination of Newton's note of October 1940 on the demarcation line in relation to a new scale map produced by the British military authorities. He pointed out that if

---

56. Ruler of Kuwait to the Political Agent, no. R-6/1493, 5 August 1941, R/15/5/208. See also Political Agent to the Political Resident, no. C/184, 2 August 1941, R/15/5/208; Political Agent to the Ruler, no. C/427, 1 August 1941, R/15/5/208; Resident to the Secretary of State for India, no. T/394, 3 August 1941, FO 371/27106.

57. Cornwallis to Foreign Office, no. 924, 13 August 1941, FO 371/27106. See also C-in-C, India, to War Office, no. 11326/G, 18 August 1941, FO 371/27106.

58. Foreign Office to Baghdad, no. 821, 25 August 1941, FO 371/27106. See also Minutes by Crosthwaite and Beckett, no. E-4647/2687/93, 18 and 19 August 1941, FO 371/27106.

the definition of 1940 was adopted, it was possible that ships coming to Umm Qasr would have to pass through Kuwaiti territorial waters.[59] Crosthwaite of the Foreign Office was delighted to hear this as he believed that since Sheikh Ahmed had already approved the British proposals of 1940, the passage of ships through Kuwaiti waters did not represent an "infringement of the Sheikh's rights". However, the Foreign Office's legal adviser, William Beckett, advised him to be "cautious in case the view should turn out to be mistaken". Beckett was also of the opinion that ships coming up to Umm Qasr would have to use Koweiti national waters (i.e. the waters of the Khor as Subiyah as well as territorial waters (the waters of the Khor Abdullah) and as such the Sheikh would have the right to disallow the use of such national waters. He, therefore, recommended that either the Sheikh's objections be overruled or some agreement should be negotiated with him over the problem of passage.[60]

While the Foreign Office was considering ways to overcome the legal implications of the Umm Qasr port, the Commander-in-Chief, India, confirmed that the proposed site for the port was inside Iraqi territory. As the Government of India endorsed this view, it advocated the establishment of a joint Iraqi–Kuwaiti harbour board given that ships might have to pass through Kuwaiti waters.[61] The Foreign Office, however, did not consider this necessary since both the Sheikh and the Iraqis had already given Britain carte blanche authority to develop and administer the new port. Moreover, the military authorities, who would be responsible for the development of the port, "would regard a joint harbour board, with two such difficult partners to reconcile, as anything but a most unwelcome complication". As the military authorities preferred to run the port and its approaches themselves, it was important that Britain should do its utmost to resolve any difficulties existing between the Iraqis and the Sheikh. Therefore, the Foreign Office thought that Britain should make a renewed effort to achieve the demarcation of the frontier on the basis agreed with the Sheikh in 1940,

---

59. Cornwallis to Foreign Office, no. 1008, 31 August 1941, FO 371/27106.
60. Minutes by Crosthwaite and Beckett, no. E-5268/2687/93, 3–5 September 1941, FO 371/27106.
61. C-in-C, India, to the War Office, no. 13535/6, 20 September 1941, FO 371/27106.

and in order to persuade the Iraqis to participate in the process, they should be told that while it was impossible to say with certainty until the frontier line had been finally traced on the ground, it was the clear impression of all the British authorities concerned that the proposed site for the new port would turn out to be in Iraq. At the same time the Sheikh should be given "some general assurance that Britain would protect his rights including his rights in the territorial waters of Kuwait".[62] This, however, represented a departure from the Political Agent's assurance of 1 August 1941 to the Sheikh that: "Your Highness may rest assured that Your Highness's rights will be fully safeguarded, both now and in any arrangements for the disposal of the port."[63] Although Sheikh Ahmed got the impression from this assurance that the port would be dismantled after the war and not handed over to Iraq, Baxter wrote to Peel at the India Office, "You will, I am sure, agree with us in thinking that it is out of the question to give the Sheikh an assurance that the port will not be handed over to Iraq. Indeed, there seems no reason why any such assurance should be given."[64] Plainly, the Foreign Office was seriously considering handing over the port to Iraq after the war without even telling the Sheikh.

The India Office, however, held a completely different view on the postwar fate of the proposed port. Since it considered it impossible to demolish the port once it was "established as a going concern", the India Office felt it necessary to give the Iraqis as well as the Sheikh some idea about the status of the port after the war. Therefore, the India Office once again called for the establishment of a joint harbour board as a concrete step towards a solution of the problem, and urged the Foreign Office to make the necessary arrangements in consultation with Iraq and Kuwait before any fresh attempt to demarcate the frontier. In addition, the India Office was no longer prepared to proceed with the demarcation of border based on Newton's definition of October 1940 (which it should be remembered was itself largely derived from Cox's vague definition of 1923, which was in turn based upon Article 7 of the Anglo-Ottoman Convention of 1913).[65] The India Office's change of

62. Baxter to Peel, no. E-5957/2687/93, 8 October 1941, FO 371/27106.
63. Political Agent to the Ruler of Kuwait, no. C/427, 1 August 1941, FO 371/27106.
64. Baxter to Peel, no. E-5957/2687/93, 8 October 1941, FO 371/27106.
65. Peel to Baxter, no. 6373/41, 20 October 1941, FO 371/27106.

attitude resulted from fresh doubts expressed by the authorities in the Gulf on the selected site of the Umm Qasr port. Major Tom Hickinbotham, the new Political Agent in Kuwait, having visited Umm Qasr in September 1941, considered that the site for the proposed port was partially inside Kuwaiti territory. Endorsing this interpretation, Charles Prior, the Political Resident, strongly urged the amendment of Newton's definition which he considered to unduly favour Iraq:

> It is clear that the definition proposed in the Ambassador's Baghdad letter no. 487 of October 7th 1940 to the Minister for Foreign Affairs represented a concession to Iraq (since it drew a line from a point south of Safwan to the junction of the Khor Zubair and Khor Abdullah and not from 'just south of Um Qasr' to the Khor function) and as the Iraqi Government did not accept the proposed definition the Sheikh is presumably no longer bound by it.
>
> Sir Percy Cox's definition was admittedly based on Article no. 7 of the Anglo-Ottoman Convention of July 29th 1913 and by that the most easterly points are (a) the mouth of Khor Zubair and (b) a point 'immediately south of the place and wells of Um Qasr'. If this is shown to be more beneficial to Koweit the Sheikh would appear entitled to claim it.[66]

Prior's campaign for the revision of Newton's definition represented something of a dilemma at the Foreign Office, which had hitherto assumed that the proposed port would be indisputably within Iraqi territory. Now there was a strong possibility that part of the port might be inside Kuwaiti territory. If this proved to be the case, it would lead to "endless complications" and affect any eventual postwar settlement. As a result, the Foreign Office preferred to halt all further discussion on the matter until a fresh survey had been carried out in order to establish once and for all whether the port installations and land approaches would in fact fall wholly within Iraqi territory. Therefore, on 20 October 1941, Cornwallis was instructed to clear up as soon as possible any doubts regarding the location of the port in relation to the frontier and procure a reliable map of the area.[67]

Accordingly, in November 1941, Edward Wakefield, an officer of

66. Prior to the Secretary of State for India, no. 108, 4 October 1941, FO 371/27106.
67. Foreign Office to Baghdad, no. 1084, 20 October 1941, FO 371/27106.

the Indian Political Service, was sent to Kuwait on special duty to find out the exact position of the Safwan–Khor Abdullah section of the Iraq–Kuwait frontier. Wakefield produced a lengthy and lucid note on the subject which reinterpreted Article 7 of the Anglo-Ottoman Convention of 1913. On the map attached to the convention the Green Line ran east-south-east from Safwan to Umm Qasr and thence south-east following the line of the Khor. It was at this point that Wakefield discovered a number of errors in the boundary line as depicted in the map: firstly, the eastern bank of the Khor Zubair below Umm Qasr was shown as the western bank of the Khor Subiya; secondly, by a complementary error of shading below Umm Qasr indicating water; and thirdly, the Green Line as shown in the map below Umm Qasr did not merely join the Red Line but extended beyond it; to do so was absurd.[68]

Wakefield further added that both the Green Line as traced on the map accompanying the convention and the definition of the line included the text were ambiguous or obscure on two points. The first point was at the position of the boundary "immediately to the south of Umm Qasr and Safwan", and the second related to the location of the beginning of the boundary line "at the mouth of the Khor Zubair". In view of this ambiguity, Wakefield put forward his own interpretation of the northern frontier of Kuwait as envisaged in the agreement of 1913:

> It sometimes happens, especially in cases affecting boundaries, that logical and precise interpretation of the words of a definition leads to a conclusion which, from a broader aspect, appears strained and unnatural. In this case, however, careful examination and logical in-terpretation of the terms used in 1913 to define Kuwait's northern frontier suggest, and indeed prove, a boundary line which, so far from being forced or artificial, demonstrably constitutes the natural link between certain well-defined points. That boundary line runs (using the nomenclature employed by Lorimer) from the junction of the thalweg of Khor Abdullah with the thalweg of the Khor Sabiyeh along the thalweg of Khor-ath-Thaalab to the junction of the thalweg of Khor Zubair with the thalweg of the Khor Umm Qasr; thence in a straight line to a point to the south of, and imme-diately adjacent to, the walls of the fort at Umm Qasr; thence in a

---

68. See the note in the Safwan–Khor Abdullah section of the Iraq–Kuwait frontier by Wakefield in Hickinbotham to Prior, no. C/654-4/22, 4 December 1941, R/15/5/209.

straight line to a point to the south of, and immediately adjacent to, the walls of the fort at Safwan. (It is to be noted that the wells of Umm Qasr and Safwan are to be left to the north of the boundary). The condition does not affect the boundary line defined above since the wells at Umm Qasr are to the north of the Umm Qasr fort and the wells at Safwan are to the west of the Safwan fort.[69]

In accordance with this reinterpretation of the convention and contrary to the interpretation of 1940, Wakefield felt that the frontier should not run in a direct line from the point south of Safwan to the junction of the Khor Zubair with the Khor Abdullah. Therefore, if the interpretation of 1940 which had already been presented to the Iraqis was used to demarcate the frontier, the projected port at Umm Qasr would fall within Iraqi territory. However, if the full implications of the Green Line were accepted and applied correctly, the port would fall mainly within Kuwaiti territory. In other words, the terms of the 1940 formula had been far too generous to Iraq. It is to be remembered, however, that the expanded definition of 1940 was accepted by Sheikh Ahmed on the understanding that it constituted merely a reaffirmation, in a more detailed form, of the existing boundary.[70] If the Sheikh had realized that this expanded definition differed from the existing boundary (i.e. the boundary intended to be delineated by the Green Line), he obviously would not have assented to it. It should also be remembered that the Iraqis had neither accepted nor rejected the definition of 1940. But it is of prime importance to note that the Iraqi government had not been informed of the Sheikh's acceptance of it. On the contrary, they were told by the Ambassador that if they agreed to the proposals, he would "endeavour to obtain, through proper channel, the formal agreement of His Highness the Ruler of Kuwait". The Sheikh was not, therefore, committed to accept the expanded definition as Wakefield believed.[71]

Thus Wakefield's reinterpretation of the 1913 convention put Hickinbotham in an awkward situation, as its acceptance would mean the abandonment or at least the significant modification of the expanded definition of 1940.[72] Therefore, before making a final judgement he

---

69. *Ibid.*
70. *Ibid.*
71. *Ibid.*
72. Hickinbotham to Prior, no. C/654-4/22, 4 December 1941, R/15/5/209.

visited Umm Qasr and Safwan in order to investigate the matter for himself. Here he discovered that while the old interpretation of the frontier placed the actual "quay" which would be built in Umm Qasr within Iraqi territory, two-thirds of the port area would be in Kuwaiti. However, according to Wakefield's interpretation of the frontier the whole area would belong to Kuwait except the railway sidings which were to the north of the Khor Umm Qasr.[73] William Hay, the Officiating Political Resident, supported these views and argued that the 1940 formula presented to the Iraqi government had "somewhat compromised" Kuwait's position and sacrificed its interests. He therefore recommended that Newton's interpretation of 1940 be disregarded, which the British government could easily do as the formula had not yet been accepted by the Iraqi government. Hay then forcefully argued that until the frontier was demarcated nothing should be done to lead Iraq to believe that Britain recognized its right to the new port.[74]

However, the Resident's plea for a retreat from the position of 1940 was not acceptable to Cornwallis, who believed that Wakefield's thesis completely discarded Cox's interpretation, which had been approved by the British government after extensive consultation with all the departments concerned. Accordingly, he preferred that the definition of 1940 be maintained as it would be extremely difficult to persuade the Iraqis to accept a less favourable interpretation.[75] Given these differing opinions, London directed both Cornwallis and Hay to visit the area in question in order to establish whether all or part of the proposed port would be inside Kuwait if Britain adhered to the definition of 1940.[76] They did so on 25 February 1942. Although they still disagreed on the exact position of the frontier, they both accepted that the 1940 formula placed the docks of the port entirely inside Iraq while with Wakefield's interpretation they would fall entirely within Kuwait. They further agreed that the area planned for administration and labour camps would

73. Hickinbotham to J. A. Jameson (Anglo-Iranian Oil Company), unnumbered, 30 January 1942, R/15/5/209. See also Hickinbotham to Prior, no. C/219, 19 March 1942, R/15/5/209.
74. Hay to Amery, no. 181-S, 20 December 1941, R/15/5/209.
75. Cornwallis to Foreign Office, no. 151, 12 February 1942, FO 371/31369.
76. Foreign Office to Baghdad, no. 193, 16 February 1942, FO 371/31369. See also Secretary of State for India to the Resident, no. 794/42, 22 February 1942, FO 371/31369.

definitely fall within Kuwaiti territory. Under these circumstances, both Cornwallis and Hay jointly recommended that the entire port and military area should be administered by the British military authorities without any Iraqi or Kuwait participation, although they felt that neither government should be informed of this until the port had been developed.[77] However, to further complicate matters, Hay, following his visit to the site, concluded that the northern frontier of Kuwait as defined in the Anglo-Ottoman Convention of 1913 and in Cox's memorandum of 1923 was neither the line described by Newton in his communication of October 1940 nor the line mentioned in Wakefield's note, but was instead "something in between". He reached this conclusion after re-examining his records and the three main pronouncements on the issue – Lorimer's description of Kuwait's northern frontier, Article 7 of the Anglo-Ottoman Convention and Cox's definition – prior to the interpretation of 1940. As Newton's definition, which had still not been accepted by Iraq, significantly differed from these pronouncements and greatly favoured Iraq, Hay recommended that "it should be regarded as abrogated". In its place, he proposed a new line, to "run from the water's edge at the right bank of the Khor ath-Thaalab [Khor Zubair] at its southern extremity up to a point immediately south of Umm Qasr port". Hay suggested that the word "immediately" could be taken as indicating a distance of around 100 yards and the total distance from the water's edge at the right bank of the mouth of the Khor-ath-Thaalab to the Umm Qasr fort should be judged as not more than 3.2 kilometres. He believed that this line would run very close to the right bank of the Khor ath-Thaalab and would leave "'little else than the actual ships' berths in Iraq territory". In support of his recommendation he further argued:

> It is true that the effect of accepting the line I now propose in place of that defined in 1940 would only be to add to Kuwait territory a narrow wedge of desert but it so happens that at the broader end of this wedge there are a few square miles of land which will become extremely valuable when the Umm Qasr port develops, and I consider that our special relations towards Kuwait make it

---

77.   Cornwallis to Foreign Office, unnumbered, 25 February 1942, FO 371/31369.

150

incumbent on us to do nothing which will prejudice the Sheikh's claim to this land.[78]

However, the Foreign Office was not inclined to adopt such a position. In fact, Crosthwaite bitterly attacked Hay for his advocacy of Kuwait. He arrogantly maintained that it was completely "out of the question to agree to Hay's Umm Qasr line and abrogate the 1940 formula", which he still considered binding upon Britain, "both now and in the future, whether it is confirmed now or not, and that we feel strongly that if the Iraqis do raise the point with Sir Cornwallis, he must tell them that we stand by the formula".[79] Endorsing this pro-Iraqi position, Baxter wrote to the India Office on 5 May 1942 defending the 1940 interpretation:

> It was a statement of what His Majesty's Government thought to be a reasonable interpretation of the admittedly somewhat obscure definition by Sir Percy Cox, and it would be extremely embarrassing to us, and might be most damaging to our reputation for fair dealing, were His Majesty's Government now to seem to abandon the formula. You will remember that it was accepted at the time by the Government of India, the Political Resident and the Sheikh of Koweit. It is certainly incumbent upon His Majesty's Government to protect the interests of the Sheikh, because of their special relations with him, but, after all, His Majesty's Government have special relations with the Iraqi Government also, and you will appreciate that the argument that the exact line which the frontier is to follow has become of greater importance since 1940 cuts both ways. It makes it desirable for the Sheikh to establish that the frontiers of the Sheikhdom run as far north as possible, but it would also make it more difficult for us to induce the Iraqi Government to give up anything to which we told them in 1940 that they were entitled.[80]

In other words, Baxter was determined not to alter the 1940 formula, though it had been proven to be faulty. This, however, was not the position of the India Office, where Peel, who was already perturbed by the Foreign Office's pro-Iraqi leanings and its earlier refusal to give any

---

78. Hay to the Secretary of State for India, no. C/78, 10 March 1942, FO 371/31369.
79. Minute by Crosthwaite, no. E-2560/134/93, 29 April 1942, FO 371/31369.
80. Baxter to Peel, no. E-2637/134/93, 5 May 1942, FO 371/31369.

weight to Wakefield's findings on Umm Qasr,[81] deplored Baxter's hard-line opposition to Hay's proposed frontier line. Considering this to be the most reasonable and logical interpretation of the relevant passage of the 1913 agreement, Peel angrily wrote back to Baxter on 16 June:

> It will be clear . . . that we are in full agreement with Hay's con-clusion that the 1940 formula is too favourable to Iraq. While we admit that the formula was not an offer but a statement of H.M.G's views as to the interpretation of certain points in the 1923/32 definition, we cannot agree that we are in any way pre-cluded from revising our views if it can be shown that the decisions taken in 1940 were based on imperfect knowledge or inaccurate interpretation. Nor, in our opinion, is it wholly irrelevant that the Iraqi Government did not accept the 1940 proposals for frontier delimitation; at least it will surely be conceded that their non-acceptance has left H.M.G. in a freer position in relation to the formula than would otherwise be the case.[82]

Unlike the Foreign Office, the India Office felt that the British govern-ment was not legally bound to abide by the 1940 definition as the Iraqis had not even been informed of the Sheikh's acceptance of it. As the formula would require a substantial change in the frontier line in the Umm Qasr area as defined in the texts of 1913 and 1932, the India Office instead wished to proceed either with Hay's line or in fact with any new formula which would preserve the rights of the Sheikh.[83]

However, given this disagreement as to the exact position of the frontier line, the India Office agreed to defer discussion of it until after the war and to instead declare the entire port area at Umm Qasr as an exclusive military zone. This was to be administered by a British military governor with absolute police, judicial and financial powers (including authority over customs arrangements), with the Basra port authorities (Colonel Sir John Ward and his team) only assisting with the piloting of vessels and the lighting and buoying of the channel in the Khor Abdullah.[84] Despite the Iraqi Prime Minister's verbal agreement to this arrangement in April 1942, an Anglo-Iraqi dispute soon developed over

---

81. For Foreign Office's views on Wakefield's report, see Harold Caccia to Peel, no. E-1747/134/93, 30 March 1942, FO 371/31369.
82. Peel to Baxter, no. EXT-2359/42, 16 June 1942, FO 371/31369.
83. *Ibid.*
84. *Ibid.* See also Peel to Baxter, no. EXT-1833/42, 18 April 1942, FO 371/31369.

the administration of the port. This resulted from the Iraqi government's promulgation of a notice purporting to empower the Basra Port Directorate to impose harbour master's fees and other dues on all ships using the port of Umm Qasr and its approaches. This notification had been issued without any opposition from the British Embassy – in fact it had even received its "tacit concurrence" – but appeared without the knowledge of the other authorities in the Gulf.[85]

As soon as this notice was brought to the attention of Hickinbotham, he argued that the Iraqi port authorities at Basra had no legal right to levy any dues on vessels entering a port which did not belong to them nor had they any right to charge dues on vessels using the approaches to that port. Such fees could only be imposed by agreement with the Sheikh of Kuwait who had equal rights with Iraq in the Khor Abdullah. He therefore argued that if this notification be allowed to pass unchallenged it might well be produced in the future as evidence to support an Iraqi claim to all the navigable waters of the Khor Abdullah and even the Umm Qasr port itself. As a result, Hickinbotham demanded that the notification should be withdrawn forthwith.[86] Both the Residency and the Government of India agreed and recommended a strong protest against the notification on the grounds that it was not only contrary to the terms of the agreement by which the British military authorities were to administer the port but that it also ignored Kuwait's rights in the waters and prejudiced its position in the channel.[87] Nevertheless, the British Embassy in Baghdad declined to raise any objection to the Iraqi government, as it believed that Iraq's cooperation in Britain's war efforts would be seriously hampered if it did so. Moreover, if at this stage Britain challenged Iraq's right to issue a notification relating to the area, it might "give rise to profound suspicion on the part of the Iraqis as to the ultimate intentions" of Britain with regard to the

---

For more details on the administration of the Umm Qasr port, see: Foreign Office to Baghdad, no. 336, 20 March 1942, FO 371/31369; and Baghdad to Foreign Office, no. 357, 4 April 1942, FO 371/31369.

85. Extract from Iraqi Government Gazette, no. 24, 14 June 1942, quoted in Cornwallis to Foreign Office, no. 50/61/42, 25 August 1942, FO 371/31369.

86. Hickinbotham to Hay, no. 852, 4 September 1942, FO 371/31369.

87. Hay to Cornwallis, no. C/884, 9 September 1942, FO 371/31369. See also Government of India to the Secretary of State for India, no. 7183, 9 September 1942, FO 371/31369.

use of the port after the war. The Embassy instead suggested that Britain should ask the Iraqi government, on behalf of the Sheikh, for an assurance that the notification had been made without prejudice to any ultimate decision regarding the demarcation of the frontier and that it was merely issued as a matter of administrative convenience to permit the port director to carry out functions necessary to meet the wartime requirements of the British force.[88]

The Embassy's pro-Iraqi stance dismayed Prior. The Resident reminded London that Kuwait's interests must be preserved and Iraq should not be allowed to prejudice its claims to the Umm Qasr area.[89] The Government of India echoed these sentiments and urged Leonard Amery, the Secretary of State for India, to take immediate steps to protect Kuwait's position. Convinced by these arguments, Amery agreed that the Iraqi notification should in no way prejudice the rights and interests of Sheikh Ahmed.[90] The Foreign Office, which realized the Embassy's error in approving the notification without first consulting the Resident, joined the India Office in its opposition to the notification.[91] Therefore, on 10 December 1942, Cornwallis was instructed to address a written communication to the Iraqi government requesting them to withdraw the controversial notification, as this greatly prejudiced the Sheikh's rights in the port area given that half the waterway leading at least part of the way to Umm Qasr from the sea belonged to Kuwait. It was also to be made clear that the British military authorities, not the Iraqi port directorate, were solely responsible for levying charges on ships going to Umm Qasr.[92]

However, the Ambassador was of the opinion that the collection of dues would be more conveniently handled by the Basra Port Directorate, than by the military authorities.[93] He therefore proposed that as no written communication had yet been made with both Iraq

---

88. Thompson (Baghdad) to Anthony Eden, no. 290, 13 October 1942, FO 371/31369.
89. Prior to Amery, no. 2301, 10 November 1942, FO 371/31369.
90. Peel to the Under-Secretary of State (Foreign Office), no. EXT-6214/42, 20 November 1942, FO 371/31369.
91. Minute by Crosthwaite, no. E-6989/134/93, 5 December 1942, FO 371/31369.
92. Foreign Office to Baghdad, no. 1126, 10 December 1942, FO 371/31369. See also Foreign Office to Baghdad, no. 1127, 10 December 1942, FO 371/31369.
93. Baghdad to Foreign Office, no. 1262, 18 December 1942, FO 371/31369.

and Kuwait concerning the British military authorities' administration of the port, the Iraqi Prime Minister should be approached "unofficially" in person to arrange the cancellation of this notification. However, while the Foreign Office believed that this idea of achieving the cancellation of the notification without anything passing in writing would meet Britain's immediate requirements, it feared that if it continued "to keep off the record any mention of the fact that part of the port area is certainly in Koweit", it might create legal difficulties for any future negotiations on the port after the war.[94] Despite this concern, the Foreign Office, following lengthy correspondence with the India Office as well as with the other authorities in the Gulf, instructed Cornwallis on 16 March 1943 to proceed with a revised version of his proposed verbal communication. It now requested that such a communication should contain a reference to the fact that the Kuwaiti ruler was concerned in the collection of port dues at Umm Qasr and that the British army would collect the dues for the use of the waterway.

Consequently, on 4 May 1943, the Ambassador called on Nuri al-Said and asked him to withdraw the notification. The Prime Minister forcefully refused to do so arguing that its cancellation would constitute an abrogation of Iraqi sovereignty in Umm Qasr. He categorically declined to admit that Kuwait was in any way concerned in the matter. Nuri al-Said then proceeded to give a wholly inaccurate account of the origins of the Umm Qasr project, stating that it had been devised at a time when Iranian–Iraqi relations were strained and as such Iraq was desperately searching for an access to the sea which would be free from Iranian interference. Nuri al-Said's uncompromising attitude convinced Cornwallis that to pursue the issue further would resurrect the whole Iraqi–Kuwaiti border problem in such a way as to seriously disrupt Anglo-Iraqi relations. He therefore recommended that as a "matter of political expediency", Britain should end its attempt to secure the cancellation of the offending notification.[95]

The Foreign Office, which was convinced that Nuri al-Said refused to cancel the notification as this would entail an admission that the

---

94. See Minutes by Crosthwaite and Baxter, no. E-7418/134/93, 21 and 22 December 1942, FO 371/31369.
95. Cornwallis to Foreign Office, no. 409, 4 May 1943, FO 371/31369. See also Cornwallis to Eden, no. 167, 18 May 1943, FO 371/31369.

ownership of the port site was in doubt, was once again confronted with the whole vexed Iraqi–Kuwaiti frontier problem. After studying the history of the case of Umm Qasr, Raymond Etherington-Smith, the Superintending Under-Secretary of the Eastern Department, produced a note on the issue maintaining that in past discussions Britain had never said or even inferred to the Iraqis that the port was wholly in Iraq but rather that it was in disputed territory. In fact, he discovered that in 1938 Suwaidi, the then Iraqi Foreign Minister, had indicated that the construction of a port at Umm Qasr would involve the cession of Kuwaiti territory to Iraq. This clearly implied that the Iraqis had already accepted that all or at least part of the proposed site lay within Kuwait. Etherington-Smith believed that the Iraqis were now refusing to accept this reality because of the new interpretation of the frontier as envisaged in the 1940 formula.[96] As he himself – unlike his predecessor Crosthwaite, who, until March 1943, had dominated the formation of Foreign Office policy towards Iraq – held "considerable doubts as to the correctness of the 1940 interpretation" and the validity of the British case for supporting it,[97] he could not agree with Cornwallis's view that the question of the notification should be left in abeyance. Etherington-Smith pleaded:

> I feel we shall have to do something to reserve our position as regards the notification. If we do not take some precautionary measure of this kind we shall merely be storing up trouble for ourselves in the future, since we shall be doing precisely what the Iraqis are accusing us now of having done in the past viz. giving the impression that we think the port is in Iraq by admitting that the Iraqis have the right to levy dues there. We shall thus be providing the Iraqis with a foundation for their assertions. I do not think we should allow this matter to rest for too long and if we are going to put the suggested proposal to the Iraqis, we should do so soon. [98]

96. Minute by Etherington-Smith, no. E-3138/124/93, 7 June 1943, FO 371/31369. See also 'Note on discussions between 1938 and 1942 regarding the construction of a port on the Khor Zubair, with reference to the question of the Koweit–Iraq frontier' by Etherington-Smith, no. E-3138/124/93, 7 June 1943, FO 371/31369.
97. See Minute by Etherington-Smith, no. E-2628/128/93, 19 May 1943, FO 371/31369.
98. Minute by Etherington-Smith, no. E-3138/124/93, 7 June 1943, FO 371/31369.

Beckett, the Foreign Office's legal adviser, endorsed this view and recommended that the Iraqis should be immediately reminded that there had always been some disagreement about their boundary with Kuwait. Beckett also advised the British government to settle the issue by international arbitration after the war and that the frontier should then be delimited in accordance with the decision of the arbitration. Pending the result of such arbitration nothing should be done with regard to the port of Umm Qasr to "affect the question of where the frontier lies".[99]

As a result of Beckett's recommendation for international arbitration of the whole frontier question, Etherington-Smith attempted to pinpoint the position of Umm Qasr within the purview of the 1940 formula in order to once again highlight its inaccuracies. In a lengthy minute, he pointed out that the significant feature of 1940 interpretation was that it made the frontier "run in a straight line from Safwan to the confluence of the waterways, thereby passing more than two miles to the south of Umm Qasr". He therefore believed that it "went too far in favour of Iraq than the 1932 definition" in which the line ran "from Safwan to a point only just south of Umm Qasr and thence to the junction of the Khors". He observed that since the Iraqis had not yet accepted the formula of 1940, Britain was not in any way legally bound by it.[100] This criticism of the 1940 interpretation was a significant departure from the Foreign Office's previous firm support of it in the face of strong opposition from the Resident, the Government of India and the India Office.[101]

Etherington-Smith, who now dominated the policy-making body in the Eastern Department, showed no enthusiasm for Beckett's arbitration proposal as he believed that the Iraqis would simply reject it out of hand. In that case the whole frontier issue would flare up again

---

99. Minutes by Beckett in FO 371/31369. See also no. 2628/28/93, 20 May 1943, FO 371/31369.

100. See the Minute on Umm Qasr and the Iraq–Kuwait frontier by Etherington-Smith, no. E-3969, 19 June 1943, FO 371/34999.

101. Etherington-Smith's former colleagues Baggallay and Crosthwaite were largely responsible for the adoption of this pro-Iraqi formula. Pointing out their marked difference of opinion with Etherington-Smith, Beckett acknowledged the biased role played by these two former Foreign Office officials in upholding the 1940 formula. See Minute by Beckett, no. E-3969, 28 June 1943, FO 371/34999.

saddling Britain "with a first-class row with the Iraqis" just at a time when it was anxious to avoid friction. He therefore concluded that Britain should again press for the withdrawal of the notification permitting the Basra Port Directorate to collect dues on ships using the Umm Qasr port without committing itself to "an expression of opinion as to whether the maritime sites of the port is in Iraq or not".[102] The India Office, backed by both the Government of India and the Resident, agreed with Etherington-Smith's position and openly opposed the idea of referring the frontier issue to international arbitration without first making renewed efforts to reach agreement between Kuwait and Iraq on the basis of a new formula. But the India Office strongly felt that before taking any fresh initiative on the issue, it was essential for both itself and the Foreign Office to resolve their differences of opinion on the actual position of the frontier line.[103]

In response, the Foreign Office called an inter-departmental meeting on 17 August 1943 to take a final decision on the problem of Umm Qasr. Sir Maurice Peterson, the former British Ambassador to Iraq who was at that time attached to the Foreign Office, chaired the meeting. Representatives of the India Office (Peel and Lumby), the Foreign Office (Baxter, Hankey and Eyres), the Military Sub-Committee (Captain Gell), the Admiralty (Colonel Spraggett), the War Office (Major Howell), and also Colman, the new Director of Basra Port, were present at the meeting. Peterson opened the proceedings by explaining the background of the decision to establish a port at Umm Qasr in 1941 and the subsequent Iraqi attempt to collect dues and charges in respect of the port itself. The former Ambassador, who was mainly concerned with the long-term strategic aspect of the port (an important point that had been overlooked by all the studies on Umm Qasr) as opposed to the possible Iraqi–Kuwaiti dispute over its location, asked the committee to decide whether Britain itself would need Umm Qasr as a deep-sea port on the Gulf to serve its postwar strategic requirements in the region. Colonel Spraggett replied that it was impossible to accurately predict the

---

102. Minute by Etherington-Smith, no. E-3969/124/93, 19 June 1943, FO 371/34999.
103. Peel to Baxter, no. EXT-3716/43, 23 July 1943, FO 371/34999. See also Government of India (External Affairs Department), no. 5220, 30 June 1943, FO 371/34999.

strategic importance of the port in the postwar era as no study had been carried out to date on the subject. But he believed that the Umm Qasr port might be a valuable asset as a supply route in the event of any Russian expansionism. Captain Gell then drew the committee's attention to a possible Persian threat to the Shatt al-Arab, stating that if Persia itself or under the influence of a hostile power denied Britain the use of the waterway, then Umm Qasr would be the only alternative supply route. He therefore urged the continued presence of British troops there following the war. Peterson supported both these views and drew the committee's attention to the terms of the tripartite treaty of 29 January 1942, which had established an alliance between Britain, the USSR and Iran. According to the treaty the Anglo-Soviet forces which had been stationed in Tehran since August 1941, in order to open up full lines of communication with Russia in view of the German attack on the country, had to be withdrawn not later than six months after the end of the war. In that case Britain would have to organize the defence of the important oil installations in Persia from bases outside Persia. Therefore, Umm Qasr could be used as a base for the defence of Abadan. In addition, he also believed that if the British-dominated Basra Oil Company developed oilfields in southern Iraq after the war, Umm Qasr would be valuable as an outlet for their oil. The committee, therefore, under Peterson's direction, agreed that Britain itself should retain the port and seek treasury sanction for the completion of the work on the port after the war. It is to be noted that the port was originally planned to contain six berths of which at this time, the middle of 1943, only two together with accommodation for personnel and a rail link between Umm Qasr and Rafidiyah had been completed; in addition, the dock cranes and gear for six berths still remained incomplete. It was therefore decided that when the port became fully operational, both Kuwait and Iraq should be approached to lease to Britain such portions of their territory as was necessary. It was next agreed to send a formal communication to the Iraqis regarding their notification to the Basra Port Directorate to serve as a statement of Britain's opposition to it. The meeting was then brought to a close without, conveniently, taking any positive step towards the settlement of the frontier dispute.[104]

---

104. See the Minutes of a meeting held in Peterson's room, no. E-5122/124/93, 27 August 1943, FO 371/34999.

Following the meeting, the Foreign Office backed by the India Office, produced an instruction for the British Embassy in Baghdad. The instruction made it clear that in order to safeguard both the British and Kuwaiti positions, Britain's reservations over the principles contained in the notification should be communicated formally to the Iraqi government. The instruction read:

> . . . it would be unwise to allow the issue of the offending notification to pass without some formal reservation. By this notification the Iraqi Government have arrogated to themselves certain rights in the port of Um Qasr which His Majesty's Government do not necessarily admit they are entitled to exercise. It is not proposed at this stage to suggest that the frontier should be delimited, and the question of what means are open to His Majesty's Government to achieve a satisfactory settlement of the Koweiti–Iraqi dispute is still under consideration. But in order to safeguard the interests of the Sheikh of Kuwait it is essential that His Majesty's Government should not by their silence lay themselves open to the imputation of having acquiesced in the notification and the claims implied in it. I consider, therefore, that a note should be addressed to the Iraqi Government which, while not inviting any reply, should make it clear that no action taken by the Iraqi Government with regard to the port of Um Qasr can be held in anyway to prejudice the question of where the frontier lies.[105]

In other words, as even the Iraqi government was well aware of the fact that the port was not entirely within Iraqi territory, the Foreign Office could not agree to the unilateral Iraqi administration of the port and was therefore determined to safeguard the Kuwaiti interests which the Ambassador was willing to sacrifice. On 30 September 1943, this instruction was sent to Cornwallis for his opinion.[106] The Ambassador approved it without comment, and on 24 November 1943 it was communicated to the Iraqi government in the form of a "Note Verbale".[107] It is, however, difficult to say whether the Iraqis made any attempt to levy dues on the port following receipt of this note.

---

105. R. M. A. Hankey to Cornwallis, no. 200, 30 September 1943, FO 371/34999.
106. *Ibid*.
107. For the full text, see the 'Note Verbale' in British Embassy to the Iraqi Foreign Ministry, no. 515, 24 November 1943, FO 371/34999.

Meanwhile, in line with the inter-departmental meeting of August 1943, the War Office calculated that Britain had already spent almost £1,000,000 on developing Umm Qasr and that it would cost at least the same again to complete the job.[108] But the Foreign Office was unable to approach the Treasury for the additional funds unless the three service departments (the Admiralty, the War Office and the Air Ministry) provided it with a joint memorandum setting out their military reasons for the postwar operation of the port.[109] Yet the service departments could not do so until the Post Hostilities Planning Committee had reviewed Britain's overall postwar requirements in the whole of the Middle East.[110] Nevertheless, as the war reached its climax the British War Cabinet's Principal Administrative Officers' Committee recommended, after studying the position of the Umm Qasr port, its immediate dismantling for the following reasons: first, the dismantling of the port installations would release material and manpower, which could be used in other areas during the remainder of the war; second, the port did not possess any commercial value during the war and it was unlikely that it would be needed for the exportation of oil either from Kuwait or Iraq in the postwar period; third, as the port was located within disputed territory, its existence after the war would remain a bone of contention between Kuwait and Iraq; fourth, the postwar strategic value of the port was in serious doubt as after the war the heavy stores for the RAF in Iraq would be transported by sea via the Arabian Gulf and aircraft personnel and light stores would be flown in from Egypt; and finally, the completion of Umm Qasr as a six-berth port retained permanently in British hands would be a continuous economic burden for the exchequer.[111] As a result of these arguments the port was largely dismantled in late 1945, to the great relief of Sheikh Ahmed.

---

108. War Office to Foreign Office, no. 0178/1188, 19 September 1943, FO 371/34999.

109. Baxter to the Secretary of the Admiralty, no. E-5638/124/93, 14 October 1943, FO 371/34999. Similar communications were also made with the Air Ministry and the War Office; see *ibid.*

110. See Minutes by C. A. F. Dundas and Baxter, no. E-5438/5438/93, 11 September 1944, FO 371/40099.

111. See the Report on the proposed disposal of Umm Qasr installations by the Principal Administrative Officers' Committee, no. C. S. A.(45)54(O), 29 March 1945, FO 371/52454. See also G. C. B. Dodda (Admiralty) to I. P. Garran (Foreign Office), no. M-07855/43, 11 September 1946, FO 371/52454.

Conclusion

The end of the Second World War also marked the end of a decade of detailed British discussion of the complicated Iraqi–Kuwaiti frontier dispute. However, the Foreign Office made no serious attempt to solve the problem until Ambassador Newton advanced a new formula in 1940, following Edmond's thesis of 1937. The Foreign Office's long delay in taking the matter of demarcation seriously was due to its fear of an unfavourable Iraqi response to any approach as well as its serious differences with the India Office and the authorities in the Gulf (who were eager to safeguard the interests of the Sheikh of Kuwait) over the nodal point at Safwan. Negotiations to achieve a settlement were further delayed by the Iraqi desire for a port at Umm Qasr. While the Foreign Office declined to endorse the British Embassy's plea for the cession of the islands of Warba and Bubiyan to Iraq, it was inclined to allow Iraq the full control of the whole channel including a portion of the Kuwaiti mainland somewhere to the south of the Umm Qasr creek in return for financial compensation. As the absolute possession of the channel might well have encouraged the Iraqis to pursue a campaign to annex Kuwait, the authorities in the Gulf as well as the Sheikh resisted the move. Sheikh Ahmed's refusal to make any territorial concession either on land or sea totally disrupted Iraq's plans for Umm Qasr and forced Britain to revise Newton's demarcation formula before it was presented in 1940. Although the 1940 definition was much more favourable to the Iraqis, they still declined to demarcate the frontier unless the islands of Warba and Bubiyan were ceded to Iraq to enable it to have absolute control of the approaches to Umm Qasr.

The British military authorities' decision to build the port at Umm Qasr for their own wartime use once again raised the issue of demarcation. As the differences between the Foreign Office and the authorities in the Gulf, backed by the India Office, widened over the frontier line at Umm Qasr, it was decided to postpone discussions over the frontier until after the war and to declare Umm Qasr a British military zone in order to avoid any Iraqi–Kuwaiti struggle for its administration. Although the port was eventually built in disputed territory the Iraqis still attempted to collect dues on vessels using the approaches to the port and completely dismissed Kuwaiti rights in the channel.

As it was eventually decided that any postwar strategic value of the controversial port, which was considered minimal, was outweighed by its economic cost to the British Treasury, it was largely demolished after the war leaving the prickly frontier issue unresolved.

6

The Frontier Disputes and the Nodal Point South of Safwan, 1945–1955

Relations between Kuwait and Iraq continued to deteriorate throughout the decade following the Second World War. This period on the one hand witnessed an increase in Iraqi incursions into Kuwaiti territory while on the other it was complicated by both agricultural development in the frontier region and the looming possibility of oil being discovered in the disputed territory. As the British officials in the Gulf, the Sheikh of Kuwait and the oil companies wanted to settle the demarcation problem in light of these developments, the British government eventually presented its second demarcation proposal to the Iraqis in an attempt to define the exact position of the point south of Safwan, the crux of the problem. Iraq, however, reacted indifferently to the note and instead resurrected its demands for the cession of Warba in order to realize its long-cherished design on Umm Qasr.

Although the smuggling of goods from Kuwait to Iraq had been reduced considerably during the course of the Second World War due to the introduction of quota controls in Kuwait, the Iraqi frontier police continued their incursions into the Kuwaiti territory, particularly at Jahra (a place near the western extremes of Kuwait Bay), on the pretext of preventing smuggling from Riyadh. Tensions surrounding these frontier violations were heightened when Iraqi police cars penetrated Kuwaiti territory as far as Mutla (near Jahra) on three separate occasions in September 1944, to the obvious annoyance of Sheikh Ahmed. While Charles Prior, the Political Resident, dissuaded the Sheikh from taking any action which might result in a direct armed clash with the Iraqi police, he drew the attention of the British Embassy in Baghdad to the worsening situation.[1] But as Iraq took no action to check the incursions,

---

1. Prior to the Ambassador in Baghdad, no. T/620, 26 September 1944, FO 371/40104. See also Prior to the Ambassador in Baghdad, no. 621, 26 September 1944, FO 371/40104.

Gordon Jackson, the Political Agent in Kuwait, produced a detailed report in January 1945 on the activities of the Iraqi police in the Iraqi–Kuwaiti frontier region, which concluded that they were directly involved in the smuggling. Jackson discovered that once a week police cars from Safwan entered Jahra under the cover of darkness to rendezvous with smugglers on the Saudi border, from whom they received 50 per cent of the value of the goods to be smuggled into Iraq. By dawn, the police would be back at Safwan reporting to their superiors of their lack of success in intercepting smugglers.[2] As William Hogg, the Chargé d'Affaires in Baghdad, was convinced that the Iraqi government would not take any action against its own force, he secretly passed Jackson's report to Colonel Arthur Sargon, the British Inspector of the Iraqi Constabulary, Southern Area.[3]

Sargon, convinced of the "substantial truth" of the British allegations, visited the Iraqi–Kuwaiti frontier zone on 2 June 1945. During his visit, he asked Major Maurice Tandy, Jackson's successor, that in the event of any future incursion he should be immediately cabled via the British Consul-General in Basra in order to improve his chances of detecting the culprits. Neither Tandy nor Colonel Arnold Galloway, the Officiating Resident, found any objection to this request. Sargon also suggested that the frontier points be marked from the area of Khidha al-Ma to that of Umm Qasr by signboards or piles of stones so that the Iraqi police could be given strict orders not to patrol to the south of them. This, however, was not acceptable either to Tandy or Galloway as they were keen to avoid any action which, at some stage in the future, might further complicate the demarcation of the frontier. Galloway was convinced that Sargon's unofficial visit to Kuwait would help prevent further incursions, thereby improving relations between Iraq and Kuwait.[4]

Contrary to this expectation, relations between the two countries soon deteriorated further when in 1945 the Iraqi government introduced visa restrictions on Kuwaitis entering Iraq. Although widely resented throughout the Sheikhdom, Kuwait did not impose similar

2. See the Note on Iraqi police incursions in Kuwaiti territory in Jackson to Prior, no. C/33, 14 January 1945, FO 371/45186. See also *PGAR* (1942), vol. X, p. 9.
3. Hogg to Prior, no. 354/7/45, 4 April 1945, FO 371/45186.
4. Tandy to Prior, no. C/528, 6 June 1945, FO 371/45186. See also Galloway to the Ambassador in Baghdad, no. 9(A), 27 June 1945, FO 371/45186.

restrictions on Iraqis. Relations continued to worsen when, on 27 October 1945, Sheikh Muhammad bin Ahmed, the second son of the Kuwaiti ruler, and his party were fired upon by an Iraqi police patrol while on a hawking expedition near Basra, seriously wounding the Sheikh and killing one of his guides. However, as the Mutassarrif of Basra expressed his regret to Sheikh Ahmed and agreed to punish the policemen involved, the Sheikh made no official protest.

By mid-1946, the frontier violations became even more threatening with plain-clothed Iraqi policemen in armed cars penetrating, almost daily, deep inside Kuwaiti territory often to a distance of around 50 kilometres, confiscating tea, sugar and cloth from travellers and Bedouins irrespective of the legitimacy of the goods. To check these increasingly violent and indiscriminate acts, Tandy accompanied by Sheikh Abdullah Mubarak, the Kuwaiti Chief of Public Security, toured the frontier zone in June 1946 to gather information to forward to Colonel Sargon. At the same time, Lieutenant Colonel William Hay, the Resident since May 1946, brought the violations to the attention of Sir Francis Stonehewer-Bird, the British Ambassador to Iraq.[5] Surprisingly, the Ambassador declined to raise the subject with the Iraqis which he justified by arguing, "a totally unmarked desert frontier is always liable to be violated by both sides." Moreover, in a communication to Sir Ernest Bevin, the Foreign Secretary, Stonehewer-Bird anticipated that, following a protest, the Iraqis would defend their actions by simply arguing that given the persistent smuggling their police have little option but to inadvertently cross the frontier at times.[6]

However, as the frontier violations intensified, the campaign for the annexation of Kuwait was resumed, most notably by Sabri Abdul-Qadir al-Hashemi, a retired army captain. In a long article in the Iraqi newspaper *al-Baath al-Qawmi* on 20 May 1946, he made an impassioned plea for the merger of the two countries. He argued, somewhat emotively:

> . . . the incorporation of this country [Kuwait] in the Kingdom of Iraq is essential and inevitable for many reasons. Kuwait is one of ⟨

---

5. Hay to Stonehewer-Bird, no. C/306, 18 June 1946, FO 371/52454. See also Tandy to Hay, no. 390, 16 June 1946, FO 371/52454.
6. Stonehewer-Bird to Bevin, no. 329, 21 August 1946, FO 371/52454.

the districts of Basrah province and has no boundaries dividing her from Iraq except the colonial boundaries separating brother from brother. The continuation of Kuwait under British protection is a military threat to Iraq. How can a country like Kuwait maintain her existence in present world currents unless (God Forbid!) she decides to remain under British protection forever thereby forgetting Arab sentiment and also the presence in Iraq of the many properties and possessions which belong to the Amir of Kuwait in the Basrah province. All these are crushing arguments in the hands of the Iraqi negotiator.[7]

These "crushing arguments", however, lacked any bases in fact, as Kuwait had never been a district of Basra province, and its boundaries with Iraq had been defined by the Anglo-Kuwaiti exchange of notes in 1923, which the Iraqis themselves later confirmed. Indeed, if one follows the logic of al-Hashimi's arguments then the Kuwaiti Sheikh should have laid claim to Basra in view of his proprietary rights there. Despite these flaws in his arguments, al-Hashimi did make the point to the Iraqi government that the question of a merger should be raised during the negotiations with the British government for the revision of the Anglo-Iraqi Treaty of 1932. He believed this to be imminent, following the declaration in May 1946 by Tawfiq Suwaidi (who had become Prime Minister the previous February) in the Chamber of Deputies that the revision of the treaty was one of his government's priorities. Al-Hashimi warned the government to keep its promise.

Although the Sheikh resented the publication of this "extremely inaccurate" article as well as the incursions into his territory, he neither took any retaliatory action nor pressed the British authorities to protest to the Iraqis. The Resident attributed the Sheikh's silence to his fear that if he was seen to rely too heavily on British support there would be an adverse reaction in the Arab world. Moreover, the Iraqi claim to Kuwait, as put forward by al-Hashimi's article, might attract more supporters if he made himself "a nuisance" to the Iraqi government.[8] Therefore, as

---

7. See Sabri Abdul-Qadir al-Hashemi, 'When will the district of Kuwait return to the Basrah province', *al-Baath al-Qawmi*, 20 May 1946. See also Enclosure in Hay to F. W. Pethick-Lawrence (Secretary of State for India), no. C/514, 22 July 1946, FO 371/52454.
8. Hay to Pethick-Lawrence, no. C/514, 22 July 1946, FO 371/52454.

both the Sheikh and the British authorities in Baghdad were unwilling to take any action against the Iraqis, the incursions into Kuwait continued unabated, and their visa regulations on Kuwaitis remained in force. However, when in April 1947 an Iraqi patrol force disarmed the Rashaida Bedouins who were encamped to the south-west of Umm Nigga, a place about 13 kilometres inside Kuwaiti territory, the British Embassy made a strong representation to the Iraqi government, but this brought nothing more than the usual denial.[9]

While the violations continued unchecked, the frontier zone was undergoing significant change with Iraqi agricultural developments, including the digging of a number of additional wells and the plantation of palm groves, taking place to the south of Safwan. Prior, who had witnessed this development first hand while travelling from Basra to Kuwait, was concerned that the phrase "the most southerly palm in Safwan" (that had been coined by the Geographical Section of the War Office in mid-1939 and incorporated into the interpretation of 1940) would soon bear an entirely different meaning in the light of this considerable agricultural activity. Moreover, he was convinced that this undemarcated area would soon be of great economic importance if the area west of Jabal Sanam, where a geological survey party had been working, proved to contain oil. He therefore considered it essential to demarcate the frontier before Iraq and Kuwait entered into a new struggle for oil.[10] Ambassador Stonehewer-Bird fully supported Prior's analysis and urged the Eastern Department of the Foreign Office to re-examine the whole question of demarcation before the existence of oil-bearing deposits made matters even more complicated than they were already.[11] The Foreign Office, after consulting with the Ministry of Fuel and Power, was instead of the view that the discovery of oil deposits in the vicinity would not present a source of future conflict and that in any case the results of APOC's surveys in Kuwait had not up until then shown any sign of oil close to the boundary. Moreover, given that even the Foreign Office and the India Office could still not agree on how best to resolve the demarcation of the border,[12] the Ambassador was told in

---

9. See *PGAR* (1947), vol X, p. 6.
10. Prior to Retaxandum (London), no. 476-S, 21 April 1946, R/15/5/185.
11. Stonehewer-Bird to T. Wikely (Eastern Department, Foreign Office), no. 928/4/46, 27 June 1946, FO 371/52454.
12. Minute by G. W. Baka, no. E-6228/4008/91, 13 July 1946, FO 371/53454.

no uncertain terms that at the present time London preferred to let the matter lie for as long as was possible. On 9 December 1946, Baxter communicated this decision to Stonehewer-Bird:

> In the circumstances we are inclined not to take the initiative at the present moment in seeking to promote a settlement between the conflicting views of Iraq and Koweit, but rather to let sleeping dogs lie as long as they are prepared to go on doing so. His Majesty's Government are, as you know, morally and legally bound to safeguard the rights of the Sheikh of Koweit, and we think it would be [wrong] to give any encouragement to Iraq to revive claims with which we might be unable to sympathize.[13]

To let sleeping dogs lie was not the position of the British in the Gulf. In the following June, Tandy concluded that although both the Iraq Petroleum Company (IPC) and the Kuwait Oil Company (KOC) were fully occupied in developing promising oilfields at some distance from the disputed area, it was possible that when these fields were brought into full production the companies might then take an active interest in the frontier zone. The Agent was convinced that the demarcation would "proceed more smoothly now when the area is not considered vitally important from an oil point of view than at some later date when the position may have changed". He therefore concluded that it was an opportune time to seek Iraqi agreement to demarcate the frontier, which they had consistently refused to do in the hope that they might be able at some future date to "annex part or all of Kuwait should British influence in the Middle East and British support for the Sheikh of Kuwait decrease as a result of developments elsewhere".[14] However, despite the fact that British influence was diminishing in other parts of the Middle East, particularly in Egypt following demands for the revision of the Anglo-Egyptian Treaty of 1936,[15] there was no sign of any decrease in British influence in the Gulf in general and in Kuwait in particular. If, as Tandy predicted, the Iraqis followed the Egyptian example and pressed

---

13. Baxter to Stonehewer-Bird, no. E-9194/4008/91, 9 December 1946, FO 371/53454.
14. Tandy to Repgu (Bahrain), no. C/444, 16 June 1947, L/P&S/12/3737. See also FO 371/61445.
15. For the full text of the Anglo-Egyptian Treaty of 1936, see *Treaty Series no. 6*, Cmd. 5360 (London, HMSO, 1937), pp. 3–29.

the Egyptians for the revision of their treaty with Britain, any agreement to do so should be entirely "conditional upon a satisfactory demarcation of the Kuwait–Iraq frontier".[16]

Tandy's assessment of the demarcation problem was accepted by the Resident without reservation.[17] On raising the matter with the India Office during his visit to London in July 1947, Hay argued that nothing would be achieved by further delaying demarcation. Convinced by these arguments, the India Office eventually agreed to again take up the issue with the Foreign Office. The following four key factors compelled the India Office to become more active in its efforts to secure a settlement of the frontier question: first, Iraqi incursions into Kuwaiti territory were still taking place; second, the Umm Qasr port project, although seemingly dormant for the time being, was considered unlikely to complicate demarcation work; third, it would be more difficult to obtain a just settlement for Kuwait after the prevailing Anglo-Iraqi Treaty had been revised; and finally, as oil had yet to be discovered near the disputed border area, it was desirable to have a demarcated frontier before any oil explorations began in earnest there.[18]

However, when the India Office referred the matter, the Foreign Office declined to make the revision of the Anglo-Iraqi Treaty of 1932 conditional on the satisfactory demarcation of the Iraqi–Kuwaiti frontier as advocated by Tandy. The Foreign Office felt strongly that if the British government was to reach agreement on the frontier issue without resort to international arbitration it was pointless to approach the Iraqis with a formula less favourable than that already put to them in 1940. Despite its serious faults, the Foreign Office still saw the "straight line formula" of 1940 as the approach most likely to secure agreement with Iraq.[19] The India Office on the other hand was still firmly opposed to this interpretation as it would strip the Sheikh of Kuwait of the

---

16. Tandy to Repgu (Bahrain), no. C/444, 16 June 1947, L/P&S/12/3737. See also FO 371/61445.
17. Hay to the Secretary of State for India, no. 1213-S, 23 June 1947, FO 371/61445.
18. See Note on Kuwait–Iraq frontier by G. W. Rendel, unnumbered, 30 August 1947, L/P&S/12/3737.
19. See Minute by L. F. L. Pyman, no. E-5792, 14 July 1947, FO 371/61445. See also Pyman to F. A. K. Harrison (India Office), no. E-5792/993/91, 7 August 1947, FO 371/61445.

ownership of the site of the fort at Umm Qasr. As a result, it considered arbitration a way to achieve an agreed frontier between the two countries, as it would then enable the British government to present a case more favourable to the Sheikh than had been provided by Wakefield's report. Moreover, the decision of the arbitrator would be given international legitimacy by its registration with the United Nations. Convinced of the merits of this approach, the India Office, on 18 September 1947, canvassed the support of Arnold Galloway, the Officiating Political Resident in the Gulf during Hay's absence.[20] As Galloway also believed the 1940 formula to be too generous to Iraq in the Umm Qasr sector, he suggested that any direct negotiations would be pointless given the ever-present possibility of the Iraqi demand for full control of the Khor Abdullah waterway, and perhaps even for the islands of Bubiyan and Warba. He therefore fully approved of the idea of arbitration subject to obtaining in advance an undertaking from the Sheikh to abide by the arbitrator's decision.[21]

However, Hay, who resumed his duties in October 1947, thought that international arbitration should be used only as a last resort. Instead, another attempt should be made to demarcate the frontier as long as the Iraqis first pledged to take the matter seriously. If they agreed to do so the British government should present them with a large-scale map showing the line it claimed on behalf of Kuwait under the definition of the frontier as reaffirmed by the Iraqi Prime Minister to the British High Commissioner in Iraq in 1932. In other words, the Resident wanted any negotiations to be based upon the 1932 definition.[22] This proposal was broadly acceptable to the Commonwealth Relations Office (which on 1 April 1947 assumed responsibility for the administration of the Residency and the Agencies in the Gulf as an interim measure until these passed into the hands of the Foreign Office scheduled for 1 April 1948).[23] It felt that it was necessary to decide on

---

20. Harrison to Galloway, no. 1699/47, 18 September 1947, FO 371/61445.
21. Galloway to Harrison, no. 1725-S, 4 October 1947, FO 371/61445.
22. Hay to E. P. Donaldson (Commonwealth Relations Office), no. 2021-S, 26 November 1947, FO 371/61445.
23. Faced with the inevitability of the independence of India, the British Cabinet decided in January 1947 to merge the India Office with the Commonwealth Relations Office. For the restructuring of responsibility in the Gulf see *PGHS*, vol. II, p. 2.

an interpretation of the 1932 definition of the frontier that would be both fair to the Sheikh and which would form the basis for any further negotiations with Iraq. Therefore, on 14 January 1948 the Commonwealth Relations Office asked the Foreign Office to put aside the 1940 formula as it provided an interpretation which would be unjust to Kuwait. It also reminded the Foreign Office that as it would assume responsibility for the conduct of British relations with Kuwait and other Gulf states in less than three months, it would soon be up to the Foreign Secretary as opposed to anyone else to protect the Sheikh's interests.[24] The Foreign Office, however, was unwilling to revise the 1940 definition of the frontier.

Although the Foreign Office had wanted to delay the opening of negotiations on the frontier, the matter soon surfaced when on 22 January 1948 Stephen Longrigg, the representative of IPC, requested permission to use Umm Qasr as a port for oil tankers in the event of oil being discovered in the Basra area.[25] As Longrigg wanted to know the exact position of Umm Qasr the Foreign Office reluctantly agreed to re-examine the issue once again and decided to proceed with the problem based on a memorandum prepared by its Research Department. In tracing the history of the boundary dispute between Kuwait and Iraq in the light of the different interpretations of the various agreements, the memorandum identified the following three major disputed points: first, at the junction of the Khor Zubair with the Khor Abdullah. The 1947 War Office map showed the Khor ath-Thaalab or the Khor Abdullah extending as far north as the Khor Umm Qasr. This justified the interpretation of the delimitation agreements that the junction point of the Khor Zubair and the Khor Abdullah was intended to be at the junction point of the Khor Zubair with the Khor Shetana, a small arm of the Khor Abdullah which merged into the main channel just north of Umm Qasr. Southwards of this point the main channel was properly called either the Khor ath-Thaalab or the Khor Abdullah. If the agreement had intended this point to be at the mouth of the Khor Zubair (which is just south of Umm Qasr) then the boundary from

---

24. Donaldson to Burrows (Foreign Office), no. EXT. 2750/47, 14 January 1948, FO 371/68346.
25. Stephen Longrigg to Donaldson, unnumbered, 22 January 1948, L/P&S/12/3737.

there to the point just south of Umm Qasr would go in a south-westerly and not a north-westerly direction as stated in the agreement. Moreover, the bend south of Umm Qasr on the Green Line on the map accompanying the agreement, "to which Kuwait partisans attach so much importance completely contradicts this view, since had the view been correct, it would have bent in a north-easterly direction at Umm Qasr". As in 1923 the Sheikh of Kuwait had claimed that it "goes south of the wells of Safwan, Jabal Sanam and Umm Qasr to the shore of the islands of Bubiyan and Warbah", it was evident that all the parties concerned subscribed to the view that the point intended in the agreement was at "the junction of the Khor Zubair with the Khor Shetana at the point at which the Khor as Sabiya also joins them near Warbah island". As the Political Resident in 1940 had agreed to this point, the memorandum concluded that there should be no further dispute over this point.[26]

The second disputed point highlighted by the memorandum was the location of the point "south of Safwan". The memorandum stated that various arguments had been forwarded for placing the point anywhere from within 100 yards (the 1913 agreement says immediately south") to "a mile south of the most southerly palm tree". Moreover, the 1940 definition referred to a notice-board which for many years had been accepted as indicating the location of the frontier at this point. The board was however removed by the Iraqi police in 1939 and when a new post was placed in position by the Political Agent of Kuwait in the presence of the Sheikh, the Iraqis removed it again. The Iraqis justified their actions by arguing that the party had erected the notice-board some 250 metres within Iraqi territory and were short of the Safwan post by 1,000 metres. Thus, although there was a difference of opinion between the two countries over the exact position of the post, the difference amounted to only 250 metres; and indeed, by implication, the Iraqi government was committed to a statement that the frontier was 1,250 metres from the Safwan post, that is 250 metres inside Iraqi territory. Therefore, the disagreement over the location of this point was in reality very slight.[27]

---

26. See 'The Iraq–Kuwait Frontier (Umm Qasr)', Memorandum by Foreign Office's Research Department, no. E-2464, January 1948, FO 371/68346.
27. *Ibid.*

The last disputed point identified by the memorandum was the route of the frontier between Safwan and the sea, which it considered "the crux of the dispute". Although the 1940 note to the Iraqi government described it as a straight line, "the 1913 agreement clearly intended the frontier to follow a line from south of Safwan to south of Umm Qasr and thence bend in a more southerly direction until it reached the junction of the Khors [the Khor Zubair, the Khor Shetana and the Khor Subiya]." The point assumed great importance when, during the war, a port was partially developed by the British military authorities at Umm Qasr to serve as an alternative to Basra (see the previous chapter). Although the port was dismantled shortly after the war, the memorandum concluded that as Umm Qasr provided the only possible site other than Basra for an Iraqi port, the Iraqis could not "be expected easily to abandon their hopes of developing it".[28]

In conclusion, the memorandum stated that the Anglo-Ottoman Convention of 1913 was irrelevant as it had never been ratified. Therefore, it considered the 1923 and 1932 agreements as the only valid documents from which to derive the frontier and claimed that the 1940 interpretation of them was accurate. As the British government was in any case morally committed to this definition, the memorandum advocated that the demarcation of the boundary be based upon it.[29] However, before taking any practical steps towards this end the Foreign Office wanted to first solve the question of the distances "south of Safwan" and "south of Umm Qasr", which was assumed to be "one mile or the same distance as south of Safwan".[30] When William Beckett, the Foreign Office's legal adviser, was consulted on 2 April 1948, he stated that in his opinion there was no legal basis for observing that "south of Umm Qasr" could be interpreted from the 1923 text to be one mile south of Umm Qasr, i.e. equal to the distance allowed in interpreting the term "south of Safwan". In other words, Beckett accepted the 1940 formula as a "natural interpretation of the 1923 agreement".[31]

With the Foreign Office involved in this lengthy re-examination of the demarcation problem, Stephen Longrigg began to lose his patience.

---

28. *Ibid.*
29. *Ibid.*
30. Minute by Thomas, no. E-2464, 24 February 1948, FO 371/68346.
31. See Minute by Beckett, unnumbered, 2 April 1948, FO 371/68346.

In a letter to the Foreign Office dated 19 April 1948, he stressed the importance of demarcating the Iraq–Kuwait frontier at Umm Qasr in view of his company's interest in using it as an oil-loading port.[32] In addition, Colonel Johnson, the Director-General of Ports and Navigation in Basra, pressed the British Consul-General in Basra for an early demarcation of the frontier as he was giving serious thought to the idea of developing port facilities at Umm Qasr. The Sheikh of Kuwait also wanted the frontier fixed as he planned to build frontier posts in order to put a stop to smuggling and the disturbances in the frontier zone.[33] The Sheikh's eagerness for an early demarcation convinced R. A. Thomas of the Eastern Department that the British government would be able to obtain his consent to negotiate on the basis of the 1940 definition.[34] Pyman agreed and argued that the Political Resident should be directed to secure the Sheikh's approval for such an approach to the Iraqi government. As there was general agreement amongst Foreign Office officials to this proposal,[35] Hay was told on 6 July 1948 that the 1940 formula was the only possible basis with which the British government could go to the Iraqis. He was also reminded that not only had this formula already been accepted by Kuwait but, crucially, had already been communicated to Iraq, which, in practice, made it impossible for the British government to put forward for negotiation another formula more favourable to Kuwait. In any case, the Foreign Office argued that this interpretation which provided the straight line from south of Safwan to the junction of the Khor Abdullah and the Khor Zubair leaving Umm Qasr and Jabal Sanam to the north of it, was a logical interpretation of the 1923 agreement and the 1932 letter.

The Resident reluctantly accepted the decision, but was still convinced that the junction of the Khor Zubair with the Khor Abdullah – the crux of the whole problem – was immediately south of Umm Qasr. However, as the mention of the "Khor Shetana" in the 1940

32. Longrigg to the Under-Secretary of State for Foreign Affairs, no. E-4911, 19 April 1948, FO 371/68346.
33. British Embassy in Baghdad to the Eastern Department, no. 367/4/48, 20 March 1948, FO 371/68346. See also Hay to Burrows, no. 21(53/67), 22 April 1948, FO 371/68346.
34. See Minute by Thomas, no. E-5444, 30 April 1948, FO 371/68346.
35. Minute by Pyman, no. E-5444, 22 June 1948, FO 371/68346. See also Minute by Evans, 28 June 1948, FO 371/68346.

communication to Iraq would make it difficult to claim this now, Hay advocated the adoption of the interpretation of the straight line formula of 1940 that was most favourable to Kuwait; he advised that the Sheikh's approval to it be secured prior to the convening of negotiations with Iraq.[36] Although the Foreign Office agreed to the latter proposal, it declined to accept the Resident's interpretation of the location of the two Khors. On 6 August 1948, the Foreign Office instructed Galloway, the Acting Resident (in Hay's absence), to take the matter up with Sheikh Ahmed to find out his opinion of the line as envisaged in the 1940 formula.[37] Later, however, the Foreign Office instructed Hay to take a more determined approach by merely showing the Sheikh a large-scale map with the line marked on it and obtaining his consent there and then and to approach the Iraqis on that basis.

Surprisingly, the Resident took more than twenty months to carry out the instruction; he blamed this unusually long delay on the frequent changes of incumbency at the Agency in Kuwait and to extensive correspondence with the successive Political Agents regarding the exact position of the frontier at Safwan, as defined by the 1940 formula, on the map that was to be shown to the Sheikh of Kuwait.[38] Therefore, it was not until 30 March 1950 that J. Gethin, the Acting Political Agent, showed the line (running 1.6 kilometres from the south of Safwan on the map) to Sheikh Abdullah bin Salem Mubarak al-Sabah, who had become the Ruler of Kuwait following the death of his cousin, Sheikh Ahmed, in January 1950. The Sheikh accepted the proposal in principle and emphasized the need of an early demarcation of the frontier in view of the continuing Iraqi incursions into his territory and the attacks on KOC personnel.[39] The following day, however, the Sheikh declared that

---

36. Hay to Pyman, no. 119(53/570), 21 July 1948, FO 371/68346.
37. R. A. Clinton Thomas (Foreign Office) to Galloway, no. E-10093/700/91, 6 August 1948, FO 371/68346. See also Minute by F. C. Waddams, no. F-10093, 1 August 1948, FO 371/68346.
38. Hay to G. W. Furlonge (Foreign Office), no. 173/18/50, 10 April 1950, FO 371/68346; Hay to the Political Agent, Kuwait, no. 4, 4 January 1949, FO 1016/7. See also Political Agent to Prodrome (Bahrain), no. C/52, 22 March 1949, FO 1016/7; Hay to G. N. Jackson (Political Agent, Kuwait), no. 21/3/49, 10 April 1949, FO 1016/7; Hay to H. G. Jakins, no. 773/5/50, 16 January 1950, FO 1016/118; Jakins to Hay, no. 75/3/50, 19 February 1950, FO 1016/27; and Hay to Jakins, no. 173/14/50, 10 March 1950, FO 1016/118.
39. It is to be remembered that the Iraqi police had continuously violated the

the point was less than 1.6 kilometres away from Safwan. Gethin supported this assessment as the term "one mile south of Safwan" had been based on Dickson's assertion that the large notice-board existing in 1935 was at a point 1.6 kilometres south of Safwan – a distance Dickson himself later disputed and considered as unreliable. After paying several visits to the area and after consulting Harold Dickson (now in the employ of KOC), Gethin provided further reasons to support the Sheikh's position and put forward his own definition of the location of the frontier at Safwan:

> The definition [Dickson's formula] has however never been communicated to the Iraqis. It appears to be faulty, and I would submit that it would be a mistake to cling to it, a) because it appears that the present Ruler will in fact question it, b) because I see no reason to present Iraq with a strip of territory 300 yards or more wide along the whole frontier unless it is certain they are entitled to it, c) because we can be sure that the Iraqis will dispute whatever we say, and it would surely be better to go in on their own definition as implied in their Note of 1940, rather than on a definition less favourable to Kuwait based on the single unsupported statement of a Political Agent fifteen years ago. I would suggest we should determine the point as being about 1250 metres south of the well,

---

frontier since 1944. By the beginning of 1950 these violations took a serious turn when a contingent of the Iraqi army forced a party of the Kuwait Oil Company to stop its drilling for water at a site near Kashm al-Adhaim, more than three kilometres east of the eastern ridge of the Batin (i.e. over three kilometres inside Kuwaiti territory). In the same month Iraqi armed vehicles entered the northern part of the Sheikh's territory to prevent the drilling operation of another KOC party. Despite British protests against these incidents, no effective measures were taken by the Iraqi government as it denied the allegations. For more details on frontier incursions, see the Note on Iraqi police incursions in Kuwait territory in Jackson to Charles Prior (Political Resident), no. C/33, 14 January 1945, FO 371/45186; Tandy to Prior, no. C/528, 6 June 1945, FO 371/45186; Tandy to Hay, no. 204, 9 March 1948, FO 371/68346; Jakins to Foreign Office, no. 7, 9 January 1950, FO 371/82038; Jakins to Foreign Office, no. 8, 9 January 1950, FO 371/82038; Note Verbales from British Embassy, Baghdad, to the Iraqi Ministry of Foreign Affairs, no. 33 and no. 211, 17 January and 19 April 1950, respectively, FO 371/82038; Consulate General, Basra, to the British Embassy, Baghdad, no. 5/7/14-C, 26 April 1950, FO 1016/27; and the Iraqi Ministry of Foreign Affairs to the British Embassy, Baghdad, no. 686/7/8601, 9 May 1950, FO 1016/27.

although it should then be defined as being at such and such a distance from the corner of the Customs compound.[40]

Cornelius Pelly, the Acting Resident, neither accepted nor rejected Gethin's suggestion and told him to measure the point "south of Safwan" from a well rather than from the corner of a building since this could easily be moved.[41] He then referred the matter to the Foreign Office.

Meanwhile, Henry Mack, the British Ambassador in Baghdad, was becoming increasingly impatient over the delay in opening the negotiations for demarcation. On 30 May 1950, in a despatch to Ernest Bevin, the Foreign Secretary, he stressed that it was essential to take positive steps towards achieving an agreed demarcation as soon as possible in view of the ever-increasing number of frontier incidents and the possibility of oil being discovered in disputed territory, together with the Iraqi intention to develop Umm Qasr as an oil-loading port. However, the Ambassador was convinced that Iraq would be unable to achieve its ambitions for Umm Qasr unless it reached an agreement with the British government covering the following points: first, the correct demarcation of the frontier from Umm Qasr; second, some exchange of territory to give the port "sufficient elbow-room" since the border joined the sea just to the south of Umm Qasr according to the 1923 and 1932 definitions; and third, agreement with Kuwait over the use of its water approaches, since ships would have to enter Kuwaiti territorial waters to reach the proposed port. Moreover, in view of Iraq's strategic interest in the development of Umm Qasr, Mack considered the time most opportune to approach the Iraqis for the settlement of the boundary issue once and for all. He, therefore, sought Bevin's authorization to conduct negotiations with Iraq.[42]

The Foreign Secretary, who was unable to issue any immediate instruction to the Ambassador as his staff were undecided as to the exact location of the point south of Safwan, preferred negotiations to be

---

40. Gethin to C. J. Pelly (Acting Resident), no. 75/9/50, 29 June 1950, FO 371/82038. See also FO 1016/27.
41. Pelly to Gethin, no. 173/32/50, 14 July 1950, FO 1016/118.
42. Mack to Bevin, no. 124/1035/24/50, 30 May 1950, FO 371/82038. For Iraq's vital economic interests in Umm Qasr, see Mack to Attlee, no. E-178/280/4/49, 14 September 1949, R/15/5/210.

postponed until this question had been resolved.[43] After lengthy internal negotiations, the Foreign Office eventually showed its inclination to accept Gethin's line 1,250 metres south of the corner of the customs compound at Safwan. In any case, Geoffrey Furlonge, now Head of the Eastern Department, pointed out that there was in fact little difference between this line and the Iraqi conception of the frontier implied at the time of the dispute over the position of the boundary post in 1940. This departure from the Foreign Office's previous firm support of the 1940 formula was due to its belief that the Sheikh would not accept a frontier 1.6 kilometres from Safwan. Therefore, on 22 January 1951, Hay was asked for his opinion on Gethin's line.[44] After consulting with the Agent, Hay gave his unqualified support to it on 28 March. To bolster his arguments, he reiterated that in September 1940, Charles Prior, the then Political Resident, had reported that the notice-board marking the frontier had originally stood "1,050 yards south of the most southerly palm of Safwan" and that Galloway in March 1949 had placed the most southerly palm "160 paces" south of the outer wall of the customs post. These two figures placed the original site of the board at rather more than 1,210 yards south of the customs post. It is to be remembered that in their note of 1940, the Iraqis had claimed that the board which they had removed in 1939 had been wrongfully erected 1,100 yards from the customs post and that as a result it was 275 yards inside the Iraqi side of the border. Thus according to their own estimate the boundary was 1,375 yards south of the customs post, which meant that the difference between their statement and Gethin's calculation amounted to no more than 165 yards. The Resident therefore concluded that the point south of Safwan from which the frontier eastwards from the Batin was to be demarcated should be regarded as no more than 1,375 yards and not less than 1,210 yards from the southern wall of the Safwan custom house. Hay recommended that the Sheikh should be informed of this position before the British government approached the Iraqis to discuss demarcation. He then suggested that the whole matter be placed before a demarcation

---

43. Minute by Rothnie, no. EA-1082/8, 12 January 1951, FO 371/82038.
44. Furlonge to Hay, no. EA-1082/8, 22 January 1951, FO 371/82038. See also Minute by Rothnie, no. EA-1082/8, 4 January 1951, FO 371/82038.

commission to determine the exact and final location of the frontier, for which the Sheikh should meet half the cost.[45]

As Hay's views were acceptable to the Foreign Office, it decided to press the Iraqis for an acceptance of the location of the point 1,210 yards south of the Safwan custom-house (one most favourable to Kuwait). The Foreign Office was determined to reach an agreement on this point before the proposed commission was appointed since on its exact location depended the demarcation of the whole northern and north-eastern section of the Iraqi–Kuwaiti frontier.[46] In fact, this section of the frontier was of particular interest to both parties with, on the one hand, the Basra Oil Company's discovery in February 1951 of high-quality oil 32 kilometres south of Zubair, and on the other, KOC's intention to conduct a survey in the northern part of its concession area – approximately 3.5 kilometres south of the Iraqi frontier.[47] As the British government thought that the oilfield in this sector possibly ran continuously from Iraq to Kuwait, the frontier, when determined, would therefore also become the boundary dividing the field between the two companies. This oil factor added additional urgency to the quest for an early settlement of the exact location of the point south of Safwan. Therefore, on 16 April 1951, Hay was instructed to make it clear to the Sheikh that although the British government believed this point to be 1,210 yards south of the Safwan post, it also accepted that the Iraqis considered it to be 1,375 yards to the south of the customs post. In addition, he was to be told that the matter would be best handled by a demarcation commission for which he would be expected to meet half the cost. The Resident agreed to this proposal and asked H. G. Jakins, the Political Agent in Kuwait, to pass this on to the Sheikh.[48]

---

45. Hay's conclusion was in fact based on a report prepared by H. G. Jakins, the Political Agent in Kuwait, who personally inspected the area accompanied by Dickson and the chauffeur who accompanied Sheikh Ali al-Khalifa, the then Governor of Kuwait Town and Director of Public Security (who in 1940 had erected the pillar to which the Iraqis objected on the score that it had been placed 250 yards within their frontier and was 1,000 yards from the Safwan post). Hay to Furlonge, no. 1034/20, 28 March 1951, FO 371/91291. See also Jakins to Hay, no. 75/13/51, 26 February 1951, FO 1016/39.

46. See Minute by C. M. Rose, no. EA–1087/4, 10 April 1951, FO 371/91291.

47. Jakins to Hay, no. 95/15/51, 26 February 1951, FO 371/91291. See also Jakins to Hay, no. 75/19/51, 13 March 1951, FO 1016/39.

48. L. A. C. Fry to Hay, no. 1087/4, 16 April 1951, FO 371/91291. See also Hay to

However Jakins, instead of clearing the way for a speedy demarcation of the frontier, suggested that an ad hoc delegation be formed to pinpoint the nodal point south of Safwan prior to the appointment of a demarcation commission. The Kuwaiti side of this delegation should consist of himself as the British government's representative, and Sheikh Abdullah Mubarak because of his local knowledge. Once the nodal point was agreed upon, Jakins suggested, professional surveyors from both Kuwait and Iraq could then draw the frontier due west to the Batin and the British government could concentrate its efforts on establishing the frontier east of the nodal point. He believed that it would be a mistake to mention any distances to the Iraqis, whether it be 1,210 or 1,375 yards, as no one had actually measured the distance in any professional way that would absolutely confirm either figure. Jakins therefore suggested that as soon as Britain had secured the consent of the Iraqi government to the appointment of this delegation and before the two sides met, he should go with Sheikh Abdullah Mubarak to the frontier to locate the spot on which the notice-board stood. They could then measure the precise distance of that spot from the Safwan customs post, so that the exact location of the nodal point could immediately and permanently be marked if an agreement were reached. Professional surveyors would then be free to delimit the western half of the frontier. On the other hand, if the two sides failed to agree then the British negotiators would have all the information to hand to start negotiations or to refer the case to arbitration. (Jakins believed that the Kuwaiti case for arbitration was a strong one because of the repeated removal of the notice-board by Iraqi officials.) Regarding the eastern half of the northern section of the frontier, Jakins argued that its demarcation should not be based on the 1940 formula, which had become outdated in 1951, "with the question of oil looming large on the northern frontier". He suggested that before Britain made any move to delimit this section of the frontier, it should first obtain a comprehensive map of the area marked with the cardinal points. On ascertaining the position of the nodal point, it should be traced on the

Fry, no. 1034/30, 28 April 1951, FO 371/91291. For the British government's approval, see Foreign Office to Bahrain, no. 222, 11 April 1951, FO 371/91291.

map indicating the frontier as envisaged by both the 1923 definition and that of the 1940 interpretation so that at least the British government would have a true picture of the issue involved.[49]

However, the Agent's suggestions failed to convince Hay, who considered them not only impractical but also contrary to his earlier agreement with the Foreign Office, an undertaking he considered impossible to renege on. He nevertheless forwarded Jakins's proposals to the Foreign Office, but reserved comment on them. Despite this, the Agent still pressed for a small ad hoc delegation to determine the point south of Safwan, as he believed that full-blown frontier negotiations could not make any real progress until the location of this crucial point was settled. On the other hand, if the point was agreed the frontier due west of it could be easily delimited. The Residency, however, simply ignored Jakins's proposals and declined to take them any further.[50] No action was taken for a further three months, but on 23 October 1951 Jakin's successor Cornelius Pelly was asked to approach the Sheikh about the frontier question. During their meeting, when Pelly raised the subject of resuming dialogue with Iraq, Sheikh Abdullah agreed without hesitation. However, he urged the British government to try and reach an agreement with the Iraqis on the point south of Safwan before a commission was appointed. He also agreed to meet half the cost of the commission.[51]

With the Sheikh's consent to proceed obtained, the Residency asked the Foreign Office to instruct Sir John Troutbeck, the Ambassador in Baghdad, to approach the Iraqis.[52] Accordingly, the Foreign Office instructed the Ambassador to do so on 7 December 1951. Three weeks later a note verbale was presented to the Iraqi government defining the position of the disputed point of the frontier as lying "1,000 metres south of the customs post at Safwan". The note was in effect the

---

49. Jakins to Hay, no. 75/30/51, 12 May 1951, FO 371/91291. See also Jakins to Hay, no. 75/31/51, 12 May 1951, FO 371/91291.
50. Jakins to Hay, no. 75/43/51, 25 July 1951, FO 371/91291. See also Quesne's remark in the same despatch, 31 July 1951, FO 371/91291.
51. Quesne to Pelly, no. 1034/57, 23 October 1951, FO 1016/39. See also Residency, Bahrain, to the Eastern Department, no. 1034/60, 3 December 1951, FO 371/91291.
52. Residency, Bahrain, to the Eastern Department, no. 1034/60, 3 December 1951, FO 371/91291.

restatement of the 1940 formula, with the significant adjustment that the point south of Safwan was now precisely defined.[53]

Although Amin al-Mumayiz, the Director-General of Arab Affairs in the Iraqi Foreign Ministry, assured Harold Beeley, the Counsellor at the British Embassy in Baghdad, at the time of receiving the note, that his government was anxious to settle the frontier question as they wanted to develop the port of Umm Qasr, Iraq did not respond immediately to the British note.[54] But on 13 January 1952, while Iraq was considering its reply, its policemen harassed the KOC employees and opened fire on the guards who were working at Rodhatain, a place about 20 kilometres south of the frontier. When the British Embassy protested against the incident eleven days later, the Iraqi authorities defended the action by arguing that their policemen were pursuing smugglers in the frontier zone and had entered Kuwait "inadvertently and without intention".[55] This latest frontier incident and al-Mumayiz's previous reference to the Umm Qasr project convinced Troutbeck that the Iraqis were eyeing enviously the potential wealth which was about to accrue to Kuwait as a result of the oil exploration taking place. He therefore considered the possibility that they might revert to their original demand for the incorporation of the Sheikhdom into Iraq. On 15 February, the Ambassador held a staff meeting to review the situation and informed his colleagues that Iraq would almost certainly lay claim to Warba Island in view of its desire to develop Umm Qasr. He was equally convinced that the Iraqis would refuse to go ahead with the proposed final demarcation of the frontier until Warba had been ceded to them. Roger Makins, a member of the Embassy staff, argued that since Warba belonged to Kuwait, Britain should not allow the Iraqis to use it as a bargaining counter in return for their acceptance of the interpretation of the frontier it had put forward and it should also try to keep the question of Iraq's claim to Warba separate from that of the frontier. It was therefore agreed to try and get the Iraqis to accept the definition of the frontier before Britain opened any discussion on Warba.[56]

---

53. For the full text of the note, see Appendix no. IV.
54. Beeley to R. F. G. Sarell, no. 1083/2/52, 9 January 1952, FO 371/98391.
55. See Note Verbale from the British Embassy, Baghdad, to the Iraqi Ministry of Foreign Affairs, no. 28, 24 January 1952, FO 371/98388. See also Iraqi Foreign Ministry to the British Embassy, no. 787/787/7/2971, 24 February 1952, FO 371/98388.
56. See the Minutes of a Meeting on 'Kuwait/Iraq problems' held at the Embassy, no.

Just as the Ambassador had feared, the Iraqi reply of 26 May 1952 demanded the cession of Warba as the construction of a harbour at Umm Qasr had become a necessity for Iraq not only from an economic but also from a military perspective. The Iraqi note alleged that in 1938 Lord Halifax, the then British Foreign Secretary, had verbally agreed to modify the Iraqi–Kuwaiti frontier by ceding Warba Island to Iraq in return for adequate compensation for Kuwait. The note asked the British government to fulfil its alleged agreement before any negotiations on the demarcation of the frontier could start. The Iraqi Ambassador in London also delivered a similar note to the British Foreign Secretary on 13 June 1952.[57]

The Iraqi note obviously annoyed Foreign Office officials. Archibald Ross, Head of the Eastern Department, after examining the texts of the conversations of 1938, considered the Iraqi "allegations" to be groundless, and decided to have an informal talk with Khedheri, the Iraqi Chargé d'Affaires in London, before he refuted them. He therefore summoned him on 17 July 1952, and read to him Halifax's despatches of 5 and 10 October 1938, which did not support the interpretation contained in the Iraqi note. Ross then asked Khedheri to read for himself the minutes of Suwaidi's meeting with Baxter on 4 October of the same year, in the course of which the Iraqi objective to acquire Warba Island was raised, but in which no undertaking to approve or to secure the transfer of the island was given on behalf of the British government. The Chargé d'Affaires was reminded that Baxter only stated: "If the Iraqi government wished the Sheikh of Kuwait to cede the island they would do well to offer him compensation elsewhere and that any communication on the subject must pass through H.M.G." Khedheri, who was not in possession of the relevant background information regarding this conversation, was unable to defend his government's position. All the same, he said that Iraq wanted the British government to inform the Sheikh of Kuwait of Iraq's desire to modify the frontier so that Warba be incorporated into Iraqi territory and to advise him to agree to this proposal. Ross demurred to the latter suggestion, arguing

---

EA-10393/5, 15 February 1952, FO 371/98388.

57. Iraqi Ministry of Foreign Affairs to the British Embassy, no. 247/247/7/8840, 26 May 1952, FO 371/98391. See also the Iraqi Ambassador to the British Foreign Secretary, no. 2/19/1508, 13 June 1952, FO 371/98388.

that such advice would jeopardize the existing friendship between Britain and Kuwait. He, however, agreed to merely inform the Sheikh that Iraq wished to acquire the island of Warba without tendering any opinion. This was not acceptable to Khedheri who argued that the British government should use its influence to convince the Sheikh to accept the Iraqi demand. As Ross categorically refused to do so, the Chargé d'Affaires explained that it was essential for Iraq to command the access to the port, which would be developed as an alternative to Basra as an outlet to the sea. When Ross suggested that Warba remaining in the hands of Kuwait would not pose a threat to Iraq given that it owned the north side of Khor Abdullah from which the island could be dominated anyway, Khedheri replied that the Iraqi government wanted to avoid any repetition of the situation in the Shatt al-Arab where Iraq was at the mercy of Iran and that there was no guarantee that "in 20 or 30 years time Kuwait would be friendly to Iraq". These arguments did not convince Ross of the Iraqi case.[58]

Ross's inconclusive conversation with Khedheri convinced Trefar Evans, the Joint Secretary of the Middle East Official Committee, that the Iraqis were trying to merge the questions of demarcation and the cession of Warba. Although he wondered "whether it was worth objecting to this" he was inclined to settle the question of Warba before discussing demarcation. David Lane, an expert on the Gulf at the Foreign Office, disagreed and maintained that the British government should not at this stage encourage the Iraqis to pursue their aim to acquire Warba, not only because the Kuwaiti Sheikh was "most unlikely" to agree to the cession of the island but also because any discussion of this issue would delay the demarcation of the frontier. He felt that whether cession of territory was discussed or not, a definition of the frontier should first be agreed through diplomatic channels and then implemented. He was, however, prepared to pass on the Iraqi proposal to the ruler if the Iraqis so wished. On the other hand, Ross, who believed that Britain's position in Kuwait was of greater importance than its relations with Iraq, was determined to dissuade the Iraqis from even asking the British government to

---

58. Minute by Ross, no. 1086/8, 17 July 1952, FO 371/98391.

convey their request for the acquisition of Warba. He then supplied his interpretation of Lord Halifax's position in 1938.[59]

In the meantime, at a meeting with Yusuf al-Gaylani, the Under-Secretary of State at the Iraqi Foreign Ministry, Beeley expressed his government's disappointment at the Iraqi note. On 16 August 1952, he informed al-Gaylani that if the Iraqi government made no new approach within ten days, the British government would have no other alternative but to "refute finally" their inaccurate account of the 1938 conversation. Al-Gaylani, however, replied that Iraq had no intention of either withdrawing or modifying its note.[60] Consequently, five days later, the Embassy wrote to the Iraqi Ministry of Foreign Affairs officially informing it that there was nothing on record to indicate any agreement on the part of the British government to the transfer of Warba Island to Iraq. Instead, it was only suggested to the Iraqi Foreign Minister in 1938 that if the Iraqi government wished the Sheikh of Kuwait to cede to it "a part of his territory, it should make proposals to him with an offer of compensation". This did not imply that the British government agreed to the cession of Warba.[61] While Iraq did not contest this explanation, it equally showed no sign of flexibility on the problem of demarcation despite repeated British efforts.

It is quite ironic to note that in June 1953 the Iraqi Ministry of Foreign Affairs complained to the British Embassy in Baghdad that a Kuwaiti armed patrol, consisting of three vehicles, had crossed the frontier and had roamed freely inside Iraqi territory.[62] The Ministry accordingly demanded the punishment of the intruders. But as the Iraqis failed to mention either the date or the location of this alleged territorial violation, the Embassy decided not to ask the Kuwaiti authorities to investigate the incident unless the Iraqis supplied detailed information about it.[63] However, following continued Iraqi protests, the

59. See Minutes by Evans and Lane, no. 1086/8, 21 and 22 July 1952, respectively, FO 371/98391. See also Ross's Minute of 23 July 1952, FO 371/98391.
60. Harold Beeley to Winston Churchill, no. 120, 21 August 1952, FO 371/98391.
61. See Note Verbale from the British Embassy to the Iraqi Ministry of Foreign Affairs, no. 393, 21 August 1952, FO 371/98391.
62. For the full text, see Ministry of Foreign Affairs to the British Embassy in Baghdad, no. 1444/387/7/14412, 11 June 1953, FO 371/104321.
63. Note Verbale from the British Embassy to the Iraqi Ministry of Foreign Affairs, no. 293, undated, FO 371/104321.

Embassy, in December 1953, used the opportunity to argue that such (alleged) incidents would diminish when the frontier had been demarcated. It once again asked the Iraqi government to respond positively to its note verbale of 28 December 1951 in order to prevent the recurrence of similar incidents in the future,[64] but the Iraqis again declined.[65]

In the following year, Iraqi–Kuwaiti relations continued to deteriorate when on 21 May 1954 an Iraqi frontier guard was shot dead and two others wounded in an exchange of fire with a Kuwaiti patrol in a border skirmish within Kuwaiti territory, 8 kilometres south-east of Safwan.[66] Two days later, the Mutasarrif of Basra made a strong protest about the incident to Sheikh Abdullah al-Salem al-Sabah, the Director of the Public Security Department, stating that the Kuwaiti patrol had crossed the border and attacked the Iraqi guards inside Iraqi territory. The Mutasarrif demanded that the family of the man killed should be compensated and that the Kuwaiti personnel responsible for security should in future be more careful and respectful of the Iraqi frontier.[67] While expressing his regret at the incident, the Director maintained that the incident took place well within Kuwaiti territory and that the Kuwaiti patrol was acting in self-defence as the Iraqi guards had opened fire first. The British Ambassador in Baghdad, who was of the same view, sent a note of protest to the Iraqi Minister of Foreign Affairs on 26 May, reminding the Iraqis of the British proposal of 1951 for demarcating the frontier.[68] However, on 30 May Yusuf al-Gaylani rejected the Kuwaiti version and demanded the establishment of a joint Iraqi–Kuwaiti commission to investigate the incident.[69] A week

---

64. Note Verbale from the British Embassy to the Iraqi Ministry of Foreign Affairs, no. 654, 4 December 1953, FO 371/104321.
65. See Mackenzie to D. A. Greenhill (Eastern Department), no. 1592/17/1953, 1 December 1953, FO 371/104321.
66. Kuwait to Foreign Office, no. 111, 22 May 1954, FO 371/109821. See also John M. Troutbeck to Foreign Office, no. 335, 26 May 1954, FO 371/109821.
67. Mutasarrif of Basra to Abdullah al-Salem al-Sabah, no. 591/1954, 23 May 1954, FO 371/109821.
68. Troutbeck to Sayid Arshad al-Umari (the Acting Iraqi Foreign Minister), no. 254, 26 May 1954, FO 371/109821. See also the President of the Public Security Department, Kuwait, to the Mutasarrif of Basra Liwa, unnumbered, undated, FO 371/109821.
69. Troutbeck to Foreign Office, no. 342, 31 May 1954, FO 371/109821.

later, the Iraqis sent a formal note to the British Ambassador giving their version of the incident (i.e. that it took place inside Iraqi territory and that the Kuwaitis fired first) and again demanded the payment of blood-money for the dead man and also the punishment of those responsible for his death.[70]

Neither the Political Agent, who had already visited the scene, nor the Sheikh of Kuwait accepted the Iraqi allegations, and declined to pay any compensation.[71] But as the Iraqis continued their clamour for a joint commission, the Foreign Office eventually agreed to it, but only on the condition that the Iraqis agree at the same time to attend to the problem of the frontier demarcation. This was conveyed to al-Gaylani by the Oriental Counsellor at the Embassy on 24 June 1954, who added that if a joint commission were established, a representative from the Political Agency in Kuwait would have to be included in the commission as the British government was still responsible for the foreign affairs of the Sheikhdom.[72] The Iraqis, however, ignored Britain's proposals and again demanded the establishment of a joint commission without any preconditions. As the Iraqis were adamant on this point, the British government was forced to tell them, on 11 January 1955, that a prolonged investigation of the alleged incident would not serve any fruitful purpose, but argued that a commission would be of use if it concerned itself exclusively with the problem of frontier demarcation.[73] The Iraqis rejected this suggestion and again insisted that the sole purpose of the commission should be to determine responsibility for the incident. They did hint, however, at the possibility of setting up another separate committee for the delineation of the frontier.[74]

---

70. Arshad al-Umari to Troutbeck, no. 1608/1608/7/13000, 7 June 1954, FO 371/109821.
71. Pelly to Foreign Office, no. 127, 10 June 1954, FO 371/109821. See also the Ruler of Kuwait to the Political Agent, no. R/6. 4806, 7 July 1954, FO 1016/364; and Donald Logan (Assistant Political Agent, Kuwait) to Foreign Office, no. 191, 31 July 1954, FO 371/109821.
72. See Baghdad to Anthony Eden, no. 142, 29 June 1954, FO 371/109821. See also Foreign Office to Baghdad, no. 513, 19 June 1954, FO 371/109821.
73. See Note Verbale, from the British Embassy, Baghdad, to the Iraqi Ministry of Foreign Affairs, no. 387/1082/1/42/54, 18 August 1954, FO 371/109821. See also British Embassy, Baghdad, to the Iraqi Ministry of Foreign Affairs no. 20(1082/3/35), 11 January 1955, FO 371/114600.
74. Iraqi Ministry of Foreign Affairs to the British Embassy, no. 882/882/7, 14 February 1955, FO 371/114644.

As the Foreign Office was convinced that the Iraqis would not agree to demarcate the frontier unless Britain consented to their demands, it closely examined the implications of establishing a commission to investigate the incident. It concluded, however, that as it would probably be impossible to agree on the circumstances surrounding the incident given the entrenched positions of the witnesses involved, such a commission would be pointless. Moreover, as the frontier had not yet been demarcated, the commission would find difficulty in deciding in whose territory the incident had taken place. Yet the Foreign Office believed that the possibility of such an inconclusive outcome would at least provide Britain with a sound argument for an early demarcation. On balance, therefore, it decided to agree to a commission of enquiry, but to suggest to the Iraqis that either the commission should also be empowered, simultaneously with its investigation, to make preliminary studies and arrangements for demarcating the frontier or that another joint commission should be set up to do so. This change of attitude was due to the Foreign Office's intention of avoiding any further disagreements with the Iraqis which might jeopardize the proposed negotiations for the supply of water from the Shatt al-Arab waterway to Kuwait,[75] as will be discussed in the next chapter.

Conclusion

The British government took over five years following the end of the Second World War to formally raise the question of demarcation with the Iraqis. This long delay was due to the wide differences of opinion between the Foreign Office and the local officials in the Gulf. While the Foreign Office – which gained much more freedom of action following the abolition of the India Office – refused to open negotiations with the Iraqis on any definition less favourable to them than that of 1940, the authorities in the Gulf strongly opposed this increasingly outdated formula as it was based on a faulty interpretation which greatly favoured Iraq at Kuwait's expense. As the pressures for its alteration mounted, the Foreign Office eventually agreed to make a minor adjustment to this

---

75. Fry to Burrows, no. EA-1089/5, 11 March 1955, FO 371/114644. See also Foreign Office Minute on Kuwait, no. EA-1089/5(A), 9 March 1955, FO 371/114644.

formula by defining the precise position of the line south of Safwan, a most important step as the whole northern frontier of Kuwait depended on determining the nodal point. But this formula was not acceptable to the Iraqis unless their demand for the acquisition of Warba Island (which they claimed was necessary for the construction of a port at Umm Qasr) was met. Neither Britain nor the Sheikh would agree to this because of the implications for Kuwait's sovereignty.

7

The Abortive Shatt al-Arab and Umm Qasr Agreements, 1954–1957

The period from the beginning of 1954 to the end of 1957 witnessed Britain's tireless efforts to win agreement between Kuwait and Iraq for the supply of fresh water from the Shatt al-Arab waterway to Kuwait and the establishment of an Iraqi port at Umm Qasr to serve as an alternative to Basra, Iraq's sole outlet to the Gulf. While Iraq agreed to meet Kuwait's water requirements without precondition, it continually declined to demarcate the frontier unless Kuwait leased it a strip of land as well as the island of Warba to develop the Umm Qasr port. Iraq's repeated refusal to demarcate the frontier compelled the Sheikh of Kuwait not only to back off from his initial pledge to meet Iraq's demands for the port but also to refuse signing the water agreement. With negotiations on Umm Qasr suspended, Iraq then turned its attention to the construction of an oil pipeline from Basra to the Mina al-Ahamedi of Kuwait, which the Sheikh attempted to use as a bargaining chip to force the Iraqis to settle the frontier issue. However, the Sheikh's strategy failed as the Iraqis themselves later abandoned the oil pipeline project. This chapter therefore attempts to analyse the underlining factors for the failure of Kuwait and Iraq, despite repeated British efforts, to reach amicable settlements to their outstanding issues.

The idea of laying a water pipeline from the Shatt al-Arab to Kuwait – first conceived in 1938 – began to gain momentum in the 1950s; hitherto Kuwait brought fresh water by ship. Trenchard Fowle, the then Political Resident, reported as early as October 1938 that there was "a proposal in the air" for fresh water to be piped from Zubair (in Iraqi territory) to Kuwait by a joint Iraqi–Kuwaiti company. Yet Fowle was concerned that this scheme would increase Iraqi influence in Kuwait, as it would place the Sheikhdom's entire water supply under Iraqi control. As he believed that Kuwait should be totally independent of Iraq for its water, he recommended that the demand for water be met by the drilling of additional wells within Kuwait. He suggested that as the British firm A. Beeby Thompson and Partners had already expressed an interest in conducting a hydrological survey of Kuwaiti territory they should be given the go-ahead, and that the British government should bear the full cost of the survey in view of the strategic and political interests involved.[1]

Although both the India Office and the Foreign Office agreed with Fowle's assessment of the dangers of making Kuwait dependent on Iraq for its water, the service departments did not consider that there was sufficient strategic need for an independent water supply for Kuwait to warrant payments from their funds. In view of this appraisal, the Foreign Office saw no prospect of obtaining Treasury funding for the project. As a result, on 7 December 1938, the Resident was instructed to ask the then Kuwaiti ruler, Sheikh Ahmed bin Jaber, to meet the cost of the survey as such expenditure was in the best interest of Kuwait.[2] Accordingly, when the Sheikh was approached he agreed to pay the necessary fee to A. Beeby Thompson. But as the firm could not accept the commission due to its commitments elsewhere the idea fell from the agenda.[3]

Nothing more was heard about the Shatt al-Arab water pipeline for almost a decade when, in December 1948, a company called Sandika submitted a scheme to Sheikh Ahmed proposing to construct a 176-kilometre-long pipeline at a cost of £1,540,000 to supply Kuwait with all the fresh water it needed from Muftieh on the Shatt al-Arab, as long as the Iraqi government consented. Although the project was acceptable to the Sheikh, the Resident warned him that despite whatever guarantees the Iraqis might give, the proposed project would give them "the whip in any period of crisis or strained relations". The Sheikh was therefore instructed to build instead a distillation plant, which at a cost of

1. Fowle to Peel (India Office), no. C/775, 13 October 1938, FO 371/21813.
2. J. P. Gibson to Fowle, no. PZ 7996/38, 7 December 1938, FO 371/21813; A. W. S. Mallaby to Peel, no. 0162/713, 10 November 1938, FO 371/21813; Ryder (Admiralty) to Peel, no. M06718/38, 30 November 1938, FO 371/21813; Baxter to Peel, no. E-6600/75/91, 1 December 1938, FO 371/21813.
3. Prior to the Secretary to the Government of India, no. C/406, 12 September 1939, FO 371/23181.

about £8,000,000 was not the Sheikh's preferred option.[4] But owing to the Resident's dogged opposition the proposed pipeline scheme was shelved. However, when Sheikh Abdullah (Sheikh Ahmed's successor) visited Baghdad in 1952, the Iraqis told him that they were prepared to allow Kuwait to pump fresh water from the Shatt al-Arab to meet its ever-growing demand for water. In August 1953, after making a thorough study of the proposal, the Sheikh formally referred the matter to the British government highlighting the desperate shortage of water in Kuwait, which was becoming increasingly acute as the 1950s drew on due to the fast pace of development and the rapidly expanding population.[5]

However, well before it received the Sheikh's application, the Foreign Office had been considering the political and economic implications of the scheme. Although it believed that one of the reasons why the Iraqis were so keen to supply water to Kuwait was to render the Sheikhdom dependent on Iraq, the Foreign Office eventually agreed to discuss the scheme with the Iraqis, on behalf of Kuwait, due to the potential advantages it offered. Yet the Foreign Office was determined to make the Sheikh's acceptance of the pipeline conditional on an Iraqi undertaking to demarcate the frontier.[6] In January 1954, with this in mind, John Troutbeck, the British Ambassador in Baghdad, entered into discussions with the Iraqis on the proposed project, which his successor Sir Michael Wright was to continue with for the next few years.

In early 1955, during the course of an informal talk with the Iraqi Prime Minister Nuri al-Said, Wright was presented with an entirely new proposal. Iraq now desired "to advance their frontier to a depth of some four kilometres, covering a desert strip, the uninhabited island of Warba and the waters of the Khor Abdullah which surround it" in order to develop Umm Qasr as a subsidiary port to Basra. In May 1955, the Iraqi Foreign Minister told the Ambassador that his government was prepared to renounce in favour of Kuwait all oil rights in the strip as well as in the said waters. Later that month, Nuri al-Said informed Wright that if Kuwait accepted these proposals, Iraq would agree to demarcate the

---

4. Hay to Ernest Bevin, no. 170, 20 December 1948, FO 371/68324. See also Foreign Office to Hay, no. E-16365/224/91, 7 January 1949, FO 371/68324.
5. The Ruler of Kuwait to the Political Agent, no. R/64704, 6 August 1953, FO 371/104380.
6. See Minute by D. J. D. Maitland, no. EA-1425/2, 8 June 1953, FO 371/104380.

frontier. This was in fact the first time that the Iraqis had formally consented to demarcation, which until then they had consistently avoided doing. As this acknowledgement could possibly be seen as a renunciation of Iraqi "pretentions" to annex the Sheikhdom, the proposal was acceptable to Wright, who believed that in any case the development of a port at Umm Qasr would also be of great strategic value to the British Empire as it could be used to defend the region. But as the Ambassador was worried that the Kuwaiti Ruler might not agree to this proposed change in his frontier, he devised a plan of linking the proposed water pipeline agreement – which the Sheikh had been eager to conclude since 1952 – with this new Iraqi scheme for Umm Qasr. In other words, both agreements should be merged into a single paper. The intention behind this was to deter the Iraqis from unilaterally abrogating the water agreement by the knowledge that if they did so their Umm Qasr lease would be simultaneously cancelled. To win over the Sheikh, Wright also proposed to try and secure a 99-year lease of the required territory instead of allowing its "outright cession" to the Iraqis.[7]

On 2 June 1955, Cornelius Pelly, the Political Agent in Kuwait, gave his unqualified support to this rather radical approach. But as the Agent was convinced that the Iraqis were pressing for the territorial concessions so that ships could sail to Umm Qasr through Iraqi waters if Iran ever attempted to block the approach to Basra, he believed the Iraqis would not be satisfied with the leasing of territory in itself. Therefore, the Kuwaiti ruler should also offer the right of passage through the waters leading to Umm Qasr as long as the agreement remained in force.[8] As this was acceptable to both the Foreign Office and the Ambassador, Gawain Bell, Pelly's successor, on 23 June 1955, placed both proposals before Sheikh Abdullah, who gave his provisional approval five days later. However, he wanted an assurance that the rights of KOC in Warba Island would be respected. This was immediately given with an additional assurance that the frontier would be demarcated following the conclusion of the Umm Qasr and Shatt al-Arab water agreements. After obtaining the Sheikh's approval, the Agent

---

7. Michael Wright to Harold Macmillan (the Foreign Secretary), no. 123, 24 May 1955, FO 371/114644.
8. Pelly to Foreign Office, no. 82, 2 June 1955, FO 371/114644. See also Wright to Foreign Office, no. 611, 23 June 1955, FO 371/114644.

produced the following points for inclusion in the proposed Umm Qasr agreement:

(a) Kuwait agrees to the lease by Iraq of area specified by Iraqis for 99 years and to use of area by Iraq for any purpose.

(b) Kuwait undertakes not to interfere with passage of ships.

(c) Rental to be agreed (or all rentals to be cancelled).

(d) Kuwait to be responsible for security (expense being cancelled on each side).

(e) Reservation of mineral rights, subject to these rights not being exercised in such a way as to interfere with navigation.[9]

No sooner had the Foreign Office and Ambassador Wright endorsed these five points, than Bernard Burrows, the Political Resident, arrived in Baghdad to take part in the negotiations. On 2 July 1955, both the Ambassador and the Resident held detailed talks with Musa al-Shahbandar, the Iraqi Foreign Minister, largely based on Bell's five points. Although the Iraqi Foreign Minister wanted to reach agreement on the two subjects simultaneously, he responded unfavourably to Wright's linked approach. The rest of their conversation was taken up by attempts to agree on the details of the Umm Qasr lease. Al-Shahbandar insisted that Iraq should be responsible for the administration and security of the leased areas, which the British negotiators were ready to accept providing Iraq met the following conditions:

(a) The explicit recognition of Kuwaiti sovereignty over the area.

(b) The guarantee that Kuwaitis, in the event of any legal action being brought against them, may remain subject to the jurisdiction of the Ruler of Kuwait.

---

9. Bell to Foreign Office, no. 107, 28 June 1955, FO 371/114644. See also 'Aide Mémoire: Water from the Shatt al-Arab', no. A1089/16, 20 June 1955, FO 371/114644.

(c) The guarantee of freedom for Kuwaiti ships in the waters of the leased areas.

(d) An undertaking that there will be freedom of passage for Kuwaiti nomads in the leased area.

(e) An undertaking that property privately owned by Kuwaitis in the area would not normally be disturbed.

(f) The Iraq government to pay for the security and policing of the water pipeline to Kuwait.[10]

Al-Shahbandar only objected to condition (e), arguing that since his government was already acquiring private land for the water pipeline, Kuwait should do the same in the proposed lease area before handing it over to the Iraqi authorities. But both the Ambassador and the Resident tried to convince the Foreign Minister that it was too simplistic to draw parallels between the two agreements; while for the proposed water agreement a precisely demarcated slice of land would be expropriated and fully utilised, with the Umm Qasr agreement the Iraqis would take over a large area, the whole of which might not be needed for the development of the port. Yet as al-Shahbandar refused to compromise on this point, the negotiations were suspended. On 4 July 1955, Wright wrote to Harold Macmilian, who had become Foreign Secretary in April, informing him of the progress of the negotiations with the Iraqis and enclosing a draft Umm Qasr agreement. The Ambassador reiterated that the Iraqi authorities were staunchly opposed to any "explicit linking" of the two agreements. However, although he believed that they might abrogate the water agreement unilaterally in the event of a deterioration in Iraqi–Kuwaiti relations, he was ready to give up his linkage formula.

Realizing that any further insistence on the adoption of Wright's linkage formula might jeopardize the water agreement which Kuwait was in dire need of, C. T. Ewart-Biggs of the Foreign Office recommended that the two agreements should proceed independently of each other, although this left Kuwait in a very weak bargaining position. However, he at least wanted the water agreement to be signed before

---

10. Wright to Macmillan, no. 149, 4 July 1955, FO 371/114645.

that of Umm Qasr in order to give the Iraqis an added incentive to be cooperative in the event of any problems arising with the implementation of the scheme. As J. L. Simpson, the Foreign Office's legal adviser agreed, to this,[11] a fresh draft of the water agreement was drawn up by Leslie Fry, Head of the Eastern Department, on 26 July 1955. The main provisions of this draft were:

(i) The Government of Iraq agree that the Government of Kuwait should take up to 100 million gallons of water per diem [day] from the Shatt al-Arab, and construct the necessary installations and pipeline for carrying it to Kuwait.

(ii) The Government of Iraq undertake to lease to the Kuwait Government the land in Iraq required for the scheme at the nominal rent of one dinar per annum.

(iii) The installations shall be managed by a resident engineer and staff appointed by the Kuwait Government, but the Government of Iraq shall be responsible for the security of the pipeline within Iraq.

(iv) Materials required for the scheme shall be exempted from Iraqi customs.

(v) The duration of the agreement shall be for 99 years and shall thereafter be terminable at five years notice.[12]

This draft was designed to safeguard Kuwait's interests and to enable the construction in Iraqi territory of the pipeline and the necessary installations for carrying water from the Shatt al-Arab to Kuwait. Charles Shuckburgh, the Assistant Under-Secretary of State for Foreign Affairs, approved the draft on the same day as it was drawn up.[13]

In the meantime, Foreign Office officials had prepared a revised Umm Qasr lease agreement, which was presented to Sheikh Abdullah on 17 July 1955. The Sheikh approved it a week later without going into details or inspecting the frontier.[14] This was possibly due to his trust

---

11. See Minute by Ewart-Biggs, no. EA-1089/18, 14 July 1955, FO 371/114645. See also Minute by Simpson, 15 July 1955, FO 371/114645.
12. See Minute by Fry, no. EA-1422/36, 26 July 1955, FO 371/114701.
13. Minute by Shuckburgh, no. EA-1422/36, 26 July 1955, FO 371/114701.
14. Bell to Foreign Office, no. 123, 17 July 1955, FO 371/114645. See also Bell to

in the British government and his belief that it would safeguard his interests. But Bell, the Political Agent, was not prepared to accept the draft until he saw the proposed route of the frontier for himself. On 31 July, accompanied by his colleagues Donald Logan and Peter Reilly as well as Saif ibn Saad of the Kuwaiti Public Security Department, Bell inspected the frontier between Safwan and the high ground just north of Umm Nigga. Bell found that the Kuwaiti frontier post at al-Qashanniya was well-guarded by a detachment of 60 soldiers under the command of a second lieutenant. These guards operated regular patrols along the frontier and maintained constant wireless communications with the Public Security Department in Kuwait Town and with other security posts. From al-Qashanniya, Bell and his team proceeded to Safwan and met with the officer in charge of the Iraqi customs post. This officer was of the opinion that the Iraqi–Kuwaiti frontier ran about 10 kilometres south of Safwan in the vicinity of ar-Raudha and on the east was about a kilometre south of Umm Qasr. To the south-east of Safwan, stretching up to 1,000 yards within the Kuwaiti side of the frontier, Bell found an extensive agricultural development and settlement claimed by the Iraqi customs officials and corroborated by Saif ibn Saad to have been in existence for the last 10 years and owned by the Iraqis of Zubair. From Safwan, Bell's party followed the proposed line of the current draft agreement as far as the high ground to the north of Umm Qasr, from where they had a clear view of Umm Qasr and the junction of the Khor Zubair with the Khor Subiya. The area was low and uninhabited, but contained a number of wells of semi-brackish water at a depth of between 20 to 25 feet.[15]

Having gained this knowledge of the frontier, the Agent suggested that the desert strip of territory south of Umm Qasr which the Iraqis wanted to lease should be extended southwards in the vicinity of Safwan in order to include the cultivated areas. In addition to this modification, Bell also urged that a reference to the note verbale of December 1951 be included in the Umm Qasr agreement, as this contained the British proposals for demarcating the frontier and a detailed interpretation of the terms of the 1932 definition. The Agent further argued that any

Foreign Office, no. 118, 11 July 1955, FO 371/114645.
15. Bell to Fry, no.1088/6/55, 8 August 1955, FO 371/114645.

agreement should safeguard Kuwait's water rights as well as their freedom of access to the leased land.[16] In view of these suggestions, the Foreign Office produced a revised Umm Qasr draft agreement in September 1955, containing the following key provisions: the leased area was defined in Article 1 and the rent fixed at 1 Iraqi dinar per annum for the duration of the agreement (Article 8); this area should be demarcated immediately after the signature of the agreement by reference to the 1932 definition (Article 2), with sovereignty over the area remaining with Kuwait but with the responsibility for public security and the administration of justice laying with the Iraqis (Article 10); Kuwait was to retain the right to all mineral resources in the land and under the waters of the leased area (Article 11); and a new article (13) was inserted to ensure that the Iraqi occupation of the leased area should not affect the ultimate division of the sea boundaries.[17] In order for the final phase of negotiations to commence, Bell was asked to obtain the approval of Sheikh Abdullah to this revised version.[18]

The Agent, however, held off from discussing the matter with the Sheikh due to an unexpected tide of opposition in Kuwait to both the proposed Umm Qasr lease and the water pipeline scheme. This campaign had been initiated by Sheikh Fahd al-Salem, the brother of the ruler and the head of the Kuwait Development Board. With this opposition gathering pace, Bell called on Sheikh Fahd on 15 August 1955 to convince him that the water scheme would be of great benefit to Kuwait and the potential disadvantages and dangers of the lease were insignificant in comparison. Sheikh Fahd disagreed and maintained that if Kuwait accepted the Shatt al-Arab agreement it would be morally bound to accept the Umm Qasr agreement which would result in the "unwelcome proximity" of an Iraqi naval base. He was convinced that the development of a large port at Umm Qasr would decimate traffic through Kuwait's port as a great deal of the Iraqi–Syrian trade which then flowed through it would be diverted to Umm Qasr. Sheikh Fahd

---

16. *Ibid.* See also Bell to Foreign Office, no. 148, 7 August 1955, FO 371/114645.

17. See the Draft Umm Qasr Agreement, no. EA1089/24, 9 September 1955, FO 371/114645. See also Minutes by Ewart-Biggs, no. EA-1089/18, 15 August and 5 September 1955, FO 371/114645.

18. Foreign Office to G. A. Gault (British Residency, Bahrain), no. 139, 9 September 1955, FO 371/114645. See also Gault to Bell, no. 28, 19 September 1955, FO 371/114645.

also believed that the draft lease agreement as it stood would give the Iraqis the right to refuse KOC permission to drill over the whole of Warba Island and the channel on the pretext that such drilling would "interfere with the installations" or "with navigation in the waters". His unproductive conversation with Sheikh Fahd convinced Bell that a small number of influential Kuwaiti merchants had induced the Sheikh to adopt this position and the ruler, who had previously given his consent to the two schemes, would now think twice before approving any fresh draft in view of this opposition. The Agent therefore decided to with-hold the new draft until the situation had stabilized.[19]

Meanwhile, Nuri Pasha, the Iraqi Prime Minister, who had already expressed his willingness to sign both of the two agreements, was beginning to loose his patience over the delay in the resumption of the negotiations.[20] In order to speed up the process, he visited Kuwait in September 1955, to discuss the pipeline project with Sheikh Fahd, but he also failed to convince him. Given this lack of progress, Nuri Pasha put forward a new proposal that if the Kuwaitis feared competition from a port at Umm Qasr and if they did not want to lease land, they could join with Iraq in developing the port on a fifty-fifty basis. Nevertheless, Sheikh Fahd remained non-committal even to this proposal.[21] Upon his return to Baghdad, the Iraqi Prime Minister related his conversation with the Sheikh to Robin Hooper, the British Chargé d'Affaires, and stressed that his government had absolutely no intention of turning Umm Qasr into a naval base. The port was instead needed as an outlet for the Zubair oilfield – which was already producing 6 million tons per annum – as well as to provide extra facilities in the event of war with Iran. Sheikh Fahd, according to Nuri Pasha, refused to understand these very simple facts. Nuri Pasha's failure to make any headway whatsoever during his mission to Kuwait convinced Hooper that Sheikh Fahd had a vested interest in the construction of distillation plants. (George

---

19. Bell to Fry, no. 1082/11/55, 16 August 1955, FO 371/114701. See also Bell to Foreign Office, no. 161, 25 August 1955, FO 371/114701; Bell to Gault, no. 10812/18/55, 2 October 1955, *ibid.*
20. Beaumont (Baghdad) to Foreign Office, no. 695, 15 August 1955, FO 371/114701. See also Foreign Office to Kuwait, no. 219, 16 August 1955, FO 371/114701.
21. Robin Hooper (Baghdad) to Foreign Office, no. 781, 4 October 1955, FO 371/114701.

Smethurst, the Head of the Water and Drainage Division of the Public Works Department of Baghdad, had in fact planted these mistaken suspicions in Hooper's mind.[22] Bell, however, refused to accept these allegations, as the distillation of water in Kuwait was a state-run business and it was "difficult to see how Fahd could have any pecuniary interest in them nor do I [Bell] know of any personal reasons why he should prefer distillation plants to the Shatt al-Arab schemes".[23]

Although the Kuwaiti Ruler still withheld his decision on both the water and the Umm Qasr proposals, the Iraqis went ahead with drawing up and planning the schemes. The Shatt al-Arab water carrier project was to consist of two pipelines, one for drinking water and the other for brackish water; and a contract for the laying of the pipes was even on the verge of being placed. At the same time, General Sammah Fattah, the former head of the Iraqi air force, who was appointed as the Director of Basra Port in 1954, personally supervised the extensive planning operation for the Umm Qasr project and was busy buying up land in the vicinity of the port in the name of the Port Directorate. A British firm of consultants, Coode and Brother, had been employed to draw up the plans were asked by the General to make 35 copies of the complete specification. The British Senior Naval Officer in the Gulf, Captain Wight-Boycott, who met with the General in October 1955, was so impressed by the scale of the designs,[24] that at a meeting of the Anglo-Iraqi Standing Committee on 12 October he openly welcomed the idea of developing Umm Qasr. He pointed out, "a large part of the difficulties involved in keeping sea communications with Iraq open were due to the fact that Iraq's only port lay at the upper end of a long approach very vulnerable to mines and difficult to watch and sweep." Wight-Boycott was therefore convinced that "if Umm Qasr were available it would certainly be less difficult to keep clear."[25] This support prompted Nuri Pasha to remind Wright of his earlier proposal to jointly develop Umm Qasr with Kuwait. The Prime Minister appealed to the

---

22. Hooper to Foreign Office, no. 1422/86/55, 5 October 1955, FO 371/114701.
23. Bell to Hooper, no. 1081220/55, 18 October 1955, FO 371/114701.
24. See an extract of a Report (top secret) by Commander-in-Chief, East Indies Station, unnumbered, 30 November 1955, FO 371/120598. See also the Enclosure no. 2 to the Report in *ibid*.
25. Robin Hooper to E. M. Rose, no. 1082/65/55, 18 October 1955, FO 371/114645.

British Ambassador to use his influence to persuade Sheikh Abdullah to come to a favourable decision on the issue as soon as possible.[26]

As a result of this continued Iraqi pressure, Burrows arrived in Kuwait on 19 November 1955, to present the latest drafts of the two agreements to the Sheikh and to explain the Iraqi position. The Resident reassured Sheikh Abdullah that in his opinion there was no "ulterior motive" behind Iraq's Umm Qasr proposals, and stressed the necessity of demarcating the frontier, which could follow an agreement, in order to avoid further border incidents. He urged the Sheikh not to miss this chance as the Iraqis had for the first time expressed their willingness to solve the problem of demarcation. Sheikh Abdullah was nonetheless unmoved by this appeal and simply stated that he needed more time to consider all the issues involved.[27]

Having failed to convince the Ruler of the chances of an early settlement of Iraqi–Kuwaiti disputes, Burrows called on Sheikh Fahd, the leading antagonist of the Umm Qasr scheme. Yet as the Sheikh was worried that the development of Umm Qasr might not only deprive Kuwait of a share in the valuable transit trade to the Mediterranean but that the Iraqis might also expropriate the possible natural resources in the leased area, he categorically stated: "Kuwait must retain effective ownership and control of its territory and not give it up on a lease which for all practical purposes would be in a perpetuity." Instead, he wanted the Kuwaiti government to carry out all the developmental work in the proposed leased territories and that non-Iraqi ships and tankers should be charged for the use of these facilities. Furthermore, these facilities should be retained and solely administered by the Kuwaitis. But Burrows told the Sheikh that if his ideas were accepted, the Iraqis would expect the same conditions for the section of the water pipeline which crossed their territory, thereby controlling both the territory and the installations there. Sheikh Fahd had no objection to this and was prepared to pay the Iraqis for the full cost of the construction of the pipelines, pumps and the like, although not for the water itself nor for the expenses of policing the pipeline.

Sheikh Fahd's uncompromising attitude towards the whole initiative convinced the Resident that the ruling Al Sabah family would never

---

26. Wright to Foreign Office, no. 36, 18 November 1955, FO 371/114645.
27. Burrows to Foreign Office, no. 14, 20 November 1955, FO 371/114645.

agree to the Umm Qasr proposal unless it was significantly modified. Therefore Burrows hit upon the idea of creating an autonomous port authority to manage the whole port area irrespective of national boundaries, which would be jointly financed by Kuwait and Iraq as both would share in the profits generated. Moreover, Iraq should only lease from Kuwait the actual sites required for harbour installations.[28] Burrows then submitted his proposals to the Foreign Office. As Derek Riches, the then Head of the Eastern Department, was worried that further wranglings would kill off the whole initiative, he supported this latest formula despite the fact that it could create some practical difficulties. He put forward the following reasons for doing so: firstly, the joint development and management of the port would give Kuwait a share in the trading and other benefits which the new port might produce; secondly, it would establish a further link between Kuwait and Iraq which would consequently help curb the growing Egyptian influence in the Sheikhdom (resulting from the increasing number of Egyptian nationals being employed in various administrative, educational and commercial establishments there); and lastly, the development of Umm Qasr as an alternative to Basra would serve the British strategic interest in the region. Burrows was then told that if the Kuwaitis declined to accept the Umm Qasr agreement in its present form, the British government would start negotiations with the Iraqis based on his latest proposal and tell them to go ahead with the water scheme, without waiting for an agreement on Umm Qasr. Yet when IPC expressed its need for an oil pipeline from their Zubair field to a loading terminal in Kuwait irrespective of Iraq's plans for the development of Umm Qasr, Riches was presented with an ideal opportunity to link the two projects together. He was sure that IPC's proposal to use a terminal inside Kuwait would reduce the importance of the development of Umm Qasr from the perspective of oil, and with regard to the water scheme would eventually provide Kuwait with a similar "hostage to that which she is giving Iraq".[29]

---

28. *Ibid.* See also Burrows to Riches, no. 10101/12/55, 12 December 1955, FO 371/114577.
29. See Minute by Riches, no. EA-1089/34, 3 December 1955, FO 371/114645. See also Foreign Office to Bahrain, no. 1154, 3 December 1955, FO 371/114645.

Riches's "hostage" formula, however, soon became irrelevant when IPC decided not to proceed with their proposed oil pipeline project following the unfavourable results of a technical survey conducted on the proposed terminal in Kuwait. Owing to Kuwait's weak bargaining position in the planned Anglo-Iraqi negotiations on the Umm Qasr scheme, the Resident suggested that the Iraqis should sign the water agreement first. If they did so, they should be permitted to go ahead with the Umm Qasr project either by leasing land or by constructing installations on Kuwaiti territory with or without Kuwaiti cooperation.[30] As Bell believed that any proposal to jointly develop Umm Qasr would be unacceptable to Sheikh Abdullah, he preferred not to present any new initiative to the Kuwaitis until they had made up their minds on the previous draft.[31] In the meantime, he gathered more information about Iraq's development plans for Umm Qasr. He discovered that the Iraqis were planning to build a four-berth harbour for general cargo as well as a grain silo and a new township on the firm land lying to the west of the harbour area to accommodate the port workers – the number of which was estimated to eventually reach a total of 4,000–5,000, which augmented by their families and an anticipated influx of other businessmen would eventually push the number to an overall population of some 30,000. Iraq was determined to go ahead with this plan with or without an Umm Qasr agreement. The Iraqis reasoned as follows:

(i) The layout of the Margil wharves is physically restricted and does not give scope for much extension beyond that already in hand.

(ii) The Karun [River] Bar is formed every year by silt brought down by the Karun floods. This is mostly removed by succeeding floods of the Tigris and Euphrates. With increased flood control of these two rivers, reliance on their floods to remove silt brought down by the Karun River will be risky.

(iii) The Karun Bar even with constant dredging provides a depth of 21/23ft. below low-water spring tides (L. W. S. T.). This

---

30. Burrows to Foreign Office, no. 900, 7 December 1955, FO 371/114645.
31. Bell to Foreign Office, no. 268, 10 December 1955, FO 371/114645.

limits the draught of vessels coming to Ashar and Margil to 27ft. draught. Ships of more than 27ft. have to complete loading at Harta Point, two miles below the Karun Bar.

(iv) With the development of Iraq as a result of oil royalties increasing demands are made on Basra, Iraq's only port. Since expansion in the Shatt al-Arab is difficult, Umm Qasr would provide additional facilities. It would be considered as an extension of the Port of Basra rather than a rival port and would come under Basra Port Directorate.

(v) The metre gauge [railway] line from Baghdad via Hindiyah to Basra is already proving a bottleneck for the movement of goods. It is proposed to build a standard gauge line from Baghdad via Kut through the fertile plains between the Tigris and the Shatt-al-Har to Umm Qasr with a branch to Basra.

(vi) With increasing irrigation it is expected that grain production in the Mosul area will expand and become an important export. There is no suitable place for a grain silo at Basra and it is suggested that one could be built at Umm Qasr.

(vii) Because there is no river to bring down silt, once the channel has been deepened, maintenance of the approaches to Umm Qasr will not call for expensive dredging.

(viii) In the event of hostilities it would provide an alternative to Basra.[32]

With these objectives in mind, Nuri Pasha told Sir Michael Wright on 23 December 1955, that his government had absolutely no intention to develop Umm Qasr for use in peacetime as this would adversely affect Basra, Iraq's main outlet to the Gulf. The main intention was to develop it for use in the event of war and as such its construction could be delayed for a year or two. To achieve this objective he was prepared, simultaneously with signing the water agreement, "to reach agreement with Kuwait that any development of Umm Qasr should be shared"

---

32. Bell to Burrows, no. 10812/35/55, 19 December 1955, FO 371/114645. See also Senior Naval Officer, Persian Gulf to the Commander-in-Chief, East Indies Station, no. PG 156/6(Secret), 16 December 1955, FO 371/120598.

between the two countries on a fifty-fifty basis.[33] But he wanted the matter resolved as soon as possible; he had even sent his son to Kuwait at the end of the previous month to urge the Sheikh to come to an early decision on the issue.[34]

Sheikh Abdullah, after canvassing the views of the prominent members of the Al Sabah family and leading Kuwaiti citizens,[35] eventually informed the Agent on 18 January 1956 that he was unable to accept the Shatt al-Arab water scheme due to the opposition to it of the majority of Kuwaitis. He personally felt that it would be a great mistake to put Kuwait at the mercy of Iraq for its principal water supply. Recalling Rashid Ali's rebellion against the Iraqi Regent and the British in 1941, the Sheikh told Bell that no one could trust Iraq and there was no guarantee that the British government would be able to safeguard the security and maintenance of this supply of water from the Shatt al-Arab indefinitely. Instead, his country's water shortage would be more reliably solved by the construction of a number of distillation plants.[36] (It should be noted that Sheikh Abdullah neither accepted nor rejected the Umm Qasr agreement at this stage, although he did raise serious objections to it.)

His conversation with Sheikh Abdullah convinced Bell that either Colonel Anwar Sadat, a member of the Egyptian Revolutionary Council and Secretary-General of the Muslim Conference, who had visited Kuwait in December 1955, or Abdullah Abu Khair, the Private Secretary to King Ibn Saud of Saudi Arabia, who had recently met with the Sheikh, had influenced the Ruler's decision to reject the scheme.[37] Riches agreed although he entirely blamed the Egyptians and not the Saudis for sabotaging the scheme:

> The Egyptians, through their technicians and school-teachers, their radio and newspapers and their visits to Kuwait, have certainly

33. Wright to Foreign Office, no. 1069, 23 December 1955, FO 371/114645.
34. Bell to Foreign Office, no. 257, 30 November 1955, FO 371/114645.
35. Bell to Burrows, no. 10812/38/55, 30 December 1955, FO 371/120598.
36. Bell to Foreign Office, no. 17, 18 January 1956, FO 371/120598. See also Bell to Burrows, no. 1422/9/56, 23 January 1956, FO 371/120598.
37. See Confidential Annex to Kuwait Diary no. 2 covering the period 23 January–26 February 1956, FO 371/120550. See also Burrows to Riches, no. 10101/3/56, 17 March 1956, FO 371/120541.

made some headway there. The Ruler is sensitive to possible criticism from Egypt; and this was probably a factor in his decision not to go on with the Iraq/Kuwait water scheme.[38]

Despite Riches's emphasis on the Egyptian influence in Kuwait, it should be remembered that Sheikh Fahd with the backing of Sabah al-Salem and Sheikh Jaber al-Ali had been campaigning against the scheme ever since it was presented.[39] Moreover, there is no evidence to suggest that the Egyptians had managed to penetrate the inner circle of the Kuwaiti court and influenced the decision-makers.

Although Iraq was disappointed by Kuwait's rejection of the water scheme, it still hoped to extend its influence over the Sheikhdom. This could be achieved by arranging exchange visits between the heads of state and high officials, by offering Kuwait Iraqi schoolteachers and by exploring other avenues of bilateral cooperation, such as the possibility of appointing a consular representative in Kuwait. On 30 January 1956, Burhan-Uddin Bashayan, the Iraqi Minister for Foreign Affairs, sought Britain's permission to send Yusuf al-Gaylani to Bahrain to discuss these ideas with Burrows.[40] While the Foreign Office welcomed the idea of sending more Iraqi teachers and technicians to Kuwait to counter the growing Egyptian influence, it declined the suggestion of consular representation as this would have set a precedent for other interested parties, particularly as Egypt had been repeatedly requesting just such an appointment in Kuwait. In any case, the establishment of non-British consulates would inevitably weaken Britain's predominant position in the Sheikhdom.[41] The Resident supported this position, adding that the Egyptian anti-British propaganda in Kuwait and other Gulf countries should also be checked by stepping up the quality and range of Iraqi radio propaganda. To achieve this there should be careful and discreet contact between all levels of the governments, and cultural and technical missions involving, for example, the sending of sports teams to the Sheikhdom.[42] It would appear that Britain at this time was more

---

38. See Riches's Note 'Kuwait', no. A-1017/4. 8 February 1956, FO 371/120550.
39. Bell to Burrows, no. 1422/9/56, 23 January 1956, FO 371/120598.
40. Wright to Foreign Office, no. 121, 30 January 1956, FO 371/120565.
41. Foreign office to Baghdad, no. 227, 3 February 1956, FO 371/120565. See also Minute by Riches, no. A-10393/2, 2 February 1956, FO 371/120565.
42. Burrows to Foreign Office, no. 194, 10 March 1956, FO 371/120565.

concerned with checking the growth of Egyptian influence in Kuwait than solving the frontier question, due to the deterioration of the Anglo-Egyptian relations following Nasser's decision to buy Soviet arms in February 1955. Moreover, Nasser had forced Britain to sign an agreement in October 1954 for the evacuation of the British troops which had been stationed in the Suez Canal Zone ever since the conclusion of the Anglo-Egyptian Treaty in 1936.[43]

While the British government had been planning to boost relations between Iraq and Kuwait in order to curb the growth of Egypt's influence in the Sheikhdom, the Iraqis made it clear that they did not consider it an "appropriate" time for a demarcation of the frontier – the ever-present stumbling-block of Iraqi–Kuwaiti relations.[44] In February 1956, the Port Directorate in Basra concluded that it was feasible to construct the port of Umm Qasr without using Kuwaiti territory provided that Kuwait permitted the use of the stretch of the Khor Abdullah between Warba and Bubiyan islands as an anchorage for shipping waiting between tides to dock in the wharves at Umm Qasr.[45] Nevertheless, Britain was not prepared to again raise the question of Umm Qasr with the Kuwaitis in any form as it was convinced that the successive Iraqi proposals on the matter was one of the reasons for Kuwait's rejection of the water pipeline scheme. Instead, Britain wanted to concentrate on a project which was likely to establish a relationship of mutual interdependency between the two countries. Therefore, IPC's proposed oil pipeline, which was still being considered by Sheikh Abdullah, became an obvious alternative. It was thought that if this project went ahead, the Kuwaitis might feel in a strong enough position to reopen negotiations with the Iraqis on the water scheme since they would then be "in a position to use the oil pipeline as a counterbalance to any difficulties which might arise over the water scheme".[46]

While the British government was searching for a way to revive the water scheme, the Kuwaitis raised it themselves following an Iraqi denial

---

43. For full Text of the Anglo-Egyptian Treaty of 1936, see Treaty *Series no. 6*, Cmd. 5360 (London, HMSO, 1937), pp. 3–29.
44. See 'Iraqi–Kuwaiti Frontier' in A. R. H. Kellas (Baghdad) to Logan (Foreign Office), no. 1638/30/56, 12 March 1956, FO 371/120598.
45. See 'Umm Qasr, Brief for Secretary of State', no. EA-1397/1. 24 February 1956, FO 371/120634.
46. Foreign Office Note on 'Kuwait', unnumbered, 16 April 1956, FO 371/120638.

that Kuwait's participation in the scheme was subject to any pre-conditions. In May 1956, the Kuwaiti Supreme Council (consisting of Sheikh Fahd al-Salem, Sheikh Sabah al-Salem, Sheikh Mubarak al-Hamad, Sheikh Jaber al-Ahmed, Sheikh Jaber al-Ali, Sheikh Sabah al-Ahmed, Sheikh Khalid al-Abdullah al-Salem, Sheikh Mubarak Abdullah al-Ahmad and Sheikh Saud al-Abdullah) once again debated the water pipeline project under the direction of the Ruler. Surprisingly the Council agreed to accept the scheme subject to the following conditions: firstly, that the Iraqis should agree to the demarcation of the frontier based on the exchange of letters of 1932; secondly, that Iraq would not at any time ask for anything that would affect the security of Kuwait's boundaries such as the building of a port at Umm Qasr; thirdly, the British government should guarantee the implementation of such an agreement in order to avoid any misunderstanding or difficulty in the future; and lastly, the negotiations with Iraq on the water project should be combined with negotiations on the oil pipeline from Zubair to Kuwait. These conditions were conveyed to Burrows, the Political Resident on 24 May 1956.[47] On 5 July, Sheikh Abdullah further informed the Agent that although he was prepared to accept the draft of the Shatt al-Arab water agreement, he preferred the Iraqis to charge a nominal rent for the land which they would make available for the pipeline.[48] The British government, however, did not put these proposals to the Iraqis immediately apparently because of its preoccupation with the Suez crisis following the nationalization of the Suez Canal Company on 26 July 1956 by the Egyptian President, Gamal Abdel-Nasser.

As soon as the Suez crisis was over in January 1957, Britain held serious negotiations with Iraq on the Shatt al-Arab water scheme and by the end of the month the Ambassador was able to obtain Iraqi approval to a fresh draft. This draft was a significant improvement upon the previous one and met almost all of Kuwait's requirements. It allowed Kuwait to pump 100 million gallons of water from the Shatt al-Arab daily, gratis for 99 years. However, the annual rent of the land required for the construction of an intake point, pipelines and all the other

---

47. Burrows to Foreign Office, no. 472, 24 May 1956, FO 371/120638.
48. Chronological Summary of Events in the Persian Gulf, 1956, in Annexure, Burrows to Selwyn Lloyd, no. 49, 15 April 1957, FO 371/126869.

necessary facilities would be 32,000 Iraqi dinars.[49] On 4 February 1957, Bell presented the draft to Sheikh Abdullah for his approval, while expressing the British government's desire to conclude an agreement as soon as possible. However, the Ruler was unable to take a final decision until he placed the draft before the Supreme Council.[50]

Eventually, on 9 March 1957, the Kuwaiti Supreme Council decided not to go ahead with the water and oil pipeline projects until the problem of demarcation had been solved.[51] Although the Ruler had previously agreed in principle to accept an IPC oil pipeline terminating in Kuwait and was ready to start final negotiations with IPC,[52] its representative was now told that these negotiations were to be suspended. Burrows, who arrived in Kuwait on 11 March, met with the Ruler as well as with the members of the Council, but failed to convince them of the benefits to Kuwait of the pipelines. The Resident, believing that this time neither Egyptian nor Saudi influence played a part in the Council's decision, attributed their opposition to the schemes to four key factors: firstly, the thinly-concealed Iraqi claim to Kuwait and their long-standing refusal to demarcate the frontier; secondly, the Iraqi attempt to lease Kuwaiti territory for the development of Umm Qasr port; thirdly, the Iraqi refusal to allow its agricultural produce to be exported to Kuwait; and finally, their conviction that the time was most opportune for settling the frontier question once and for all not only because the Iraqis required the oil pipeline agreement more than the Kuwaitis needed the water but also because Nuri Pasha, who recognized the frontiers in 1932, was now once again in power. Burrows, who had considerable sympathy with the Kuwaiti cause, was convinced that there was no way out of this stalemate unless their demand for demarcation was met. Britain's refusal to accept it would jeopardize Anglo-Kuwaiti relations, which had already been shaken by the Suez crisis and the British bombing of Egypt on 1 November 1956, which

---

49. For full text, see the Enclosure in R. A. Beaumont to Bell, no. 1422/4/57, 31 January 1957, FO 371/126869.
50. Bell to Foreign Office, no. 57, 4 February 1957, FO 371/126869.
51. The members of the Supreme Council to the Ruler, no. 31-2/2, 9 March 1957, FO 371/126869.
52. See Wright to Foreign Office, no. 117, 29 January 1957, FO 371/126869; Bell to Foreign Office, no. 104, 4 March 1957, FO 371/126869; Minute by A. R. Walmsley, no. EA-1421/6(A), 7 March 1957, FO 371/126869.

triggered anti-British feeling throughout the Arab world including Kuwait, where demonstrations against the British action in Egypt took place. A committee of merchants was also formed to boycott British goods in Kuwait; it even asked the Ruler to set up an office to recruit volunteers for service with the Egyptian forces. So before any permanent damage was done to Anglo-Kuwaiti relations, Burrows urged the Foreign Office to try and persuade the Iraqis to at least send a letter or issue a statement concerning their recognition of the frontier as defined in the 1932 document and their willingness to demarcate it as soon as possible. The Resident believed that this would help to ease Kuwaiti suspicions of Iraq's intentions and lead to a closer relationship between the two countries, which was the only way to curb Egyptian influence in the Sheikhdom.[53]

However, the British Ambassador in Baghdad strongly opposed Burrow's proposals which, he believed, the Iraqis would not accept given that they had already made the key concession of dropping their demands for Umm Qasr. Yet he was prepared to push for a partial solution to fix and mark the frontier where the water and oil pipelines would cross it.[54] Like the Ambassador, the Foreign Office similarly believed that the Iraqis would not agree to demarcate the frontier as this was a "valuable bargaining counter which they may later need to persuade the Kuwaitis to agree on Umm Qasr".[55] Instead, it introduced the following fresh suggestions in the ongoing quest for a solution:

(a) Her Majesty's Government give to the Ruler an unpublished assurance that they will uphold the 1932 frontier.

(b) The Iraqi Government give Her Majesty's Government an unpublished assurance that they for their part do not intend to raise the frontier issue.

(c) The Iraqi Government agree to mark the frontier at the points where the pipelines cross it.[56]

---

53. Kuwait to Foreign Office, no. 7, 14 March 1957, FO 371/126869. See also Kuwait to Foreign Office, no. 114, 14 March 1957, FO 371/126869.
54. Baghdad to Foreign Office, no. 333, 17 March 1957, FO 371/126869.
55. See Walmsley's Minute on Kuwait water and pipeline schemes, no. EA-1421/11, 18 March 1957, FO 371/126869.
56. Foreign Office to Baghdad, no. 786, 20 March 1957, FO 371/126869.

This package of proposals was sent to Wright with an instruction that he should not reveal it to the Iraqis until he had ascertained their reaction to the Kuwaiti demand for an assurance concerning the demarcation of the frontier prior to the signature of the water and oil pipeline agreements.[57] On 27 March 1957, when Wright broached the subject with Nuri Pasha, the Prime Minister vehemently opposed it and stated that he had absolutely no intention of trading a frontier for an oil pipeline, which in any event was a matter for Kuwait and the oil companies. He warned the Ambassador that if the Kuwaitis persisted in raising this issue, the Iraqi government would be forced "by public opinion" to re-examine the whole frontier problem and demand adjustments in Iraq's favour.[58]

Although Nuri Pasha showed no wish to compromise, Wright presented him with the Foreign Office's latest proposals on 3 April. But the Prime Minister simply reiterated that it was impossible for any Iraqi government to agree to reaffirm the frontier "as it stood". The best thing for the Kuwaitis was, therefore, to leave the question alone, just as he was prepared to do. However, at the end of the conversation Nuri Pasha retreated slightly by admitting that if he was forced demarcate "the greater portion of the frontier" he would do so on the condition that the Kuwaitis granted Iraq the "small wedge of unoccupied land in the Umm Qasr area" for which he had already asked. He needed this concession in order to "save the face of the Iraq Government in the eyes of their own people".[59] Although it is difficult to judge the strength of Iraqi public opinion on the frontier matter, Wright genuinely believed the Prime Minister. Expressing his complete solidarity with Nuri Pasha, the Ambassador in a long letter to Burrows pressed the Iraqi case:

> Apart from the fact that Nuri acknowledged the 1923 Memorandum in his letter of July 21, 1932, the Iraq Government are not otherwise, I believe, on public record as having ever agreed to the Iraqi–Kuwait frontier. So far as the public are aware, it is a frontier fixed by the 'imperialists' for their own interests and should therefore be subject to rectification in the interest of Iraq or of 'the Arab people', e.g. in the event of Arab unity. There undoubtedly

---

57. *Ibid.*
58. Baghdad to Foreign Office, no. 386, 27 March 1957, FO 371/126869.
59. Wright to Burrows, no. 1422/37/57, 4 April 1957, FO 371/126869.

exists in Iraq a considerable body of opinion which looks forward to seeing not only frontier rectification but the absorption of Kuwait in Iraq as part of a Fertile Crescent scheme [that is the formation of a union of Iraq, Syria, Jordan and Lebanon] . . .

Many Iraqis, with envious eyes on Kuwait, contend that it was separated from the Basra vilayat for reasons of British policy prior to World War I and that this separation is invalid. Kuwait would further provide an additional and easily accessible sea port for Iraq. There are also the questions of the Shia minorities in north-eastern Nejd and a military adventure in the al Hasa oil fields which lurk in some minds.

There are a number of reasons which lead less thoroughgoing nationalists to wish for frontier rectification in their favour. There is first the fact that the Basra Petroleum Company's Rumaila oil wells lie within a few kilometres of the frontier about 10 kilometres west-north-west of Safwan and some 5–6 kilometres from the present frontier. The formation very probably stretches into Kuwait territory. Second, there is a genuine desire to develop Umm Qasr, if only as a strategic port.

I think, therefore, that Nuri's opposition to delimitation is not so much a whim as a real fear. Any publicity on the question of the Kuwait frontier is liable to let loose some or all of these aspirations, both in the Press and in Parliament. His Government may well be pressed to do something about them with ourselves and the Kuwaitis and his signature to the 1932 Exchange of Letters will then be revealed and will be a political embarrassment to him, being used by the nationalists to show he has already signed away to Kuwait (i.e. Britain) Iraq's interests. For this reason he wants to cover himself *vis-à-vis* his political opponents, either by not allowing the issue to be raised at all or, if it is, by extracting something from Kuwait which would appear to counter-balance what he personally is probably quite willing to give to Kuwait . . .[60]

In short, Nuri Pasha's hands were tied by the possibility of an unfavourable public reaction to any solution of the frontier problem without any real gain to Iraq. But in pointing this out Wright exposed his staunch support of the Iraqi Prime Minister, due not only to his pro-Iraqi leanings but also to his conviction that Nuri Pasha was the most moderate and practical man in Iraq as well as a great friend of Britain.[61]

---

60. *Ibid.*
61. *Ibid.*

He did not hesitate to place the blame squarely on the Kuwaitis for the unresolved state of Iraqi–Kuwaiti disputes:

> The frontier question is a political storm signal for him [Nuri Pasha] and an irritant to him, but also because the Kuwaitis have kept on changing their minds or thinking up something further whenever matters look set for an agreement. It was after all the Ruler who insisted on the oil scheme as the only possible counterbalance to the water scheme. I have deliberately let Nuri have time to calm down. I have had to.[62]

This extract reveals the extent to which Wright had also lost his patience and temper over Kuwait's uncompromising stance. He then stressed that if the frontier was ever to be demarcated, the Kuwaitis had no option but to make concessions by agreeing to the following:

(a)   to the Water Agreement and the Oil Agreement going forward in principle, and at the time,

(b)   to either

    (i)   a deal whereby they leased territory (including possibly Warba) to Iraq for the development of Umm Qasr granting rights of anchorage in Kuwaiti waters, or

    (ii)   an offer of co-operation by making available land and a certain amount of capital for the joint Iraqi–Kuwaiti exploitation of Umm Qasr as a port.[63]

Although there was no practical difference between this formula and the Nuri Pasha's position, the Ambassador considered this compromise as the only option available to break the deadlock.

However, the Foreign Office was not in favour of taking any new initiative until Sheikh Fahd, who remained suspicious of Iraqi intentions, was persuaded to change his mind. In the hope of allaying his suspicions, the Iraqi government, at Britain's suggestion, invited him

---

62. *Ibid.*
63. *Ibid.*

to Baghdad.[64] As soon as the Sheikh accepted the invitation, Bell called on him on 27 April 1957 to impress upon him that Kuwait would have to make concessions if the Iraqis were to agree to demarcate the frontier. Sheikh Fahd was, however, unreceptive and explained that as Kuwait needed Iraqi water and Iraq needed an additional outlet for its oil, a water pipeline in exchange for an oil pipeline was a fair arrangement.[65] Sheikh Fahd left for Baghdad a week later, but surprisingly neither he nor the Iraqis raised either the question of the Shatt al-Arab scheme or the demarcation of the frontier during the course of his visit.[66]

On the Sheikh's return to Kuwait, Bell had a long talk with him about the three outstanding issues of the water and oil pipelines and the frontier. Although Sheikh Fahd stated that the demarcation of only part of the frontier was unacceptable to Kuwait, he hinted that it might be possible to reconsider, after the demarcation of the frontier, the question of leasing Warba and a strip of Kuwaiti territory to Iraq so long as Kuwait was given a share in the project to develop Umm Qasr. As this was a significant advance on anything he had said previously, the Agent immediately referred it to the Resident, who felt confident enough to devise a new deal. Just two days later, Bell was instructed to explore whether a package deal was acceptable to the Ruler as well as Sheikh Fahd on the following lines:

(i) The water scheme should go forward.

(ii) The oil pipeline scheme should go forward, subject only to negotiation of detailed terms between Kuwait and I.P.C.

(iii) The frontier between Kuwait and Iraq should be that agreed in 1932 and demarcation should begin immediately.

(iv) If Iraq wished to develop Umm Qasr this should be done by a joint enterprise in which Iraq and Kuwait would share equally. Kuwait would make available for this purpose any facilities

---

64. See Minute by Moberly, no. EA-1421/18, 11 April 1957, FO 371/126869. See also Minute by Walmsley, no. EA-1421/18, 25 April 1957, FO 371/126869.

65. Kuwait to Foreign Office, no. 168, 30 April 1957, FO 371/126961. See also Foreign Office to Kuwait, no. 196, 26 April 1957, FO 371/126960; Bell to Burrows, no. 1422/47/57, 24 April 1957, FO 371/126961.

66. Bell to Burrows, no. 1422/56/57, 16 May 1957, FO 371/126961.

which . . . on technical grounds were necessary for the construction and operation of the port in Kuwait territory or waters including if necessary the use of Warba which should, however, remain part of Kuwait.[67]

This proposal was not far in advance of Sheikh Fahd's ideas and was fairly close to Nuri Pasha's position. Burrows further suggested as a possible refinement that the work on demarcation should start in the area in which the water and oil pipelines would cross the frontier.[68]

On 27 May 1957, Bell presented this package to Sheikh Fahd and discussed it with him at length. To his great surprise and disappointment he found that the Sheikh had reverted to his original position. On the following day, the Agent then approached the Ruler with the proposals, but he also declined to accept them and demanded that the demarcation of the frontier should be accomplished before any settlement on the water and oil pipelines could be reached. He was not prepared to give any ground on the Umm Qasr project beyond telling the Iraqis that they were free to develop it within their own territory. When Bell explained the impossibility of reaching any agreement with the Iraqis unless he made some concessions, the Ruler reminded him that the demarcation of the frontier was the responsibility of the British government and that he expected it not to fail to fulfil its duty.

Despite this lack of progress in Kuwait, Wright discussed Burrows's package deal with the Iraqis. Although the Iraqi Prime Minister was ready to conclude the water agreement either on its own or in conjunction with the oil pipeline scheme, he was still reluctant to accept the demarcation of the frontier on the basis of the 1932 definition unless Kuwait agreed to cede or lease the strip of land near Umm Qasr as well as Warba Island.[69] Although Bashayan, Nuri Pasha's Foreign Minister, echoed these sentiments, he hinted that his government might agree to a "counter concession of an adjustment of the boundary elsewhere in favour of Kuwait" if the Kuwaitis accepted Iraq's requirements for Umm Qasr.[70] This encouraged both the Ambassador and the Foreign

---

67. Bahrain to Foreign Ofice, no. 577, 20 May 1957, FO 371/126961.
68. *Ibid.*
69. Baghdad to Foreign Office, no. 680, 25 May 1957, FO 371/126961. See also Baghdad to Foreign Office, no. 701, 28 May 1957, FO 371/126961.
70. Baghdad to Foreign Office, no. 701, 28 May 1957, FO 371/126961.

Office to think that an agreement based on Burrow's package deal would eventually be possible.[71] Therefore, the Resident, at the Ambassador's request, arrived in Baghdad on 5 June 1957 to expound his formula. Upon his arrival, he visited Nadim Pachachi, the Minister of Economics and the Director-General of Political Affairs in the Foreign Ministry, to explain the attitude of Sheikh Abdullah towards the frontier problem. He stressed that in view of previous public statements in Iraq calling for the annexation of the Sheikhdom, the Ruler was still suspicious of Iraqi intentions and therefore wanted the frontier indisputably demarcated once and for all. However, although Pachachi confirmed that the Iraqis still wanted the oil pipeline as well as the development of Umm Qasr, he was careful to avoid the question of demarcation. As Burrows continued to press the point, the Minister told him that the issue was to be referred to a higher authority and was thus out of his hands. This unsuccessful mission convinced the Resident that as neither Iraq nor Kuwait were willing to make any concessions, it would be impossible to reach settlement. He was also worried that the British government would be attacked by both the parties; while the Kuwaitis would blame it for not sufficiently promoting their cause, the Iraqis would accuse Britain of failing to prevent the Kuwaitis from hardening their attitude towards the oil pipeline agreement. Therefore, the Ambassador and the Resident agreed that the best course of action would be to "lie low on the whole question and wait for such developments to occur as would heighten the interest of at least one of the parties in reaching an agreement".[72]

While Britain was following this policy of wait and see, there was a change of government in Iraq. Nuri Pasha lost the premiership to Ali Jawdat al-Ayyubi in the third week of June 1957. The new Iraqi Foreign Minister, Ali Mumtaz, reopened discussions about the outstanding issues when Bell paid a courtesy visit to him on 2 July 1957. During the course of the talks, the Foreign Minister reiterated that Iraq urgently required a pipeline from Zubair to Ahmadi in order to increase the output of the Basra oilfield from 8 to 25 million tons a year. If the Kuwaiti Ruler agreed to this project, it would create a favourable atmosphere in Iraq which would make it easier for the Iraqi government

---

71. See Minute by Moberly, no. EA-1421/27, 30 May 1957, FO 371/126961. See also Minute by Walmsley, no. EA-1421/25, 27 May 1957, FO 371/126961.
72. Richard Beaumont to Bell, no. 1422/66/57, 20 June 1957, FO 371/126961.

to demarcate the frontier. Demarcation would, however, have to include an adjustment to allow the long-term lease of Warba in order to develop Umm Qasr as a second port for Iraq's growing trade and commerce. Ali Mumtaz then offered Kuwait as much water as it needed from the Shatt al-Arab without any conditions as Iraq attached great importance to the establishment of friendly relations with Kuwait. After considering these proposals, Bell suggested that Ali Mumtaz should take them directly to Sheikh Abdullah, with an assurance that the demarcation of the frontier would follow soon after the completion of an oil pipeline agreement.

Although the Foreign Minister agreed to meet privately with the Kuwaiti Ruler during the course of the Sheikh's forthcoming holiday in Lebanon, he was not prepared to give any assurances about demarcation in advance. But Wright anticipated, mistakenly as it turned out, that this face to face meeting would convince Iraq that it must give a quid pro quo if there was to be an agreement.[73] It is important to remember here that the British government had hitherto declined to allow the Iraqis any direct contact with the Kuwaitis on political matters due to the terms of the Anglo-Kuwaiti Exclusive Agreement of 1899. However, the British now fostered this direct approach between the two countries in the hope that each side might become aware of the strength of objection on the other, thereby making both of them realize that the British government had not obstructed the negotiations for their own ends as had been previously alleged.[74]

Upon his return to Kuwait, on 3 July 1957, Bell immediately spoke to the Ruler about Ali Mumtaz's proposed visit. Sheikh Abdullah was receptive to the idea and agreed to send an invitation,[75] which was conveyed to the Iraqi Foreign Minister by the British Ambassador on 17 July 1957. But Ali Mumtaz told the Ambassador to make it clear to the Ruler that he should not raise the question of demarcation as it was politically impossible for any Iraqi government, particularly the present one, to agree to demarcate the frontier at that time. Wright was warned that if this question was raised, his visit far from improving relations would severely damage them since his response would be entirely

---

73. Wright to Riches, no. 1422/80/57, 2 July 1957, FO 371/126961.
74. Minute by Riches, no. EA-1421/37, 10 July 1957, FO 371/126961. See also Minute by Moberly, no. E-11421/41, 9 August 1957, FO 371/126961.
75. Bell to Foreign office, no. 258, 3 July 1957, FO 371/126961.

negative. However, he was assured that if a healthy atmosphere was created and the oil pipeline project agreed to in principle, it might be possible later to talk about the problem of demarcation "without the appearance of having given way to Kuwaiti blackmail". Wright replied that Sheikh Abdullah might not agree to a visit which excluded the discussion of such a crucial issue.[76] Indeed, when the Foreign Office was informed of this stipulation it was unsure as to whether a visit on this basis would be useful or not. John Moberly of the Foreign Office was convinced that the Ruler would not be deterred from asking for "demarcation now or nothing".[77] Bell, who had been working tirelessly for the settlement of the question of demarcation since his arrival in Kuwait, was dismayed by Ali Mumtaz's stubborn insistence on this precondition. He even declined to convey his message to the Ruler arguing that if Ali Mumtaz was not prepared to discuss demarcation he should abandon the idea of visiting Sheikh Abdullah as his refusal to talk about it would only serve to increase the Ruler's suspicions of Iraq and thereby all chances of an immediate settlement would be lost.[78] This was conveyed to the Iraqi Foreign Minister on 21 July, who replied by sending a warm message to Sheikh Abdullah expressing his earnest desire to see him as soon as possible.[79] The Sheikh, however, preferred the Foreign Minister to write to him in advance of the meeting putting down his ideas for a settlement of all the outstanding Iraqi–Kuwaiti problems.[80] When Richard Beaumont, the Chargé d'Affaires in Baghdad, passed on the Sheikh's request Ali Mumtaz declined to do so, arguing that he was still not fully acquainted with all the problems between their two countries as he had only been appointed to his position in the previous month. He then told Beaumont that as his planned visit was intended to be informal and purely exploratory, Sheikh Abdullah would be free to raise any issue he wished. If any significant point came up during the course of this fact-finding mission, Ali Mumtaz would be ready to pay another visit to the Sheikh or put proposals in writing.[81]

---

76. Baghdad to Foreign Office, no. 869, 17 July 1957, FO 371/126913.
77. See Minute by Moberly, no. EA-10393/1, 18 July 1957, FO 371/126913.
78. Kuwait to Foreign Office, no. 281, 20 July 1957, FO 371/126913.
79. Baghdad to Foreign Office, no. 885, 21 July 1957, FO 371/126913.
80. Kuwait to Foreign Office, no. 287, 24 July 1957, FO 371/126913.
81. Baghdad to Foreign Office, no. 906, 25 July 1957, FO 371/126913.

Ali Mumtaz's enthusiasm to see the Ruler should be viewed within the context of his government's growing interest in the future of the Gulf. This was given added impetus by Iran's search for friends in the Gulf and its lavish entertainment of the Ruler of Dubai during his visit to Tehran in August 1957. This convinced the Iraqis that they had to pay more attention to their interests in the region than ever before. The growing communist activities in Syria became a further cause of Iraqi concern, due to their fear that the Syrians might at some future date cut the Kirkuk oil pipeline. If this were to happen, Iraq would be entirely dependent on exporting its oil through the Gulf. But British support of Oman and Abu Dhabi in their dispute with Saudia Arabia over the possession of the Buraimi Oasis (resulting in Britain using force in October 1955 to evict the Saudi troops occupying Buraimi) might even endanger this sole alternative route for Iraqi oil. These factors, therefore, combined to make it more necessary than ever for Iraq, to "cling tight" to King Ibn Saud. The Iraqis felt that in the face of the potential danger from Syria, minor differences between the British, the Americans, the Saudis and themselves should be resolved quickly so that they could face the common threat together. For this reason Iraq wanted Britain to reach some form of agreement with both it and Saudi Arabia over the future of the Sheikhdoms in the Gulf. The Iraqis were prepared to work closely with the British government towards a revised political regime in the Arabian Gulf states, a regime which would have the full support of King Ibn Saud. Beaumont wrote to the Foreign Office:

> They [the Iraqis] maintain that the disappearance of the British–Indian Empire makes a purely British relationship with the Gulf states anomalous. They feel also that the security of the Gulf as their own vital supply line, which was in the past guaranteed by the British presence in India and Iraqi friendship with Britain, has now been diminished, and they call in witness the political storms which arise whenever we are forced to intervene in Gulf affairs, as in Bahrain in November or in Oman on the present occasion. They feel that they must now take an active part to find an up-to-date substitute for the *Pax Britannica* which for fifty years or more has reigned in the Gulf. At the back of their minds there always lurks the idea of establishing a predominant position for themselves in Kuwait. They express themselves as ready if asked by the Gulf

Rulers to find experts and teachers from their own rather meagre cadres, and acknowledge, albeit reluctantly, that they are being out-distanced by the Egyptians, both because of the ability of Egypt to produce personnel and because of the fact that Iraq is an unknown quantity with many of the Gulf states and with some is downright unpopular. They would like to find some means whereby in conjunction with themselves and King Saud we could ensure both our own interests in the Gulf and security there. But to avoid friction it would all have to be done with the concurrence of Saudi Arabia and, may be, under the aegis of some new political arrangements.[82]

In short, the Iraqis wanted to be actively involved in the affairs of the Gulf states under the umbrella of a new political set-up, an arrangement which would give them a chance to play a dominant role in Kuwait in particular and in the Gulf in general.

As a result of this overambitious policy of Iraq, Ali Mumtaz was very keen to find a basis for agreement with Kuwait, Iraq's gateway to the Gulf. He therefore sent another conciliatory message to Sheikh Abdullah appealing to him to respond to his call and fix a date for a meeting.[83] Upon receipt of this message, the Sheikh sent a cordial telegram to the Foreign Minister, formally inviting him to visit him during his holiday in Beirut.[84] Ali Mumtaz eagerly accepted his invitation, arriving in the Lebanese capital on 21 August 1957 and talks were held between the two men six days later. Although minutes of the meeting are not available, upon his return to Baghdad the Foreign Minister gave Beaumont a full account of the discussions, stating that the Sheikh had agreed in principle to the idea of an Iraqi oil pipeline through Kuwait and that the Ruler had not mentioned the demarcation of the border. On the question of a water pipeline, he had told the Sheikh that Iraq was still prepared to sign an agreement for the supply of water to the Sheikhdom without attaching any conditions. He further stated that Sheikh Abdullah had assured him that he would take up the

---

82. Beaumont to Sir William Hayter (Foreign Office), no. 1073/17/57, 23 August 1957, FO 371/126913.
83. Baghdad to Foreign Office, no. 906, 25 July 1957, FO 371/126961.
84. Kuwait to Foreign Office, no. 296, 30 July 1957, FO 371/126961. See also Baghdad to Foreign Office, no. 1010, 19 August 1957, FO 371/126961.

matter of the oil pipeline with the representatives of IPC on his return to Kuwait.[85]

To the great astonishment of A. K. Rothnie, the Acting Political Agent in Kuwait, Ali Mumtaz's version of the talks was disputed by Sheikh Abdullah who maintained that there had been serious discussions of the frontier issue. He said that while he had agreed with the Iraqi Foreign Minister that the four issues of the oil pipeline, the water project, the development of Umm Qasr and the demarcation of the frontier could be regarded as unconnected, a frontier settlement should be considered as a precondition of any discussion of the other three. Sheikh Abdullah also disclosed that he had told Ali Mumtaz that he would only consider a frontier settlement provided Iraq submitted a letter stating its readiness to demarcate the boundary in accordance with the exchange of letters of 1932. As the Iraqi Foreign Minister had declined to accept this, the Ruler made it clear to Rothnie that as the question of demarcation was of vital importance to Kuwait the British government should settle the matter without delay, if necessary by "some strong action".[86]

On hearing this, the Resident felt that it was crucial for Britain's relationship with Kuwait that it should respond positively to the Ruler's call for an early settlement of this question. As a result, Burrows suggested that Mumtaz should first be confronted with Sheikh Abdullah's version of the frontier discussions in Beirut. The Foreign Minister could then be asked whether his government would agree to something on the lines of the letter proposed by the Sheikh. The next step should then be to arrange a tripartite conference – consisting of Britain, Kuwait and Iraq – in Kuwait to discuss the issue in detail. As the Foreign Office approved these suggestions,[87] the Resident arrived in Kuwait on 4 October 1957 and told the Sheikh that he now had two choices: to either remain firm to his stated position that full demarcation must take place before any progress was made on the water and oil issues or to allow Britain to find an intermediate agreement which would both

---

85. See Beaumont to Riches, no. 1422/99/57, 6 September 1957, FO 371/126961. See also Foreign Office to Baghdad, no. 535, 11 September 1957, FO 371/126961.

86. Kuwait to Foreign Office, no. 334, 15 September 1957, FO 371/126961. See also Rothnie to Foreign Office, no. 347, 28 September 1957, FO 371/126938; Kuwait to Foreign Office, no. 351, 29 September 1957, FO 371/126938.

87. Bahrain to Foreign Office, no. 1243, 29 September 1957, FO 371/126938. See

safeguard Kuwait's rights and be acceptable to Iraq. Although Sheikh Abdullah accepted the idea of tripartite talks, he reserved comment on such an intermediate step until he discussed the idea with the members of the Supreme Council. Nevertheless, Burrows's conversations with the Sheikh convinced him that despite Mumtaz's assertion to the contrary, the question of demarcation had been discussed in Beirut. Therefore, the Resident asked the Foreign Office to become more forceful with the Iraqis and issue a public statement pointing out that Iraq's non-cooperation was responsible for the failure to solve the boundary issue. He argued:

> The frontier is generally known and respected by both parties but in spite of numerous requests in the past the Iraqi Government has never been willing to take the practical steps necessary to arrange demarcation on the ground.[88]

As the publication of this sort of statement would greatly offend the Iraqis, Derek Riches of the Foreign Office declined to issue one as he believed it would wreck any chance of a settlement. He further reasoned that it would draw even more attention to the Iraqi–Kuwaiti frontier problem causing embarrassment to Nuri Pasha over his affirmation of the frontier in 1932.[89] Thus, the Resident was informed that London was unable to issue any public statement as this would only cause "friction and polemics detrimental to further negotiations".[90] Burrows did not share this view as he believed Britain's failure to strongly support Kuwait in its endeavour for demarcation would place the British in the Sheikhdom in a difficult position:

> My main conclusion is that we must take this business of looking after Kuwait's foreign relations extremely seriously as a factor in the maintenance of our position in Kuwait and in the Gulf generally. I fully realize that firm support by us for Kuwait's position about the Iraq frontier may make things awkward for us in Iraq, but failure to do so may equally well make things awkward for us in Kuwait and

---

also Minute by Riches, no. EA-10812/2, 1 October 1957, FO 371/126938.
88. Kuwait to Foreign Office, no. 360, 6 October 1957, FO 371/126938.
89. Minute by Riches, no. EA-10812/8, 8 October 1957, FO 371/126938.
90. Foreign Office to Bahrain, no. 1724, 8 October 1957, FO 371/126938.

in view of the importance which we so often say we attach to the Gulf I suggest that the balance between the two is fairly close.[91]

In other words, the Resident was reminding the Foreign Office that it was Britain's responsibility to protect Kuwait's interests rather than Iraq's if for no other reason than because of the growing importance of the Sheikhdom to British strategy in the Gulf. Britain should protect Kuwait's interests both directly and indirectly in order to ensure the uninterrupted and increasing flow of oil to the West.[92]

While the authorities in the Gulf were debating Kuwait's economic importance to Britain, Mumtaz arrived in London on 10 October 1957 to discuss the outstanding Iraqi–Kuwaiti problems. During a meeting with David Ormsby-Gore, the Minister of State for Foreign Affairs, the latter raised the question of his apparently controversial meeting with the Kuwaiti Ruler in Beirut. However, Ali Mumtaz reiterated that Sheikh Abdullah had at no time during their discussions raised the issue of demarcation. He further explained that he had made it clear to the Sheikh that the Iraqi government was unable to accept frontier demarcation as a precondition of an agreement on the oil pipeline and that he was of the impression that the Ruler had accepted his point of view. Mumtaz was equally convinced that the Ruler changed his mind soon after his return to Kuwait due to the influence Sheikh Fahd and the Egyptians had over him. Ormsby-Gore at this point interjected in defence of the Ruler that this could not have been the case, especially as prior to the meeting in Beirut Sheikh Abdullah had told the British government that something had to be said about demarcation if any progress was to be made in the negotiations on the oil pipeline. In response to this, Mumtaz declared that the Ruler's conditional offer to agree to the pipeline if the frontier was first demarcated was not acceptable to Iraq.[93] The meeting then ended, without achieving any progress on either issue.

---

91. Burrows to Beeley, no. 1034, 9 October 1957, FO 371/126905.
92. Burrows to Beeley, no. EA-1022/2, 3 December 1957, FO 371/126905. See also Aubrey Halford (Political Agent in Kuwait) to Burrows, no. 1034/6/57, 14 November 1957, FO 371/126905.
93. See Minute by David Ormsby-Gore, no. EA-10812/9, 10 October 1957, FO 371/126938.

As the Kuwaitis remained adamant that negotiations on the oil pipeline scheme were entirely dependent on the demarcation of the frontier, the Iraqis decided on an alternative route for the exportation of its oil from the Basra field. Therefore, Ali Mumtaz, upon his return to Baghdad, informed Wright on 18 October 1957 that while his government was still ready to complete the proposed Shatt al-Arab water agreement with Kuwait without any conditions simply as a mark of friendship, it was no longer interested in the idea of a pipeline from Basra to Kuwait as it had instead decided to build a deep-water terminal in Iraqi waters off Fao.[94] In fact, the idea of this Fao project was not entirely new as on 28 September 1957 *The Times* had reported that the terminal would enable oil to be shipped from Basra in tankers of up to 100,000 tons.[95] While the scheme would ensure a higher revenue for Iraq, it would deprive Kuwait of transit revenue worth between two and three million pounds per annum. The Iraq Petroleum Company, which had been following the political debate over the pipeline project for over a year, also favoured the Fao option as it would not involve any political difficulties and would be completed in a comparatively shorter time – in two and a half years – than the abortive pipeline project.[96]

The Iraqi government's decision to go ahead with the Fao terminal meant the virtual end of Kuwait's bargaining power with regard to frontier demarcation as there was no longer any need for Iraq to agree to any settlement. This simple fact was overlooked by the Resident, who still wanted the British government to continue with its efforts to find common ground between the Kuwaitis and the Iraqis on the question of demarcation and that it should try to persuade both parties to at least agree to an exchange of letters.[97] However, London did not agree with this suggestion. While Riches refused to go on acting as a broker in an attempt to bring both the parties together, Beeley, who was then at the Foreign Office, believed that the Iraqis would never agree to demarcate the frontier now that the pipeline project had been abandoned, and as such Kuwait should be told, for its own sake, to settle the frontier

94. Baghdad to Foreign Office, no. 1255, 18 October 1957, FO 371/126938.
95. See 'New basis for oil pacts?', *The Times*, 28 September 1957.
96. See Minute by P. Gore-Both, no. EA-10812/6(B), 14 October 1957, FO 371/126938. See also Baghdad to Foreign Office, no. 1208, 7 October 1957, FO 371/126938.
97. Bahrain to Foreign Office, no. 1324, 21 October 1957, FO 371/126938.

question as soon as possible even at the "cost of ceding the territory necessary to provide Iraq with a deep water channel to Umm Qasr under Iraqi sovereignty".[98] In other words, he urged the resolution of the problem on Iraqi terms, although Kuwait considered these as derogating its independence. Despite this, Ormsby-Gore accepted Beeley's views and instructed the Resident on 24 October 1957 to inform Sheikh Abdullah of the Iraqi decision to construct the Fao terminal. Moreover, Burrows was told to ask the Sheikh to consider accepting Iraq's unconditional offer of a water pipeline by inviting an Iraqi official to visit Kuwait to discuss it further. If he agreed to do so the British government would try to convince the Iraqis of the necessity of demarcating the frontier at least "at the point where the pipeline would cross it".[99] When Aubrey Halford, the Political Agent, related this to the Ruler, the Sheikh, who mistakenly believed that the Iraqis were not seriously intending to build the terminal but were actually still interested in the pipeline project, maintained that he would neither accept the Iraqi offer of water nor receive its envoy unless it first agreed to demarcate the frontier. He even requested the British government to put pressure on the Iraqis to bring this about.[100] In view of the Sheikh's attitude, Halford had no other option but to leave the Ruler to reconsider his position.

As a result of this failure to settle the frontier dispute, relations between Kuwait and Iraq remained cool with no sign of improvement. The Iraqis, without any justification, openly blamed this on Britain who, they claimed, had encouraged the Sheikh to adopt an inflexible attitude towards them. As the Ambassador tried but failed to dispel this suspicion from Iraqi minds, he asked the Foreign Office on 22 November 1957 to make a concerted attempt to put Iraqi–Kuwaiti relations on a better footing. Nevertheless, Wright felt that the main initiative behind any attempt to improve relations must first come from Iraq. The ball could be started rolling by sending some professional Iraqi officials to Kuwait

---

98. Minute by Riches, no. EA-10812/12, 22 October 1957, FO 371/126938. See also Minute by Beeley, no. 10812/12, 23 October 1957, FO 371/126938.
99. Foreign Office to Bahrain, no. 1782, 24 October 1957, FO 371/126938.
100. Kuwait to Foreign Office, no. 392, 28 October 1957, FO 371/126938. See also Kuwait to Foreign Office, no. 397, 30 October 1957, FO 371/126938.

to assist in its administration and by posting carefully chosen police and customs officers to the frontier to prevent any incidents.[101]

The Iraqis, however, had no wish to do so unless their relations with the Sheikhdom deteriorated further. To complicate matters they soon resurrected their long-cherished designs on Umm Qasr. In view of the previous Kuwaiti refusal to lease any land for the project, the Iraqis revised the plan so as not to need the strip of Kuwaiti territory. But the plan still required the placing of navigation marks and lights on the north shore of Bubiyan Island and the use of Kuwaiti waters between Warba and Bubiyan as an anchorage. The Foreign Office was concerned that if Iraq went ahead with this plan, Britain would then be placed in a difficult position as the Ruler would expect it to prevent ships from entering his waters without his prior permission. Therefore, the Foreign Office felt that the Iraqis should be instructed to consult with Sheikh Abdullah at some stage in order to avert any serious problems in the future. However, R. S. Crawford, the Chargé d'Affaires in Baghdad, opposed this idea as he believed that the Iraqis were progressing at such a slow pace that it would take at least three years or more to complete the project, during which time he expected relations between the two countries to have improved to such an extent that the Kuwaitis would not object to Iraq's minor request.[102] Indeed, Wright even openly encouraged Abdul-Wahab Mirjan, the new Iraqi Prime Minister, to believe that it was possible to proceed with the revised Umm Qasr plan without consulting the Kuwaitis at all. But Moberly of the Foreign Office disagreed and argued that it was dangerous to proceed without first gaining the consent of the Kuwaiti Ruler. Therefore, the Embassy was instructed to tell the Iraqis that even if the port itself was exclusively within Iraqi territory, the Kuwaiti Ruler's agreement would still be required for the placement of navigation marks on his territory and for the use of his waters as an anchorage.[103] It is difficult to say whether the Chargé

---

101. Wright to Beeley, no. 1034/9/57, 22 November 1957, FO 371/126913. See also R. S. Crawford's conversations with Tahsin Qadri (Master of Ceremonies at the Iraqi Palace), unnumbered, 18 November 1957, FO 371/126913.

102. Crawford to Walmsley, no. 3391/1/9/57, 20 December 1957, FO 371/126961. See also Walmsley to Crawford, no. EA-1421/48, 6 December 1957, FO 371/126961.

103. Riches to Crawford, no. 1421/49, 3 January 1958, FO 371/126961. See also Minute by Moberly, no. EA-1421/49, 1 January 1958, FO 371/126961.

d'Affaires conveyed this message to the Iraqis. In any event, the Iraqis began work on Umm Qasr without the knowledge of the Kuwaitis, and in January 1959 officially announced that the Baghdad–Basra railway line was to be extended from Basra to Umm Qasr.[104]

Conclusion

Although there was some initial optimism that the three interconnected issues – of the Shatt al-Arab water scheme, the leasing of Kuwaiti territories to Iraq for the development of the Umm Qasr port and the demarcation of the frontier – could be settled by a package deal drawn up by the British, no such settlement was reached. Kuwait would not go ahead with the water project because it felt it could not trust the Iraqis, who had previously waged public campaigns for the annexation of the Sheikhdom. The Kuwaitis feared placing their country at the mercy of an unfriendly Iraq for their vital water supply. Moreover, they were worried that if they accepted the Shatt al-Arab water agreement, it would oblige them morally to accept the Umm Qasr agreement, whereby, they believed, Iraq would develop Umm Qasr into a naval base to dominate the Gulf. Moreover, the Kuwaitis feared that, anyway, the establishment of Umm Qasr as a subsidiary port would in time severely affect the profitability of Kuwait port.

Despite the British government's earnest efforts to conclude the Umm Qasr agreement – partly because of its own military interest in the project – it eventually became clear that Iraq's proposal concerning Umm Qasr was one of the major factors behind Kuwait's refusal to sign the water agreement. With both of the proposed agreements abandoned, the British concentrated their efforts on securing agreement to an oil pipeline project from Zubair to the Kuwaiti port of Mina al-Ahmadi, in the hope that this might induce the Kuwaitis to accept the water agreement since they would then be in a position to use the oil pipeline as a counterbalance in the event of any problems with the supply of water. However, as Sheikh Abdullah believed that the Iraqis needed the oil pipeline more than Kuwait needed Iraqi water, he made the

---

104. J. M. Hunter (Head of Chancery, Baghdad), no. BA-1371/1, 22 January 1959, FO 371/140199.

demarcation of the frontier a precondition of any oil pipeline agreement. In fact, Iraq's persistent refusal to attend to the issue of demarcating its frontier with Kuwait, forced Kuwait to use all the weapons at its disposal, such as its obduracy regarding the pipeline project, to bring pressure to bear on Iraq. But by the end of 1957, Iraq had abandoned its plans for the oil pipeline in favour of a deep-sea terminal at Fao, thereby depriving Kuwait of whatever bargaining power it potentially had enjoyed. Therefore, despite Britain's efforts, Iraqi–Kuwaiti relations continued to stagnate.

8

Qasim's Claims and British Intervention, 1958–1962

Kuwait eventually gained its independence from Britain in May 1961, before any other protected state in the region. But no sooner had the country emerged as a sovereign state than Brigadier General Abdul-Karim Qasim – who had gained power in Iraq by overthrowing the monarchy in 1958 – repeatedly threatened to annex the fledgling state under the pretext of Iraq's spurious historical claim to Kuwait. However, unlike the 1990 crisis, Qasim did not deploy troops on the Kuwaiti border to execute his threats. Without waiting to see whether Qasim was serious or not, Britain responded by landing troops in Kuwait against the advice of the British Ambassador in Baghdad. These troops were withdrawn following the arrival of Arab League forces in Kuwait. Nevertheless, the British preserved their right of re-entry into Kuwait and formulated a long-term military strategy for the future security of the country.

Before discussing Qasim's claims to Kuwait and the resultant British intervention, it is first necessary to give a brief account of both Iraqi–Kuwaiti relations just before the military *coup* in Iraq and the Sheikhdom's gradual move towards full independence. Ever since the collapse of the water and Umm Qasr agreements as discussed in the previous chapter, attempts to demarcate the frontier had been suspended and Kuwait's attention drawn to another issue. This was the Iraqi plan to bring the Sheikhdom under the purview of the Iraq–Jordan Federation, which had been formed on 14 February 1958 to counter the Egyptian–Syrian Union established thirteen days earlier. But the Iraqis had an ulterior motive behind their offer of membership in the Federation. Nuri al-Said, who became the Prime Minister of Iraq on 3 March 1958 for the last time,[1] intended to treat Kuwait – which had

---

1. Nuri al-Said served as Prime Minister of Iraq fourteen times: March–October 1930; October 1930–October 1932; December 1938–April 1939; April

now emerged as one of the most important countries in the Gulf due to its massive oil production – not as an equal partner but as a protégé of Iraq to be exploited economically. The Premier believed that the British government would support Iraqi efforts to bring Kuwait under the umbrella of the Federation following Iraq's active cooperation with Britain in the formation of the Baghdad Pact in 1955 and its vigorous propaganda campaign against the Egyptian President Gamal Abdel-Nasser, Britain's arch-enemy.[2]

With these objectives in mind, Nuri al-Said invited Sheikh Abdullah to Baghdad on 10 May 1958. However, although the Sheikh came under great pressure to join the Iraq–Jordan Federation, he declined to do so and the talks ended without any progress being made. As a result, Bernard Burrows, the Political Resident and a strong advocate of the Federation, arrived in Kuwait towards the end of May to convince the Ruler of the benefits of associating himself with it. But as the Ruler correctly believed that the central aim of the Federation was to wage a propaganda war against Egypt, with which he had developed friendly relations, he declined to accept the Resident's suggestion to join and stated that prevailing public opinion in Kuwait made outright accession to the Federation impossible, at least for the time being. However, the Sheikh did agree to receive an Iraqi delegation to negotiate limited agreements on such matters as the frontier dispute, the promotion of trade, the investment of Kuwaiti capital in Iraq and the exchange of information on security issues. But as the Kuwaiti Ruler linked the demarcation of the frontier with the discussion of these other issues, Iraq refused the offer.[3] Instead, in a note to the British government dated 6 June 1958, the new Iraqi government headed by

---

1939–February 1940; February–March 1940; October 1941–October 1942; October 1942–December 1943; December 1943–June 1944; November 1946–March 1947; January–December 1949; September 1950–July 1952; August 1954–December 1955; December 1955–June 1957; and March–May 1958. See Hanna Batatu, *The Old Social Classes and the Revolutionary Movements of Iraq* (Princeton, New Jersey, Princeton University Press, 1987), p. 184.

2. Schofield, *Kuwait and Iraq*, p. 101.

3. See Confidential Annex to Kuwait Diary no. 6, 19 May–19 June 1958, in Halford to Foreign Office, no. 1014/58, 19 June 1958, FO 371/132751. See also Persian Gulf Monthly Report, 30 April–2 June 1958, in Bahrain to Foreign Office, no. 10101, 29 May 1958, FO 371/132751.

Ahmad Mukhtar Baban, painted itself as the successor of the Ottoman Empire in the Basra Vilayet and reasserted Iraq's claim to Kuwait. Pointing to the problems of smuggling, public security and Iraq's need for an additional outlet to the waters of the Gulf, the note insisted that the ideal "solution would be the accession of Kuwait [to the proposed Arab Federation] . . . otherwise they would unilaterally straighten out the frontier and appropriate all the islands in their territorial waters".[4]

However, calls for Kuwait to be brought under Hashemite rule ended abruptly with the military *coup d'état* in Iraq on 14 July 1958, headed by Brigadier General Abdul-Karim Qasim, in which King Faisal II, the Crown Prince and former Regent Abdul-Ilah, Nuri al-Said and a number of prominent Iraqi leaders were killed.[5] The new regime in Iraq not only abandoned the Federation but also brought about the eventual collapse of the Western-sponsored Baghdad Pact, an alliance that had been devised to counter the growing Soviet influence in the Middle East. Qasim also sought to restrict any further strengthening of Britain's privileged status in Iraq.[6] The revolution also had wider repercussions in Kuwait and throughout the Middle East. In the absence of the Ruler who was on holiday in Damascus, Sheikh Abdullah al-Mubarak, the Chief of Public Security, placed the army on a high state of alert. Forces were strengthened at the oil centres at Ahmadi and Raudatain (in the north of Kuwait) and troops deployed on the border. With British forces landing in Jordan in an attempt to stabilize the region, Halford, the Political Agent, offered the Acting Ruler military assistance to help control the internal situation and to protect the oil installations. The Sheikh, however, declined the offer arguing that Kuwait was well able to maintain order. On 17 July 1958, Burrows, the Political Resident, arrived in Kuwait and pressed Sheikh Abdullah to accept some British troops, but the Sheikh once again declined the offer making it clear that

---

4. For the 1958 Iraqi claim to Kuwait see 'Historical Note on the Iraqi claim to Kuwait' by Foreign Office Research Department, no. BK1083/181, 19 July 1961, FO 371/156852.

5. For more details of the 1958 *coup* in Iraq see Humphrey Trevelyan, *The Middle East in Revolution* (London, Macmillan, 1970), pp. 135–40.

6. Ever since the emergence of Iraq as a separate entity Britain had been providing it with military and administrative experts and played a vital role in shaping its foreign policy. These British officials in the Iraqi administration had also been supplying vital information to the British government. This privilege ended once and for all with their expulsion following the *coup*.

the Sheikhdom intended to pursue a policy of non-involvement and to remain neutral.[7]

Yet despite Kuwait's stated neutrality the military regime in Baghdad soon closed its frontier with Kuwait and imposed restrictions on the exportation of foodstuffs to the Sheikhdom.[8] These measures forced the Kuwaiti Ruler to cut short his holiday and return home on 24 July. The Sheikh, deeply concerned by these actions of the new regime in Iraq, was anxious not to suffer a repetition of the events of the previous May, when he had felt that the British government had "deserted" him in face of Nuri Pasha's pressure to join the Arab Federation. He therefore sought the British government's permission for Kuwait to become a full member of the Arab League which, he believed, would give him greater authority in his dealings with Iraq and would also be a tangible expression of the Sheikhdom's solidarity with the rest of the Arab world. As Burrows opposed this request, the Ruler compromised by asking for a reaffirmation of Britain's undertaking to his country.[9] This was given to him on 23 October 1958 by the Political Agent with an added pledge that the Ruler was now free to conduct his own relations with other Arab states.[10] The abolition of this long-standing restriction paved the way for Kuwait's push for greater autonomy.

With the Sheikhdom edging towards independence, Qasim wrote to Sheikh Abdullah expressing his desire to establish a "co-operative relationship between Iraq . . . [and its] sister Kuwait".[11] This friendly message encouraged the Sheikh to visit Qasim in Baghdad on 25 October 1958 to discuss outstanding bilateral issues. Ashraf Lutfi, the Assistant Secretary of State of Kuwait, drafted some broad areas of agreement with the Secretary-General of Iraqi Foreign Affairs on such issues as the frontier, trade exchanges, extradition, the investment of Kuwaiti funds in Iraq and the exchange of information about subversive

---

7. Confidential Annex to Kuwait Diary no. 7, 20 June–28 July 1958, in Halford to Foreign Office, no. 1014/58, 28 July 1958, FO 371/132751
8. Kuwait to Foreign Office, no. 500, 18 August 1958, FO 371/132751.
9. Confidential Annex to Kuwait Diary no. 8, 29 July–25 August 1958, in Halford to Foreign Office, no. 10101, 25 August 1958, FO 371/132523.
10. Persian Gulf Monthly Summary, 29 September–2 November 1958, in Bahrain to Foreign Office, no. 10101, 3 November 1958, FO 371/132523.
11. Mustafa M. Alani, *Operation Vantage: British Military Intervention in Kuwait 1961* (Surrey, LAAM, 1990), p. 53.

activities. Both parties, however, agreed to defer detailed negotiations until the internal political situation in Iraq had stabilized.[12] In an attempt to deal more directly with the Sheikhdom, Qasim in December 1958 sought the Ruler's permission to establish an Iraqi Consulate there. Although this request was denied, it at least implied Iraq's acknowledgement of Kuwait as an independent state. In fact, Qasim's government had always referred to Kuwait as an independent state in its official correspondence, and even he himself had addressed Sheikh Abdullah as the Ruler of Kuwait. Moreover, ever since he seized power, Qasim had been tacitly encouraging Kuwait to assert its full independence, probably as he reasoned that by attaining its sovereignty the Sheikhdom would be kept free from British political and military control.[13]

Meanwhile, the Ruler signed up to the international conventions on the Load Line and the Safety of Life at Sea on 12 April 1959 to enhance Kuwait's status in the international arena. On 24 July, the Sheikhdom was elected a full member of the International Telecommunication Union, without Iraqi objection.[14]

Despite the improving state of Iraqi–Kuwaiti relations, unusual Iraqi troop movements took place in March 1959 on Kuwait's northern frontier. This aroused suspicion in diplomatic circles that Qasim was preparing to attack Kuwait to boost his floundering position at home. Upon receipt of these reports, the Foreign Office requested its Ambassador in Baghdad, Sir Humphrey Trevelyan, to submit a detailed analysis of the situation. Trevelyan however dismissed claims that Iraq was preparing to invade the Sheikhdom on the grounds that: firstly, the military regime itself felt threatened on its Syrian, Turkish and Iranian borders; secondly, the army was preoccupied with maintaining internal order and protecting Qasim himself; and finally, such a move against Kuwait was likely to antagonize all of Iraq's Arab neighbours.[15] All the same, this perceived Iraqi threat on his frontiers forced the Sheikh to

---

12. See Confidential Annex to Kuwait Diary no. 11, 27 October–24 November 1958, in Halford to Foreign Office, no. BA1013/63, 25 November 1958, FO 371/132523.

13. Alani, *Operation Vantage*, p. 74. See also Schofield, *Kuwait and Iraq*, pp. 102–3.

14. See Persian Gulf Monthly Summary, 5 January–1 February 1959, in Bahrain to Foreign Office, no. 10101, 2 February 1959, FO 371/140066. See also 'Kuwait: Annual Review for 1959' in Richmond to Middleton, no. 1, 4 January 1960, FO 371/148896.

15. Baghdad to Foreign Office, no. 301, 9 April 1959, FO 371/140963.

seek renewed assurances from Britain that it would defend Kuwait in the event of an Iraqi attack. In response, the Gulf Military Co-ordination Committee formulated a military plan for the defence of Kuwait. British troops were placed on stand-by in Bahrain to leave for Kuwait at short notice in the event of any emergency. A military delegation under the command of Major-General Bry was sent to the Sheikhdom to assess its military requirements. Following this visit the Committee, at a meeting on 11 June 1959, decided to train Kuwaiti crews for Centurian tanks within six months at the Royal Armoured Corps' base at Catterick.[16] This Anglo-Kuwaiti military cooperation continued until the apparent Iraqi threat began to subside towards the end of the year.

In the meantime, Kuwait made further progress towards achieving full independence. In 1960, with British backing and Iraqi votes, Kuwait became a full member of the Universal Postal Union and World Health Organization and was unopposed in its bid to join the International Civil Aviation Organization, the Intergovernmental Maritime Consultative Organization and UNESCO.[17] Kuwait also became a founder member of the Organization of Petroleum Exporting Countries (OPEC) on 14 September 1960. At the same time, the Sheikhdom assumed more direct control of its foreign relations.[18] As the Sheikh felt confident enough to deal with his country's external affairs, he paid a visit to Riyadh in October 1960 and persuaded King Saud to agree in principle to the demarcation of the Kuwaiti–Saudi neutral zone as soon as possible.[19] Encouraged by this diplomatic success, Sheikh

---

16. See Minutes of the Eleventh Meeting of the Persian Gulf Military Co-ordination Committee, no. MCC(PG)59, 11 June 1959, FO 371/140175. See also Minutes of the Sixth Meeting, no. MCC(PG)59, 13 March 1959, FO 371/140175.

17. See the Memorandum by Arabian Department on Kuwait's Foreign Affairs, no. BA1073/11, 27 October 1960, FO 371/148948. See also 'Kuwait's Membership of International Organization' by Foreign Office Research Department, no. BK1083/181, 14 July 1961, FO 371/156852.

18. Memorandum by the Secretary of State on Kuwait, no. C(60)81, 10 May 1960, CAB/129/101.

19. At the conference of Uqair in December 1922, Sir Percy Cox solved the problem of the no man's land in the Kuwait–Hasa border region by the formation of a neutral zone in which the two rulers – Ibn Saud and Sheikh Ahmed – were to have equal and individual rights. See Stephen Hemsley Longrigg, *Oil in the Middle East* (London, Oxford University Press, 1968), p. 100. See also Kuwait to Foreign Office, no. 486, 15 October 1960, FO 371/148966.

Abdullah wrote to Qasim on 29 October, asking him whether Iraq would be prepared to discuss in general terms the question of their land and sea boundaries. In fact, the Ruler wanted to settle the frontier question as quickly as possible in view of the progress of the construction of the Iraqi section of the Basra–Kuwait road.[20] As Qasim did not reply, the Ruler sent him another letter on 3 January 1961 repeating his earlier request. Eventually, on 1 March 1961, Hashem Jawad, the Iraqi Foreign Minister, replied that the proposal was being given his government's active consideration.[21]

However, while reluctant to discuss the frontier problem, the revolutionary regime instead resurrected the Umm Qasr project which had lain dormant for over three years. Although the Foreign Office thought that there might be "something sinister" in Iraq's sudden revival of the project, it had no wish to resume its role as a go-between as it had done in the past, especially since the Kuwaitis had themselves approached Iraq.[22] As a result, the foundation-stone for the port at Umm Qasr was laid on 26 March 1961, without Kuwaiti protest.[23] This acquiescence on the part of Kuwaiti ruling family with regard to Umm Qasr was due to their belief that the Iraqis had finally dropped all intention of asking Kuwait for the use of Kuwaiti territory to the south of Umm Qasr.[24]

Meanwhile, in January 1961, Britain formally relinquished its control of Kuwait's foreign policy, a move warmly applauded by the Iraqis. They therefore reacted most unfavourably when three months later it was rumoured that Kuwait was planning to join the British Commonwealth. Denouncing this publicly on 30 April, Qasim urged

---

20. Kuwait to Foreign Office, no. 510, 29 October 1960, FO 371/148966. See also J. C. B. Richmond to R. A. Beaumont (London), no. 10814/60, 15 October 1960, FO 371/148966.

21. Ahmad al-Mayyal, 'The political boundaries of the State of Kuwait: a study in political geography' (Ph.D. thesis, School of Oriental and African Studies, University of London, 1986), pp. 116–17. See also Schofield, *Kuwait and Iraq*, p. 104.

22. 'Approach to port of Umm Qasr' by R. A. Beaumont, no. BK1082/6, 28 February 1961, FO 371/156844.

23. British Embassy (Baghdad) to Arabian Department, no. 392/3/61, 30 March 1961, FO 371/156844; Richmond to Foreign Office, no. 97, 22 March 1961, FO 371/156844.

24. Richmond to R. A. Beaumont (Foreign Office), no. 1086/61, 25 March 1961, FO 371/156844.

the Ruler to resist "such imperialist schemes". Significantly the Iraqi dictator then offered Kuwait his support in the event of any external threats, maintaining that there were no frontiers between the two countries.[25] This was Qasim's first major statement concerning the status of Kuwait. Although it is not clear what he actually meant by this absence of frontier, it perhaps referred to Qasim's underlying ambition of annexing Kuwait. The statement was disturbing to both the British and the Kuwaitis, who were still engaged in the final phase of negotiations for independence. To pacify Iraq, the Kuwaiti government officially denied in 2 May that it had any intention of joining the Commonwealth after independence.[26] In Baghdad, when Trevelyan sought an explanation of Qasim's statement, he was assured by Hashem Jawad that his comments were "purely historical" and bore no political significance. This explanation seemed to be borne out when, on 13 June, Iraq sponsored Kuwait's application for membership of the International Labour Organization.[27] However, despite this gesture, the real meaning of Qasim's earlier reference to Kuwait soon became clearer when Kuwait eventually emerged as a sovereign state.

On 19 June 1961, the formal independence of Kuwait was announced, with the Exclusive Agreement of 1899 replaced by an Exchange of Notes, which contained the following clauses:

(a) The Agreement of the 23rd January 1899, shall be terminated as being inconsistent with the sovereignty and independence of Kuwait.

(b) The relations between the two countries shall continue to be governed by a spirit of close friendship.

(c) When appropriate the two Governments shall consult together on matters which concern them both.

---

25. See Majid Khadduri, *Republican Iraq: A Study in Iraqi Politics since the Revolution of 1958* (London, Oxford University Press, 1969), p. 169. See also Alani, *Operation Vantage*, p. 55.
26. Kuwait to Foreign Office, no. 173, 3 May 1961, FO 371/156838.
27. Schofield, *Kuwait and Iraq*, p. 105. See also Alani, *Operation Vantage*, pp. 55–6; Trevelyan, *The Middle East in Revolution*, pp. 184–5; 'Kuwait's Membership of International Organization' by Foreign Office Research Department, no. BK1083/181, 14 July 1961, FO 371/156852.

(d) Nothing in these conclusions shall affect the readiness of Her Majesty's Government to assist the Government of Kuwait if the latter requests such assistance.[28]

Although Qasim congratulated the Sheikh for the abrogation of the 1899 agreement, he went on to say that the British, who had in any case "unlawfully" concluded this agreement with Sheikh Mubarak al-Sabah, were still engaged in "plots and intrigues" against Kuwait as well as the rest of the Arab world.[29] Qasim's statement convinced the Sheikh (who had taken the title of Emir) that the Iraqi leader was beginning to take a more hostile attitude towards Kuwait. As the Emir had anticipated, Qasim, just six days after the announcement of Kuwait's independence, laid claim to the whole country on the grounds that Kuwait had been part of Basra right up to the outbreak of the First World War. He declared that Kuwait was still an "integral and indivisible part" of Iraq and as such the Sheikh of Kuwait would be appointed Qaimaqam of Kuwait under the Liwa (Province) of Basra. Qasim warned that Iraq was determined to protect the Iraqi population of Kuwait and acquire all the territory rightfully belonging to the Liwa of Basra. If the Sheikh "misbehaved" he would be "seriously punished and considered a rebel. Kuwait was part of Iraq and no one could behave despotically with the rights of the Iraqi people."[30] No previous Iraqi Prime Minister or leader had made such a public statement concerning Kuwait. Qasim apparently did so to stem a rising tide of opposition at home to his dictatorial policies. Moreover, the signing of the new Anglo-Kuwaiti agreement had angered him and convinced him that with the possibility of Kuwait joining the Arab League and the United Nations, time was running out for Iraq to reassert its claim to Kuwait.[31]

---

28. The full text is in E. Lauterpacht, C. J. Greenwood, M. Weller and D. Bethlehem (eds.), *The Kuwait Crisis: Basic Documents* (Cambridge, Grotius, 1991), p. 50.

29. Alani, *Operation Vantage*, p. 61. See also Trevelyan, *The Middle East in Revolution*, p. 186.

30. Trevelyan to Foreign Office, no. 635, 26 June 1961, FO 371/156845; Trevelyan to Foreign Office, no. 637, 26 June 1961, FO 371/156845. See also Alani, *Operation Vantage*, pp. 61–2.

31. See Note on Qasim's policy towards Kuwait by G. F. Hiller, no. K1083/3, 26 June 1961, FO 371/156845.

As Qasim's claim to Kuwait had forced the Foreign Office to investigate the validity of his assertion, it concluded that there was nothing of substance in it.[32] However, Trevelyan was instructed to make a strong protest to the Iraqi Foreign Minister against Qasim's statement. Hashem Jawad replied that Iraq's long-standing claim to Kuwait, though ignored for so long, was well-known to the British government. The Ambassador did not hesitate to inform him that Britain "had never recognized Iraq's claim" and pointed out that the new agreement "marked no change of status but was merely a reflection of the fact that Kuwait had already, for some time, been exercising responsibility for her international relations".[33]

While Trevelyan believed that Qasim would not resort to military intervention due to his own internal problems, he alerted his Military Attaché at the Embassy as well as the Consul in Basra to remain vigilant. As neither witnessed any unusual military movements – there were no extra military or police patrols in Baghdad and no abnormal activity was noticeable on the part of the Iraqi navy anchored at Basra – early indications did not suggest that an attack on Kuwait was imminent. Nevertheless, the Ambassador was inclined to think that Qasim might be planning a *coup* in Kuwait supported by limited Iraqi military action on 14 July 1961, the third anniversary of the Iraqi revolution, under cover of the usual troop movements.[34] However, John Richmond, the new Consul-General in Kuwait, immediately discounted the possibility of an Iraqi-engineered *coup* in Kuwait as he could neither find any evidence to support such a theory nor was there an adequate network of pro-Iraqi organizations in the Emirate to carry it out. Rather, there were anti-Iraqi demonstrations throughout Kuwait with citizens of all classes waving the Kuwaiti flag and displaying pictures of Sheikh Abdullah to demonstrate their loyalty to the Emir and his government.[35] The Emir's position was further boosted by messages of support from King Hussein

---

32. See 'Kuwait' in Burrows to C. F. Hiller, no. 225290/61, 8 July 1961, FO 371/156847.
33. Trevelyan to Foreign Office, no. 633, 26 June 1961, FO 371/156845.
34. Trevelyan to Foreign Office, no. 639, 26 June 1961, FO 371/156873; Basra to Foreign Office, no. 45, 27 June 1961, FO 371/156873; Trevelyan to Foreign Office, no. 640, 27 June 1961, FO 371/156873.
35. Richmond to Foreign Office, no. 288, 28 June 1961, FO 371/156873. See also Richmond to Foreign Office, no. 284, 27 June 1961, FO 371/156845.

of Jordan and King Saud of Saudi Arabia, who even sent his Chief of Staff to consult with the Kuwaitis.[36] Despite such support, Sheikh Abdullah still felt threatened enough to request a formal assurance of support from the British government in order to bolster the morale of his people.[37] The British government agreed to do so and the Consul-General was instructed to deliver the following message to the Emir:

> Her Majesty's Government wish to assure His Highness the Ruler of Kuwait and the Kuwaiti people of their support and sympathy in the present situation and to reaffirm their determination to carry out all the obligations entered into in the exchange of Notes signed on June 19, 1961.[38]

This was conveyed to the Emir on the morning of 28 June 1961. That afternoon, Lord Home, the British Foreign Secretary, declared in the House of Commons that the notes exchanged nine days previously between Britain and Kuwait were an agreement between two independent and sovereign states in which Britain's obligations were laid down, obligations which it was ready to honour. He added that the British government had been in touch with the government of Kuwait to assure the Emir of its continued support.[39]

As a result of this pledge, the British Joint Planning Staff drew up plans for possible British military intervention in Kuwait under the code-name "Operation Vantage", which could be enacted at a moment's notice to forestall an Iraqi occupation of Kuwait.[40] A timetable was framed for a rapid response to Iraqi aggression. HMS *Bulwark*, which was lying off Karachi and carrying a commando contingent of the Royal Marines, was placed on full alert to be ready to sail to Kuwait at short notice. RAF aircraft had been ordered up from Aden to Sharjah and

---

36. Richmond to Foreign Office, no. 281, 27 June 1961, FO 371/156845. See also Amman to Foreign Ofice, no. 506, 27 June 1961, FO 371/156845.
37. Richmond to Foreign Office, no. 281, 27 June 1961, FO 371/156845.
38. Foreign Office to Kuwait, no. 378, 27 June 1961, FO 371/156845.
39. For the full text of the parliamentary question, see no. K1083/21, 2S June 1961, FO 371/156846.
40. See 'Military Preparations for Intervention in Kuwait' by A. R. Walmsley, no. BK1193/18G (Top Secret), 26 June 1961, FO 371/156874.

Bahrain. Tanks were loaded into landing-craft off Bahrain and could reach Kuwait in just 24 hours.[41]

While this military planning was going on, Trevelyan sent alarming reports to the Foreign Office on 28 June that Baghdad was "full of rumours of troops movements". Although unable to confirm these rumours, he believed that Qasim was most likely to make a quick dash against Kuwait from Basra with one mechanized infantry brigade supported by Centurion tanks with artillery and air support. This force could be assembled and moved under the guise of military rehearsals for the 14 July parade in Basra, the last rehearsal for which was to be held on the night of 2 July. Based on this intelligence, Trevelyan strongly recommended that British forces including HMS *Bulwark* be despatched immediately to Kuwait to act as a visible deterrent and, if it came to it, to defend the Emirate.[42]

However, Lancelot Pyman, the British Consul-General in Basra, sent contrary reports on the military situation the following day. Based on his own reliable source, Pyman cabled the Foreign Office that there had been no clear indications of intended aggressive action. There was still no increase in the number of troops in the main Basra barracks; security patrols remained normal and Iraqi Airways continued to fly to Kuwait; the Basra Petroleum Company was still allowed to use their aircraft within the country and on the same day, as further proof of the normalcy of the situation, the garrison commander permitted the oil company to resume drilling at a new well at the extreme northern end of the Rumaila oilfield which he had previously stopped. He further added that nothing of military significance was moving into Basra by rail.[43]

Because of these conflicting reports, Sir William Luce, the Political Resident, later that day called an urgent meeting of the Arabian Gulf Military Co-ordination Committee to review the military situation. The committee made the following hurried assessment: first, Qasim had

---

41. Brief by A. R. Walmsley for the Secretary of State's Statement in the Cabinet, no. BK1193/30/A, FO 371/156874. See also Foreign Office to Baghdad, no. 819, 28 June 1961, FO 371/156873.
42. Trevelyan to Foreign Office, nos. 655, 658 and 659, 28 June 1961, FO 371/156873. See also Trevelyan to Foreign Office, no. 685, 29 June 1961, FO 371/156875.
43. Pyman (Basra) to Foreign Office, nos. 46 and 48, 29 June 1961, FO 371/156874.

declared publicly that Kuwait was to be merged with Iraq; second, his propaganda machine was building the case for Iraqi intervention in Kuwait; third, he was moving an armoured regiment to Basra where an infantry brigade was already stationed; fourth, he would be in a position to invade Kuwait within the next three days; fifth, no military action by any other Arab state could prevent Iraq's sudden seizure of Kuwait; and sixth, the Emir of Kuwait had shown that he relied entirely on British assistance. In view of these factors, the committee recommended that as the threat to Kuwait was both "grave and imminent", "Operation Vantage" should be put into partial effect forthwith to the extent of concentrating British forces in Bahrain.[44]

Luce's recommendation alarmed London. An emergency meeting of the Cabinet was held on the same day, 29 June, to decide whether to mobilize British forces to defend Kuwait. Lord Home opened the proceedings by informing the Cabinet that as there were now clear indications that General Qasim, in pursuance of his claim to Kuwait, might shortly launch an attack on the Emirate, British troops were ready to intervene. But he felt that if British forces were to act with sufficient speed and legitimacy, the Emir should make a formal request for British military assistance. Lord Home then proposed that the United States should be kept abreast of developments with a view to obtaining their prompt support if it became necessary for Britain to take military action. It was important to impress on the White House the gravity of the threat facing Kuwait and the serious consequences of failing to maintain its independence.[45]

Following the conclusion of this meeting, Sir Harold Caccia, the British Ambassador in Washington, was instructed to enlist the full political backing of the United States government. He was to inform them that British units were moving into the area in order to pre-empt an Iraqi attack and that these forces would stay there no longer than was absolutely necessary.[46] The United States, which had been developing a close relationship with Kuwait well before it had even achieved

---

44. Sir W. Luce (Bahrain) to Foreign Office, no. 374, 29 June 1961, FO 371/156874.
45. Conclusions of a Meeting of the Cabinet, no. CC(61), 36th Conclusions, 29 June 1961, CAB128/35/PT1.
46. Foreign Office to Washington, no. 4344, 29 June 1961, FO 371/156874.

independence, assured Caccia of their support in the defence of the Emirate. Dean Rusk, the US Secretary of State, also agreed that both the American and British missions in New York should "concert about tactics at the United Nations".[47]

Later that day, Richmond was instructed to tell Sheikh Abdullah to prepare for an imminent Iraqi attack. In so doing he should permit British forces to take up defensive positions within Kuwait before the Iraqis assembled a strike force close to the border. He then told the Emir that to enable British forces to mobilize quickly the British government needed a formal written request from Kuwait for assistance under section (d) of the agreement of 19 June 1961, but he stressed that this request would not be made public until the actual arrival of British forces made this necessary.[48] The following morning, the Consul-General met the Sheikh and obtained this written request for the immediate landing of British troops.[49]

While Kuwait was making preparations to receive the British troops, Trevelyan sent a series of urgent despatches to London about military movements in Baghdad. At 10.45 a.m. on 30 June, the Ambassador reported that there was unusual activity involving the Centurion tank regiment in Baghdad and that some of the tanks had been transported by rail to southern Iraq the previous night. He added that there were also rumours that troops from Jaloula and from Baghdad had moved south overnight. At 1.39 p.m. on the same day, Trevelyan further reported that the force stationed at Basra possibly consisted of a mobile infantry brigade, 1 squadron of Centurion tanks, 1 artillery regiment, some paratroopers, and 12 Soviet torpedo-boats with Soviet crews. But he stressed that this information was based on unconfirmed reports, rumours and the known strength of the permanent Basra garrison. The previous night, his Military Attaché, based on sources close to General Officer Commanding 1 Division, Baghdad, had reported that tanks, troops and elements of the 20th Infantry Brigade had been

---

47. Washington to Foreign Office, no. 1596, 29 June 1961, FO 371/156874. See also Washington to Foreign Office, no. 1589, 30 June 1961, FO 371/156874.
48. Foreign Office to Kuwait, no. 413, 29 June 1961, FO 371/156874. See also Foreign Office to Kuwait, no. 427, 30 June 1961, FO 371/156874.
49. For the full text, see Kuwait to Foreign Office, no. 314, 30 June 1961, FO 371/156874. See also Kuwait to Foreign Office, nos. 313 and 316, 30 June 1961, FO 371/156874.

moved to Basra.[50] Pyman, however, still disputed these reports of an Iraqi build-up as there had been no movement of troops or military supplies, including tanks, in Basra and that the evidence available from Basra simply did not suggest that an attack on Kuwait was under preparation. Nevertheless, he did concede that due to the proximity of the Kuwaiti frontier a surprise attack could be mounted without the need of large-scale preparations.[51] Given these conflicting assessments of the situation, Trevelyan recommended that British forces should not be deployed in Kuwait until they were satisfied that Qasim had assembled a force in the Basra area which could be considered a threat to Kuwait. Otherwise Qasim, who had sympathy both within Iraq and "elsewhere in the Arab world" for his claim to Kuwait, would capitalize on the presence of British troops and "convert an inter-Arab quarrel into a first-class anti-British issue". He therefore strongly recommended that it was essential before the arrival of British troops in the Emirate to conduct air reconnaissance of the Iraqi–Kuwaiti border area in order to discover whether there was a concentration of Iraqi forces.[52]

The Ambassador's recommendation for delaying the landing of troops until strong evidence of an Iraqi build-up was available, was controverted by the Consul-General in Kuwait. Richmond, who was seriously concerned for the Emirate's security, argued that since the Emir had formally requested British assistance, it would be extremely damaging to British interests in Kuwait if this was not given.[53] Luce was of the same opinion and stated that it was most important politically that Britain should not risk forfeiting the Emir's confidence in British "determination to help him, by appearing to drag our feet". Accordingly, he urged the immediate implementation of the following measures to reassure Sheikh Abdullah, pending the decision on whether to launch "Operation Vantage":

    (i) Forty two commando from [HMS] Bulwark with half squadron of tanks from [HMS] Striker, under his command,

---

50. Trevelyan to Foreign Office, nos. 690, 693, 700 and 703, 30 June 1961, FO 371/156875.
51. Pyman (Basra) to Foreign Office, nos. 51 and 52, 30 June 1961, FO 371/156874.
52. Trevelyan to Foreign Office, no. 692, 30 June 1961, FO 371/156875.
53. Richmond to Foreign Office, no. 325, 1 July 1961, FO 371/156875.

should take up defensive position Mutla Ridge and secure the airfield.

(ii) Eight Squadron Royal Air Force, based in Bahrain, should provide air defence and armed reconnaissance patrols in the area, refuelled as necessary in Kuwait.

(iii) Crews for Kuwait stockpiled tanks should be sent to Kuwait directly as early as possible.[54]

London agreed to deploy troops despite the lack of concrete information about Iraqi troop movements on the Kuwaiti border. The first British contingent, including 42 Royal Marine Commando, 1 squadron of Centurion tanks, 1 squadron of the 11th Hussars (armoured cars), and 10 Hunter aircraft in addition to 50 Canberras from British bases in Germany and Cyprus, had arrived in Kuwait by 1 July. In addition to these, 10 more Hunters in Bahrain and 11 Canberras in Sharjah as well as a further 8 in Cyprus were placed on stand-by.[55] The United States and French governments were duly informed of the landing of British sea, air and land forces in Kuwait in an attempt to gain their full political support in bringing the matter before the Security Council.[56] In addition to these British forces, an advance Saudi army detachment also arrived in Kuwait on 1 July, which was placed under the command of the Kuwaiti Commander-in-Chief and ordered to the Iraqi–Kuwaiti frontier. In fact Britain encouraged the presence of Saudi forces in Kuwait as this could have some political value in proving that the Emirate had Arab support and was not entirely dependent on Britain.[57]

---

54. Luce to Foreign Office, no. 380, 30 June 1961, FO 371/156875.
55. For details of the military build-up see Foreign Office to New York, no. 2570, 2 July 1961, FO 371/156876; Richmond to Foreign Office, no. 336, 1 July 1961, FO 371/156875; Cabinet Conclusions, no. CC(61), 38th Conclusions, 3 July 1961, CAB128/35/PT1.
56. Foreign Office to Washington and Paris, nos. 4394 and 2204, 30 June 1961, FO 371/156874. Many other governments including those of Egypt, Jordan and Turkey were also informed of the British decision to send troops to Kuwait. See Foreign Office to Cairo, Amman, Ankara, Beirut, Benghazi, Tunis, Khartoum, Rabat and Tehran, nos. 1352, 812, 697, 745, 193, 361, 625, 369 and 934, 30 June 1961, FO 371/156874.
57. Richmond to Foreign Office, no. 331, 1 July 1961, FO 371/156877; Foreign Office to Kuwait, no. 505, 1 July 1961, FO 371/156877; Richmond to Foreign

The Kuwaiti government soon publicly announced this arrival of British and Saudi forces, which it justified by stating: "Qasim had begun to mass his forces on the frontiers in preparation for the invasion of Kuwait." The statement added that these troops had come in response to the Emir's request for the defence of Kuwait and would be withdrawn as soon as the crisis was over.[58]

Although at this stage the balance of forces was still in Iraq's favour, the relative strength of the Iraqi forces at Basra was gradually declining in the face of the continued British build-up.[59] Despite this, Qasim did not attack Kuwait during the night of 2 July as had been anticipated; Basra remained quiet and there were no extra police or military patrols either there or in Safwan. Indeed, everything was normal and there was no sign of hostility towards Britain or any action taken against British companies.[60] Britain completed its deployment in Kuwait on 6 July 1961 with the troops taking up defensive positions along the frontier.

Although there was no unusual Iraqi troop movements in the frontier zone, the crisis was gaining momentum in the UN Security Council. The Emir of Kuwait, at Britain's direction, sent an urgent telegram to the President of the Security Council on 1 July, informing him of the Iraqi threat to the independence and territorial integrity of his country.[61] The Emir requested an immediate meeting of the Council under Article 35.2 of the UN Charter in view of the expected Iraqi armed aggression.[62] On the same day, Sir Patrick Dean, Britain's permanent representative in the UN, wrote to the President supporting

---

Office, no. 359, 3 July 1961, FO 371/156877; Richmond to Foreign Office, no. 350, 2 July 1961, FO 371/156875.

58. For the full text of the statement issued to the press and radio by the State Secretariat, see Richmond to Foreign Office, no. 333, 1 July 1961, FO 371/156846.

59. For the relative strength of the forces as on the morning of 2 July, see Foreign Office to New York, no. 2570, 2 July 1961, FO 371/156876.

60. For more details on the situation in Basra, see Pyman to Foreign Office, nos. 58, 59 and 60, 2, 3 and 4 July 1961 respectively, FO 371/156876.

61. The Emir's message to the President of the Security Council was drafted by the British Foreign Office. For the full text, see Foreign Office to Kuwait, no. 477, 30 June 1961, FO 371/156875.

62. The copy of the text is in Richmond to Foreign Office, no. 329, 1 July 1961, FO 371/156875.

this request. He also sent a letter to the UN Secretary-General explaining that the actions Britain had taken in Kuwait were in accordance with the terms of the Anglo-Kuwaiti Exchange of Notes of 19 June. In response to these requests, the Security Council held a series of meetings on the crisis in Kuwait between 2 and 6 July. During these meetings there were charges and counter-charges between Dean and Adnan Pachachi, the Iraqi permanent representative. Dean argued that his government had deployed troops in Kuwait because Qasim's claims to the country had greatly undermined its independence and the presence of a considerable Iraqi military force in Basra, only 48 kilometres from the Kuwaiti border, meant that Iraq was able to invade Kuwait within a few hours of an order to attack.[63] Adnan Pachachi retorted that the British action in Kuwait was "motivated entirely by considerations of Kuwaiti oil and the need to safeguard Kuwaiti investments in London". Describing the historical basis of Iraq's claim to Kuwait he maintained, "Kuwait was not and never had been a sovereign and independent State".[64] He then demanded the immediate withdrawal of the British troops, whose number he estimated to be in the region of 20,000.

A crucial meeting of the Security Council was held on 5 July, following the arrival of a Kuwaiti delegation headed by Abdul-Aziz Hussein. During the meeting, Hussein made a statement refuting Iraq's claim to Kuwait and argued: "The independence of Kuwait had been recognized de facto or *de jure* by most of the countries of the world including both the pre- and post-revolutionary Iraq." He further assured the Council that the British forces would leave Kuwait as soon as the Iraqi threat was removed. The US representative then made a brief statement reaffirming his country's recognition of Kuwait's independence and supporting Britain's actions. The final speech of the day was delivered by the representative of the UAR who reiterated his government's opposition to the landing of British troops in Kuwait and stressed that the differences between Kuwait and Iraq should be resolved by the mediation of the League of Arab States.[65]

---

63. For the full text, see New York to Foreign Office, no. 1075, 2 July 1961, FO 371/156848.
64. New York to Foreign Office, no. 1076, 2 July 1961, FO 371/156848.
65. New York to Foreign Office, no. 1094, 5 July 1961, FO 371/156847.

The debate continued throughout the following day. Opinion in the Council with the exception of the Soviet Union and the UAR was solidly against Iraq. Members of the Council recognized that Kuwait was an independent state and that the Iraqi claims were totally unjustified. The British representative tabled a draft resolution calling upon the Security Council to respect the independence of Kuwait and for all concerned to work for peace and stability in the region.[66] On 7 July, voting took place on the resolution. Although Britain, Chile, China, France, Liberia, Turkey, and the United States voted in favour, Russia vetoed it and the delegations of the UAR, Ecuador and Ceylon abstained.[67] Although the resolution was not passed due to the Soviet veto, its approval by seven delegations at least indicated their explicit recognition of Kuwait's independence and their endorsement of the British action – a considerable moral victory for Britain according to Sir Patrick Dean.[68] Nevertheless, the meeting had convinced Dean that with each passing day it would become increasingly difficult for many to "stomach the presence" of British troops in a newly independent country like Kuwait. He was particularly worried that the Arab and Afro-Asian countries, with Russia's encouragement, would soon call for the immediate withdrawal of British troops from Kuwait. He therefore asked London to prepare to face "an instinctive and emotional opposition" to the use of British forces in Kuwait under any circumstances.[69] Dean was in fact convinced of the necessity of an early British withdrawal from Kuwait. P. H. Scott of the Foreign Office agreed, adding that an early withdrawal of British forces would clear the way for Kuwait's full membership of the United Nations as their continued presence would give the USSR an excuse to veto Kuwait's application.[70] The authorities in the Gulf, however, were not in favour of a total evacuation. Instead, they preferred to reduce the British force to the minimum considered necessary to deter Qasim from attacking Kuwait.[71]

---

66. For the full text of the British draft resolution, see Dean to Foreign Office, no. 1099, 6 July 1961, FO 371/156849.
67. New York to Foreign Office, no. 1120, 7 July 1961, FO 371/156850.
68. New York to Foreign Office, no. 1121, 7 July 1961, FO 371/156850.
69. *Ibid.* See also Dean to Earl of Home, no. 18, 12 July 1961, FO 371/156851.
70. See the Note on 'Kuwait and the United Nations' by P. H. Scott, no. BK1193/183, 7 July 1961, FO 371/156883.
71. Richmond to Foreign Office, no. 429, 9 July 1961, FO 371/156880. See also

As the Foreign Office endorsed this recommendation, the local planners devised a programme for the reduction of troops which would involve the withdrawal to Bahrain of substantial elements of all three services, including two units of commandos, one parachute battalion, one Royal Artillery battery and half a tank squadron. HMS *Bulwark* would also sail to Singapore. On 13 July 1961, Harold Watkinson, the Minister of Defence, presented this plan to the Cabinet, stating that such a withdrawal would be possible in the near future in view of the improving military situation in Kuwait.[72]

Having reached the decision to reduce troops, the British government recognized the need to formulate a long-term strategy for the defence of Kuwait. The Foreign Secretary gave serious consideration to the idea of stockpiling equipment in the Emirate and strengthening Kuwaiti forces by means of a small British training contingent. He also wanted to maintain a British military presence there, albeit much smaller that that presently assembled, until the training of the Kuwaiti forces was completed. This was to consist of two infantry battalions, a tank squadron, two armoured car squadrons, a field regiment of the Royal Artillery and one squadron of Hunters.[73] On 16 July, Richmond discussed this plan for the future defence of Kuwait with the Emir. Sheikh Abdullah, however, wanted a decision on the matter delayed until after the forthcoming meeting of the League of Arab States in Cairo, to which he had already sent a delegation headed by Sheikh Jaber al-Ahmed to seek an Arab solution to the problem in view of the Russian veto in the Security Council.[74]

Meanwhile, Qasim, in a speech delivered at the Daura refinery, made a fierce attack on Kuwait and on "British imperialism". Renewing his claim to Kuwait, he declared that he would fix in the mind of every Iraqi child that Kuwait belonged to Iraq. In an interview with Inam Rad, a Lebanese journalist, given the following day, Qasim again pressed

Secretary of State's Draft Minute to the Prime Minister, undated, no. BK1193/191/G, FO 371/156883.

72. See the Cabinet Conclusions, no. CC(61), 40th Conclusions, 13 July 1961, CAB128/35/PT1. See also Foreign Office to Kuwait, no. 759, 11 July 1961, FO 371/156880.

73. Foreign Office to Kuwait, no. 803, 14 July 1961, FO 371/156882; Foreign Office to Tunis, no. 398, 15 July 1961, FO 371/156882.

74. Richmond to Foreign Office, no. 484, 16 July 1961, FO 371/156882.

his claim to Kuwait.[75] As it was obvious that his intentions towards the Emirate remained unchanged, the Foreign Office was concerned that Qasim might attempt to seize the country by a surprise attack, unless an effective military deterrent existed in the Emirate.[76] Therefore, the Foreign Secretary was forced to urgently consider how best to ensure its long-term defence. Lord Home also felt that it was essential to try to improve British relations with Iraq in order to reduce the risk of Qasim becoming more heavily dependent upon Russian support. In a minute to Harold Macmillan, the Prime Minister, he suggested that all the departments concerned should immediately prepare reports setting out possible alternatives and recommendations for the future protection of Kuwait.[77] Macmillan was in total agreement with his Foreign Secretary and wrote: "Something must be done and quickly. Kuwait's election to the Arab League may help. The sooner we can reduce to a mission . . . or retire altogether, the better."[78]

While the British government was considering reducing the number of troops (5,500) currently stationed in Kuwait, in order to avoid antagonizing the Arab world,[79] the League of Arab States in their meeting of 20 July admitted Kuwait as a full member despite the strong opposition of the Iraqi delegation. The League offered troops to replace British forces and Abdul-Khaliq Hassuna, the Secretary-General of the League, personally asked the members to contribute troops. The League also decided to send a delegation to Kuwait to assess the country's military requirements.[80] The admission of Kuwait to the League was however based on the following formula:

---

75. Trevelyan to Foreign Office, no. 958, 19 July 1961, FO 371/156851; Trevelyan to Foreign Office, no. 961, 20 July 1961, FO 371/156851. Again on 3 August at the time of laying the foundation-stone of a railway sleeper factory, Qasim announced: "We want to liberate Kuwait. However, if they prefer the word annexation then we will annex Kuwait forcibly and despite their wishes." See Foreign Office to New York, no. 3227, 4 August 1961, FO 371/156852.
76. Minute by A. R. Walmsley, no. DK1193/174, 20 July 1961, FO 371/156882.
77. See Lord Home's Minute, no. BK1198/248/G, 21 July 1961, FO 371/156886.
78. Minute by Macmillan, no. BK1198/248/G, 23 July 1961, FO 371/156886.
79. For the number of British troops in Kuwait see Minute by Sir Roger Stevens (Foreign Office), no. BK1193/196/G, 18 July 1961, FO 371/156883 and Luce to Stevens, no. 1036, 22 July 1961, FO 371/156886.
80. Minute by A. R. Walmsley, no. BK1193/154, 24 July 1961, FO 371/156881.

First: (a)   The Government of Kuwait undertakes to request the withdrawal of British forces from Kuwaiti territory as soon as possible.

         (b)   The Government of the Republic of Iraq undertakes not to use force in the annexation of Kuwait to Iraq.

         (c)   The Council [of the League of Arab States] undertakes to support every wish Kuwait may express for a union or a federation with other countries of the Arab League in accordance with the League's Pact.

Second: (a)   The Council decides to welcome the State of Kuwait as a member of the Arab League.

         (b)   To assist the State of Kuwait in joining the United Nations.

Third: The Arab States undertake to provide effective assistance for the preservation of Kuwait's independence, upon its request, and the Council confers upon the Secretary-General the power to take the necessary measures for the urgent implication of this resolution.[81]

The League's granting of membership to Kuwait together with its pledge to send Arab troops was a major diplomatic victory for the Emirate. However, although Britain welcomed this development, it believed that the stationing of League forces might not be wholly effective in deterring an Iraqi attack on Kuwait. Nevertheless, the presence of Arab contingents would enable Britain to soon withdraw its troops and might prove a sufficient enough political deterrent to Iraq, at least while Kuwaiti forces were being expanded and trained.[82]

Having decided to extend Britain's support to an Arab League force for the short-term defence of Kuwait, Lord Home, after consulting with the Joint Planning Staff and with the agreement of the Prime Minister, cabled the authorities in the Gulf with Britain's long-term defence strategy for Kuwait. It was re-emphasized that the Kuwaiti forces should be expanded and strengthened with the assistance of a British military

---

81. See Lauterpacht *et al.*, *The Kuwait Crisis*, p. 55.
82. Foreign Office to Baghdad, no. 1309, 21 July 1961, FO 371/156882.

mission to enable them to carry out a holding operation for at least 36 hours in the event of a surprise Iraqi attack, thereby allowing time for British reinforcements to arrive. A stockpile of heavy military equipment would be maintained in Kuwait for British use and British forces in Bahrain would be strengthened to a greater degree than ever before, in order to be able to respond immediately and effectively to an attack on Kuwait. Finally, the Anglo-Kuwaiti agreement of 19 June should be maintained regardless of any criticism from the Arab States.[83] Luce presented this plan to the Emir on 31 July, asking him to also request a strong Arab force. The Emir, who fully understood the realities of the Iraqi threat and the importance of a military deterrent, agreed to press for as large an Arab force as he could realistically get away with. In addition, the Emir agreed to expand his forces by 150 per cent from its present strength of 1,600 men and to purchase heavy British equipment from Britain such as armoured cars, tanks and so on.[84] With this in mind, the British Chiefs of Staff set out to determine the actual size and composition of the new Kuwaiti armed forces and of the British mission necessary to train them. The main objectives of the expansion of these armed forces were: firstly, to provide "a forward screen" near the Iraqi frontier to give early warning of an attack; secondly, to delay the enemy advance; and finally, to protect points of entry – at the port and new airport – for 36 hours to enable British reinforcements to land. The proposed land force should be of about brigade strength, composed of 2 infantry battalions, 1 armoured car regiment including 1 squadron of armoured personnel carriers, 2 squadrons of tanks, 2 field batteries, 1 troop of field engineers, 1 reconnaissance flight together with head-quarters and administrative personnel. This would amount to approximately 3,000 men. The proposed Kuwaiti air force should consist of 6 Provosts jets equipped with 3 rockets in addition to front guns. The navy should consist of about 8 fast gunboats to prevent the mining of Kuwaiti waters and small Iraqi raids. Training of these forces, estimated to take from 15 to 18 months,[85] would come under the command of a

---

83. Foreign Office to Bahrain and Kuwait, nos. 1258 and 1259, 29 July 1961, FO 371/156886; Lord Home's Minute on Defence of Kuwait, no. PM/61/102, 28 July 1961, FO 371/156886; Security of Kuwait, Report by the Joint Planning Staff, no. JP(61), no. 92 (Final), 21 July 1961, DEFE 6/72.

84. Kuwait to Foreign Office, nos. 548 and 549, 31 July 1961, FO 371/156886.

85. See 'Build-up of the Kuwaiti Armed Forces and the Size and Composition of the

Brigadier and would include 5 army officers and 12 other ranks, 2 air force officers, 2 naval officers and 4 ratings. The stockpile of heavy equipment for use by British reinforcements on arrival would include 16 Centurion tanks, 24 armoured cars, 12 field guns, together with ammunition and weapons, and spares for the RAF and the Royal Navy. This stockpile would have to be maintained for use at 24 hours notice by 48 officers and men drawn from each of the three services. Therefore, the entire mission proposed by the Chiefs of Staff required a 74-strong British contingent.[86] Luce arrived in Kuwait on 7 August and presented this list to Sheikh Abdullah the following day.[87]

While the Resident waited for the Emir's response, Sheikh Abdullah held detailed negotiations with the League's mission, resulting in an agreement with Abdul-Khaliq Hassuna on the status of the Arab League force to be stationed in Kuwait. This stipulated that any aggression against these forces would be regarded as aggression against all the Arab States of the League. Following the signing of this agreement on 12 August, the Emir wrote to Luce formally requesting the withdrawal of British troops as soon as the Arab League force arrived.[88] Before making any reply, Luce met the Sheikh two days later to discuss the unresolved issues of the stockpile and the training mission. Although Sheikh Abdullah was anxious to press ahead with the build-up, he preferred to postpone discussion of both measures until after Kuwait's entry into the United Nations.[89] Yet despite the Sheikh's reluctance to discuss the British proposals, he was informed officially on 16 August that all British troops would be withdrawn from Kuwait as soon as they

---

Associated British Military Mission' by Joint Planning Staff, no. JP(61), no. 105 (Final), 3 August 1961, DEFE 6/72. See also Annex to *ibid.*

86. The British contingent required to maintain the stockpile consisted of (a) Avmy – 2 officers and 40 other ranks; (b) RAF – 3 other ranks; (c) Royal Navy – 3 ratings. Therefore, the entire mission (both training and stockpiling) involved 12 officers and 62 other ranks. See Appendix A and B to Annex to JP(61), no. 105 (Final), 3 August 1961, DEFE 6/72. See also Foreign Office to Bahrain, no. 1317, 4 August 1961, FO 371/156886.

87. For more details see 'Build-up of the Kuwait Armed Forces' in Luce to Sheikh Abdullah al-Salem al-Sabah, no. 44, 8 August 1961, FO 371/156886.

88. Kuwait to Foreign Office, no. 595, 12 August 1961, FO 371/156887; Kuwait to Foreign Office, no. 598, 13 August 1961, FO 371/156887.

89. Kuwait to Foreign Office, no. 605, 14 August 1961, FO 371/156888.

could be replaced by an Arab force.[90] Luce then went to London to discuss the schedule for the withdrawal with the Foreign Secretary.

Upon his arrival in London on 19 August, Luce attended a meeting chaired by Lord Home. Also present at the meeting were J. Godber, the Minister of State for Foreign Affairs, Sir Roger Stevens, the Superintending Under-Secretary of the Eastern Department, as well as Arnold Walmsley, the Head of the Arabian Department. Straightaway the Resident was questioned as to how Britain's position in the rest of the Gulf would be compromised if it abandoned its military protection of Kuwait. Luce replied that in such an eventuality Britain could not count on retaining its position elsewhere in the Gulf indefinitely as the other Gulf rulers would lose confidence in Britain. Then Lord Home asked of the Emir's attitude towards the proposed British training mission and the stockpiling of equipment. Luce, who believed that Sheikh Abdullah was opposed to the training mission on political grounds, told the meeting that he had serious doubts as to whether such a mission was actually necessary from the British point of view. He however felt that it was essential to have the stockpile (including the maintenance personnel) for use by British soldiers in the event of an emergency. The Resident maintained that if the Emir declined to accept the stockpile, he should be told categorically that Britain would no longer be able to intervene effectively if his country was attacked. Stevens agreed and added that Britain should not wait until after Kuwait had become a member of the United Nations as the Emir had suggested to begin stockpiling equipment. Godber even went a step further by arguing that the Emir should be forced to agree to the stockpile. Lord Home, however, was of the opposite view and maintained that whether the Emir agreed or not, it was a matter of national policy to defend Kuwait in view of Britain's economic interests there. Indeed, the Foreign Secretary was quite prepared to drop the idea of a training mission and instead put all energies into achieving the stockpiling of British equipment.[91]

---

90. For the full text, see Foreign Office to Kuwait, no. 1060, 15 August 1961, FO 371/156887. See also Kuwait to Foreign Office, no. 614, 16 August 1961, FO 371/156887.

91. For more details, see Record of Conversation between the Secretary of State and Sir William Luce, no. BK1193/297, 19 August 1961, FO 371/156888.

On 24 August 1961, at another departmental meeting convened to discuss British obligations to Kuwait, Luce stated that so long as Qasim remained in power there was "no prospect of a diminution in the threat". It was therefore important, according to Luce, "to ensure the independence of Kuwait and to prevent its oil from falling into the hands of third parties". Supporting this view, Walmsley added that if Kuwait fell to the Iraqis there would be a complete revision of the policies governing the production of oil throughout the Middle East to the detriment of the major British oil companies. Consequently, this might translate into a loss to Britain's balance of payments of anywhere between £100 to £400 million per annum. Stevens, also present at the meeting, was worried that if the Emir refused to accept a British stockpile, Britain would have no option but to review all of its military and financial commitments to the region. It is important to note that at this time Kuwait was a major investor in Britain to the tune of £300 million.[92]

Following the conclusion of this meeting, Luce was instructed to return to Kuwait and tell the Emir that although the training mission was no longer considered essential, he must agree to allow Britain to stockpile heavy equipment along with an additional eight tanks and a mobile radar station as well as pushing ahead with the expansion of his own forces if he was to expect Britain to effectively defend the independence of his country once British forces had been withdrawn.[93] When the Resident relayed this to the Emir on 31 August, the Sheikh, despite his earlier reservations, readily agreed to all the points and even volunteered to bear the full cost of the stockpile. However, he emphasised that the British personnel required for its maintenance and the operation of the mobile radar should be kept to an absolute minimum. Luce assured Sheikh Abdullah that the necessary personnel could be reduced to no more than 45 (including 2 officers), a figure to which the Emir readily gave his consent. His change of attitude was due to talks he had had in the meantime with some members of the Arab League, in which he had encountered little opposition to the idea of a continued British military presence in Kuwait.

---

92. Record of a Meeting held in the Foreign Office, no. B1052/36, 24 August 1961, FO 371/156674. For Kuwait's investments in Britain, see Minute by A. R. Walmsley, no. BK1193/222, 17 July 1961, FO 371/156885.
93. Foreign Office to Bahrain, nos. 1469 and 1470, 25 August 1961, FO 371/156888.

With the resolution of the stockpile issue, Harold Watkinson, the British Minister of Defence, stated in a memorandum to the Cabinet that the British government was committed to withdraw its forces from Kuwait as soon as they were replaced by an Arab force. The Minister assured the Cabinet that this withdrawal would not affect Britain's obligation to the Emir, given in the Exchange of Notes of 19 June, to go to his assistance in the event of an emergency. Nevertheless, to forestall any future Iraqi attack on Kuwait, British land and air forces should be redeployed in Bahrain, Sharjah, Aden and Kenya to enable effective intervention in Kuwait within 36 hours. Watkinson then asked for funds of around £500,000 to be made available for the construction of barracks in Bahrain to house the additional British forces necessary for the implementation of this rapid response plan.[94] On 5 September, the British Cabinet approved these proposals adding that urgent action should also be taken on the despatch of the stockpile to Kuwait.[95]

In response to this Cabinet conclusion, Brigadier MacDonald, the Chief of Staff, told Brigadier Mubarak, the Deputy Commander-in-Chief of the Kuwaiti army, on 6 September that the equipment for the stockpile, such as tanks, armoured cars, field guns, ammunition and so on, was due to leave Aden shortly for Kuwait. Mubarak agreed to MacDonald's request that this equipment should be stockpiled in the barracks and workshops attached to the Mishrif Palace, to the south of Kuwait Town. Both men agreed that the size of the maintenance team should not exceed 2 officers and 28 other ranks as well as 15 RAF personnel in civilian clothes. MacDonald then put forward a tentative plan to Mubarak for the withdrawal of British troops in two phases; first the withdrawal from operational areas to a base camp followed by the total evacuation from the country. Although this phased withdrawal was acceptable to the Brigadier, no definite timetable was agreed due to their lack of information on the arrival of the Arab League forces.[96]

---

94. See 'Kuwait', a Memorandum by the Minister of Defence, no. C(61), no. 133, 1 September 1961, CAB129/106.
95. Conclusions of a Meeting of the Cabinet, no. CC(61), 49th Conclusions, 5 September 1961, CAB128/35/PT2.
96. Kuwait to Foreign Office, nos. 577, 578, 579 and 580, 7 September 1961, FO 371/156889. See also Troopers to HQ Middle East (Aden), no. MO4/125, 6 September 1961, FO 371/156889.

With both Britain and Kuwait preoccupied with the logistics of the British withdrawal, General Qasim once again renewed his claim to the Emirate. In an interview with the editor of *al-Thawra* newspaper on 4 September 1961, he reiterated that Iraq would never surrender its "rights in the usurped Qadah" of Kuwait and he was determined to recover it by peaceful means. He justified this statement by citing reports of the alleged Kuwaiti maltreatment of Iraqi nationals resident in the Emirate and warned Sheikh Abdullah that he would not hesitate to punish him if this proved to be the case.[97] Kuwait immediately denounced this allegation, stating: "The Emir treats Iraqis on an equal footing with all other Arabs in Kuwait, not because he is intimidated by threats from Iraq but because they are bound to the Kuwaitis with close religious and amicable ties." Regarding Qasim's claim, the Kuwaiti government reminded him that all successive Iraqi governments, including his own, had recognized the Iraqi–Kuwaiti boundary in the past on their own maps. Kuwait also made a strong protest to the UN Security Council against Qasim's latest assertion.[98] Nevertheless, to the great dismay of the Kuwaitis, Qasim repeated his claims at a function at the Iraqi Ministry of Education on 7 September, stating:

> It is a pledge and resolve that Kuwait will return to the homeland within not a long period . . . When Iraq restores Kuwait and has reached the sea shores, when the South of Arabia is liberated, then imperialism will inevitably go out and the iron curtain will be torn out and the decaying, corrupt regimes now prevailing in South Arabia as well as in the Arabian Peninsula, will vanish too. This is the logic of history and development.
>
> Some people do not know why we are attaching this importance to Kuwait. The matter is clear. The importance is a strategic one and relates to our safety and integrity.[99]

---

97. Trevelyan to Foreign Office, nos. 15 (Saving) and 1159, 5 September 1961, FO 371/156853.
98. Rothnie, Acting Consul-General (Kuwait) to Foreign Office, no. 678, 7 September 1961, FO 371/156853. See also Bader Mulla to the President of the Security Council, no. BK1083/172, 7 September 1961, FO 371/156853.
99. As quoted in Trevelyan to Foreign Office, no. 1191, 12 September 1961, FO 371/156853.

In view of these repeated claims, Sheikh Abdullah hurriedly concluded an agreement with the Secretary-General of the League of Arab States for the deployment of about 3,000 Arab troops mainly from Saudi Arabia, Jordan, Sudan, Tunisia and the UAR to replace the British troops. With these forces beginning to land in Kuwait, the Emir was under pressure from the League to announce that he had requested Britain to finally withdraw its troops. So on 14 September, he told Rothnie, the Acting Consul-General, that as the build-up of Arab forces would be completed in two days British forces should start withdrawing on 17 September. However, Rothnie declined to set a firm date for Britain to start withdrawing its units until he himself was convinced that the Arab League forces had taken up secure defensive positions throughout Kuwait. He added that Britain was ready to withdraw a significant number of troops very quickly but it might take up to two to three weeks from the date of starting to effect a total withdrawal. This was acceptable to Sheikh Abdullah.

Luce, after consulting with the Middle East Defence Committee, confirmed that it would be possible to begin the evacuation of British forces at any time from 19 September – a process that would be completed within 15 days.[100] This timetable was backed by Sir Humphrey Trevelyan as he believed any further delay would give credibility to Qasim's repeated claim that Britain was intending to establish a permanent military base in Kuwait.[101]

London moved quickly on the question of withdrawal. On 15 September, the Resident was instructed to go to Kuwait to finalize the withdrawal procedure and inform the Emir that the British government was ready to start withdrawing its troops on 19 September. Initially, however, this would be only a token withdrawal, with a detachment of one company to leave Kuwait by that date. Luce was to explain to Sheikh Abdullah that the further stages of withdrawal should take place in relation to the implementation of a plan for the Arab forces to take over without leaving a gap during which time Kuwait would be at the mercy of Iraq. Therefore, the Kuwaiti government's first priority should be to arrange the coordination of the Arab League and British plans.[102]

---

100. Rothnie to Foreign Office, no. 712, 14 September 1961, FO 371/156890. See also Luce to Foreign Office, no. 603, 14 September 1961, FO 371/156890.
101. Trevelyan to Foreign Office, no. 1214, 15 September 1961, FO 371/156890.
102. Foreign Office to Bahrain, no. 1621, 15 September 1961, FO 371/156890.

The Resident conveyed this to the Emir on 16 September, adding that after the completion of the first phase of withdrawal, the timing of subsequent withdrawals should be as flexible as possible. The Emir agreed and confirmed that he would instruct Brigadier Mubarak to arrange tripartite coordination involving Kuwait so as not to leave a gap in its defences.[103]

After obtaining these assurances, the Resident returned to Bahrain and his military spokesman announced on 19 September that elements of one unit would leave Kuwait later that day as the first step in complying with the Emir's request for a total British withdrawal, with the remaining units to follow progressively in agreement with the Kuwaiti authorities. Sir Edward Heath, the Lord Privy Seal, relayed this to the Cabinet.[104]

As soon as this first phase was completed, a Saudi battalion as well as the Kuwaiti armoured unit were deployed along the length of the border.[105] Following this deployment, Brigadier Mubarak, on behalf of the Emir, pressed Rothnie on 24 September to commence the second phase of withdrawal as soon as possible. The main reason for requesting such a rapid evacuation of the remainder of the British troops was due to Kuwait's expectation that the question of its membership of the United Nations might be raised in the current session of the Council, which had begun on 19 September. Although the Acting Consul-General understood Mubarak's eagerness for membership, he stressed that the British government was unable to start phase two for at least two to three weeks.[106] Luce, however, did not agree and, due to the state of preparedness of the deployed Arab force and the absence of any unusual Iraqi military activity in southern Iraq, he recommended beginning the operation straight away. He was worried that any further delay in implementing the second phase would both jeopardize the "politico-military deterrent" provided by the combined Arab League and the Kuwaiti force and embarrass the Emir in his relations with the

---

103. Luce to Foreign Office, no. 718, 16 September 1961, FO 371/156890.
104. Conclusions of a Meeting of the Cabinet, no. CC(61), 5th Conclusions, 19 September 1961, CAB128/35/PT2. See also Commonwealth Relations Office to Ottawa, no. W522, 19 September 1961, FO 371/156890.
105. Rothnie (Kuwait) to Foreign Office, no. 760, 24 September 1961, FO 371/156891.
106. Rothnie to Foreign Office, no. 761, 24 September 1961, FO 371/156891.

League. It might also prejudice Kuwait's application for admission to the United Nations due to the possibility of a Soviet veto. Therefore, on the afternoon of 24 September, the Resident, strongly recommended that authority be delegated to the C-in-C, Middle East, to begin the withdrawal of the remaining forces as early as 27 September, which should be completed within ten days.[107] Although Luce's timetable for an early withdrawal was acceptable to both Macmillan and Lord Home, the Chiefs of Staff found his ten-day schedule too optimistic. They wanted at least 18 days to complete the job due to the shortage of transport aircrafts, which were engaged in the dislocation of troop programmes in many parts of the world, particularly in Berlin.[108] The Foreign Office accepted their arguments and told the Resident that it did not see any reason to reduce the period of withdrawal by about one week as he had proposed.[109]

Despite this, the second phase of withdrawal did in fact begin on 27 September and was scheduled for completion by 15 October. Nevertheless, Brigadier Mubarak told Rothnie the following day that the withdrawal of the British forces should be speeded up in view of the continuous pressures on Kuwait from the Arab League. He further emphasized that it was necessary to get the British troops out before Kuwait could make an application to the United Nations for member-ship. But as Rothnie did not believe the pressure from the Arab League on Kuwait to be "very great", he refused point-blank to meet the Kuwaiti request for the acceleration of the British withdrawal as it was a complex and considerable operation which had to be achieved in orderly manner.[110] However, Luce argued from Bahrain that Britain's failure to make any attempt to speed up the withdrawal could jeopardize future Anglo-Kuwaiti relations. He therefore recommended that Britain should try to complete the withdrawal by 6 October, before the arrival of the Arab League Secretary-General in Kuwait.[111] The Foreign Office once

---

107. Luce to Foreign Office, no. 640, 24 September 1961, FO 371/156891. See also Luce to Foreign Office, no. 643, 25 September 1961, FO 371/156891.
108. Minute by Lord Home, no. BK193/350, 25 September 1961, FO 371/156891; Foreign Office to Bahrain, no. 1704, 26 September 1961 FO 371/156891; Minutes by A. R. Walmsley, no. BK1193/367, 27 September 1961, FO 371/156892.
109. Foreign Office to Bahrain, no. 1714, 27 September 1961, FO 371/156872.
110. Rothnie to Foreign Office, no. 779, 28 September 1961, FO 371/156891.
111. Luce to Foreign Office, no. 657, 29 September 1961, FO 371/156891.

again declined to do so as it did not think that the saving of a week would make any difference to Kuwait's efforts to secure UN membership. London's opposition to the acceleration of the rate of the British withdrawal was further strengthened by a right wing *coup* in Syria on 28 September headed by Lieutenant Colonel Abdul-Karim Nahlawi, which brought Syria's union with Egypt to an end. Now the Foreign Office, with reference to the instability in Syria, emphasized: "It is surely unwise, both in the Kuwaiti interest and our own, to hurry over the withdrawal of our forces before the reactions of the Syrian *coup* can be estimated."[112]

Contrary to this statement, Ambassador Trevelyan not only advocated an early withdrawal but also called for a permanent political solution of the Iraqi–Kuwaiti problem by the formation of a tripartite confederation of Iraq, Kuwait and Jordan. The aim of this would be to establish a formal link between the three states, without compromising Kuwait's essential independence, to provide permanent joint councils for the coordination of political and economic policy. Trevelyan believed that this would safeguard British interests in Iraq and prevent both the communists and Nasser from increasing their hold over Qasim.[113] However, Sir Roger Stevens considered Trevelyan's confederation plan as purely reflecting a pro-Iraqi standpoint. He was convinced that the Emir of Kuwait would reject such an idea outright, and the Saudis would "hotly contest" it. Robert Crawford, the Assistant Under-Secretary of State for Foreign Affairs, was in full agreement, and added: "The Saudis can certainly be relied upon to resist any form of association which excludes them, and perhaps any which includes Iraq."[114] Yet before shelving the idea the views of Harold Beely, the British Ambassador to Egypt, were sought because of his long experience of Iraqi affairs. Beely explained that the Iraqi threat to Kuwait would not be removed even after the departure of Qasim as he was merely following a long line of Iraqi leaders who had laid claim to Kuwait, and "even Nuri al-Said was

---

112. See 'Acceleration of Withdrawal from Kuwait', Minute by A. R. Walmsley, no. BK1193/359, 29 September 1961, FO 371/156891. See also Foreign Office to Bahrain, no. 1736, 29 September 1961, FO 371/156891.
113. Trevelyan to Stevens, no. 10510/61G, 28 September 1961, FO 371/156892.
114. Minutes by Stevens and Crawford, no. BK1193/374(A), 3 and 5 October 1961 respectively, FO 371/156892.

not above an occasional covetous glance in that direction". Beely instead argued that the resolution of Kuwait's problems should be sought within the context of an inter-Gulf Convention involving the major regional powers:

> As for the remote future, I used to think that the only safe and honourable way of extricating ourselves from our responsibilities in the Persian Gulf would be to negotiate some kind of Gulf Convention with the Governments of Saudi Arabia, Iraq and Iran, which would recognize the common interest of the signatories in maintaining the territorial status quo. Since all three of the major Gulf powers are themselves rich in oil, it should be possible for them in the long run to resist the temptation to swallow up their smaller neighbours provided each of them could feel sure that one of the others was not going to steal a march on it.[115]

This far-sighted and logical analysis of the long-term security of the Gulf failed to convince the Foreign Office. However, less than a decade after Beely's recommendation the British abandoned the Gulf without making any such convention or agreement among these three major Gulf powers – a failure which perhaps eventually emboldened Iraq to invade Kuwait in August 1990.

Having failed to convince London of the merits of a tripartite confederation, Trevelyan made a hasty assessment of the implications of the Syrian *coup* for Kuwait's security so that the authorities in London could take a decision on an early withdrawal. He concluded that the situation in Syria would not encourage Qasim to launch a surprise attack on Kuwait as more than two divisions of his army were now committed in Kurdistan to suppress the movement for independence there.[116] Some troops were also kept ready in case of a counter-*coup* in Syria. In the event of this, according to Rothnie, Qasim would have to "choose between also intervening in Syria to gain a share of the spoils

---

115. Beeley to Stevens, no. 10625/61G, 17 October 1961, FO 371/156892.
116. In September 1961, Qasim launched a military campaign against the Kurds of northern Iraq when they, under the leadership of Mustafa al-Barzani, proclaimed an independent state as a result of Qasim's failure to meet their demands for investment, jobs and cultural autonomy. However, Qasim's forces failed to suppress them and the Kurdish rebels (who had grown to a strength of around 15,000) established their hold over much of the countryside in Kurdistan. See M. E. Yapp, *The Near East since the First World War* (London, Longman, 1991).

and influence and taking a chance against Kuwait while the attention of the Arab world was diverted towards Syria." Rothnie concluded that the Syrian *coup* did not pose any threat to the security of Kuwait even if another revolution in Syria forced King Hussein of Jordan to intervene militarily, thereby resulting in the withdrawal of his battalion – numbering more than 1,000 – from Kuwait. [117]

As the situation in Syria began to stabilize quickly, London eventually agreed to complete the withdrawal by 10 October, 5 days earlier than originally planned, which was announced publicly from both London and Kuwait City.[118] However, a large party of personnel consisting of 212 soldiers and 55 RAF technicians were left behind to handle the stockpiling of equipment as well as to operate a radar installation left in Kuwait with the Emir's agreement for the use of British forces in the event of a renewed threat.[119] Although it was decided not to reveal the presence of such a large British contingent, it became public when on 11 October the BBC Arabic Service mentioned that a rear party was still in Kuwait.[120] This disclosure embarrassed the Emir as he had already told the Secretary-General of the Arab League that all British troops would be withdrawn by 10 October. Because of this undertaking he pressed Rothnie, who had now become the Chargé d'Affaires in Kuwait following the appointment of Richmond as its first British Ambassador on 7 October, to remove this party. The Emir argued that he did not want to stand "condemned as a liar to the world and could only beg that his friends, the British, would help him in the dilemma". As Rothnie was convinced that the Arab League Secretary-General had warned the Emir that neither the League nor Egypt would push the case for Kuwait's membership of the United Nations until the rear party was removed, he recommended its withdrawal by 19 October.[121] Eventually, after consulting Air Marshal Sir Charles Elworth,

---

117. Trevelyan to Foreign Office, no. 1334, 2 October 1961, FO 371/156891. See also Rothnie to Foreign Office, no. 792, 2 October 1961, FO 371/156891.

118. Foreign Office to Bahrain, no. 1776, 5 October 1961, FO 371/156892; Rothnie to Foreign Office, no. 821, 8 October 1961, FO 371/156892; Rothnie to Foreign Office, no. 840, 10 October 1961, FO 371/156893.

119. Foreign Office to Certain of Her Majesty's Representatives, no. 422 (Guidance), 25 October 1961, FO 371/156893.

120. Rothnie to Foreign Office, no. 848, 12 October 1961, FO 371/156893.

121. Rothnie to Foreign Office, nos. 860, 861 and 862, 16 October 1961, FO

C-in-C, Middle East, the Foreign Office instructed the Resident to go to Kuwait and arrange the complete withdrawal of the remainder of the British forces, with the exception of a liaison team of 5 officers and 41 other personnel to train the Kuwaiti army in the use of British military equipment.[122] Luce carried out the instruction immediately and completed the withdrawal on scheduled.[123]

Most of the evacuated troops and equipment were flown to Bahrain, Aden and Kenya. Air Marshal Sir Charles Elworth, who had the authority to act without prior reference to London in the event of Iraqi aggression on Kuwait, formulated a plan code-named "Operation Sodabread" for rapid intervention in Kuwait either in brigade strength without any warning of an attack or in divisional strength with some four days notice.[124] In addition, Kuwait decided to expand its own army to about 3,000 men and upgrade its equipment, particularly with tanks, armoured cars, anti-tank guns and jet aircraft. An agreement was signed with Britain for the purchase of this equipment.[125]

The total evacuation of British troops therefore cleared the way for the submission of Kuwait's application for membership to the United Nations, with Egypt's sponsorship. Nevertheless, it was again vetoed by the Soviet Union because of its deteriorating relations with Nasser and its growing interest in Baghdad. Meanwhile, the Arab League forces – with the exception of the 300-strong Egyptian contingent which was withdrawn on 13 December due to differences between Nasser and King Hussein – having taken up strategic positions in Kuwait imposed a boundary line in order to minimize the risk of any clashing with Iraqi

371/156893. See also Rothnie to Foreign Office, no. 852, 14 October 1961, FO 371/156893.

122. Foreign Office to Bahrain, no. 1879, 20 October 1961, FO 371/156893.

123. Luce to Foreign Office, nos. 708 and 711, 17 October 1961, FO 371/156893. See also Political Office Middle East Command (Aden) to Foreign Office, no. 82, 17 October 1961, FO 371/156893; Luce to Foreign Office, no. 726, 21 October 1961, FO 371/156893; Foreign Office to Bahrain, no. 1861, 17 October 1961, FO 371/156893.

124. For more details see 'Intervention in Kuwait', Report by the Joint Planning Staff, no. JP(61), no. 140 (Final), 21 October 1961, DEFE6/73. For authority delegated to C-in-C, M. E., to intervene in Kuwait after British withdrawal see Watkinson to Macmillan, no. BK1193/405G, 30 October 1961, FO 371/156894.

125. Rothnie to Foreign Office, no. 834, 9 October 1961, FO 371/156893.

troops. This line, designed to serve as a working boundary until such time as Kuwait and Iraq could agree on its final demarcation, ran about 350 metres south of and parallel to Kuwait's northern frontier with Iraq. Although Qasim made no attempt to push back this boundary line despite the departure of the well-equipped British troops, he renewed his claims to Kuwait throughout the month of December 1961, threatening its annexation to Iraq by force: "I wish to remind Britain to step aside from Kuwait or else we will kindle fires of a ferocious war in the Middle East compelling them to abandon that territory." He continued that ultimately the Iraqi army and its people would meet and "combine with each other in the usurped Qadah of Kuwait".[126]

The re-emergence of Qasim's aggressive stance towards Kuwait once again alarmed Britain. On 24 December, the British government decided as a precaution to immediately despatch an aircraft-carrier and four or five Britannias and one Comet aircraft from Transport Command to Aden as well as eight Canberras to Nairobi from Cyprus. Middle East Command was also placed on full alert.[127] Nevertheless, as there were no unexpected troop movements either in Baghdad or Basra, Britain decided not to take any further action except to assure the Emir that it was ready at his request to counter any Iraqi act of aggression.[128] Moreover, British anxiety not to provoke a political outcry from the League of Arab States as well as among some Kuwaitis such as Sheikh Jaber al-Ahmed, the then Minister of Finance, was an additional reason for not persuading the Emir to let them move even a small force into Kuwait. It was in fact Luce who had managed to convince London not to take the risk of a military re-entry into Kuwait as he believed that such a move would undoubtedly jeopardize Britain's entire "defence

---

126. In fact, Qasim made five statements renewing his claims to Kuwait during the period 3 to 23 December 1961. See Foreign Office to Her Majesty's Representatives, no. 1, 1 January 1962, FO 371/162898.
127. Foreign Office to Baghdad, no. 2353, 27 December 1961, FO 371/156854. See also Foreign Office to Khartoum, nos. 1371 and 1373, 26 and 27 December 1961 respectively, FO 371/156895.
128. Richmond to Foreign Office, no. 1006, 27 December 1961, FO 371/156854. For a report on the absence of any unusual military activity in the Basra area, see the correspondence between Basra to Foreign Office, nos. 151–76, 23–7 December 1961, FO 371/156854. For the military situation in Baghdad, see Sir Roger Allen (Baghdad) to Foreign Office, nos. 1690 and 1696, 23 and 24 December 1961 respectively, FO 371/156854.

arrangements for Kuwait and even imperil the position of the Emir himself".[129]

Although Britain made no attempt to redeploy troops in Kuwait, it kept its forces both in Bahrain and Aden on a high state of alert. Iraq wasted no time in drawing the attention of the UN Security Council's to this increased military activity. In a memorandum to the Security Council dated 28 December, the Iraqi Foreign Minister Hashem Jawad complained that British military manoeuvres in the Gulf had created a very tense atmosphere, endangering the peace and stability of the region and threatening the security of Iraq.[130] Although this kind of statement did not deserve to pass unanswered, Britain avoided refuting the Iraqi charges and defending its position. This was due to Britain's keen wish not to exacerbate the situation by provoking Iraqi counter-measures and also to avoid creating difficulties for the Iraqi Petroleum Company, which was trying to obtain additional oil production rights in the Basra area. In addition, London was worried that a public display of support for Kuwait from the British government might reduce the chances of support for Kuwait from the Arab League and the rest of the Arab world. It therefore tried to diffuse the situation by ignoring the memorandum.[131] On the other hand, Kuwait did not fail to refute the Iraqi accusations. In a telegram to the Security Council, the Kuwaiti Foreign Minister Sheikh Sabah strongly protested against the continuation of the Iraqi campaign. Defending the increased British military measures in Bahrain, the Foreign Minister emphasized that his country had no other alternative but to take every possible precautionary measure to preserve of its sovereignty.[132]

Relations between the two countries further deteriorated when Iraq decided, quite unexpectedly, to freeze Kuwaiti accounts in Iraqi banks (amounting to KD 2,000,000) and seized a number of Kuwaiti vessels.[133] In January 1962, with tensions running high, the Syrian Prime Minister Maarouf Dawalibi offered Iraq his services as a mediator in its

---

129. Luce to Foreign Office, no. 916, 26 December 1961, FO 371/156895.

130. *The Times*, 29 December 1961.

131. Foreign Office to New York, no. 4, 1 January 1962, FO 371/162898.

132. Kuwaiti Foreign Minister to the President of the Security Council, unnumbered, 28 December 1961, FO 371/156898.

133. British Embassy in Kuwait to the Arabian Department, no. 1035/61, 30 December 1961, FO 371/156898.

dispute with Kuwait.[134] Ignoring this offer, Qasim, in an interview with the editors of *al-Ahd al-Jadid* and *al-Zaman* on 14 March, stated that Iraq was now well on the way to recovering Kuwait.[135] A week later, the Iraqi dictator declared at a dinner party in Baghdad: "Kuwait has become a ripe fruit and we shall gather it at a suitable time." On 14 March, he further stated at the Fourth Conference of the Iraqi Railway Workers Union that the planned route of the railway would stretch from Baghdad to the "usurped Qadah of Kuwait". Kuwait denounced these provocative statements and protested to the Secretary-General of the League of Arab States that they constituted a threat to the peace of the whole region.[136]

Despite this protest, Iraqi aircraft violated Kuwaiti air space on 21 March and again a week later. Although these flights were tracked by the RAF radar in Kuwait, they were not intercepted as there were no British fighter planes in the vicinity at that time. However, the military authorities in the Gulf reacted angrily to these incidents and suggested that new military measures should be taken against Iraq.[137] On 17 April 1962, after prolonged inter-departmental discussions, the Cabinet finally approved an extension to the delegated authority of the C-in-C, Middle East, to cover the following action:

(a) Carrying out offensive air action against Iraqi ground and air forces in and over Kuwait. This authority covers hot pursuit of Iraqi aircraft to a distance of 30 miles inside Iraqi territory.

(b) Deploying forward to Kuwait DF/GA forces and any extra men to activate the stockpile and operate Type T radar on more than a one-watch basis together with ground forces to protect the airfields.

---

134. For Syria's efforts in solving the Iraqi–Kuwaiti dispute, see Bromely (Damascus) to Foreign Office, nos. 29 and 30, 30 January 1962, FO 371/156898.
135. Sir Roger Allen (Baghdad) to Foreign Office, no. 204, 5 March 1962, FO 371/162898.
136. As quoted in Richmond to Foreign Office, no. 12, 18 March 1962, FO 371/156898.
137. See Watkinson to the Prime Minister, no. BK1193/50/G, 11 April 1962, FO 371/162916. See C-in-C, M. E., to MOD (London), no. MIDC 05.28, 4 April 1962, FO 371/162916.

(c) Completing all necessary measures for intervention short of deploying its remaining forces in Kuwait.

(d) Extending photographic reconnaissance into Iraqi territory, but this must be limited to high altitude flights that do not penetrate beyond the Basra area.[138]

In other words, British fighter planes could follow and take action against Iraqi aircraft up to the Basra and Shuaiba area. This permission allowing offensive air action against Iraq if necessary should be enacted swiftly, but was subject to the approval of the Resident and the submission of a formal request for assistance from the Emir. The C-in-C, Middle East, should also be sure prior to launching any offensive that Iraqi land forces had crossed the frontier or that the Iraqi Air Force had attacked Kuwaiti targets.[139] Kuwait itself took some measures to strengthen its frontier forces, equipping them with Vickers Vigilant anti-tank missiles and heavy machine guns.[140]

Kuwait's position in the international arena had meanwhile been enhanced considerably due to its recognition as a sovereign and independent state by all the Arab states (with the obvious exception of Iraq) as well as more than 70 other countries. However, despite this diplomatic boost, Kuwait was still unable to secure UN membership. In the UN session of September 1962, Kuwait even avoided applying for membership due to its fear of a Soviet veto prompted by Iraq. Indeed, the decision was taken to defer indefinitely its quest for UN membership until such a time as the Soviet Union had changed its position.[141]

Along with its opposition to Kuwaiti entry into the United Nations, the Iraqi government also persisted with its contention that Kuwait was an integral part of Iraq.[142] Although Qasim continued to

---

138. Foreign Office to Kuwait, no. 486, 7 June 1962, FO 371/162917.
139. *Ibid.*
140. M. I. Goulding (British Embassy, Kuwait) to F. D. W. Brown, no. 1194/62, 3 October 1962, FO 371/162914; War Office to Foreign Office, no. MU/2C/0371, 3 June 1962, FO 371/162913; M. W. Errock (Kuwait) to M. A. Marshall (Foreign Office), no. 11914/652, 27 June 1962, FO 371/162913.
141. C. T. Crowe (UK Mission to the UNO), no. 22229/143/62, 10 December 1962, FO 371/162896. See also Richmond to Foreign Office, no. 623, 1 November 1962, FO 371/162896.
142. For Kuwait's complaint against the Iraqi Foreign Minister's statement at the UN

deliver militant speeches about Kuwait, he made no attempt to cross the frontier throughout his rule. The British Military Attaché in Baghdad argued that the following factors deterred Qasim from attacking Kuwait:

(a) The standard of training (especially at the Command level) throughout the Army, the poor standard of technical ability, the lack of logistical support, the shortage of officers in units and the inter-formation transfers made necessary of officers and men as a result of the Kurdish ops.

(b) The deterrent of British troops in Bahrain. (A major factor and referred to in the press and in conversation by army officers.)

(c) The Kurdish Operations which tie down 2 Division and other troops from Baghdad. (Although this operation is officially finished the Kurds are bloody-minded as a result of the indiscriminate bombing and killing of their women, children and relations and even if the Mulla fled or was captured the Kurds in the hills are certain to continue holding down troops and be a constant concern.)

(d) The deterrent of the Arab Forces in Kuwait and any attack against his brother Arabs bringing into effect the opposition of the whole of the Arab League.

(e) The long Saudi Arabia–Iraqi Frontier which the Saudis would be likely to cross especially in the South to exploit the discontent prevailing because of drought, no crops and suspicions of Qasim's Communist leanings.

(f) Qasim cannot be absolutely sure of the loyalty of his army. He also has strong Baathist and other opposition in Baghdad making it necessary to contain certain troops in and around the capital.

General Assembly, see the Permanent Observer of the State of Kuwait to the UN, unnumbered, 17 October 1962, FO 371/162899. For Qasim's interview with the Lebanese press reiterating his claims to the Emirate, see Roger Allen to R. S. Crawford, no. 1082/49/62, 12 June 1962, FO 371/162899.

(g) Qasim will not commit suicide by putting in an attack that failed like the UAR against Israel thereby showing how useless his army and air force is.

(h) By character he is likely to try and achieve his aims by subversion and political means.[143]

Although Qasim badly needed a military campaign in Kuwait in order to strengthen his ever-vulnerable position in the face of growing discontent within Iraq – which was being whipped up by Nasserite and Baathist anti–Qasim underground movements – the factors in favour of an attack were far outweighed by those against. Nevertheless, the dictator showed no sign of relinquishing his claims to Kuwait, claims which were producing wider repercussions in the internal politics of the Emirate. For example, the Emir introduced democratic reforms in the country in order to "demonstrate that what his people could gain under his benevolent rule was denied to the people of Iraq".[144] The Constituent Assembly, elected in late 1961, framed a constitution which was approved by the Emir on 11 November 1962. Under the terms of this constitution Kuwait's first ever democratic elections were held on 23 January 1963 to elect 50 members to the National Assembly. However, due to a constitutional restriction of the franchise, only 17,000 male voters cast their votes out of a total population at the time of around 321,000.[145]

Conclusion

The overthrow of the monarchy in Iraq not only brought about a dramatic change in Iraqi politics, but also seriously disrupted Iraqi–Kuwaiti relations. Kuwait's eventual emergence as an independent sovereign state (replacing the 1899 agreement with Britain with an Anglo-Kuwaiti Exchange of Notes), was soon greeted by Iraq's reassertion of its historical

---

143. Military Attaché (British Embassy, Baghdad) to War Office, no. MA/IF/11/36, 12 October 1961, FO 371/156894.
144. Schofield, *Kuwait and Iraq*, p. 110. See also al-Mayyal, 'The political boundaries of the State of Kuwait', pp. 122–40.
145. Jill Crystal, *Oil and Politics in the Gulf*, p. 86. See also Khadduri, *Republican Iraq*, p. 111.

claim to the country. However, Qasim's claim was inconsistent with his government's recognition of the independence of Kuwait expressed in a variety of ways up to 13 June 1961; on this date Iraq itself sponsored Kuwait's application for full membership of the International Labour Organization. Despite his threats, however, Qasim made no attempt to invade the country. This was apparently due to the timely arrival of British troops in Kuwait and his own weak position at home. British troops stayed in the Emirate until they were replaced by Arab League forces, which served as a politico-military deterrent against Qasim's designs on Kuwait. As Qasim persisted with his militant claims, Britain had little option but to devise a new strategy – "Operation Sodabread" – for the long-term defence of the Emirate and, not least, for the preservation of its vital interest in the country – oil.

9

The Struggle for Warba and Bubiyan in the Period of Recognition, 1963–1989

From 1963 to the end of the 1980s Iraqi–Kuwaiti relations significantly improved following Iraq's recognition of Kuwait as a sovereign and independent state with a well-defined boundary. Yet despite Iraq's change of attitude towards Kuwait, no serious attempt was made to settle the problem of the demarcation of the border except for the formation of a joint Iraqi–Kuwaiti frontier commission. During this period, the border issue was further complicated by the Iranian abrogation of their border agreement of 1937 with Iraq. Indeed, Iraq's increasingly hostile relations with Iran forced the Iraqi government to seek direct access to the Gulf water through the acquisition of Warba Island and at least a part of Bubiyan. Accordingly, Iraq made demarcation conditional on the cession or lease of these two islands. This remained Iraq's position with regard to the frontier during the prolonged Iran–Iraq War despite the unprecendented scale of Kuwait's economic support of the Iraqi war effort.

General Qasim was overthrown on 3 February 1963 by the Baath military coalition headed by Abdul-Salam Muhammad Aref, paving the way for an improvement in Iraqi–Kuwaiti relations. Sheikh Abdullah bin Salem Mubarak al-Sabah, on 8 February, was the first Gulf leader to publicly congratulate the new Iraqi President and in reply Aref expressed his desire to establish friendly relations with the new Emirate. In a further sign of reconciliation, Aref on the same day removed all the travel restrictions between the two countries which his predecessor had imposed. In return, Kuwait offered to invest in the Iraqi economy.[1] Due to these improving relations, the Soviet Union withdrew its opposition to the Emirate's entry into the United Nations and, on 4 March 1963, Kuwait was admitted unanimously. The Soviet Union then established

---

1. Schofield, *Kuwait and Iraq*, p. 111.

diplomatic relations with Kuwait at the ambassadorial level.[2] Simultaneously, steps were taken to resolve all the outstanding differences between Kuwait and Iraq in an attempt to establish a lasting peace. Negotiations were opened between the two countries in June which continued until the end of September 1963. As soon as Kuwait offered to terminate its agreement of 1961 with Britain and grant Iraq an interest-free loan the Iraqi government expressed its willingness to recognize Kuwait as an independent state with a fixed boundary. Accordingly, a high-level Kuwaiti delegation headed by Sheikh Sabah al-Salem al-Sabah, the Heir Apparent and Prime Minister, arrived in Baghdad on 4 October 1963 to finalize the recognition procedure. Later that day, a joint communiqué signed by Major-General Ahmed Hasan al-Bakr, the Iraqi Prime Minister, and Sheikh Sabah, was issued expressing their agreement on the following points:

> The Republic of Iraq recognizes the independence and complete sovereignty of the State of Kuwait and its boundaries as specified in the letter of the Prime Minister of Iraq dated 21.07.1932 and which was accepted by the Ruler of Kuwait in his letter dated 10.08.1932.

> The two Governments shall work towards reinforcing the fraternal relations subsisting between the two sister countries, inspired by their national duty, common interest and aspiration to a complete Arab Unity.

> The two Governments shall work towards establishing cultural, commercial and economic co-operation between the two countries and the exchange of technical information.

> In order to realize all the foregoing objectives, they shall immediately establish diplomatic relations between them at the level of ambassadors.[3]

This Iraqi recognition of Kuwait's independence and its reconfirmation of the boundaries as defined in the 1932 Exchange of Letters was a major diplomatic victory for Kuwait, as it clearly implied the renunciation

---

2. Tim Niblock, 'Iraqi politics towards the Arab states of the Gulf 1958–1981' in Tim Niblock (ed.), *Iraq: The Contemporary State* (London, Croom Helm, 1982), pp. 134–5. See also Khadduri, *Republican Iraq*, p. 172.
3. Schofield, *Kuwait and Iraq*, P. 111.

of all Iraqi claims to Kuwait including the islands of Warba and Bubiyan. While Britain had failed repeatedly to extract such a concession from Iraq, the independent Kuwait was able to achieve it with relative ease. Although the Agreed Minutes of 1963 made no reference to the eventual demarcation of the frontier between the two countries, it at least established a status quo in the border area.[4] Nevertheless, in return for this significant concession the Emirate had to pay a KD30 million interest-free loan to Iraq (which to this day remains unpaid).[5] It also agreed to terminate the Anglo-Kuwaiti agreement of 1961, the only effective deterrent in the event of any threat to the security of Kuwait. (The treaty was not actually abrogated until 13 May 1968, following the British announcement of withdrawal from the east of Suez.) Therefore the Emirate, although emerging as one of the most important countries in the Middle East due to its burgeoning oil production, left itself open to future Iraqi encroachment. The Arab League force had withdrawn completely by 4 February 1963.

The accord was soon implemented and diplomatic relations were established between Kuwait and Iraq at the ambassadorial level as stipulated. An agreement to pump fresh water from the Shatt al-Arab to Kuwait was signed on 11 February 1964 followed by another on 25 October abolishing all custom duties and taxes on such items as mineral resources and animal products traded between them. In the following year, both countries explored the possibility of establishing joint projects to develop their iron, steel, sulphur, and petrochemical industries, and over the next few years a number of other agreements were signed including a loan agreement for a paper-mill at Basra (1966) and another for the Samarra flood control project (1967).[6]

Despite these improving relations, the question of frontier demarcation laid dormant at a time when the oil companies were

---

4. The Agreed Minutes were deposited with the Treaty Section of the United Nations by the Kuwaiti government on 10 January 1964. Notice of this registration was mentioned in the UN monthly publication of January 1964, and in the following year it appeared in volume no. 485 of the UN treaty series. See David H. Finnie, *Shifting Lines in the Sand: Kuwait's Elusive Frontier with Iraq* (Cambridge, Mass., Harvard University Press, 1992), p. 152.
5. For Kuwaiti payment to Iraq see C. T. Gandy to Foreign Office, No. 36, 11 August 1964, FO 371/174594.
6. See Niblock, *Iraq: The Contemporary State*, p. 135. See also Lauterpacht *et al.*, *The Kuwaiti Crisis*, p-. 153.

expanding their operations in the frontier area. For instance, throughout the 1960s the Iraq Petroleum Company increased production in the southern oilfields of Zubair and Rumaila to about 18 million long tons per year by 1965. On the Kuwaiti side of the frontier the Kuwait Oil Company continued its exploration work and in 1964 it drilled two wildcat wells at Jirfan, just to the south of Iraq's Rumaila field, although these proved to be unproductive. Deep-pool tests were also drilled at Sabriya and Raudatain close to Kuwait's northern frontier.[7]

As a result of this flurry of activity in the frontier zone, Sheikh Abdullah attempted to revive the demarcation issue. In a bid to negotiate a settlement of the problem, the Emir paid a visit to Baghdad in August 1965 accompanied by his Foreign Minister, Sheikh Sabah al-Ahmed al-Sabah, and proposed the establishment of a joint Iraqi–Kuwaiti boundary committee to demarcate the frontier. However, the subsequent discussion of the proposal came to nothing, due largely to the Iraqi Foreign Minister's revival of Iraq's old claim to Warba and Bubiyan islands and to a strip of Kuwaiti territory to the south of Umm Qasr in an attempt to gain complete control of the newly built port. Although these demands were totally rejected by Sheikh Abdullah, the Iraqis later circulated a report (published rather conveniently after the Emir's death on 24 November 1965) stating that during the talks he had not ruled out the possibility of leasing Warba Island to Iraq for 99 years.[8]

Nevertheless, in the following year there were signs of *rapprochement* between the two governments on the frontier issue, when in August 1966 the new Emir of Kuwait, Sheikh Sabah (III) bin Salem, visited Baghdad and met with General Abdul-Rahman Aref, who had become President on 16 April 1966 following the death of his brother Abdul-Salam Aref in a helicopter crash. The two men agreed to establish a joint boundary committee within two months to demarcate the frontier. This committee was soon formed (with the Iraqi delegation headed by Nuri al-Jamil, a senior official at the Iraqi Ministry of Foreign Affairs, and with Abdul-Latif al-Thuwayni, the Under-Secretary of the Ministry of Interior, leading the Kuwaiti team) and held three meetings in Baghdad from 26 February to 3 March 1967. However, instead of discussing the mandate of the committee, the Iraqis raised the question of the position

---

7. *Ibid.*, pp. 135–6. See also Longrigg, *Oil in the Middle East*, p. 405.
8. Schofield, *Kuwait and Iraq*, p. 114.

of the existing Iraqi–Kuwaiti border stating that it was essential to both carry out a new survey and prepare new maps of the border zones in order to be able to agree on a borderline with Kuwait. They also insisted that such a survey should be conducted by Iraq alone without any Kuwaiti participation despite the fact that significant parts of Kuwaiti territory would be included in it. As the Kuwaiti delegation assumed from this that the Iraqis wanted to readjust the frontier in their favour by drawing a new line in the Safwan and al-Batin areas, they insisted upon demarcating the frontier on the basis of the 1932 Exchange of Letters as endorsed in the Agreed Minutes of 1963. The Iraqi delegation maintained, however, that as the 1932 agreement had been imposed by British "imperialists", the Iraqi public as well as the opposition parties would never accept any agreement based upon it. The Kuwaiti team replied that it was not the function of the committee to question the validity of the 1932 Exchange of Letters but rather to discuss the *modus operandi* of its implementation. Despite this marked difference of purpose, the committee met again on 7 October 1967 at the insistence of Iraq, which was in dire need of financial assistance from Kuwait. However, the negotiators again failed to make any real progress except for the issuing of a joint communiqué stating that a comprehensive survey of the Iraqi–Kuwaiti frontier would begin soon. Nevertheless, as no steps were taken to implement this undertaking the joint committee was eventually dissolved.[9]

On 30 July 1968, the Baathists, again in collaboration with the army, staged their second *coup* under the leadership of Ahmed Hasan al-Bakr. As al-Bakr had signed the Agreed Minutes of 1963 recognizing Kuwait's independence the Kuwaitis hoped that a settlement of the long-standing frontier dispute would at last be possible. Despite this expectation, no serious attempt was made to settle the issue. This inaction may be attributed to the eruption of hostilities between Iran and Iraq over the Shatt al-Arab. Ever since the establishment of the first Baathist government in Iraq, Iran had been pushing for a revision of the 1937 boundary treaty, which had redefined the frontier between the two

---

9. Lauterpacht *et al.*, *The Kuwait Crisis*, pp. 76–7. See also Panel of Specialists, *Kuwait–Iraq Boundary Demarcation: Historical Rights and International Will* (Kuwait City, Centre for Research and Studies on Kuwait, 1994), pp. 48–9.

countries at the low-water mark on the eastern side (that is the Iranian side) of the Shatt al-Arab. As the treaty gave Iraq control of the Shatt al-Arab waterway except for two small areas opposite Khorramshahr and Abadan, the Iranian government requested in February 1969 its replacement by a more balanced treaty. Rejecting this outright, the new Iraqi regime told Tehran that it considered the Shatt al-Arab part of its territory. Relations deteriorated further when the Iraqi authorities, in an attempt to establish their full control over the waterway, instructed Iranian vessels not to fly the Iranian flag upon entering the Shatt al-Arab and warned that if they failed to comply Iraq would not allow any ship en route for the ports of Iran to enter the Shatt. This ultimatum obviously presented a great threat to the Iranian national interest as free passage through the Shatt al-Arab was of vital importance to Iran's economy. Operations in the Khuzistan oilfields and refineries as well as the oil terminal and petrochemical industries in Abadan would cease if denied use of the waterway. Therefore, Iran decided that it had no option but to unilaterally abrogate the 1937 treaty on 19 April 1969, justifying its decision by stating that not only had Iraq never fully implemented the terms of the treaty but also that it was concluded at a time when Iraq was under British influence.[10] Iran, which had already emerged as one of the most important factors in the politics of the Middle East as a result of military assistance and political backing from the US since 1959, also took military measures to protect Iran-bound shipping in the Shatt al-Arab. Yet despite its threats to the contrary, Iraq did not attempt to challenge the Iranian warships patrolling the waterway. Instead, the Iraqis turned their attention once again towards Kuwait.[11]

The Iraqi–Kuwaiti frontier dispute at this time should therefore be viewed against the background of worsening relations between Iran and Iraq. With tensions mounting, Iraq requested Kuwait in April 1969 to allow its troops to be posted on the Kuwaiti side of the undemarcated frontier to protect the Umm Qasr port from a possible Iranian attack. Yet Iraq did not even wait for a Kuwaiti reply. Long before permission

10. Majid Khadduri, *Socialist Iraq: a Study in Iraqi Politics since 1968* (Washington DC, The Middle East Institute, 1978), pp. 148–55; al-Mayyal, 'The political boundaries of the State of Kuwait', pp. 124–5.
11. Jasim M. Abdulghani, *Iraq and Iran: The Years of Crisis* (London, Croom Helm, 1984), pp. 118–19. See also Syed Hassan Amin, *Political and Strategic Issues in the Gulf* (Glasgow, Royston, 1984), pp. 59–60.

was officially given, Iraqi troops were deployed within the Kuwaiti territory just to the south of Umm Qasr. The Emirate therefore had no alternative but to reluctantly agree to the presence of Iraqi troops on its soil.[12]

Although there was no outbreak of hostilities between Iraq and Iran, Iraq declined to withdraw its troops from Kuwait maintaining that Umm Qasr needed to be protected as long as the problem of the Shatt al-Arab remained unsettled.[13] Iranian occupation of the strategic islands of Abu Musa and the Greater and the Lesser Tunbs, situated at the western entrance to the Strait of Hormuz, towards the end of 1971, gave Iraq a further excuse to keep its troops on Kuwaiti territory. Iranian efforts to become predominant in the Gulf following the occupation of these islands induced Iraq to become more aggressive in its efforts to gain direct access to Gulf waters through the acquisition of Warba and Bubiyan, which in any case had become crucial with the Iraqi development of the north Rumaila oilfield and the expansion of the Umm Qasr port.[14] Undoubtedly Iraq also calculated that its possession of the two islands would enable it, by extending its limited Gulf coastline, to acquire the right to exploit the seabed oil resources. With these objectives in mind, Murtada Said Abdul Baqi, the Iraqi Foreign Minister, arrived in Kuwait City on 2 May 1972 and proposed that his government was prepared to demarcate the frontier based on the 1932 and 1963 agreements provided the Emirate agreed to the following conditions: firstly, to invest Kuwaiti capital in Iraq; secondly, to allow Iraq to ensure the security of Kuwait through the implementation of joint defence policies; thirdly, to recruit Iraqi labour for employment in Kuwait; and finally, to allow Iraq to acquire Warba and Bubiyan for the establishment of military bases to ensure direct naval access to the Gulf and for the construction of an offshore oil terminal with pipelines crossing Bubiyan Island. Kuwait, unsurprisingly, rejected the proposal.[15]

As the Emirate showed no wish to compromise over these issues, Iraq reinforced its military position in the occupied territory to the south of Umm Qasr in November 1972 and started to build a road

12. Schofield, *Kuwait and Iraq*, p. 115.
13. Khadduri, *Socialist Iraq*, pp. 155–6.
14. *Ibid.*, p. 156.
15. Alan J. Day (ed.), *Border and Territorial Disputes* (London, Longman, 1982), p. 224. See also Panel of Specialists, *Kuwait–Iraq Boundary Demarcation*, p. 50.

about 100–150 metres inside Kuwait.[16] On 5 November, the Kuwaiti Ambassador in Baghdad, at his government's instruction, lodged a strong protest to the Iraqi Foreign Minister against this territorial violation and asked him to halt all work immediately. Although Baqi assured him that his government had no intention of creating unnecessary problems for Kuwait, he stressed that he was unwilling to stop the work as he was unsure as to whether the new road was inside Kuwaiti or Iraqi territory. However, the Ambassador insisted that the work should be stopped immediately and although the construction of the road was halted following this protest it was resumed a few days later. When the Kuwaiti Ambasador drew the attention of the Iraqi government to this, the Iraqi Under-Secretary in the Foreign Ministry denied that the construction work had resumed, and so the Ambassador accompanied by the Kuwaiti Consul in Basra travelled to Umm Qasr to find out the situation for themselves. The progress of the new road convinced the Ambassador that the Iraqis were trying to encircle the al-Samitah border post (two kilometres inside Kuwaiti territory) in order to be able to control it if the need arose, given that it was strategically situated on top of a hill.[17]

As a the result of Iraq's provocative actions, Kuwait despatched a high-level delegation, headed by its Foreign Minister Sheikh Sabah al-Ahmed al-Sabah, to Baghdad on 26 February 1973 to thrash out a balanced solution to the frontier problem with Taha al-Gizrawi, the Iraqi Minister of Industry. While Sheikh Sabah insisted that the demarcation had to be based on the 1932 and 1963 agreements, al-Gizrawi would only agree to do so if the islands of Warba and Bubiyan along with the strip of land south of Umm Qasr were ceded to Iraq as without them Iraq could not play a vital role in the region's politics. Unable to agree to these demands, the Sheikh stated categorically that Kuwait would "never cede any inch of its territory" to Iraq. However, he was prepared to start negotiations to enable Iraq to use the waterway to the north of the Gulf, but such negotiations could only be opened after the demarcation of the boundary was completed. Two days later he

---

16. Al-Mayyal, 'The political boundaries of the State of Kuwait', pp. 130–5. See also Schofield, *Kuwait and Iraq*, pp. 116–7; Anthony H. Cordesman, *The Gulf and the Search for Strategic Stability* (Boulder, Colorado, Westview Press, 1984), pp. 403–5.

17. Panel of Specialists, *Kuwait–Iraq Boundary Demarcation*, pp. 51–2.

repeated this conditional offer to Saddam Hussein, the then Vice-President, stating: "It is unthinkable to dispose of any Kuwaiti territory; no one in Kuwait is capable of doing that."[18] Consequently, the negotiations ended in deadlock and Sheikh Sabah returned home empty-handed.

Following the collapse of these talks, Iraq moved a step closer to achieving its territorial ambitions. On 20 April 1973, Iraqi troops attacked the border post at al-Samitah killing two Kuwaiti frontier policemen and forcing the garrison to withdraw. They also penetrated a further 4.8 kilometres inside Kuwait, later claiming that they had done so only in response to a Kuwaiti armed attack on them. The Kuwaiti Minister of the Interior instantly rejected the Iraqi claims and argued that the Kuwaiti policemen at al-Samitah had been overpowered by heavily armed Iraqi troops carrying out a premediated plan of attack. He demanded that all provocative actions and movements in the frontier area should be stopped forthwith and that Iraq should respond to Kuwait's repeated requests for frontier demarcation in order to diffuse the tension between their two countries.[19]

The al-Samitah raid was the first major incident in the frontier zone since the clash of 1954 which had resulted in the death of an Iraqi frontier guard. However, unlike this earlier crisis, the attack on al-Samitah produced a wave of anti-Iraqi feeling in both Kuwait and other Gulf states. While Kuwaitis took to the streets in anti-Iraqi demonstrations, both the Saudi and Iranian governments denounced the aggression and offered military assistance to the Emirate. As a result of this widespread support together with the efforts of Muhammad Riyad, the Secretary-General of the League of Arab States, Iraq withdrew its troops from al-Samitah. Nevertheless, the granting of a substantial Kuwaiti loan to Iraq contributed significantly to this decision. The looming Arab–Israeli conflict and the Soviet Union's disapproval of the Iraqi aggression on Kuwait and its advice to settle the boundary dispute peacefully, were further factors for the Iraqi withdrawal.[20] But the Iraqis still retained their troops in the area to the

---

18. *Ibid.*, pp. 52–3. See also Schofield, Kuwait and Iraq, p. 117.
19. Panel of Specialists, *Kuwait–Iraq Boundary Demarcation*, p. 53.
20. *Ibid.*, p. 54. See also al-Mayyal, 'The political boundaries of the State of Kuwait', p. 138; Schofield, *Kuwait and Iraq*, p. 117. The pressure on Iraq from the Soviet

south of Umm Qasr which had been under their occupation since 1969.

Following the evacuation of al-Samitah, both countries made a greater effort to settle the frontier dispute. On 28 April 1973, negotiations were held in Kuwait between the two parties which continued until the middle of May. Sheikh Sabah al-Ahmed, heading the Kuwaiti delegation, continued to press for the settlement of the problem on the basis of the 1932 and 1963 agreements, which he considered as binding international instruments. But Murtada Said Abdul Baqi again declined to do so as, he argued, both agreements had never been "ratified in accordance with Iraqi constitutional procedure". Instead he pressed for the right to construct and maintain at least one oil pipeline through Kuwait to the deep waters off Bubiyan Island in return for the settlement of the frontier dispute. As Sheikh Sabah believed that once this right was granted the Iraqis would seize not only Bubiyan but also Warba, he rejected the proposal outright.[21]

Despite this impasse, Kuwait made another attempt to demarcate the border in August 1973. In an effort to defuse tensions and improve bilateral relations, Sheikh Jaber al-Ahmed al-Sabah (the then Kuwaiti Heir Apparent and now the current Emir) arrived in Baghdad on 20 August. As soon as Sheikh Jaber raised the issue with Saddam Hussein, the Iraqi Vice-President asked for the cession of Warba and a strip of land to the south of the northern Kuwaiti town of Abdaly. Saddam also pressed for the division of Bubiyan into two halves with the eastern portion leased to Iraq for 99 years, leaving Kuwait the territory to the west. As Sheikh Jaber found these proposals to be unacceptable, the negotiations broke up.[22]

The improvement of Iranian–Iraqi relations following the conclusion of the Algiers Agreement of 6 March 1975, which resolved their dispute over the Shatt al-Arab with the adoption of the "thalweg principle" (where the frontier was fixed at the median line in the mid-channel of

---

Union to settle the border dispute peacefully was all the more acute given that they had just signed the Treaty of Friendship and Co-operation with each other on 9 April 1972 for a 25-year period.

21. Panel of Specialists, *Kuwait–Iraq Boundary Demarcation*, p. 54. See also al-Mayyal, 'The political boundaries of the State of Kuwait', pp. 139–56.

22. *Ibid*. See also Khadduri, *Socialist Iraq*, p. 157.

the waterway),[23] presented yet another opportunity for the reopening of the Iraqi–Kuwaiti frontier question. The Kuwaitis strongly believed that there was no longer any justification for Iraqi troops to remain on their territory to defend Umm Qasr. Moreover, Iraq's plans for Warba and Bubiyan became irrelevant in view of its *rapprochement* with Iran. But to the contrary, Iraq became even more determined to acquire the two islands after having lost full sovereignty over the Shatt al-Arab. In May 1975, the Baathists, stating that the islands were still "indispensable to enhance the Iraqi deep water port at Umm Qasr",[24] put forward their own proposals for the settlement of the boundary problem. These consisted of nothing more than a simple rehashing of their previous demands for the long-term lease of the eastern half of Bubiyan Island and the ceding of Kuwaiti sovereignty over Warba in return for their recognition of Kuwait's land frontiers.[25] Saddam maintained that Iraq needed the two islands in order to promote itself as an Arabian Gulf power so as to defend itself and its neighbours against any external pressure. Therefore, the Iraqi Vice-President made it clear that frontier demarcation would only take place when Kuwait fulfilled Iraq's security and defence requirements.[26] Before giving a formal reply, the Kuwaiti government placed these proposals before its National Assembly, which declined to endorse them as Kuwait's sovereignty over all the islands was recognized in international agreements.[27] In addition, the National Assembly was unable to accept Saddam's demands on Warba and Bubiyan as allowing Iraq to acquire the islands for military purposes would seriously jeopardize Kuwait's declared policy of neutrality with its neighbours and would thereby invite trouble for itself, at least from Iran.[28]

The frontier question was further complicated by Syria's closure of the Tripoli–Banias oil pipeline, an act which further convinced Iraq of the necessity of acquiring Warba and Bubiyan as a way of safeguarding

---

23. Al-Mayyal, 'The political boundaries of the state of Kuwait', p.158. See also Schofield, *Kuwait and Iraq*, p. 118.

24. For the full text of the Algiers Agreement of 1975, see Abdulghani, *Iraq and Iran*, pp. 244–6.

25. *Ibid.*, p. 159. See also Khadduri, *Socialist Iraq*, p. 158.

26. Day, *Border and Territorial Disputes*, p. 225.

27. Abdulghani, *Iraq and Iran*, p. 159.

28. Khadduri, *Socialist Iraq*, p. 158.

its oil exports through the Gulf. Therefore, in December 1976 Tariq Aziz, the Iraqi Minister of Information, announced without reference to Kuwait that Warba and Bubiyan were Iraqi islands. At the same time, there were frequent Iraqi frontier violations along the length of the border.[29] On 13 December, the Kuwaiti Acting Minister of Information, Sheikh Jaber al-Ali, denounced these actions and reiterated that Warba and Bubiyan belonged to Kuwait as defined in the 1932 Exchange of Letters and the 1963 Iraqi–Kuwaiti Agreed Minutes. The Sheikh also condemned the continuing Iraqi military presence in the Kuwaiti territory south of the Umm Qasr area.[30]

However, there were signs of an improvement in the uneasy state of Iraqi–Kuwaiti relations in the following year. This was largely due to Iraq's avoidance of raising the question of Warba and Bubiyan because of its desire to concentrate on other political and economic aspects of its relations with Kuwait. With these objectives in mind, an Iraqi delegation headed by Izzat al-Dury, the Iraqi Interior Minister, visited Kuwait to discuss how to boost relations between their two countries. The visit was reciprocated on 17 June 1977 by Sheikh Saad al-Abdullah. On this occasion both parties agreed to establish a joint ministerial committee to discover ways of improving relations and solving the boundary issue. Following the conclusion of Sheikh Saad's mission, Iraq, in a move to restore peace and order in the frontier zone, at last withdrew the troops that had been stationed on Kuwaiti territory ever since 1969. In addition, the border which had been closed ever since the al-Samitah incident of 1973 was reopened in the July. In an attempt to build on this progress, a high-level Kuwaiti delegation headed by Sheikh Sabah, the Foreign Minister, arrived in Baghdad on 1 November 1977 to examine other ways of improving bilateral cooperation. The two sides soon agreed to set up a number of committees in order to study the feasibility of various joint projects, such as a rail link between Kuwait and Basra and the supply of electricity from Kuwait to southern Iraq. The old proposal of supplying fresh water from the Shatt al-Arab to Kuwait (see Chapter 7) was also added to the list.[31] Although all

---

29. *Ibid.*, p. 159.
30. Al-Mayyal, 'The political boundaries of the State of Kuwait', pp. 169–72.
31. Day, *Border and Territorial Disputes*, p. 225. See also Schofield, *Kuwait and Iraq*, p. 119.

these projects eventually came to nothing, relations between the two countries improved considerably.

In the following year, Kuwait attempted to resurrect the question of demarcation when Sheikh Jaber al-Ahmed acceded to the throne following the death of Sheikh Sabah (III) on 31 December 1977. Yet again there was no change in the Iraqi position towards demarcation, with the two sides merely agreeing to form a joint committee headed by their respective Interior Ministers to re-examine the issue. But this committee failed to make any progress despite the visit of Sheikh Saad al-Abdullah, the new Heir Apparent, to Baghdad in May 1980.[32] In any event, the frontier issue was soon overshadowed by the increased tensions and border enchroachments between Iran and Iraq which eventually led to the outbreak of war. Saddam, who became the President of Iraq on 16 July 1979 (just six months after the fall of the Iranian Shah),[33] attacked Iran on 22 September 1980. In also abrogating the Algiers Treaty of 1975, he claimed Iraqi sovereignty over the whole of the Shatt al-Arab, ordering all ships in the waterway to fly the Iraqi flag.[34] Saddam struck at a time calculated to take full advantage of the political chaos in Iran, anticipating, mistakenly as it turned out, a quick and decisive victory over the disintegrating Iranian forces. Saddam, who had already spent over two billion dollars in 1979 on upgrading his armed forces, was aiming at assuming the leadership of the Arab world by dominating the whole of the Gulf both politically and militarily as soon as Iran was defeated. Although initially Saddam was able to besiege

---

32. Al-Mayyal, 'The political boundaries of the State of Kuwait', pp. 176–8; Schofield, *Kuwait and Iraq*, p. 120.

33. Well before Saddam became President he had been heavily involved in subversive activities. In 1963, he was appointed as the head of the secret intelligence wing of the Baath Party. He took an active part in Bakr's *coup* of 30 July 1968 against Prime Minister Abdul-Razzak al-Nayif's faction. Although Saddam held no official post following the *coup*, he emerged as "the strongman in Iraq" because of his prominent position in the Baath Party's Regional Command and his strong hold over the party which monopolized the government. In early 1970, Bakr appointed him as his deputy, making him the de facto ruler of Iraq. Eventually, he placed Bakr under house arrest and declared himself President in 1979. See Daniel Dishon (ed.), *Middle East Record: 1968* (Jerusalem, Israel University Press, 1973), vol. 4, pp. 520–3. See also John Bulloch and Harvey Morris, *Saddam's War: the Origins of the Kuwait Conflict and the International Response* (London, Faber and Faber, 1991), p. 28.

34. Day, *Border and Territorial Disputes*, p. 225.

Abadan and Khorramshahr, he was soon beaten back and locked into a prolonged and bloody war. The Iranian bombardment of the Iraqi deep-sea oil terminals at Khor al-Amaya and Mina al-Bakr in the first week of the war forced Iraq to cut its oil output from a pre-war total of around three and a half million barrels a day to just half a million. Oil production from the Rumaila and Zubair fields was brought to a standstill following the closure of Iraq's only ports at Basra and Umm Qasr.[35] Iraq's position became even more precarious following Iran's capture of the Fao peninsula in early February 1986.

Kuwait's relations with Iraq were therefore dictated to a large extent by both Iraq's failure to achieve any significant success in its war with Iran and its increasing economic hardship. Iraq's inability to conduct any major naval offensive against Iran from Basra and Umm Qasr amplified the strategic importance of Warba and Bubiyan to its war efforts. While Iraq's forces were in retreat, its Interior Minister arrived in Kuwait in February 1981 to hold the first ever meeting of the joint boundary commission formed before the war. At this, he pressed his Kuwaiti counterpart to lease the islands of Warba and Bubiyan to Iraq so that they could be turned into major naval bases. If the Emirate agreed to do so, Iraq would demarcate the frontier based on the 1932 and 1963 agreements. Kuwait, however, once again rejected the Iraqi proposal as it had already been warned by the Iranian Foreign Minister Hussein Mussawi that Iran would not hesitate to take military action against the Emirate if it allowed Iraq any military privileges on the two islands.[36] Yet in an interview with a correspondent of the Kuwaiti daily *al-Anba'* on 4 July 1981, Saddam repeated his government's earlier request for the lease of Bubiyan to enhance its naval capability against Iran and placed the blame for the absence of a frontier settlement squarely on Kuwait.[37] Disregarding Saddam's comments, the Emirate instead set about strengthening its hold on Bubiyan in 1983 by starting construction work on a bridge to connect it to the mainland at a total cost of $52 million.[38] Later, plans were made for a speedy development of the island,

---

35. Edgar O'Ballance, *The Gulf War* (London, Brassey's Defence Publishers, 1988), p. 12.
36. Schofield, *Kuwait and Iraq*, p. 121.
37. Al-Mayyal, 'The political boundaries of the State of Kuwait', p. 179.
38. *Ibid.*, p. 185.

including the construction of another bridge linking it with Warba Island and the establishment of recreational and research centres as well as fish-canning factories.[39]

However, in light of Iran's naval supremacy in the Gulf, Saddam was not prepared to let the frontier issue rest. In an another interview with *al-Watan* in April 1984, the Iraqi President once again blamed Kuwait for not solving the problem of demarcation and expressed his keen desire to establish naval bases on Warba and Bubiyan from which to fight back at the Iranian navy. Admitting the disadvantaged position of his own navy in the Gulf, Saddam stated: "We are in an impossible position worse than anywhere in the Gulf. If our navy sailed away two steps it could be hit so easily."[40] In view of this handicap, Saddam was prepared to demarcate the frontier in exchange for a 20-year lease of the two islands rather than the 99 years sought previously.[41] To this end, the Kuwaiti Crown Prince Sheikh Saad was invited to Baghdad on 12 November 1984. However, the visit produced no tangible result on the frontier issue except for an undertaking that both countries were willing to press ahead with the as yet unimplemented joint economic projects agreed upon in 1977.[42]

Although no deal on the islands was reached, Sheikh Saad's mission angered the Iranians. Ali Akbar Hashemi Rafsanjani, the then Speaker of the Iranian Majlis (Parliament), who was of the mistaken belief that Sheikh Saad was considering the lease of Warba and Bubiyan to Saddam, warned Kuwait that if it did so the islands would be occupied by Iran. Kuwait was therefore forced to deny the allegation in the strongest possible terms and to take precautionary military measures to defend the islands by installing rockets and anti-aircraft guns. In fact, in December 1984, the Warba and Bubiyan area was declared a prohibited military zone.[43] Yet despite Kuwait's unambiguous statement that it had absolutely no intention of granting Iraq any military privileges on either island, Iran issued another strong warning to Kuwait as soon as its forces

---

39. Cordesman, *The Gulf and the Search for Strategic Stability*, p. 570. See also Schofield, *Kuwait and Iraq*, p. 124.
40. As quoted in al-Mayyal, 'The political boundaries of the State of Kuwait', p. 192.
41. *Ibid.*, p. 193. See also Schofield, *Kuwait and Iraq*, p. 121.
42. Al-Mayyal, 'The political boundaries of the State of Kuwait', p. 195.
43. *Ibid.*, p. 198.

captured Fao in February 1986. Rafsanjani stated that any Kuwaiti move to allow the retreating Iraqis to use Bubiyan Island would be regarded as an act of hostility against Iran. He also threatened to occupy the neutral zone oilfields (jointly owned by Saudi Arabia and Kuwait), which had been supplying oil to Iraq's customers during the war.[44]

Following the loss of Fao, Saddam concentrated his entire energies on rebuilding his army and the problem of the frontier fell from his agenda. Although no progress was made on demarcation, Kuwait gave Iraq generous economic support. As soon as Saddam launched his full-scale assault on Iran, Kuwait gave it its full political backing and used its own main port to transport Iraqi supplies. The land routes that ran through Kuwait to the Mediterranean became main Iraqi supply lines from the onset of the war. By the end of the war in 1988, Kuwait had given Iraq interest-free loans totalling $10 billion (still to this date not repaid) to meet its growing economic problems. From 1983 to 1988, Kuwait allocated to Iraq the revenues earned from an output of up to 125,000 barrels per day from the oilfields in the northern part of the Kuwaiti–Saudi neutral zone.[45] Despite Kuwait's unprecedented generosity and support of Iraq throughout the war, the Iraqis still saw the leasing of Warba and at least part of Bubiyan as a non-negotiable precondition of any demarcation of the frontier.

The demarcation issue resurfaced as soon as the Iran–Iraq War came to an end, when in February 1989 Sheikh Saad arrived in Baghdad to discuss the border. While Saddam expressed his willingness to resolve the dispute, he still demanded absolute right over Bubiyan and Warba in order to prevent Kuwait from controlling Iraq's access to the sea. The Heir Apparent rejected this demand as Kuwait itself was planning to develop Bubiyan into a resort centre and intended to create a new city for 100,000 people on the Subiya peninsula just opposite Bubiyan. Consequently, the talks followed a familiar pattern by ending without any agreement being reached with each party blaming the other for the lack of progress. Yet despite this impasse there was no sign of a deterioration in the relations between the two countries. For instance,

---

44. O'Ballance, *The Gulf War*, p. 176. See also Shahram Chubin and Charles Tripp, *Iran and Iraq at War* (London, I. B. Tauris, 1988), p. 171.
45. See Schofield, *Kuwait and Iraq*, p. 121. See also Bulloch and Morris, *Saddam's War*, p. 132.

Sheikh Jaber was invited to Baghdad in September 1989 to receive the Rafadin Medal, Iraq's highest civil decoration. Saddam warmly received the Emir with a 21-gun salute and the Iraqi media referred to him as "a brave Arab leader". Although Sheikh Jaber did discuss the border issue directly, he suggested that the problem of demarcation should be solved through international arbitration. However, as Saddam was against the idea of internationalizing the dispute,[46] the 1980s drew to a close with the question of the frontier yet to be decided.

Conclusion

The overthrow of Qasim's government by the first Baathist revolution paved the way for Iraq's recognition of Kuwait's independence with a fixed boundary as defined in the 1932 Exchange of Letters. This diplomatic victory, however, had been achieved at a cost to Kuwait of £32 million and an undertaking to scrap the Anglo-Kuwaiti Exchange of Notes of 1961 which covered the defence of Kuwait in the event of any external threat. Although Iraqi–Kuwaiti relations improved during this period, Kuwait's repeated attempts throughout the 1970s to demarcate the frontier came to nothing due to Iraq's dogged insistence on certain preconditions. These were the cession or the leasing of Warba and Bubiyan – where it wanted to establish military bases to gain direct naval access to the waters of the Gulf – as well as the leasing of a strip of territory south of Umm Qasr. Kuwait could not agree to these demands as it feared not only the permanent Iraqi tenure of the islands but also an unfavourable Iranian reaction to such a move. Eventually, the frontier question was overshadowed by the outbreak of the Iran–Iraq War, but this only served to heighten the strategic importance of Warba and Bubiyan to Iraq. Saddam Hussein's failure to achieve absolute control of the Shatt al-Arab waterway – one of his prime objectives during the war – together with the destruction of the Basra port by the Iranians made Hussein more desperate than any previous Iraqi ruler to gain better access to the sea. Indeed, this lack of access to the Gulf waters rendered Iraq's navy considerably inferior to that of Iran, and it was this handicap

---

46. Elaine Sciolino, *The Outlaw State: Saddam Hussein's Quest for Power and the Gulf Crisis* (New York, John Wiley and Sons, 1991), p. 196.

which prompted Saddam Hussein to renew his efforts to gain a foothold on the two Kuwaiti islands. In order to achieve this, the necessities of the war forced him to offer to demarcate the frontier in return for a 20-year lease of the islands as opposed to the 99-year lease he had sought earlier. But Kuwait could not compromise over this issue and responded by fortifying the islands. Thus, despite its wholehearted political and economic support of Iraq during the war, Kuwait's efforts to bring about the demarcation of its northern frontier remained unrewarded.

10

The Gulf War and its Aftermath

On 2 August 1990 Saddam Hussein invaded Kuwait and occupied it for seven months. The Iraqis were driven out of Kuwait by a US-led multinational force following a well-planned military strategy. Prior to the use of force, efforts were made for a peaceful solution to the crisis. While Iraq's invasion of Kuwait brought it only defeat and economic hardship, for Kuwait it heralded a UN-initiated settlement of its long-standing boundary problem with Iraq and paved the way for the signing of a series of defence pacts with Western countries for the future security of Kuwait.

According to Salinger and Laurent, the end of the Iran–Iraq War on 8 August 1988, marked "the beginning of the Gulf crisis of 1990–91".[1] This bloody and prolonged war had ravaged the Iraqi economy draining it of its entire oil revenue of $25 billion; in 1990 Iraq was unable to even service the interest on its huge foreign debt of $80 billion. As a result of an annual rate of inflation of over 40 per cent, public sector workers faced severe hardship as their pay had been frozen since the beginning of the war. Saddam had had to cut his economic programme curtailing many ambitious developmental projects, such as the building of highways, railway lines, hydroelectric dams and even an underground system in Baghdad.[2] While economically the Iran–Iraq War caused severe hardship in Iraq, it brought no benefit to the country, except that Saddam could declare a "victory" over Iran. Saddam had failed to gain control of the Shatt al-Arab waterway which remained closed. More than 120,000 Iraqis had been killed, around 300,000 wounded and 65,000 had been taken prisoners.[3] The Iraqi President's

---

1. Pierre Salinger and Eric Laurent, *Secret Dossier: the Hidden Agenda behind the Gulf War* (London, Penguin Books, 1991), p. 1.
2. *Ibid.*, pp. 8–9.
3. Judith Miller and Laurie Mylroie, *Saddam Hussein and the Crisis in the Gulf* (New York, Times Books, 1990), pp. 126–7.

long-cherished dream to style himself as the leader of the Arab world remained unrealized. In the course of the war he had built up an army of more than one million and equipped it with the most sophisticated armaments his hard-earned oil dollars could buy. Between 1982 and 1990 Iraq had spent about $42.8 billion on various kinds of weapons from the USSR, China, North Korea, Britain, the USA, France, Italy, Germany, Austria, Switzerland and Belgium. Yet despite Iraq's severe economic difficulties, this programme of militarization continued after the war with Iran.[4]

Saddam Hussein, aware of the need to keep his one-million-strong army fully occupied partly to prevent the possibility of it turning against him, intended to use it to fulfil the following objectives: firstly, to realize Iraq's long-standing claim to Kuwait; secondly, to gain direct access to the open waters of the Gulf through the acquisition of Warba and Bubiyan; thirdly, to occupy the land opposite the high-yielding Rumaila oilfield situated in the disputed frontier zone; fourthly, to create a situation in which he would not have to repay (fully) the huge sums borrowed from the Gulf states during the Iran–Iraq War; and finally, to help fashion himself as the unrivalled leader of the Arab world.[5] However, before resorting to military action to achieve these objectives, Saddam first put diplomatic pressure on his wartime economic allies. On 24 February 1990, at a closed meeting in Amman of the Arab Co-operation Council (ACC) – a regional association of Egypt, Jordan and Iraq formed in 1989 – the Iraqi President told Hosni Mubarak, the Egyptian President, and King Hussein of Jordan that they should persuade both King Fahd of Saudi Arabia and Sheikh Jaber, the Kuwaiti Emir, to write off their loans totalling $30 billion which he had used to finance his war effort. He argued: "If they don't cancel the debt and give me another $30 billion I shall take steps to retaliate."[6] While Mubarak left the meeting in protest and returned immediately to Cairo, King Hussein journeyed to both Kuwait and Saudi Arabia on 26 February to convey Saddam's demands. As neither King Fahd nor Sheikh Jaber were prepared to accept Saddam's terms, King Hussein returned to Baghdad on 3 March to relay their reply to the Iraqi

---

4. Salinger and Laurent, *Secret Dossier*, pp. 17–18.
5. *Ibid.*, p. 11.
6. As quoted in *ibid.*, p. 7. See also Elaine Sciolino, *The Outlaw State*, p. 199.

President. Consequently, Saddam secretly directed his military high command to formulate plans for the deployment of troops on the Kuwaiti border.[7]

Tensions were mounting rapidly. At an Arab summit meeting held in Baghdad on 28 May 1990 to discuss Soviet Jewish emigration to Israel, Saddam told his guests that the Gulf states, particularly Kuwait and the United Arab Emirates (UAE), were exceeding their quotas fixed by OPEC, thereby keeping oil prices low. He claimed, "every time the price of a barrel drops by one dollar, Iraq loses $1 billion a year." He accused Kuwait of consistently extracting 2.1 million barrels a day despite its OPEC allocation of only 1.5 million barrels. This overproduction, he added, was tantamount to an act of economic war against Iraq.[8] Stating that Iraq suffered most as a result of these violations, he demanded that Kuwait, the UAE and Saudi Arabia cancel their wartime loans of $30 billion and give him a further $10 billion to help return his country to its pre-war economic position. But the leaders of the three states kept calm and remained non-committal.

Less than a month after this meeting the Iraqi Deputy Prime Minister Saadoun Hammadi travelled to Riyadh to tell King Fahd that he should persuade the Gulf states to call an emergency OPEC meeting in order to set lower quotas for oil production so that prices could increase. Although the King was in favour of bringing some harmony among the oil-producing countries, he decided not to act on the Iraqi request as he did not find any justification for calling a special meeting of OPEC, especially as the oil ministers were due to meet the following month anyway. Displeased with this answer, Hammadi then went to Abu Dhabi to repeat the message, but the response there was the same. His next destination was Kuwait City. During an audience with Sheikh Jaber, he reiterated Saddam's earlier demand for financial assistance. As Hammadi estimated Kuwait's worldwide assets to be in excess of $100 billion, he demanded that the Kuwaiti Emir contribute $10 billion to Iraq. To pacify Hammadi Sheikh Jaber agreed to pay Iraq $500 million over three years but only on condition that Saddam agreed to demarcate

---

7. Salinger and Laurent, *Secret Dossier*, pp. 11–12.
8. *Ibid.*, p. 31. See also Bishara A. Bahbah, 'The crisis in the Gulf: why Iraq invaded Kuwait' in Phyllis Bennis and Michel Moushabeck (eds.), *Beyond the Storm: A Gulf Crisis Reader* (Edinburgh, Canongate Press, 1992), p. 52.

the Iraqi–Kuwaiti frontier and to ratify this immediately. This proposition, however, was not acceptable to Baghdad.

Hammadi's unsuccessful Gulf mission helped convince Saddam that the Gulf states would not bow readily to diplomatic pressure alone.[9] He therefore decided to step up the pressure on the Gulf states. His Foreign Minister Tariq Aziz, in a memorandum dated 17 July to the then Secretary-General of the League of Arab States Chadli Klibi, openly accused both Kuwait and the UAE of being the "culprits" of the overproduction. The memorandum complained that Kuwait, having taken advantage of Iraq's preoccupation with the war with Iran, had pushed its border further northwards, established military and oil installations inside Iraqi territory and had stolen Iraqi oil worth around $2.4 billion from the Rumaila field.[10] (The Rumaila oilfield is one of the largest oil deposits in the Middle East spreading over an 80-kilometre area inside Iraq. But the southern part of the field is well within Kuwaiti territory, touching the Ratga oilfield.) Klibi was surprised by the memorandum and sent a copy to the Kuwaiti Ambassador in Tunis. As soon as it reached Kuwait City, the Kuwaiti government flatly denied the allegation reiterating that the Emirate only drew oil from wells within its own territories at a reasonable distance from the border.[11] An emergency meeting of the Kuwaiti Cabinet was also held to discuss Aziz's memorandum. Ali Khalifa al-Sabah, the Finance Minister, opened the proceedings by claiming that the Iraqis were trying to blame the Gulf states for their own economic hardship. He did not believe that Saddam would change his behaviour even after the forthcoming OPEC meeting in Geneva. But when he suggested that the problem should be solved through the Gulf Co-operation Council (GCC), his Cabinet colleagues disagreed. Instead of taking a decision on the question of Iraq's debt and Saddam's demand for a $10 billion donation, the Cabinet moved on to examine the Iraqi threat facing Kuwait. Sheikh Sabah al-Ahmed al-Sabah, the Foreign Minister, prophetically observed that there was a strong possibility of an Iraqi attack on Kuwait since Iraq

---

9. Salinger and Laurent, *Secret Dossier*, pp. 35–7.
10. *Ibid.*, p. 40.
11. For more details on Kuwait's reply to Iraqi accusations, see *Kuwait Diplomacy Against Iraq's Invasion of Kuwait* (Cairo, Kuwait Information Centre, 1992), pp. 13–25. For more details on the location of the Rumaila field, see Schofield, *Kuwait and Iraq*, p. 126.

had already started moving troops towards the Kuwaiti frontier. Sheikh Saad al-Abdullah al-Sabah, the Crown Prince and Prime Minister, however, believed that the Iraqis would not launch a full-scale attack and would not go beyond the limits of Ratga and Umm Qasr. Dhari al-Othman, the Minister of Justice, disagreed and argued: "The question of oil prices is only a pretext. In reality, Iraq is a wolf and we are the sheep." As Abd al-Wahab al-Fawzan, the Health Minister, and Fahd al-Hasawy, the Minister of State for Municipal Affairs, were in full agreement with this far-sighted prediction, they urged the Cabinet to take immediate measures to counter the Iraqi threat. The Cabinet concluded its meeting by cancelling the leave of all service personnel, although it apparently took no decision on any strategy to defend the country against an Iraqi attack.[12]

In the meantime, Saddam continued his build-up. By 21 July, he had assembled 30,000 troops along the Kuwaiti border. Even at this late stage the United States did not see any immediate danger to Kuwait but instead took this display of military might as an attempt to force Kuwait to agree to raise oil prices. Its spokeswoman Margaret Tutwiler made this somewhat unclear statement: "We remain determined to defend the principle of freedom of navigation and to ensure the free flow of oil through the Strait of Hormuz." In other words, the United States was primarily concerned with the safe flow of oil rather than the security of the Emirate, a major oil exporter to the West. Meanwhile, tensions mounted in the border area when the Egyptian intelligence agency reported that about 6 to 8 Iraqi armoured divisions as well as a similar number of its mechanized infantry were moving in the direction of the Kuwaiti frontier. The report alarmed Hosni Mubarak, who, on 24 July, hurriedly left for Baghdad in an attempt to persuade Saddam not to take any hasty action. Saddam told Mubarak that he had no intention of invading the Emirate but was simply holding a normal military exercise in the frontier zone. After passing on this explanation to Sheikh Jaber, the Egyptian President managed to persuade the Emir to agree to an Iraqi–Kuwaiti meeting in Jeddah to discuss all the outstanding

---

12. Salinger and Laurent, *Secret Dossier*, pp. 39–44. See also Adel Darwish and Gregory Alexander, *Unholy Babylon: the Secret History of Saddam's War* (London, Victor Gollancz, 1991), pp. 264–5.

issues between the two countries. Mubarak then went on to Riyadh to update King Fahd on his progress in Baghdad and Kuwait City.[13]

While Mubarak was shuttling from one capital to another in an attempt to diffuse tensions, Tutwiler made another ambiguous statement pointing out that the United States was committed to support the individual and collective self-defence of its friends in the Gulf with whom it had "deep and long-standing ties". But in reply to reporters' questions, she stressed that the United States was under no obligation to defend Kuwait in the event of an Iraqi attack as it had no defence agreement with Kuwait.[14] In view of these contradictory statements, Saddam was apparently eager to know where exactly the United States stood with regard to his military build-up on the Kuwaiti frontier. Therefore, on 25 July 1990, he summoned April Glaspie, the American Ambassador in Baghdad, and gave her a long lecture on the economic difficulties of his country and his people and again accused Kuwait and the UAE of waging an economic war against Iraq ever since the end of the Iran–Iraq War. These two states, he continued, were largely responsible for the suffering of Iraqis and had been disregarding Iraq's rights as detailed in Aziz's memorandum eight days earlier. He then complained that the United States in favouring a lower oil price encouraged them to overproduce. Ambassador Glaspie told Saddam that President Bush had no wish to harm Iraq economically and not only did he want better and deeper relations with Iraq but also "an Iraqi contribution to peace and prosperity in the Middle East". The Ambassador then drew Saddam's attention to the concentration of troops in the frontier zone. He assured her that he had already told Kuwait through Mubarak that he would not invade the Emirate at least until after the representatives of Iraq and Kuwait had met in Jeddah towards the end of July. But he made it clear that if the meeting failed to reach an agreement, "then it will be natural that Iraq will not accept death, even though wisdom is above everything else". In effect, Saddam was saying that he would take military action against Kuwait if the proposed talks in Jeddah failed to produce a favourable outcome. Whether Glaspie understood this or not she made this assuring statement: "We have no opinion on Arab–Arab conflicts

---

13. Darwish and Alexander, *Unholy Babylon*, pp. 265–6.
14. As quoted in *ibid.*, p. 266.

like your border disagreement with Kuwait."[15] This statement apparently convinced the Iraqi President that the United States would not get involved, at least militarily, if he crossed the Kuwaiti border. It is difficult to say whether Glaspie gave him this impression at the State Department's instruction or not. In any event, following this meeting, Saddam increased the number of troops on the border to 50,000 and sent his new Oil Minister, Isam al-Shalabi, to Geneva to attend the crucial OPEC meeting. The Iraqi Minister pressed for a $25 per barrel benchmark price – $7 above the price at the time. While Libya and the revenue-hungry Nigeria supported him, other members disagreed. Eventually after heated discussions a compromise formula was reached fixing the benchmark price at $21 with a limit on production of 22.5 million barrels per day.

Although the outcome of this meeting placated the Iraqis, Saddam showed no sign of withdrawing his forces from the Kuwaiti border. On the contrary, he continued the build-up, increasing the number of troops to 100,000 supported by 300 tanks and 300 pieces of artillery. By 28 July, Saddam had also established major supply lines for his troops on the frontier. Although CIA headquarters in Washington was flooded with intelligence reports of the accelerated build-up along the Kuwaiti frontier, the decision-makers in Washington, London and Cairo were of the opinion that it was nothing more than a bluff on Saddam's part designed to put pressure on the Kuwaitis on the eve of the Jeddah talks. Meanwhile, King Hussein and the PLO Chairman Yasser Arafat made last-ditch efforts, on 28 July, to convince the Kuwaiti government that they should pay Iraq the $10 billion demanded by Saddam to diffuse the crisis. But both Sheikh Jaber, the Emir, and Sheikh Saad, the Crown Prince, declined to do so, stating: "If Saddam comes across the border, let him come. The Americans will get him out."[16]

With no visible sign of compromise from either side, the Jeddah meeting was held on 31 July. The Kuwaiti delegation headed by Sheikh Saad also included Sheikh Sabah al-Ahmed al-Sabah, the Foreign Minister, and Dhari al-Othman, the Justice Minister. The Iraqi team

---

15. *Ibid.*, pp. 267–70. See also Salinger and Laurent, *Secret Dossier*, pp. 47–62.
16. As quoted in Salinger and Laurent, *Secret Dossier*, pp. 66–7. For the CIA's assessment of the situation, see Darwish and Alexander, *Unholy Babylon*, pp. 272–3.

included Izzat Ibrahim, the Vice-President of the Revolutionary Command Council and a die-hard Baathist, Saadoun Hammadi, the Deputy Prime Minister, and Ali Hassan al-Majid, Saddam's cousin. The meeting was chaired by Prince Saud al-Faisal, the Saudi Foreign Minister. Though all issues from finance to the concentration of forces were discussed during the meeting nothing was achieved. Although minutes are not available, it was later reported that when Kuwait agreed to write off the Iraqi debts, the Iraqis moved the goalposts by insisting on the lease of Bubiyan along with an additional $10 billion in aid. The meeting was reconvened the following morning, but in the absence of any official statement from either the Kuwaiti or Iraqi side, it is difficult to say what exactly transpired at this meeting. In any event, the meeting was soon concluded after agreeing to meet again in a few days in Baghdad.[17]

Following this inconclusive outcome, Sheikh Saad immediately reported back to Kuwait on the lack of progress and the gravity of the situation. Meanwhile Ibrahim, the leader of the Iraqi delegation, gave Saddam a detailed account of the unsuccessful talks. Saddam at once summoned the members of the Revolutionary Command Council to announce his decision to invade the Emirate later that night.[18]

Saddam's forces crossed the Kuwaiti border on 2 August 1990 at 1.30 a.m. Kuwaiti time. Sheikh Saad was the first to receive news of the invasion from the Defence Ministry and immediately alerted the Emir and the other members of the Al Sabah family. The Emir, realizing that it would be futile to face the advancing Iraqi masses reluctantly fled, along with his ministers and other dignitaries, to Saudi Arabia and began the task of mobilizing world opinion against the invasion.[19] Although some Kuwaitis offered stiff resistance to the invaders, within

---

17. Darwish and Alexander, *Unholy Babylon*, pp. 276–8.
18. Salinger and Laurent, *Secret Dossier*, p. 81.
19. In a move to show the unity and solidarity of the Kuwaiti people against Saddam's invasion, the exiled Kuwaiti government held a three-day conference (from 13 to 15 October) in Jeddah for Kuwaiti people. The conference was attended by more than 750 Kuwaitis from all walks of life including former ministers, parliamentarians, diplomats, businessmen, judges and civil servants. Sheikh Jaber al-Ahmad al-Sabah and Sheikh Saad al-Abdullah al-Sabah both addressed the conference and promised greater democracy in Kuwait after its liberation. The Kuwaiti Emir then underlined the following conditions for a

six hours the Iraqi forces had occupied the entire country, contrary to the general expectation that Saddam would confine the invasion to the two strategic islands of Warba and Bubiyan and the Ratga oilfield. The Iraqi government attempted to justify its actions by announcing that its troops had entered Kuwait at the invitation of so-called Kuwaiti revolutionaries who had overthrown the Al Sabah government. In actual fact, there were no such revolutionaries in Kuwait. Saddam apparently thought that the Kuwaiti opposition headed by Ahmed al-Saadoun might join with his troops, thereby making it easier to install a puppet government. To Saddam's great dismay, no one in Kuwait except some expatriate Palestinians and Jordanians cooperated with the invaders. Nevertheless, thousands of Iraqi troops soon reached Kuwait City from Basra and took over all of the key installations.

As news of the invasion spread around the globe, world leaders re-acted immediately and with unprecedented unity. Washington, London and Paris strongly condemned the invasion and called for an immediate Iraqi withdrawal. President Bush called it "naked aggression" and said he was leaving all options open. While China joined the chorus for an immediate halt to military action, the Soviet Union called for a prompt and unconditional Iraqi withdrawal, as did Britain and France. Bush then went a step further by ordering the aircraft-carrier USS *Independence* to the Gulf. All Iraqi and Kuwaiti assets and property in the US were frozen to foil any Iraqi attempt to expropriate them. On the evening of 2 August, the UN Security Council unanimously passed Resolution 660 condemning the Iraqi aggression and ordering Iraq to withdraw all its forces immediately and unconditionally from Kuwaiti territory.[20]

Although this worldwide condemnation surprised Saddam, he still refused to withdraw his troops. With reports of the movement of Iraqi

---

political settlement of the crisis: (i) Kuwait's sovereignty and territorial integrity cannot be a subject for negotiation or bargaining; (ii) full implementation of UN Security Council resolutions calling for unconditional Iraqi withdrawal and the return to Kuwait of the legitimate government; (iii) reparation for all damages Iraq has caused Kuwait; and (iv) the unconditional Iraqi withdrawal should precede any attempt for a peaceful solution to the conflict which Iraq has used as a pretext to invade Kuwait. See 'Kuwait is in a show of unity', *Gulf Times*, 14 October 1990.

20. See BBC World Service (compilation), *Gulf Crisis Chronology* (London, Longman, 1991), pp. 1–2.

troops towards the Saudi frontier, King Hussein devised a possible Arab solution to the crisis. Even though this was very generous to Saddam, allowing him to take enormous wealth from Kuwait and retain the Raudatain oilfield as well as Warba and Bubiyan, the King's proposal failed to gain the support of either President Mubarak or King Fahd.[21]

Following further reports of Iraqi tank movements on the Saudi border both Richard Cheney, the US Secretary of State for Defence, and General Norman Schwarzkopf, the Commander-in-Chief, US Central Command, along with a number of high-level military experts rushed to Jeddah on 6 August and obtained King Fahd's permission for the deployment of US troops on his territory to defend Saudi Arabia from a possible Iraqi attack. Two days later, President Bush declared in a televised address to the American people that elements of the 82nd Airborne Division as well as key units of the US Air Force were being sent to Saudi Arabia to take up defensive positions under the command of General Schwarzkopf.[22] This was the beginning of Operation "Desert Shield", the largest US deployment since Vietnam. Bush outlined the four guiding principles of the operation: first, the immediate, unconditional and complete withdrawal of all Iraqi forces from Kuwait; second, the restoration of Kuwait's legitimate government; third, the reaffirmation of the US commitment to the security and stability of the Arabian Gulf; and fourth, the protection of US citizens abroad.[23]

Meanwhile, on 6 August, the UN Security Council imposed some of the toughest economic sanctions in the UN's 45-year history (Resolution 661) ordering an arms embargo on Iraq and a ban on its oil exports.[24] Turkey immediately implemented the resolution and banned the loading of Iraqi oil at its Mediterranean ports, thereby effectively cutting off more than half of Iraq's crude exports and leaving it with no option but to shut the pipeline through Turkey. Other countries soon followed suit, and in order to tighten the maritime enforcement of the embargo some 70 warships from different countries were sent to patrol the Gulf and the Red Sea in September 1990. The embargo was to cost

21. Darwish and Alexander, *Unholy Babylon*, pp. 282–3. See also Salinger and Laurent, *Secret Dossier*, pp. 102–6.
22. General H. Norman Schwarzkopf, *It Doesn't Take a Hero* (London, Bantam Press, 1992), pp. 305–6.
23. For the text of President Bush's televised speech, see *Gulf Times*, 9 August 1990.
24. For the full text, see *Gulf Times*, 7 August 1990.

Iraq $20 million a day and the crisis more than $20 billion in lost oil revenues per year. To further tighten the ring around Iraq, the Security Council, on 25 September, passed another resolution (670) imposing an air embargo on Iraq.

In the meantime, Saddam proclaimed the "formal union" of Kuwait and Iraq on 8 August. This was the first annexation of a sovereign and independent state since the Second World War. It was inevitably denounced by the UN Security Council which unanimously adopted Resolution 662 outlawing the annexation and calling on all states not to recognize it.[25] The annexation also resulted in Iraq's isolation from the Arab world. On 9 August, Arab leaders held an emergency summit meeting in Cairo, which was also attended by the Iraqi Foreign Minister Tariq Aziz and the Deputy Prime Minister Taha Yasin Ramadan. The following day, the majority of those present approved a resolution condemning Iraq for annexing Kuwait and calling for the deployment of a joint Arab force in Saudi Arabia to defend the kingdom against Iraqi attack.[26]

Following the Cairo summit, the deployment of multinational troops gathered momentum. With Egypt, Syria and Morocco deploying 15,000, 13,000 and 1,200 troops, respectively, in Saudi Arabia, the US had increased its military strength by the first week of October to a land force of 150,000 supported by 35,000 marines, 45 warships, 180 jet fighters and a further 300 aircraft on sea-based carriers. On 3 October, the United States further bolstered its forces in the Gulf with the arrival of the aircraft-carrier USS *Independence*, with its 70 combat aircraft, and other warships along with several escort ships. Britain, which had already sent 2 squadrons of Tornado fighters and 1 squadron of Jaguar ground attack aircraft as well as 2 frigates and minesweepers with support ships, began to airlift an armoured brigade from Germany to Saudi Arabia including more than 9,000 "Desert Rat" soldiers and 2 armoured regiments equipped with 120 Challenger tanks. Britain completed its deployment by mid-November 1990 with Lieutenant

---

25. *Gulf Times*, 11 August 1990.
26. Eleven out of the twenty member states voted for the resolution: Kuwait, Saudi Arabia, Egypt, UAE, Bahrain, Djibouti, Morocco, Oman, Somalia and Syria. While Iraq, Libya and Palestine voted against, Algeria and Yemen abstained. Jordan, Mauritania and Sudan expressed reservations on the resolution and took no stand. Tunisia did not attend the summit. *Gulf Times*, 11 August 1990.

General Sir Peter de la Billière, a former SAS commander, placed in command of the British land, air and naval forces in the Gulf. France had already sent 8,950 soldiers and 14 warships as well as a Foreign Legion force under the command of Lieutenant General Michel Roquejeoffre. Other countries, namely Argentina, Australia, Belgium, Canada, Denmark, Holland, Norway and Spain either sent warships or fighter planes to the region.[27] Even comparatively poor countries like Pakistan and Bangladesh, appalled by Saddam's blatant disregard of international norms and practices, sent 5,000 and 2,500 troops, respectively, as their contribution to the multinational force. In addition, Kuwait, Bahrain, Qatar, the UAE and Oman placed their active forces at the disposal of Saudi Arabia, which itself had already deployed 38,000 troops, 7,200 marines and its modern air force. Saudi and the other GCC troops together with all other Islamic forces were placed under the command of Lieutenant General Prince Khalid bin Sultan al-Saud. The Coalition's fighter planes were spread throughout Saudi Arabia, Qatar, Bahrain and the UAE.[28] In response to the multinational build-up, Saddam continued to strengthen his forces in southern Iraq and Kuwait, deploying by the first week of October 1990 nearly 400,000 of his one-million-strong army and 3,500 tanks.[29]

Despite the military build-up and the economic sanctions, diplomatic efforts were continuing for a peaceful solution to the crisis. In the first week of September, UN Secretary-General Javier Perez de Cuellar met with Tariq Aziz in Amman and requested the withdrawal from Kuwait of Iraqi forces in order to avoid war. In an unprecedented display of superpower solidarity, George Bush and Mikhail Gorbachev held a summit meeting in Helsinki on 10 September. Both leaders told Iraq in no uncertain terms to get out of Kuwait and seek a peaceful solution to its grievances. Moscow, which had a long-standing treaty of friendship with Iraq predating Saddam's accession to power, sent a top envoy, Yevgeny Primakov, a member of Gorbachev's Presidential Council, to Baghdad on 6 October. Primakov handed Saddam a

---

27. See *Gulf Times*, 15 September 1990. See also Schwarzkopf, *It Doesn't Take a Hero*, p. 358.
28. *Gulf Times*, 4 October 1990; see also Schwarzkopf, *It Doesn't Take a Hero*, p. 414.
29. For the full text, see Resolution 670 (1990) in E. Lauterpacht, *et al., The Kuwait Crisis*, pp. 94–5.

message from Gorbachev, the content of which though not definitely known, would seem, from Primakov's observations, to have stressed the need for a political solution. Saddam told Primakov that Iraq would withdraw from Kuwait as long as it could retain the southern Rumaila oilfield and the islands of Warba and Bubiyan.[30] Despite these ambitious demands, Primakov was optimistic at the prospects of reaching a peaceful end to the crisis and expressed great satisfaction over his talks with Saddam and Tariq Aziz. Yet following Primakov's mission, Saddam still showed no sign of withdrawing his troops but instead tried to draw attention to the inconsistency of "the implementation of international law in the Gulf and its implementation regarding the Palestinian problem."[31]

Meanwhile, Primakov shuttled between the Middle East and Europe advocating the policy of a partial Iraqi withdrawal which would cede Warba and Bubiyan as well as the Kuwaiti end of the disputed Rumaila oilfield to Iraq. He arrived in Washington on 19 October to present this formula to the American administration. However, President Bush rejected it outright and made it clear that the United States would "stay the course" until Iraq's invasion of Kuwait was reversed. The President added:

> I am as determined as I was when the first troops left [for Saudi Arabia] that Saddam Hussein's aggression not be rewarded by some compromise, not be rewarded by failing to get him totally out of Kuwait and restoring the legitimate rulers.[32]

Echoing this, Douglas Hurd, the British Foreign Secretary at a press conference in Cairo, ruled out any compromise which would allow Iraq to carve out any part of Kuwait. He stated: "There is no future in a compromise which would leave Saddam Hussein in possession of part of Kuwait or a privileged position in Kuwait." In view of this firm Anglo-American stand, Primakov dropped his proposals for a partial withdrawal and stressed that Moscow and Washington remained united behind the UN resolutions which demanded Iraq's total withdrawal from Kuwait.[33] In addition, Kuwaiti leaders, determined not to make

---

30. See *Gulf Times*, 8, 9, 11 and 12 October 1990.
31. See *Gulf Times*, 2 and 7 October 1990.
32. As quoted in *Gulf Times*, 20 October 1990.
33. *Ibid*.

any territorial compromise with Iraq, also rejected any solution of the Gulf crisis short of Iraq's complete withdrawal from their homeland and their restoration to office.[34] Nevertheless, Moscow still held out hope of reaching a peaceful solution. As a result, Primakov arrived in Baghdad on 27 October and delivered another letter from Gorbachev demanding an Iraqi withdrawal from Kuwait. Although the letter also said that the Soviet Union would do all it could to find a peaceful settlement, Primakov failed to persuade Saddam to pull his forces out of Kuwait. On 29 October, the Soviet envoy left Baghdad empty-handed.[35]

Following Primakov's second unsuccessful peace mission, the UN Security Council hurriedly passed Resolution 674 on 29 October, which held Iraq responsible for war damages and the mistreatment of civilians arising from the Iraqi occupation of Kuwait.[36] In fact, the resolution was designed to keep up the pressure on Iraq in order to give the sanctions strategy, which had already started to bite, more time to work; the embargo had halted all Iraqi oil exports except for a small amount to Jordan and virtually cut off all its imports forcing the Iraqi government, on 19 October, to introduce the rationing of petrol and other essential commodities.[37]

Yet despite these severe economic difficulties within his country, Saddam had increased the number of his troops in Kuwait to 420,000 by the last week of October. With the Coalition continuing its military build-up in Saudi Arabia and the Gulf region (reaching a total of 350,000 troops), Saddam put his army on a high state of alert on 30 October. The Iraqi President warned the United States that his army would no sooner "withdraw from Kuwait than he imagined the United States would give up Hawaii", to which James Baker immediately retorted: "Let no one doubt; we will not rule out a possible use of force if Iraq continues to occupy Kuwait."[38]

Preparations for war continued at full speed. On 5 November, the US Defense Department called up major units from the military reserves for duty in the Gulf, a move that would add thousands of men to the forces already massed there. At this stage the United States alone

34. *Gulf Times*, 23 and 27 October 1990.
35. *Gulf Times*, 30 October 1990.
36. See 'UN adopts move on damages', *Gulf Times*, 30 October 1990.
37. *Gulf Times*, 24 October 1990.
38. See 'Iraqi army put on high alert', *Gulf Times*, 31 October 1990.

had 220,000 soldiers, sailors and airmen serving in the military net surrounding Kuwait and Iraq. The Pentagon had called up some 34,000 reservists since the Gulf crisis began, although all of them were in support units as opposed to being infantry or other combat reserve forces. In addition, on 5 November, the American aircraft-carrier USS *Midway* cruised into the Gulf with its 7 escort ships placing targets in Iraq and Kuwait within the range of the carrier's 75 warplanes without the need for refuelling. There were 3 other carriers in the region: the *Independence* in the northern Arabian Sea, the *Saratoga* in the Red Sea and the *John F. Kennedy* in the Mediterranean.[39] Therefore, although US military objectives initially were to deter an Iraqi attack on Saudi Arabia and to enforce the effective implementation of the UN sanctions, preparations for war were in full swing.

On 4 November, Baker arrived in Jeddah to discuss military plans with King Fahd and soon signed an agreement on the operational control of more than 200,000 American troops and nearly 100,000 GCC soldiers spread throughout Saudi Arabia. In the defence of the kingdom, these forces would operate under joint Saudi–US command.[40] The accord also allowed the US to deploy at least an additional 140,000 troops and virtually gave it a free hand to command its own troops in an attack on Iraq or against its troops in Kuwait. Following his Saudi mission, Baker arrived in Cairo and obtained Mubarak's approval to the formula, maintaining the Egyptian military contingent in a defensive role in Saudi Arabia. On 7 November, the Secretary of State flew to Ankara to discuss Allied military requirements in Turkey in the event of war with Iraq. The Turkish government agreed to open up airports in the southern towns of Diyarbakir, Mus, Tatvan as well as the strategic Incirlik airbase in return for American financial support. Baker then visited Moscow and London to brief Mikhail Gorbachev and Margaret Thatcher, respectively, of the situation in the Gulf.[41]

On his return to Washington on 10 November, after his successful week-long mission in the Middle East and Europe, Baker concentrated all his efforts in working out a resolution for the United Nations authorizing the use of force against Iraq. His only problem was China,

---

39. 'US call-up for combat reserves', *Gulf Times*, 6 November 1990.
40. Schwarzkopf, *It Doesn't Take a Hero*, pp. 372–4.
41. *Gulf Times*, 11 November 1990.

the most reluctant of the five permanent members of the Security Council to approve the use of force. The Chinese Foreign Minister Qian Qichen had already stated that Beijing would not be rushed into supporting any UN resolution authorizing military action against Iraq.[42] But Baker did not give up hope of bringing China into line, and in the second week of November he embarked on a diplomatic mission to enlist the support of the majority of the fifteen members of the Security Council for such a UN resolution. Within ten days he had met the Foreign Ministers of most of the members of the Council – Britain, Canada, Colombia, Ethiopia, Finland, France, the Ivory Coast, Malaysia, Romania, the Soviet Union, Yemen and Zaire. All of these member states except Yemen agreed to support the US in its quest for votes in the Security Council.[43]

While Baker prepared the way for a war resolution, President Bush, on 8 November, signed deployment orders to increase the US force in the Gulf region to a total of 430,000 in order to enable an adequate military offensive should this become necessary to oust Iraq from Kuwait. Once this deployment was completed, about one-third of the US army would be in the Saudi desert.[44] In response, Iraq announced on 19 November that it was sending more troops to bolster its forces in Kuwait.[45] Following this statement, Tom King, the British Secretary of State for Defence, announced that an additional 14,000 British troops as well as tanks, ships and combat helicopters would soon be sent to the Gulf, bringing the total number of British troops there to 45,000, the second largest contingent in the US-led Coalition. Britain did so despite the resignation of Margaret Thatcher, Saddam's "harshest critic", on 23 November.[46]

As soon as this new wave of Anglo-American troops began arriving in Saudi Arabia, the United States, on 29 November, sponsored Resolution 678 that gave Iraq until 15 January 1991 to withdraw from Kuwait or face being expelled by force. While twelve members of the Security Council supported the resolution, Cuba and Yemen opposed it

---

42. See 'Iraq pins hope on China', *Gulf Times*, 11 November 1990.
43. See *Gulf Times*, 15 and 24 November 1990.
44. The US forces in Saudi Arabia as of the first week of November 1990 totalled 230,000. See *Gulf Times*, 10 November 1990.
45. *Gulf Times*, 20 November 1990.
46. See 'Tough Gulf policy likely to continue', *Gulf Times*, 24 November 1990.

while China was absent for the vote.[47] This resolution was Saddam's last chance to withdraw from Kuwait peacefully. Hostilities in the Gulf could legitimately break out at any time after 15 January, if Saddam had made no attempt to pull back. This final ultimatum signified two things: firstly, that the coalition members had become "throughly disgruntled at Saddam's stubborn attitude in rejecting almost every move aimed at resolving the Kuwait crisis peacefully"; and secondly, that they were now determined to see the liberation of Kuwait sooner rather than later.[48]

However, following the adoption of Resolution 678, Bush offered Saddam an olive branch, explaining that he was prepared to "go the extra mile" in an effort to avert war. Bush invited Tariq Aziz for talks at the White House and was prepared to send Baker to Baghdad to meet Saddam. But in making this gesture, the President stressed that the United States would not accept anything less than a total and unconditional Iraqi withdrawal from the Emirate. Iraq agreed to the proposed meeting but reiterated its earlier demand that the Palestinian question be included in the talks. It should be noted here, however, that since Saddam came to power he had made no significant contribution to the Palestinian cause. His attempts to link the Palestine issue with his annexation of Kuwait was a mere propaganda exercise to win the support of the conservative Muslim world. In response, the US Vice-President Dan Quayle stated that there could be no linkage between the two issues in the talks. The new British Prime Minister John Major echoed this and stated: "There can be no question of negotiations, concessions, partial solutions or linkage of other issues."[49] While this seemed to end further discussion of any linkage, both countries became locked into a dispute over dates for the proposed meeting. Iraq stuck to 12 January for a Baker–Saddam meeting in Baghdad, but the United States was unable to agree to this date as it considered it too close to the UN deadline for withdrawal. Eventually, Bush withdrew his proposal of sending Baker to Baghdad for peace talks, and in its place offered to

---

47. For the full text, see Resolution no. 678 (1990) in Lauterpacht *et al., The Kuwait Crisis*, p. 98. See the editorial 'Quit Kuwait, or else . . .', *Khaleej Times*, 1 December 1990.
48. As quoted in *Gulf Times*, 2 December 1990.
49. *Gulf Times*, 5 December 1990.

send the Secretary of State to meet Aziz in Geneva on 9 January 1991, six days before the expiry of the deadline. As this was acceptable to Iraq the proposed Baker–Aziz meeting took place on the scheduled date. The six-hour meeting, however, failed to produce any result as Aziz was not prepared to withdraw Iraqi troops from Kuwait. He also attempted to raise the Palestinian problem, arguing that all Middle East conflicts should be tackled simultaneously, but Baker rejected this approach outright.[50]

Following the Baker–Aziz conference, during which time Bush had obtained the US Congress's authorization to use force to compel Iraq to withdraw from Kuwait, the UN Secretary-General arrived in Baghdad on 12 January and made a final appeal to Saddam to withdraw from Kuwait within the next three days. Javier Perez de Cuellar apparently suggested that a UN peacekeeping force could replace the foreign troops in the Gulf once Iraq had left Kuwait. But Saddam rejected this proposal saying: "Kuwait is the nineteenth province of Iraq. There can be no compromise on that." These eleventh hour crisis talks finally convinced the UN Secretary-General that Saddam would not withdraw. With all hope of a peaceful settlement gone, he returned to New York fearing a war would break out any moment now.

In Washington at midnight on 15 January, both Dick Cheney and General Colin Powell, the Chairman of the Joint Chiefs of Staff, signed the order for an air attack on 17 January at 03.00 a.m. (Saudi Arabian time). On 16 January, warplanes in airfields across Saudi Arabia, Bahrain, the UAE and Qatar were loaded with hundreds of tonnes of missiles, rockets and bombs and made ready for action. The first shots of Operation "Desert Storm" were fired at 2.40 a.m. (Saudi Arabian time) on 17 January at various Iraqi military targets. The carriers in the Gulf and the Red Sea also joined in the barrage. In the first 24 hours, over 100 missiles and 600 air sorties were launched by the US Navy alone.[51]

Iraq retaliated by striking at Israeli targets. Scud missiles were fired towards Tel Aviv and Haifa in an attempt to draw Israel into the conflict, in order to create disharmony amongst the coalition's Arab partners. Riyadh, Dhahran, Bahrain and later Qatar also became Iraqi

---

50. *Gulf Times*, 10 and 11 January 1991.
51. *Gulf Times*, 13, 14, 15 and 18 January 1991.

Scud targets, but these failed to hit any strategic locations or even cause any significant damage. In contrast, the aerial bombing of vital Iraqi facilities, communication lines, bridges and strategic installations continued without interruption at the rate of more than 800 missions every 24 hours. Iraqi targets inside Kuwait were also bombed. The American, British, French, Canadian, Saudi as well as other GCC states' aircraft participated in this campaign. US F-15, F-16 and F-111 fighter bombers were launched from the Turkish–US base at Incirlik. Iraqi anti-aircraft batteries were taken out, aircraft destroyed in their shelters on the ground, and airfields and airbases bombed. Although initial coalition efforts were centred on annihilating Iraq's air capacity, it was later reported that only 15 per cent of Iraq's 800 combat aircrat had been destroyed. Iraqi fighter planes made no attempt to engage Coalition warplanes in dogfighting and most had been either "hunkered down in bunkers" or dispersed in mountains, agricultural fields or residential areas, and more than 100 had even escaped to neighbouring Iran. As a result, the Allies declared "air supremacy" by 27 January, and virtually controlled the skies over Iraq.[52] Moreover, by mid-February, it was reported that the Coalition had destroyed 30 per cent of Iraq's 5,000 tanks, 31 per cent of its 2,800 armoured vehicles and 44 per cent of its 3,200 artillery pieces. Iraq's supplies into Kuwait had been cut by half due to the Coalition's bombing of roads, railways and bridges. Iraqi units along the front lines were down to 50 per cent strength and the second line of defence had been reduced by a quarter as a result of the bombings. The Iraqi naval forces were considered to be combat ineffective because of the destruction of all the Iraqi patrol craft that were capable of firing missiles at Allied ships. Meanwhile, the Allies had lost only 18 planes and a very small number of men. Despite these facts, the first phase of the Allied strategic bombing campaign took longer than the 10 days originally estimated because of bad weather, the diversion of fighter planes for Scud hunts and the sheer scale of the Iraqi military machine. In fact, according to Colonel Lalonde, the Commander of the Canadian task force in Qatar, "a significant part of Iraq's military

---

52. For more details of the air war, see Schwarzkopf, *It Doesn't Take a Hero*, pp. 408–40. See also General Sir Peter de la Billière, *Storm Command: A Personal Account of the Gulf War* (Dubai, Motivate Publishing, 1992), pp. 201–30.

strength still remained intact despite the infliction of heavy damage to Iraqi forces by the Allied bombing."[53]

Although it had not been part of the Allied strategy to launch a ground assault to dislodge Iraqi forces from Kuwait until the Iraqi army's fighting capability had been reduced by 50 per cent, General Schwarzkopf was under heavy pressure from Washington by the middle of February 1991 to order a land offensive. However, the military authorities in the Gulf widely believed that a costly war on the ground, which was bound to cause heavy Allied casualties, was unnecessary. This was due to their conviction that the Iraqi army, which was now as Lieutenant General de la Billière put it, "in a poor state, starving with lice and sores, and not defending their own country", would collapse before the land war began if the air campaign continued for an indefinite period.[54] Therefore, General Schwarzkopf wanted to allow more time to knock out more of the Iraqi tanks and artillery from the air, thereby reducing the risks inherent in a ground attack.

Washington, however, was against this tactic due to the production of a peace proposal by President Gorbachev, which involved an immediate Iraqi withdrawal from Kuwait to begin the day after a cease-fire had been called so that the retreating Iraqis could return home safely with their arms and ammunitions. The timetable for complete evacuation had still to be negotiated. Saddam had accepted the proposal on the condition that an immediate cease-fire be called together with the lifting of the UN sanctions as soon as Iraq had withdrawn two-thirds of its troops from the Emirate. The Iraqis also demanded six weeks to pull out and as soon as the withdrawal was complete, all the Security Council resolutions against Iraq should be cancelled. As Washington believed that it would be dangerous for the future peace of the region if Iraq was allowed to simply pull out of Kuwait with its war machine relatively intact, it proposed that the Iraqis should complete their withdrawal within one week leaving behind their supplies and the bulk of their equipment to be destroyed by the Allied forces who would enter Kuwait as soon as the Iraqis had withdrawn. But the Iraqis declined to accept such a short timetable for evacuation, arguing that they still

---

53. See the interview of Colonel Romeo Lalonde, *Gulf Times*, 16 February 1991. See also 'Iraqi damage up to 40%', *Gulf Times*, 17 February 1991.
54. De la Billière, *Storm Command*, pp. 273–4.

needed the extra time as most of their roads and bridges had been damaged or destroyed by Allied bombings.[55]

Washington was now worried that Moscow might come forward with another peace initiative which would be more acceptable than a land war to the coalition countries. This would present political difficulties for the American administration in the international sphere, especially in the leadership of the coalition forces. Moreover, with the month of Ramadan starting in the middle of March, the coalition's Islamic forces might then feel unwilling to fight. Conditions in the desert would also deteriorate in March due to the rising temperatures. Therefore, any further delay could well do more harm than good to the ground forces, which had already taken their positions for a major offensive. Washington then pressed Schwarzkopf to launch the land offensive before Saddam "could withdraw of his own accord and thereby keep his enormous army intact".[56] The General had no other alternative but to clear the way for an immediate land war.

As Schwarzkopf gave way, President Bush, on 22 February, issued an unequivocal ultimatum to Iraq to start withdrawing its troops from Kuwait within 24 hours or face the grave consequences. The White House Spokesman Marlin Fitzwater, in clarifying the US-led alliance's requirements for averting a ground offensive, stated that Iraqi forces must be out of Kuwait City within 48 hours and the full withdrawal must be completed within one week of George Bush's deadline.[57] As Iraq showed no sign of capitulating, some 700,000 Allied troops received the final order to take action to expel the 500,000-strong Iraqi force from Kuwait. By the time President Bush had announced that the liberation of Kuwait had entered its final phase, US Marines had already penetrated Iraq's eastern border and the French 6th Light Armoured Division along with the US 82nd Airborne had pushed 48 kilometres into the western sector of Iraq in an attempt to cut off the highway from Baghdad to Basra. Simultaneously, Saudi, Qatari and other Gulf forces were advancing on Kuwait City from the north. The 101st Assault Division (the Screaming Eagles) soon established a forward operating base, known as Cobra, 80 kilometres within Iraq from which to strike

---

55. *Ibid.*, p. 275. See also Schwarzkopf, *It Doesn't Take a Hero*, pp. 441–5.
56. De la Billière, *Storm Command*, p. 274.
57. For the full text, see the *Khaleej Times*, 23 February 1991.

at the highway leading to Baghdad. Meanwhile, the Allied air forces gave extensive support to the ground troops and the US Navy shelled the coast.[58]

Within ten hours of the launch of the ground offensive, the Allied forces, facing no significant resistance, made remarkable progress on all fronts. General Schwarzkopf therefore revised his original battle plan (which was based on the assumption that the Iraqis would put up fierce resistance) to speed up the schedule of the offensive so that the Iraqis could not escape "relatively intact". As the campaign progressed rapidly, Radio Baghdad made an unexpected announcement on the morning of 26 February (at 2.15 a.m.), ordering the Iraqi forces occupying Kuwait to pull out immediately, although it gave no indication whether Iraq was willing to accept all the UN resolutions. But by this stage the Iraqis were surrendering *en masse* and abandoning their positions on all fronts while a convoy of hundreds of vehicles was making a dash from Kuwait City towards Basra. These retreating troops destroyed over 700 Kuwaiti oil wells as well as a water plants and a number of buildings including hospitals. As General Schwarzkopf was worried that this retreat would soon lead to a cease-fire allowing the majority of Iraqi troops, particularly the elite Republican Guard, to escape unhurt, he immediately ordered an attack on the retreating forces as well as the Republican Guard in and around Basra. Consequently, the fierce campaign against the Iraqis continued until about 30 of the 42 divisions deployed in the area were either destroyed or rendered ineffective.[59] Kuwaiti, Saudi, Qatari, Egyptian and other Arab soldiers liberated Kuwait City on 26 February. Elsewhere, the Anglo-American contingent occupied a substantial part of southern Iraq after destroying a large number of Iraqi tanks and other heavy equipment. As the prime object of the Coalition – the liberation of Kuwait – had been fulfilled, on the night of 27 February President Bush made an announcement declaring the cessation of offensive operations and the end of the war in the Gulf with effect from 8 a.m. (Saudi Arabian time), 28 February 1991.

---

58. For Schwarzkopf's military planning for the defeat of the Iraqi forces, see Schwarzkopf, *It Doesn't Take a Hero*, pp. 452–4. See also de la Billière, *Storm Command*, pp. 279–80.
59. Schwarzkopf, *It Doesn't Take a Hero*, p. 467.

Bush's declaration cleared the way for a meeting on 2 March 1991 at Safwan (an Iraqi military landing strip just north of the Kuwaiti border), between the Allied and the Iraqi military commanders in order to arrange a formal cease-fire. The Allied commanders General Schwarzkopf and General Prince Khalid spoke on behalf of the coalition while Lieutenant General Sultan Hashim Ahmad, the Chief of Operations at the Iraqi Defence Ministry, and Lieutenant General Saleh Abbud Mahmoud, the Commander of the Iraqi 3rd Corps, represented Iraq. Instead of negotiating a postwar peace or settlement, General Schwarzkopf simply dictated a set of military conditions to the Iraqis for the cease-fire to become permanent. These conditions were: firstly, the immediate release of all Coalition prisoners of war including the 3,000 detained Kuwaitis; secondly, an exchange of information on troops listed as missing in action; thirdly, the disclosure of the locations of both the minefields in Kuwait and the Gulf waters and any storage sites the Iraqis had established for chemical, biological or nuclear weapons; and finally, the acceptance of a cease-fire line deep within Iraqi territory to avoid any military clashes between Allied and Iraqi forces. The Iraqi delegation accepted these conditions without reservation.[60]

Following the conclusion of the Safwan meeting, Allied troops began to withdraw from the region, a process accomplished within three months. Arrangements were also made for the speedy repatriation of the Iraqi prisoners of war whose number had reached 170,000 and the Allied prisoners numbering below 50. The next step for Iraq was to accept the terms of the Security Council's latest resolution of 2 March, which demanded that Iraq repealed its order annexing Kuwait and its declaration that the Emirate was its nineteenth province. Iraq met this condition on 5 March, annulling the annexation order and repealing all Iraqi laws and regulations involving Kuwait. However, Iraq as yet showed no sign of fulfilling other conditions imposed on it, such as the release of all the detained Kuwaitis as well as the return of expropriated Kuwaiti property. Moreover, Saddam was still reluctant to relinquish Iraq's territorial claim to Kuwait by accepting a defined borderline. Consequently, on 3 April 1991, the Security Council passed Resolution 687 ordering Iraq to respect the boundary with Kuwait as envisaged in "the Agreed Minutes" between the two countries on 4 October 1963.

---

60. *Ibid.*, pp. 479–89. See also *Gulf Times*, 4 March 1991.

The Iraq–Kuwait Boundary Demarcation Commission (IKBDC), comprising experts from Kuwait, Iraq, New Zealand and Sweden, was soon formed under UN patronage to demarcate the border. In April 1992, after making a thorough study of the matter from the historical and legal perspectives, and based on the 1932 Exchange of Letters and the British formulas of 1940 and 1951, the commission produced its findings on the undemarcated 200 kilometre section of the Iraqi–Kuwaiti boundary. The commission accurately drew the point south of Safwan on their maps and made the following recommendations: first, this point should lie at a distance of 1430 metres from the south-western extremity of the wall of the old customs post; second, the boundary line from this point south of Safwan to the point south of Umm Qasr should be the shortest line between the two points; and third, the boundary line from the point south of Umm Qasr on the shore should follow "the line of the low water springs up to the point directly opposite and nearest to the junction point of Khor al-Zobeir and Khor Abdullah". The commission also demarcated the intersection of the boundary with the shoreline of Umm Qasr, leaving the Umm Qasr port area and Umm Qasr village within Iraqi jurisdiction. While Kuwait lost 430 metres of its original boundary with Iraq in and around Safwan, it recovered its portion of the Rumaila oilfield extending to about 1.5 kilometres inside Kuwaiti territory. The commission further demarcated, with reference to the 1932 Exchange of Letters and the Agreed Minutes of 1963, the 64-kilometre maritime boundary between the two countries in the Khor Abdullah following the median line principle, giving both countries an "equitable" sea access. But the commission, despite Kuwait's objections, allocated the whole of the waters of the Khor Zubair to Iraq.[61]

Although Iraq did not attend the final session of the IKBDC, the findings were binding on it. While Kuwait hailed this demarcation of the frontier as a "historic achievement", Iraq rejected it reiterating its previous argument that Kuwait was an integral part of Basra under the Ottoman Empire and that no Iraqi government had ever agreed to

---

61. For more details, see the UN's *Final Report on the Demarcation of the International Boundary between the Republic of Iraq and the State of Kuwait*, no. S/25811 (New York, United Nations Security Council, 1993), pp. 8–43. See also Panel of Specialists, *Kuwait–Iraq Boundary Demarcation*, pp. 65–84; Schofield, *Kuwait and Iraq*, pp. 117–92.

demarcate the border with Kuwait. Yet as both Kuwait and the UN Security Council dismissed this Iraqi argument, the commission went ahead with the physical demarcation of the boundary between the two countries based on its earlier proposals and this was completed by May 1993.[62] For the first time in the history of Iraqi–Kuwaiti relations their border had been drawn up and demarcated in a definitive manner – a great diplomatic victory for Kuwait which had been struggling for this ever since the 1930s. (See Map 5.)

As Iraq still refused to formally accept the UN-demarcated boundary, the Security Council continued to keep its economic sanctions in place. Yet on 7 October 1994, Iraq, in an attempt to put pressure on the UN to lift the sanctions, deployed more than 60,000 troops in southern Iraq, about 20 kilometres from the UN-controlled buffer zone along the Kuwaiti border. President Bill Clinton immediately responded by despatching 30,000 troops to Kuwait and placing 156,000 more on alert. The United States also warned Iraq that any attempt to either violate the UN buffer zone or cross the frontier would invite an immediate and massive air strike on his troops. However, instead of backing down, Saddam fixed a deadline of 10 October – the date set by the Security Council for the review of Iraq's compliance with UN resolutions – for announcing a date for the lifting of sanctions. The Iraqi President stated that there would be serious consequences if the sanctions were not removed on or around that date. But by the end of the week Iraq had abandoned its threat following Russian intervention. The Russian Foreign Minister Andrei Kozyrev had flown to Baghdad and had worked out a deal with Iraq on 13 October, promising Russia's help in getting the sanctions lifted within seven months in return for an Iraqi recognition of Kuwait's sovereignty and the UN-demarcated frontier. On 15 October, Iraq started pulling back its troops in the face of another unanimous Security Council resolution (949) which demanded that Iraq immediately withdraw all the units it had deployed in southern Iraq or face grave consequences.[63]

---

62. For Kuwaiti and Iraqi reactions to the IKBDC's land and maritime boundaries demarcation, see *Khaleej Times*, 18 June 1992. See also Panel of Specialists, *Kuwait–Iraq Boundary Demarcation*, pp. 80–137.
63. See 'Saddam's phoney crisis', *Middle East International*, 21 October 1994, pp. 4–5. See also 'Russia's measured response', *ibid.*, pp. 5–6.

Less than a month later, on 10 November 1994, Iraq, in a statement signed by Saddam and endorsed by its National Assembly, recognized "the sovereignty of the State of Kuwait, its territorial integrity and political independence". Moreover, in a move calculated to win the UN Security Council's permission to resume its oil exports, Iraq also recognized the international boundary with its neighbour as demarcated by the IKBDC and agreed to respect its inviolability.[64] Therefore Iraq, in accepting the border, officially dropped its claim to Kuwait. But the United States, Britain and Kuwait decided that the Iraqi recognition of Kuwait was not in itself enough, as it was just the fulfilment of one of a number of requirements established by the Security Council. Therefore, the US and Britain, two of the permanent members of the Security Council, pressed for the continuation of the embargo until Iraq had complied with all the other UN resolutions including the issue regarding the Kurds and Shiites in Iraq, the return of the Kuwaiti prisoners of war and Kuwaiti stolen property as well as Iraq's full cooperation with the UN commission monitoring its nuclear weapons programme. However, on 14 April 1995, in order to ease economic hardship caused by the sanctions, the Security Council unanimously authorized Iraq to sell oil worth $2 billion over six months to purchase badly needed food and medical supplies. But two days later, the Iraqi Cabinet chaired by Saddam Hussein categorically rejected the resolution as a "dangerous violation of Iraq's sovereignty and national unity". The UN economic sanctions against Iraq remain in force at the time of writing this book although Russia, France and China, the three other permanent members of the Security Council, are in favour of lifting them.

Conclusion

The Allied aims of driving the Iraqis out of Kuwait and shattering Saddam's military capability were achieved with very limited loss of life (on the Allied side), while Iraqi political and economic objectives that inspired Saddam to invade Kuwait remain unfulfilled. This total failure may partially be attributed to his lack of finesse as a military strategist. Believing and actively espousing brutal strength as the means to any

---

64. For full text, see *Khaleej Times*, 11 November 1994.

end, Saddam, obsessed with a desire to annex Kuwait, had overlooked the fact that the subjugation and forcible occupation of a sovereign state was simply a thing of the past. In overlooking the option of deploying his troops on the Kuwaiti frontier and thereafter negotiating a permanent settlement of his strategic requirements in Kuwait, he had left the multinational force with no other option but to unleash a unified attack. General de la Billière made this observation:

> We also knew from his military record that he was an extraordinarily bad strategist and tactician; even so, we could hardly believe that he would be idiotic enough to sit and wait while the fire-power facing him rapidly increased. His shrewdest move would have been to conduct a partial withdrawal from Kuwait, perhaps retaining Bubiyan Island and the Raudatain oilfield in the north of the state. Had he done that, he would have undermined the United Nations' resolution calling for his removal, and placed the Coalition in an awkward position. Equally, he could have launched pre-emptive attacks, with either aircraft or Scud missiles, before the Coalition was organized, and seriously disrupted our preparations.[65]

Although Saddam's army, on whom he had relied to achieve his political and economic goals, was one of the world's largest, it was not only poorly trained but also suffered from low morale, weary after the prolonged war with Iran. On the other hand, the Coalition troops were far superior in all aspects and ready to fight in a well-planned air and land campaign. Saddam's 42-division army was easily crushed by the Allied fire-power and strategy.[66]

Both parties miscalculated the other's position. While Saddam wrongly thought that the deployment of Coalition troops was nothing

---

65. General Sir Peter de la Billière, *Looking for Trouble: SAS to Gulf Command* (Dubai, Motivate Publishing, 1994), p. 403.
66. It was later reported that the United States grossly exaggerated Iraqi losses during the war. For example, the US claimed to have killed 150,000 Iraqi soldiers, but the real figure is now thought to be closer to 15,000. Similarly, the 1991 US figure for tanks destroyed in the war was 3,956, but a more recent assessment shows that this was the total number of Iraqi tanks deployed during the war. There was also a discrepancy in the artillery figures; it was reported that 3,092 artillery pieces were destroyed, but it is now reckoned that the Iraqis only deployed 2,475 heavy guns. See 'Up and running again', *Middle East International*, 21 October 1994, p. 8.

other than an elaborate bluff, the Coalition believed that Saddam would withdraw from Kuwait if faced with an economic embargo, together with a military build-up and an ultimatum. The Coalition also mistakenly believed that the Iraqi forces would fight in the same manner as they had done in the Iran–Iraq War and thereby engage the Coalition troops in a protracted and bloody war. Instead, the demoralized and war-weary Iraqi troops surrendered or fled after having been relentlessly bombed and starved for several weeks.

While the war put paid to Saddam's ambitions in Kuwait and crippled his military machine, it prompted Kuwait to reassess its defence requirements. Following the end of the war, Kuwait concluded a ten-year defence pact with the US, allowing US forces access to Kuwaiti ports and airports. The pact also permits the US to stockpile supplies in the Emirate and makes provision for the purchase of equipment. Similar defence agreements have been signed with Britain and France and a limited one with Russia. Since the conclusion of these agreements, regular joint military manoeuvres have been taking place in and around the Emirate. Kuwait's conclusion of the military pacts with the Western powers demonstrates that the Emirate no longer relies on the GCC or any other Arab force for its security. Indeed, Kuwait's military relations with the Western powers have plugged the gap in its military defences that had existed ever since the aborgation in 1968 of the 1961 Anglo-Kuwaiti Exchange of Notes.

11

Concluding Remarks

Saddam Hussein's invasion of Kuwait, ostensibly a reaction to Kuwait's alleged overproduction of oil, to its supposed extraction of oil from the Rumaila oilfield as well as to its refusal to write off Iraq's wartime debts, was in fact prompted by Hussein's personal ambition of becoming the most powerful man in the Arab world.

To his people, he would have become Iraq's unrivalled hero this century for having fulfilled his country's long-standing claim to Kuwait. Indeed, he may have used this 'noble' cause to achieve his end of becoming the undisputed leader in the region, since the combined oil reserves of Iraq and Kuwait would have vastly increased his clout, not only regionally but worldwide.

Despite the worldwide condemnation and unprecedented inter-national unity in opposing the illegality of Iraq's occupation of Kuwait (since Kuwait had never been part of the Basra administration), Saddam Hussein successfully held his ground for seven long months. As mentioned in the text, the fact that during the critical years of war with Iran Saddam Hussein had desperately tried to secure only a short-term leasehold of Warba and a part of Bubiyan islands and, unlike his predecessors, had never made any military attempts to assert sovereignty claims either over these islands or over the whole of Kuwait, makes his annexation of the whole country all the more unexpected and sur-prising. The seizure of the whole country, therefore, shows that Saddam's objectives were not limited to the islands only. If so, he would have confined his military action to seizure of these islands and then demanded negotiations for concessions.

The long-standing Kuwait–Iraq boundary dispute that seemingly led to the invasion of Kuwait in 1990 had its roots in the beginning of the twentieth century when the Ottoman Empire extended its power as far as Safwan, Umm Qasr and Bubiyan Island, establishing military outposts there. The Ottomans did so in the belief that the British, who had concluded the Exclusive Agreement with Kuwait in 1899 and had established it as a veiled protectorate, might soon block all access to the Gulf for the proposed Baghdad Railway. But Ottoman encroachment in Kuwaiti territory justifiably alarmed Sheikh Mubarak and prompted him to re-examine the limits of his own frontier and thereafter lay claim to the ownership of Safwan, Umm Qasr, Bubiyan and Warba. Mubarak asserted his right to these places despite the lack of firm support from the British until the question of the status of Kuwait and its territories came up in the Anglo–Ottoman negotiations of 1911 which culminated in the conclusion of an agreement in 1913 defining the frontiers of Kuwait. Although the Anglo–Ottoman Convention of 1913 recognized Kuwait's ownership of Warba and Bubiyan, it intentionally ignored Sheikh Mubarak's claims to Safwan and Umm Qasr because Britain wanted to secure its objectives regarding the Baghdad railway project without incurring Ottoman opposition. Though the definition of the northern frontier of Kuwait in the Convention of 1913 formed the basis for the present-day Kuwait–Iraq border, its ambiguities, however, remained unsolved until the UN demarcation of the boundary in 1993. And even though the Convention of 1913 was not ratified due to the outbreak of the First World War, Britain recognized Kuwait's independence under its protection.

Despite British recognition of Kuwait's sovereignty over Umm Qasr and Safwan following the end of the war, Sheikh Mubarak's successor, Sheikh Jaber, did not feel the need to physically occupy these two places; and by not doing so he had left the doors open for years of controversy over the course of Kuwait's frontier from Safwan to Umm Qasr. However, further significant changes in the status of Kuwait resulted from the fact that the defunct Ottoman Empire had lost the last vestiges of whatever suzerainty it had had over Kuwait following the conclusion of the treaties of Sèvres (1920) and Lausanne (1923). The question of the demarcation of Kuwait's northern frontier was brought up again when Mesopotamia became the Kingdom of Iraq under British mandate. The British government's recognition of Kuwait's boundary with Iraq in 1923, reproducing the 1913 definition and giving specific reference to Kuwait's ownership of Warba and Bubiyan, once again indicated that Kuwait was a separate entity with a well-defined boundary with southern Iraq. Iraq itself reconfirmed this frontier in an exchange of letters with Kuwait in 1932, on the eve of its application for membership of the League of Nations. But both Kuwait and Britain failed to comprehend the importance of the physical demarcation of this Kuwaiti–Iraqi frontierline which would have been easy to accomplish while Britain held a mandate over Iraq. Once Britain abandoned its mandatory power over Iraq and granted it political independence, albeit limited by a treaty, it lost its power of dictating a settlement of the frontier issue.

Therefore, as soon as Iraq emerged as an independent state it revived the Ottoman policy of accusing Kuwait of engaging in smuggling goods into Iraq thereby undermining Iraqi commerce. In the name of an 'anti-smuggling drive' Iraqi officials continued their infiltrations into Kuwaiti territory despite repeated complaints from the Sheikh. While uncertainty over the actual line of the frontier was at the root of many of the frontier incidents, high tariffs in Iraq compared to extremely low tariffs in Kuwait was the main reason for smuggling from Kuwait. Overlooking the basic factor behind the growth of the illicit trade, the Iraqis blamed the Sheikh for the smuggling and insisted that he should stop it on their own terms which were derogatory to the territorial integrity of the Sheikhdom. Several attempts to solve the twin problems of smuggling and frontier violations failed as neither party was ready to accept the blame. Matters were made worse by the divergent views held by the British on the two issues souring the Kuwaiti–Iraqi relationship, and it can be said with some certainty that the British were partly responsible for adding fuel to the fire for their own diplomatic reasons. The two problems thus complemented each other in forming a vicious circle, for whenever a Kuwaiti protest was made to the Iraqis about police infiltrations into Kuwaiti territory the Iraqis would counter it with charges of Kuwaiti smuggling, and whenever attempts were made to deal with the smuggling issue the Kuwaiti ruler would protest that no proper attention had ever been paid to his own protests of Iraqi violations of his territory.

The Iraqi press did not lag behind in promoting the aims of the government. With full governmental support the press soon launched an unprecedented campaign for the annexation of Kuwait claiming that Kuwait had previously been part of Iraq. The press propaganda aimed at mobilizing public opinion in support of the government's designs on Kuwait as well as stirring up anti-Sabah feelings within the Sheikhdom. Against this background, Iraq finally in September 1938 made the first move. In an *aide-mémoire* to the British government, Iraq made an official claim to Kuwait, it being the successor of Ottoman sovereignty over the Ottoman vilayet of Basra to which, it alleged, Kuwait was subordinate. But in the same *aide-mémoire* this demand softened significantly by the proposition that its claim to the whole of Kuwait could be sacrificed in return for Kuwaiti agreement to a customs union or to certain territorial concessions to Iraq or for combined security action. This flexibility on the part of Iraq, therefore, revealed that Iraq was not wholly serious about its claim to the whole of Kuwait; it was mainly a tactical move to gain some territorial concessions possibly in and around Warba Island, the acquisition of which would enable it to become the guardian of the whole Khor Abdullah channel. While no attempt was made by the Iraqi government to pursue the matter with urgency, a military plot to destabilize Kuwait was hatched, which, however, fizzled out with the death of King Ghazi of Iraq, the main instigator of the plot.

The 1940s witnessed a serious move aimed at settling the Kuwaiti–Iraqi frontier dispute by defining the controversial frontier line running from Safwan to the junction of Khor Abdullah and Khor Zubair. While the Kuwaiti ruler accepted the 1940 formula as a solution to the frontier dispute, Iraq declined to do so unless both Warba and Bubiyan were handed over to it. This way, Iraq would gain full possession of the approaches to Umm Qasr where it wanted to build a new port as an alternative to Basra, Iraq's only seaport. In the event, Iraq had to abandon its plan for a second port at Umm Qasr because the British military authorities hastened to build one themselves for their own military requirements during the Second World War. The port was, in fact, built largely on Kuwaiti territory and partly on Iraqi territory. The port was demolished at the end of the war, but the question of the demarcation of the frontier remained unresolved.

In the postwar period three basic factors induced the British government to revive the question of demarcation of the northern frontier. These were: continuous Iraqi violations of Kuwaiti territory, the agricultural development in the Safwan area and, not least, the oil companies' scramble for oil in the disputed territory. After debating for more than half a decade amongst themselves – because of the sharp differences between the Foreign Office in London and the local officials on the precise position of the line south of Safwan – the British government in 1951 proposed to Iraq that the frontier be demarcated according to a new formula which differed slightly from the 1940 proposal. To the dismay of the British and the Sheikh, the Iraqis refused to consider the demarcation issue unless Kuwait ceded Warba to it. Interestingly, this time the Iraqis confined their requirement to Warba only and made no mention of Bubiyan.

From 1954 to 1957 the question of Iraq leasing Warba as well as a strip of Kuwaiti territory for the construction of a port at Umm Qasr was linked to the issue of demarcation and Kuwait's water requirement from Shatt al-Arab waterway. For the first time there were positive indications that a solution of the problem of demarcation based on a compromise formula drawn by the British was about to be reached. But the whole initiative suddenly collapsed when the Kuwaiti ruler pulled back from the deal at the last moment. He did so because of his genuine suspicion of Iraqi intentions in Kuwait and possibly because of strong pressure from senior members of the ruling family who believed that the development of an Iraqi port at Umm Qasr would in time erode the economic value of their own Kuwaiti port. The British, who initiated the scheme, washed their hands of it and put the blame on the Egyptians for its collapse.

Iraq's repeated failure to achieve its objective at Umm Qasr – because of Kuwait's persistent refusal to compromise on Warba or any other part of Kuwait – prompted Iraq to reaffirm its claim to the whole of Kuwait for the second time; the trigger for this action was Kuwait's refusal to join the Iraq–Jordan Federation. The *coup d'état* in Iraq in 1958 put an end to both the Federation and the monarchical system, and brought a lull in the frontier dispute. The military regime showed no sign of pursuing its predecessors' claims to Kuwait, but three years later, when Kuwait emerged as a fully independent state in June 1961, the Iraqi military leader General Abdul-Karim Qasim revived his country's old claim with threats of invasion and annexation. His claim to the fledgling Emirate and the reported deployment of Iraqi troops to the south compelled Britain to take counter measures by landing troops in Kuwait. This timely British military intervention effectively prevented Qasim from fulfilling his objectives in Kuwait. British troops were eventually replaced by Arab League forces whose task was to ensure Kuwait's security. The obstacle to the Emirate's membership of the United Nations was thus removed.

However, Qasim's claim to Kuwait continued until he was overthrown by a military coup in February 1963, one which brought a dramatic change in the hostile relations between Iraq and Kuwait. The new regime affirmed its recognition of Kuwait as a sovereign and independent state and its recognition of the boundary as delineated in the 1932 exchange of letters. The subsequent registration of this recognition accord with the UN put a legal stop to Iraq's age-old claims to Kuwait. Iraq adhered strictly to this position for more than a quarter of century and confined its hopes only to Warba and half of Bubiyan, the strategic importance of which was reinforced by Iran's bombardment of Iraq's only port at Basra during the Iran–Iraq war and Iraq's inability to engage the Iranian naval forces in the Arabian Gulf. Iraq had always been loath to develop an effective navy because of its poor access to the sea. A leasehold of Warba and a part of Bubiyan to the Iraqi's would have enabled Iraq to establish a naval base there from which to challenge Iran's naval supremacy.

Despite its military weakness *vis-à-vis* Iraq and the absence of natural defences, Kuwait still refused to grant a privileged position to Iraq on those two strategic islands even for a short period; this is because of its conviction that, with a foothold on Kuwaiti territory, the Iraqis would seize not only the islands but also the whole of the Emirate – eventually. In the event, no such precautions worked. Once Saddam Hussein found himself relieved from the war which he had initiated against Iran, and free to employ the huge army he had built up in the course of it, he directed it towards Kuwait to quickly realize the hitherto unfulfilled Iraqi dream of becoming a major power in the Gulf. By dislodging the Al Sabah leadership from the seat of government and laying hands on Kuwait's oil wealth, Saddam Hussein believed he could get away with the prize of the century, one he asserted was Iraq's by right. But his military adventure proved foolhardy and boomeranged against himself and his country. He was ignominiously ejected from Kuwait, his army destroyed by a coalition of nations led by the United States. The Iraqis not only had to renounce their annexation of Kuwait, for which they had been campaigning ever since their independence in 1932, but also accept a demarcated boundary with Kuwait. While Iraq's recognition of Kuwait's sovereignty and territorial integrity including a UN-demarcated boundary heralded an end to Kuwait's long-running territorial dispute with Iraq, it did not prompt the UN to lift the sanctions it had imposed on Iraq.

The Gulf War produced wider military repercussions throughout the region. An eight-nation (the six GCC states, Egypt and Syria) security and economic pact was signed in Damascus in March 1991, for the establishment of a new Arab order and the elimination of all weapons of mass destruction from the whole of the Middle East. In addition to this arrangement, Kuwait and other Gulf states made defence arrangements with Western powers, particularly with the USA, allowing the stationing of their troops with their military hardware on their territories to act as an effective deterrent against any future military threat from Iraq or any other hostile power. In effect, these arrangements have plugged the security gap that had existed since Britain's withdrawal from East of Suez.

APPENDIX I

Agreement with the Sheikh of Koweit, 1899
Translation of Arabic Bond

Praise be to God alone ("Bissim Illah Ta'alah Shanuho", lit. in the name of God Almighty [*sic*])

The object of writing this lawful and honourable bond is that it is hereby covenanted and agreed between Lieutenant-Colonel Malcolm John Meade, I.S.C., Her Britannic Majesty's Political Resident, on behalf of the British Government on the one part, and Sheikh Mubarak-bin-Sheikh Subah, Sheikh of Koweit, on the other part, that the said Sheikh Mubarak-bin-Sheikh Subah of his own free will and desire does hereby pledge and bind himself, his heirs and successors not to receive the Agent or Representative of any Power or Government at Koweit, or at any other place within the limits of his territory, without the previous sanction of the British Government; and he further binds himself, his heirs and successors not to cede, sell, lease, mortgage, or give for occupation or for any other purpose any portion of his territory to the Government or subjects of any other Power without the previous consent of Her Majesty's Government for these purposes. This engagement also to extend to any portion of the territory of the said Sheikh Mubarak, which may now be in the possession of the subjects of any other Government.

In token of the conclusion of this lawful and honourable bond, Lieutenant-Colonel Malcolm John Meade, I.S.C., Her Britannic Majesty's Political Resident in the Persian Gulf, and Sheikh Mubarak-bin-Sheikh Subah, the former on behalf of the British Government and the latter on behalf of himself, his heirs and successors do each, in the presence of witnesses, affix their signatures on this, the tenth day of Ramazan 1316, corresponding with the twenty-third day of January 1899.

M. J. MEADE,
Political Resident in the
Persian Gulf.

MUBARAK-AL-SUBAH

Witnesses:

E. WICKHAM HORE, *Capt., I.M.S.*

J. CALCOTT GASKIN.

MUHAMMAD RAHIM
BIN ABDUL NEBI
SAFFER.

APPENDIX II

Extract from Convention between the United Kingdom and Turkey Respecting the Persian Gulf and Adjacent Territories, 29 July 1913 (Cmd. 10515)

1. Koweit

Article 1
The territory of Koweit, as delimited by articles 5 and 7 of this convention, forms an autonomous kaza of the Ottoman Empire.

Article 2
The Sheikh of Koweit shall, as heretofore fly the Ottoman flag, with the word "Koweit" inscribed in the corner, if he so desires, and he shall enjoy complete administrative autonomy in the territorial zone defined in article 5 of this convention. The Imperial Ottoman Government shall abstain from any interference in the affairs of Koweit, including the question of the succession, and from any administrative act or occupation, and from any military act, in the territories forming part thereof. In the event of a vacancy, the Imperial Ottoman Government shall appoint the successor of the late Sheikh, by Imperial firman, to be kaimakam. The Imperial Ottoman Government shall also be free to accredit to the Sheikh a commissioner to protect the interests and the natives of other parts of the Empire.

Article 3
The Imperial Ottoman Government recognize the validity of the conventions previously concluded by the Sheikh of Koweit with His Britannic Majesty's Government, dated the 23rd January, 1899, the 24th May, 1900, and the 28th February, 1901, the texts of which are annexed to this convention (Annexes I, II, III). They recognize also the validity of the concessions of land granted by the said Sheikh to His Britannic Majesty's Government and to British subjects, and the validity of the engagements enclosed in the note dated the 24th October, 1911,

addressed by His Britannic Majesty's Principal Secretary of State for Foreign Affairs to the Ambassador of His Imperial Majesty the Sultan in London, the text of which is annexed (Annex IV).

Article 4

With the view of confirming the understanding already reached between the two Governments by the assurances exchanged on the 6th September, 1901, between His Britannic Majesty's Embassy at Constantinople and the Imperial Ministry for Foreign Affairs. His Britannic Majesty's Government declare that, so long as no change be made by the Imperial Ottoman Government in the status quo in Koweit, as defined by this convention, they will make no change in the nature of their relations with the Government of Koweit, and will establish no protectorate over the territory which is assigned to it. The Imperial Ottoman Government take note of this declaration.

Article 5

The Sheikh of Koweit exercises autonomy in the territory of which the boundary forms a semi-circle with the town of Koweit at the centre, the Khor-Zoubair at the northern extremity and el-Kraine at the southern extremity. This line is marked in red on the map annexed to this convention (Annex v). The islands of Warba, Bubiyan, Mashjan, Failakah, Auhah, Kubbar, Qaru, Makta and Umm-el Maradim, with the adjacent islets and waters, are included in this zone.

Article 6

The tribes lying within the boundaries laid down in the following article are recognized as dependent on the Sheikh of Koweit, who shall collect their titles as heretofore, and shall exercise over them the administrative functions which attach to him in his capacity of Ottoman kaimakam. The Imperial Ottoman Government shall carry out no administrative act in this zone independently of the Sheikh of Koweit, and shall abstain from placing garrisons there or taking any military step there whatsoever without having previously come to an understanding with His Britannic Majesty's Government.

Article 7
The boundaries of the territory referred to in the preceding article are fixed as follows:–

The line of demarcation runs north-west from the coast at the mouth of the Khor-Zoubeir and passes immediately south of Um-Kasr, Safwan and Jebel-Sanam, leaving these places and their wells to the vilayet of Basra; on reaching the Batin the line follows it towards the south-west of Hafr-el Batin, which it leaves on the side of Koweit; thence the said line runs south-east, leaving to Koweit the wells of Es-Safa and El-Garaa, El-Haba, Wabra and Antaa, and reaches the sea near Jebel-Munifa. This line is marked in green on the map annexed to this convention (Annex v).

Article 8
In the event of the Imperial Ottoman Government agreeing with His Britannic Majesty's Government to extend the Baghdad–Basra Railway to the sea at the terminus of Koweit, or to any other terminus in the autonomous territory, the two Governments shall come to an understanding as to the measures to be taken with respect to the guarding of the line and stations, and with regard to the establishment of customs offices, warehouses and any other installation accessory to the service of the railway.

Article 9
The Sheikh of Koweit shall enjoy in full security the private proprietary rights which he possesses in the territory of the Basra vilayet. These private proprietary rights must be exercised in accordance with Ottoman law, and the real estate concerned shall be subject to such taxes and charges, method of registration and of transfer, and to such jurisdiction as are imposed by Ottoman law.

Article 10
Criminals of the neighbouring provinces shall not be allowed to enter the territory of Koweit, and shall be expelled if found there; similarly criminals of Koweit shall not be allowed to enter the neighbouring provinces and shall be expelled if found there.

It is understood that this stipulation shall not afford a pretext to the Ottoman authorities to interfere in the affairs of Koweit; nor, on the other hand, shall it afford a pretext to the Sheikh of Koweit to interfere in the affairs of the neighbouring provinces.

APPENDIX III

The British Frontier Definition of 1940 [FO 371/24545]

No. 487

British Embassy,
Bagdad.
7th October, 1940.

Your Excellency,

I have the honour to inform you that my Government consider it desirable that the frontier between Iraq and Koweit should be demarcated and I have received instructions to propose to the Iraqi Government that arrangements should be made to do this at an early date.

2. With this end in view, His Majesty's Government suggest that there should be an exchange of notes providing that the work of demarcating the frontier and erecting pillars should be carried out in a manner similar to that laid down in the notes exchanged for the same purpose between the Iraqi and Saudi Arabian Governments in February 1938. In order, however, to avoid difficulties which might otherwise arise, His Majesty's Government think it desirable that the proposed notes should include agreement on the interpretation of certain points in the wording of the definition of the frontier as reaffirmed by the Prime Minister in his letter to the High Commissioner No. 2944 of July 21st, 1932.

3. In that letter the definition of the frontiers was re-affirmed in the following terms:–

> From the intersection of the Wadi al Audja with the Batin and thence northwards along the Batin to a point just south of the latitude of Safwan; thence eastwards passing south of Safwan wells, Jebel Sanam and Um Qasr leaving them to Iraq and so on to the junction of the Khor Zobeir with the Khor Abdullah. The islands of Warba, Bubian, Maskan (or Mashjan), Failakah, Auhah, Kubbar Qaru and Um el Maradin appertain to Koweit.

4. The point to be interpreted and the interpretation which it is suggested should be given to them are as follows:–

(i) "Along the Batin" the frontier line shall follow the *thalweg*, i. e. the line of the deepest depression.

(ii) The "point just South of the latitude of Safwan" shall be the point on the *thalweg* of the Batin due West of the point a little to the South of Safwan at which the post and notice-board marking the frontier stood until March, 1939.

(iii) From the Batin to the neighbourhood of Safwan the frontier shall be a line along the parallel of latitude on which stands the above-mentioned point at which the post and notice-board formerly stood.

(iv) The "junction of the Khor Zubair with the Khor Abdullah" shall mean the junction of the *thalweg* of the Khor Zubair with the *thalweg* of the north-westerly arm of the Khor Abdullah known as the Khor Shetana.

(v) From the neighbourhood of Safwan to the junction of the Khor Zubair with the Khor Abdullah the frontier shall be the shortest line between the point defined in sub-paragraph (ii) and the point defined in sub-paragraph (iv). But if this line shall be found, when followed on the ground to strike the right bank of the Khor Zubair before it reaches the point defined in sub-paragraph (iv), it shall be modified in such a manner as to follow the low water line on the right bank of the Khor Zubair until a point on the bank immediately opposite the point defined in sub-paragraph (iv) is reached, thus leaving the whole of the Khor Zubair to Iraq.

(vi) From the point defined in sub-paragraph (iv) to the open sea the boundary shall follow the *thalweg* of the Khor Abdullah.

5. In the hope that Your Excellency will agree in principle with my Government's view of the advantage to both the Iraqi and Koweiti Governments of a demarcation of their common frontier, I am enclosing, as a basis for discussion, a draft of a Note which I suggest Your Excellency should, on behalf of the Iraqi Government, address to me. I

will then endeavour to obtain, through the proper channel, the formal agreement of His Highness the Ruler of Koweit to these proposals.

I avail myself of this opportunity to express to Your Excellency the assurance of my highest consideration.

(Sgd.) Basil Newton.

APPENDIX IV

British Note Verbale concerning Demarcation of the Frontier between Kuwait and Iraq, 1951 [FO 371/98391]

No. 626

Note Verbale

His Britannic Majesty's Embassy presents its compliments to the Ministry of Foreign Affairs and has the honour to state that His Britannic Majesty's Government in the United Kingdom have had under consideration the question of the demarcation of the frontier between Iraq and Kuwait. In July 1948 His Excellency Sayid Jalal Baban, who was then Acting Prime Minister of Iraq, informed Sir Henry Mack, then His Britannic Majesty's Ambassador, that the Iraq Government were about to reopen this whole question with His Britannic Majesty's Government. No written communication has been received by His Britannic Majesty's Embassy on this subject and the Embassy has accordingly been instructed to inform the Iraq Government of His Britannic Majesty's Government's views on the exact line of the frontier and to make certain proposals about the demarcation of the frontier.

In his letter No. 2944 of the 21st July, 1932, to the United Kingdom High Commissioner in Iraq the then Prime Minister of Iraq defined the frontier between Iraq and Kuwait as follows:

> From the intersection of the Wadi el Audja with the Batin and thence northwards along the Batin to a point just south of the latitude of Safwan; thence eastwards passing south of Safwan wells, Jebel Sanam and Um Qasr leaving them to Iraq and so on to the junction of the Khor Zobair with the Khor Abdullah. The islands of Warba, Bubuyan, Maskan (or Mashjan), Failakah, Auhah, Kubbar, Qaru and Um el Maradin appertain to Kuwait.

His Britannic Majesty's Government interpret this definition of the frontier as follows:–

(a) "Along the Batin" means that the line of the frontier shall follow the *thalweg*, i. e. the line of the deepest depression.

(b) The "point just south of the latitude of Safwan" means the point on the *thalweg* of the Batin due west of the point 1000 metres due south of the customs post at Safwan, i. e. the building which on the 25th June, 1940, was used as the customs post at Safwan.

(c) From the Batin to the neighbourhood of Safwan the frontier shall be the line along the parallel of latitude between the two points described in sub-para (b) above.

(d) The "junction of the Khor Zubair with the Khor Abdullah" means the junction of the *thalweg* of the Khor Zubair with the *thalweg* of the north-westerly arm of the Khor Abdullah known as the Khor Shetana.

(e) From the point 1000 metres south of the customs post at Safwan the frontier shall follow the shortest line between that point and the point defined in sub-para (d) above (the "junction of the Khor Zubair with the Khor Abdullah"), but only as far as the spring tide low water mark on the right bank of the Khor Zubair.

(f) From the point of the spring tide low water mark on the right bank of the Khor Zubair mentioned in the preceding sub-para to the point on that same low water mark nearest to the point defined in sub-para (d) above (the "junction of the Khor Zubair with the Khor Abdullah") the frontier shall follow the low water mark.

(g) From the point on the low water mark on the right bank of the Khor Zubair nearest to the point defined in sub-para (d) above (the "junction of the Khor Zubair with the Khor Abdullah") to that point itself the frontier shall be the shortest line which can be drawn.

(h) From the point defined in sub-para (d) above (the "junction of the Khor Zubair with the Khor Abdullah") to the open sea the frontier shall follow, first, the *thalweg* of the north westerly arm of the Khor Abdullah known as the Khor Shetana and then the *thalweg* of the Khor Abdullah proper.

His Britannic Majesty's Embassy have also been instructed to suggest that the arrangements for the actual demarcation of the frontier should be similar to those proposed in paragraph 4 of the draft note enclosed in Sir Basil Newton's letter No. 487 of the 7th October, 1940, to the then Iraqi Minister for Foreign Affairs. These proposals were as follows:–

(a) A Joint Technical Commission shall be set up to:–

(I) complete where defective a network of triangulation along the frontier zone from the intersection of the Wadi al Audja with the Batin to the western extremity of the land frontier;

(ii) erect frontier pillars which shall be visible one from another along the whole length of the land frontier and to mark by buoys or other means which may be agreed upon that part of the boundary which follows the Khor Zubair, the Khor Shetana and the Khor Abdullah down to the sea.

(b) For the purpose of (i) and (ii) above, the frontier shall be deemed to be the line re-affairmed in the Prime Minister's note to the High Commissioner, No. 2944 of the 21st July, 1932, as interpreted above.

(c) The frontier pillars shall be iron stakes 5" x 5" and 11' in length. On the upper extremity an iron disque 1' in diameter shall be fixed in a perpendicular position bearing in relief the number of the pillar.

(d) The pillars shall be numbered consecutively beginning with the first pillar which shall be placed at the point where the Joint Commission begins its work.

(e) The Joint Commission shall consist of a first representative and a second representative with the necessary technical and other assistants nominated by each Government, that is to say His Britannic Majesty's Government and the Iraq Government. It shall be permissible, in case of necessity, for the second, representative to replace and enjoy the same privileges as the first representative. The first representative of each country shall preside alternately over the work of the Commission.

(f) In case of differences between the representatives, they shall submit the question in dispute to their Governments with a view to a solution being reached through the diplomatic channel.

(g) The *procès verbaux* of the Commission shall be prepared in Arabic and English and, in case of difference, the English text shall prevail.

(h) The date on which the Joint Commission shall begin work shall be fixed by agreement between His Britannic Majesty's Government and the Iraq Government.

(i) It is confirmed that the costs of demarcation shall be shared equally between the Governments of Kuwait and Iraq.

His Britannic Majesty's Embassy look forward to receiving in due course the views of the Iraq Government on the proposals set forth above.

His Britannic Majesty's Embassy avails itself of this opportunity to renew the expression of its highest consideration.

APPENDIX V

The Al Sabah Rulers/Emirs of Kuwait, 1752–1996

Sheikh Sabah (I) bin Jaber	1752–1756
Sheikh Abdullah bin Sabah	1756–1814
Sheikh Jaber bin Abdullah	1814–1859
Sheikh Sabah (II) bin Jaber	1859–1866
Sheikh Abdullah (II) bin Sabah	1866–1892
Sheikh Muhammad bin Sabah	1892–1896
Sheikh Mubarak bin Sabah	1896–1915
Sheikh Jaber bin Mubarak	1915–1917
Sheikh Salem bin Mubarak	1917–1921
Sheikh Ahmed bin Jaber	1921–1950
Sheikh Abdullah bin Salem Mubarak	1950–1965
Sheikh Sabah bin Salem	1965–1977
Sheikh Jaber al-Ahmed	1977–

APPENDIX VI

British Political Agents in Kuwait, 1904–1961

Capt. Stuart George Knox	Aug. 1904 – Apr. 1909
Capt. William Henry Irvine Shakespear	Apr. 1909 – Jan. 1914
Lt. Col. William George Grey	Jan. 1914 – June 1916
Lt. Col. Robert Edward Hamilton	June 1916 – Mar. 1918
Capt. Percy Gordon Loch	Mar. 1918 – Sept. 1918
Capt. Daniel Vincent McCallum	Sept. 1918 – Feb. 1920
Maj. James Carmichael More	May 1920 – May 1929
Maj. Cyril Charles Johnson Barrett (Acting)	Apr. 1927 – Oct. 1927
Lt. Col. Harold Richard Patrick Dickson	May 1929 – Feb. 1936
Asst. Surg. Allen Leslie Greenway (Acting)	May 1931 – Sept. 1931
Maj. Ralph Ponsonby Watts (Acting)	June 1934 – Oct. 1934
Capt. Gerald Simpson de Gaury	Feb. 1936 – May 1939
Maj. Arnold Crawshaw Galloway	May 1939 – May 1941
Capt. Andrew Charles Stewart. (Acting)	Apr. 1937 – May 1937
Dr Allen Lesslie Greenway (Acting)	May 1937 – June 1937
Lt. Col. Harold Richard Patrick Dickson	May 1941 – Aug. 1941
Maj. Tom Hickinbotham	Aug. 1941 – Sept. 1943
Gordon Noel Jackson (Acting)	June 1943 – Aug. 1943
Cornelius James Pelly	Oct. 1943 – June 1944
Gordon Noel Jackson	June 1944 – Apr. 1945
Maj. Maurice O'Connor Tandy	Apr. 1945 – Mar. 1946
Capt. Richard Ernest Rowland Bird	Mar. 1946 – May 1946
Maj. Maurice O'Connor Tandy	May 1946 – Apr. 1948
Maj. Arnold Crawshaw Galloway	Apr.1948 – Apr. 1949
Gordon Noel Jackson	Apr. 1949 – Nov. 1949
H. G. Jakins	Nov. 1949 – Sept. 1951
Cornelius James Pelly	Sept. 1951 – June 1955
Gawain Westry Bell	June 1955 – Aug. 1957
A. K. Rothnie (Acting)	Aug. 1957 – Oct. 1957
Aubrey Seymour Halford	Oct. 1957 – Dec. 1959
John Christopher Blake Richmond	Jan. 1960 – July 1961.

APPENDIX VII

British Political Residents in the Gulf, 1852–1966

Capt. Arnold Burrowes Kemball	Mar. 1852–July 1855
Capt. James Felix Jones	Oct. 1855–Apr. 1862
	(Offg. until July 1856)
Capt. Herbert Frederick Disbrowe (Offg.)	Apr. 1862–Nov. 1862
Lt. Col. Lewis Pelly	Nov. 1862–Oct. 1872
	(Acting until Mar. 1863)
Lt. Col. Edward Charles Ross	Oct. 1872–Mar. 1891
	(Acting until 1877)
Lt. Col. William Francis Prideaux (Acting)	May 1876–1877
Lt. Col. Samuel Barrett Miles (Acting)	1885–Oct. 1886
Lt. Col. Adelbert Cecil Talbot	1891–May 1893
	(Offg. under Sept. 1891)
Capt. Stuart Hill Godfrey (i/c)	May 1893–June 1893
Maj. James Hayes Sadler (Acting)	Dec.1893–Jan. 1894
Col. Frederick Alexander Wilson	Jan. 1894–June 1897
Lt. Col. Malcolm John Meade (Offg.)	June 1897–Apr. 1900
	(Offg. until Mar. 1898)
Lt. Col. Charles Arnold Kemball (Acting)	Apr. 1900–Apr. 1904
Maj. Percy Zachariah Cox	Apr. 1904–Dec. 1913
Maj. Arthur Prescott Trevor (i/c)	Aug. 1909–Mar. 1910
John Gordon Lorimer	Dec. 1913–Feb. 1914
Capt. Richard Lockington Birdwood (i/c)	Feb. 1914–Mar. 1914
Maj. Stuart George Knox (i/c)	Mar. 1914–Nov. 1914
Maj. Percy Zachariah Cox	Nov. 1914–Oct. 1920
Maj. Stuart George Knox	
(Officer on Special Duty)	Jan. 1915–Apr. 1915
Lt. Col. Sir Arnold Talbot Wilson (Offg.)	Oct. 1920–Nov. 1920
Lt. Col. Arthur Prescott Trevor	Nov. 1920–Apr. 1924
Lt. Col. Stuart George Knox (Acting)	Apr. 1923–Oct. 1923
Lt. Col. Francis Veville Prideaux	Apr. 1924–Jan. 1927
Lt. Col. Charles Gilbert Crosthwaite	
(Acting)	June 1925–Oct. 1925

Lt. Col. Sir Lionel Berkeley Haworth	Jan. 1927–Nov. 1928
Sir Frederick William Johnston	Nov. 1928–Apr. 1929
Lt. Col. Cyril Charles Johnson Barrett	Apr. 1929–Nov. 1929
Lt. Col. Hugh Vincent Biscoe	Nov. 1929–July 1932
Lt. Col. Trenchard Craven Fowle (Acting)	May 1931–Oct. 1931
Lt. Col. Trenchard Craven Fowle	July 1932–Aug. 1939
Lt. Col. Percy Gordon Loch (Acting)	Apr. 1933–Oct. 1935
Lt. Col. Percy Gordon Loch (Acting)	July 1936–Oct. 1936
Olaf Kirkpatrick Caroe (Acting)	Aug. 1937–Nov. 1937
Hugh Weightman (Acting)	Aug. 1938–Sept. 1938
Lt. Col. Charles Geoffrey Prior	Sept. 1939–May 1946
Lt. Col. William Rupert Hay (Offg.)	Oct. 1941–Sept.1942
Lt. Col. Arnold Crawshaw Galloway (Offg.)	May 1945–Nov. 1945
Lt. Col. William Rupert Hay	May 1946–1953
Lt. Col. Arnold Crawshaw Galloway (Offg.)	June 1947–Oct. 1947
Sir Bernard A. B. Burrows	July 1953–Oct. 1958
Sir George Humphery Middleton	Oct. 1958–Oct. 1961
Sir William Henry Tucker Luce	May 1961–1966

APPENDIX VIII

British Representatives in Iraq, 1920–1961

Sir Percy Cox	High Commissioner	Oct. 1920–May 1924
Sir Henry Dobbs	High Commissioner	May 1924–Mar. 1929
Sir Gilbert Clayton	High Commissioner	Mar. 1929–Oct. 1929
Sir Francis Humphrys	High Commissioner	Oct. 1929–Oct. 1932
Sir Francis Humphrys	Ambassador	Nov. 1932–Mar. 1935
Sir Archibald Clark Kerr	Ambassador	Mar. 1935–Mar. 1938
Sir Maurice Drummond Peterson	Ambassador	Mar. 1938–1939
Sir Basil Newton	Ambassador	1939–1941
Sir Kinahan Cornwallis	Ambassador	Apr. 1941–Mar. 1945
Sir Francis Hugh Stonehewer-Bird	Ambassador	Mar. 1945–1947
Sir Henry B. Mack	Ambassador	1948–1950
J. M. Troutbeck	Ambassador	1950–1954
Michael Wright	Ambassador	Jan. 1955–Dec. 1958
Sir Humphrey Trevelyan	Ambassador	Dec. 1958–Oct. 1961

APPENDIX IX

Iraqi Kings, Prime Ministers and Presidents, 1921–1996

Faisal (I) bin Hussein	King	Aug. 1921–Sept. 1933
Ghazi (I) bin Faisal	King	Sept. 1933–Apr. 1939
Faisal (II) bin Ghazi	King	Apr. 1939–July 1958
Abdul-Illah	Regent	Apr. 1939–1953
Abdul-Rahman al-Gaylani	Prime Minister	Sept. 1921–Nov. 1922
Abdul-Muhsin as-Sa'dun	Prime Minister	Nov. 1922– Nov. 1923
		June 1925–Nov. 1926
		Jan. 1928–Jan. 1929
		Sept. 1929–Nov. 1929
Ja'far al-'Askari	Prime Minister	Nov. 1923–Aug. 1924
		Nov. 1926–Jan. 1928
Yasin al-Hashemi	Prime Minister	Aug. 1924–June 1925
		Mar. 1935–Oct. 1936
Tawfiq al-Suwaidi	Prime Minister	Apr. 1929–Aug. 1929
		Feb.1946–May 1946
		Feb. 1950–Sept. 1950
Naji al-Suwaidi	Prime Minister	Nov. 1929–Mar. 1930
Nuri al-Said	Prime Minister	Mar. 1930–Oct. 1930
		Oct. 1930–Oct. 1932
		Dec. 1938–Apr. 1939
		Apr. 1939–Feb. 1940
		Feb. 1940–Mar. 1940
		Oct. 1941–Oct. 1942
		Oct. 1942–Dec. 1943
		Dec. 1943–June 1944
		Nov. 1946–Mar. 1947
		Jan. 1949–Dec. 1949
		Sept. 1950–July 1952
		Aug. 1954–Dec. 1955
		Dec. 1955–June 1957
		Mar. 1958–May 1958.

Naji Shawkat	Prime Minister	Nov. 1932–Mar. 1933
Rashid Ali al-Gaylani	Prime Minister	Mar. 1933–Oct. 1933
		Mar. 1940–Jan. 1941
		Apr. 1941–May 1941
Jamil al-Midfa'i	Prime Minister	Nov. 1933–Feb. 1934
		Feb. 1934–Aug. 1934
		4 Mar. 1935–16 Mar. 1935
		Aug. 1937–Dec. 1938
		June 1941–Oct. 1941
		Jan. 1953–Sept. 1953
Ali Jawdat al-Ayyubi	Prime Minister	Aug. 1934–Feb. 1935
		Dec. 1949–Feb. 1950
		June 1957–Dec. 1957
Hikmat Sulaiman	Prime Minister	Oct. 1936–Aug. 1937
Taha al-Hashimi	Prime Minister	Feb. 1941–Apr. 1941
Hamdi al-Pachachi	Prime Minister	June 1944–Aug. 1944
		Aug. 1944–Jan. 1946
Arshad al-Umari	Prime Minister	June 1946–Nov. 1946
		Apr. 1954–July 1954
Salih Jabr	Prime Minister	Mar. 1947–Jan. 1948
Muhammad as-Sadr	Prime Minister	Jan. 1948–June 1948
Muzahim al-Pachachi	Prime Minister	June 1948–Jan. 1949
Mustafa al-Umari	Prime Minister	July 1952–Nov. 1952
Nur-ud-Din Mahmud	Prime Minister	Nov. 1952–Jan. 1953
Fadil al-Jamali	Prime Minister	Sept. 1954–Apr. 1954
Abdul-Wahhab Mirjan	Prime Minister	Dec. 1957–Mar. 1958
Ahmad Mukhtar Baban	Prime Minister	May 1958–July 1958
Abdul-Karim Qasim	Prime Minister	July 1958–Feb. 1963
Abdul-Salam Muhammad Aref	President	Feb. 1963–Apr. 1966
Abdul-Rahman Aref	President	Apr. 1966–July 1968
Ahmad Hasan al-Bakr	President	July 1968–July 1979
Saddam Hussein.	President	July 1979–

Bibliography

Unpublished Sources

    1. India Office Library and Records, London:

(a) Political and Secret Department
      Departmental papers (1902–1928)
      L/P&S/10/606, 937, 1271.

(b) Political and Secret Department
      External files and collections (1931–1950)
      L/P&S/12/3737.

(c) Political and Secret Department
      Memorandum (1840–1947)
      L/P&S/18/B133, B165, B166, B166a, B188.

(d) Political Residency, Bushire (1899–1948)
      R/15/1/472, 479, 505, 523–5.

(e) Political Agency, Kuwait (1908–1949)
      R/15/5/18, 58, 59, 65, 67, 113, 126, 127, 130,
      131, 184, 185, 194, 207–10, 218.

    2. Public Record Office, London:

(a) Cabinet Conclusions (1961)
      CAB 128/35/PT1–PT2.

(b) Cabinet Memorandum (1960–1961)
      CAB 129/101, 104–6.

(c) Chiefs of Staff Committee (1960–1961)
      DEFE 6/61–4, 66, 67, 71–3.

(d) Foreign Office (1912–1962)
      FO 371/1485, 16852, 19967–9, 20774, 21813,
      21858, 21860, 23180–1, 23200, 24545, 24559,
      27106, 31369, 34999, 40104, 45186, 52454, 61445,
      68346, 82038, 91291, 98388, 98391, 104321,104380,

109821, 114577, 114600, 114644–5, 114701,
120550, 120556, 120559, 120634, 120638, 126869,
126913, 126938, 126960–1, 132523, 132751,
140066, 140125, 140199, 140963, 148896, 148948,
148966, 156838, 156844–54, 156872–7,
156880–5, 162896–9, 162913–7.

FO 1016/7, 27, 39, 118, 364.

Published Documents

Aitchison, C. U. *A Collection of Treaties, Engagements and Sanads Relating to India and Neighbouring Countries*, Delhi, Manager of Publication, 1933.

Hansard Parliamentary Debates: House of Commons, 5th series, vol. CCCXLIV, London, HMSO, 1938–9.

Hurewitz, J. C. *Diplomacy in the Near and Middle East: A Documentary Record 1914–1956*, 2 vols., New York, Octagon Books, 1972.

Lauterpacht, E. and C. J. Greenwood, Marc Waller and Daniel Bethlehem (eds.). *The Kuwait Crisis: Basic Documents*, Cambridge, Grotius Publications, 1991.

Lorimer, J. G. *Gazetter of the Persian Gulf, Oman and Central Arabia*, Historical, Part 1B, and Geographical and Statistical, Parts 2A and 2B, Calcutta, Government Printing, 1908.

Iraqi Responses to International Demands: A Chronicle from March 1991 to April 1994, Kuwait City, Centre for Research and Studies on Kuwait, undated.

—*Kuwait–Iraq Boundary Demarcation: Historical Rights and International Will*, Kuwait City, Centre for Research and Studies on Kuwait, 1994.

The Persian Gulf Administration Reports: 1873–1947, vols. IX and X, Gerrards Cross, Archive Editions, 1986.

The Persian Gulf Historical Summaries: 1907–1953, vol. II, Gerrards Cross, Archive Editions, 1987.

Political Diaries of the Persian Gulf: 1938–1939, vol. XIII, Oxford, Archive Editions, 1990.

Rush, Alan de Lacy (ed.). *Records of Kuwait: 1899–1961*, vols. I, VI and XII, Oxford, Archive Editions, 1989.

Saldanha, J. A. *Precise of Kuwait Affairs, 1896–1904*, Calcutta, Government of India, 1904.

—*Precise of Turkish Affairs 1801–1905*, Simla, Government of India, 1906.

Schofield, Richard (ed.). *Arabian Boundary Dispute*, vol. VI, Gerrards Cross, Archive Editions, 1992.

Schofield, Richard and Gerald Blacke (eds.). *Arabian Boundaries Primary Documents 1853–1957: Political Control and Sovereignty*, vol. I, Farnham Common, Archive Editions, 1988.

Thomas, R. Hughes (ed.). *Arabian Gulf Intelligence: Selections from the Records of the Bombay Government*, vol. XXIV, New York, The Oleander Press, 1985.

Tuson, Penelope. *The Records of the British Residency and Agencies in the Persian Gulf*, London, India Office Library and Records, 1978.

United Nations Iraq–Kuwait Boundary Commission *Final Report on the Demarcation of the International Boundary between the Republic of Iraq and the State of Kuwait*, no. S/25811, New York, Security Council, 21 May 1993.

United Nations. *Demarcation of the International Boundary between the State of Kuwait and the Republic of Iraq*, Kuwait City, Center for Research and Studies on Kuwait, undated.

Newspapers and Periodicals

al-Arab (Doha)
The Economist (London)
Gulf Times (Doha)
al-Ikha' al-Watani (Baghdad)
Khaleej Times (Dubai)
Middle East Economic Digest (London)
Middle East International (London)
Newsweek (New York)
The Observer (London)
al-Raya (Doha)
al-Sharq (Doha)

The Times (London)
Time International (New York)

Special Articles

Busch, B. C. 'Britain and the status of Kuwait, 1896–1899', *The Middle East Journal*, vol. XXI (1967).

Gott, Richard. 'The Kuwait incident', *The Survey of International Affairs* 1961 (1962).

Hay, Sir Rupert. 'The Persian Gulf States and their boundary problems', *Geographical Journal*, vol. LXX (1954).

Karabell, Zachary. 'Backfire: US policy toward Iraq, 1988–2 August 1990', *The Middle East Journal*, vol. IL, no. I (1995).

al-Najjar, M. A. 'The political history of Iraq's international relations with the Arabian Gulf', *Journal of the Basra University* (1975).

Rahman, H. 'Kuwaiti ownership of Warba and Bubiyan Islands', *Middle Eastern Studies*, vol. XXIX, no. II (1993).

Salih, Kamal Osman. 'The Salih, Kamal Osman 'The Kuwait Legislative Council', *Middle Eastern Studies*, vol. XXIIV, no. I (January 1992).

Unpublished Thesis

al-Mayyal, Ahmad Y. A. 'The political boundaries of the State of Kuwait: A study in political geography', Ph.D. thesis, School of Oriental and African Studies, University of London, 1986.

Books

Abdulghani, Jasim M. *Iraq and Iran: the Years of Crisis*, London, Croom Helm, 1984.

Abu-Hakima, Ahmad Mustafa. *History of Eastern Arabia 1750–1800: The Rise and Development of Bahrain, Kuwait and Wahhabi Saudi Arabia*, London, Probsthain, 1988.

Alani, Mustafa M. *Operation Vantage: British Military Intervention in Kuwait 1961*, Surrey, LAAM, 1990.

Amin, Syed Hassan. *International and Legal Problems of the Gulf*, London, Middle East and North African Studies Press, 1981.

—*Political and Strategic Issues in the Gulf*, Glasgow, Royston, 1984.

Amirsadeghi, Hossein (ed.). *The Security of the Persian Gulf*, London, Croom Helm, 1981.

Batatu, Hanna. *The Old Social Classes and the Revolutionary Movements of Iraq*, Princeton, N.J., Princeton University Press, 1987.

BBC World Service. *Gulf Crisis Chronology*, London, Longman, 1991.

Bennis, Phyllis and Michel Moushabeck (eds.). *Beyond the Storm: A Gulf Crisis Reader*, Edinburgh, Canongate Press, 1992.

de la Billière, General Sir Peter. *Storm Command: A Personal Account of the Gulf War*, Dubai, Motivate Publishing, 1992.

—*Looking for Trouble: SAS to Gulf Command*, Dubai, Motivate Publishing, 1992.

Bulloch, John and Harvey Morris. *Saddam's War: the Origins of the Kuwait Conflict and the International Response*, London, Faber and Faber, 1991.

Busch, B. C. *Britain and the Persian Gulf, 1894–1914*, Berkeley, University of California Press, 1967.

Chubin, Shahram and Charles Tripp. *Iran and Iraq at War*, London, I. B. Tauris, 1988.

Cordesman, Anthony H. *The Gulf and the Search for Strategic Stability*, Boulder, Colorado, Westview Press, 1984.

Crystal, Jill. *Oil and Politics in the Gulf: Rulers and Merchants in Kuwait and Qatar*, Cambridge, Cambridge University Press, 1990.

—*Kuwait: the Transformation of an Oil State*, Boulder, Colorado, Westview Press, 1992.

Darwish, Adel and Gregory Alexander. *Unholy Babylon: the Secret History of Saddam's War*, London, Victor Gollancz, 1991.

Day, Alan J. (ed.). *Border and Territorial Disputes*, London, Longman, 1982.

Dickson, H. R. P. *Kuwait and Her Neighbours*, London, George Allen and Unwin, 1968.

Finnie, David H. *Shifting Lines in the Sand: Kuwait's Elusive Frontier with Iraq*, Cambridge, Mass., Harvard University Press, 1992.

al-Ghunaim, Abdullah and Mufid Shehab, Gamal Zakariyya Qasem, Mohammad Murci Abdullah and Ahmed al-Mayyal. *Kuwait: Statehood and Boundaries*, Kuwait City, Kuwait Foundation for the Advancement of Sciences, 1992.

Graubard, Stephen R. *Mr Bush's War: Adventures in the Politics of Illusion*, London, I. B. Tauris, 1952.

El-Hakim, Ali A. *The Middle Eastern States and the Law of the Sea*, Manchester, Manchester University Press, 1979.

Heikal, Mohamed. *Illusions of Triumph: An Arab View of the Gulf War*, London, Harper Collins, 1992.

Kelly, J. B. *Britain and the Persian Gulf*, Oxford, Clarendon Press, 1968.

Khadduri, Majid. *Republican Iraq: A Study in Iraqi Politics since the Revolution of 1958*, London, Oxford University Press, 1969.

—*Socialist Iraq: A Study in Iraqi Politics since 1968*, Washington DC, The Middle East Institute, 1978.

Kumar, Ravinder. *India and the Persian Gulf Region 1858–1907: A Study in British Imperial Policy*, Bombay, Asia Publishing House, 1965.

Lenczowski, George. *The Middle East in World Affairs*, London, Cornell University Press, 1980.

Longrigg, Stephen Hemsley. *Oil in the Middle East*, London, Oxford University Press, 1968.

Lutsky, V. *Modern History of the Arab Countries*, Moscow, Progress Publishers, 1969.

Mezcrik, A. G. (ed.). *Kuwait–Iraq Dispute 1961*, New York, International Review Service, 1961.

—Miller, Judith and Laurie Mylroie. *Saddam Hussein and the Crisis in the Gulf*, New York, Times Book, 1990.

Niblock, Tim. *Iraq: The Contempory State*, London, Croom Helm, 1982.

O'Ballance, Edgar. *The Gulf War*, London, Brassey's Defence Publishers, 1988.

Peterson, Sir M. *Both Sides of the Curtain*, London, Allen and Unwin, 1950.

Ramazani, R. K. *International Straits of the World: the Persian Gulf and Strait of Hormuz*, The Netherlands, Sijthoff & Noordhoff, 1979.

Rush, Alan de Lacy. *Al Sabah: History and Genealogy of Kuwait's Ruling Family, 1752–1987*, London, Ithaca Press, 1987.

Salinger, Pierre and Laurent, Eric. *Secret Dossier: The Hidden Agenda Behind the Gulf War*, London, Penguin Books, 1991.

Schofield, Richard. *Kuwait and Iraq: Historical Claims and Territorial Disputes*, London, Royal Institute of International Affairs, 1991.

Schwarzkopf, General H. Norman. *It Doesn't Take a Hero*, London, Bantam Press, 1992.

Sciolino, Elaine. *The Outlaw State: Saddam Hussein's Quest for Power and the Gulf Crisis*, New York, John Wiley and Sons, 1991.

Sharabi, H. B. *Government and Politics of the Middle East in the Twentieth Century*, New York, D. Van Nostrand, 1962.

Silverfarb, Daniel. *Britain's Informal Empire in the Middle East: A Case Study of Iraq, 1922–1941*, Oxford, Oxford University Press, 1986.

Sultan, HRH General Khaled bin. *Desert Warrior*, London, Harper Collins, 1995.

Trevelyan, Humphrey. *The Middle East in Revolution*, London, Macmillan, 1970.

Wilkinson, John C. *Arabia's Frontiers: the Story of Britain's Boundary Drawing in the Desert*, London, I. B. Tauris, 1991.

Woodward, Bob. *The Commanders*, London, Simon and Schuster, 1991.

Yapp, M. E. *The Making of the Modern Near East, 1792–1923*, London, Longman, 1987.

—*The Near East since the First World War*, London, Longman, 1991.

Index

361